Mary Forbes Winslow

Life in Jesus

A memoir of Mrs. Mary Winslow

Mary Forbes Winslow

Life in Jesus
A memoir of Mrs. Mary Winslow

ISBN/EAN: 9783337125936

Printed in Europe, USA, Canada, Australia, Japan

Cover: Foto ©Lupo / pixelio.de

More available books at **www.hansebooks.com**

LIFE IN JESUS:

A MEMOIR

OF

MRS. MARY WINSLOW,

ARRANGED FROM HER

Correspondence, Diary, and Thoughts.

BY HER SON

OCTAVIUS WINSLOW, D. D.,

AUTHOR OF
"MIDNIGHT HARMONIES," "PERSONAL DECLENSION AND REVIVAL," "THE PRECIOUS THINGS OF GOD," ETC.

"In her had Nature bounteously combined
The tenderest bosom with the strongest mind ;
I view the Mother and the Saint in one,
And pay beyond the homage of a Son."—*Knight.*

"Her children arise up, and call her blessed."—*Prov.* xxxi. 28.

NEW YORK:
ROBERT CARTER & BROTHERS,
No. 530 BROADWAY.
1860.

PREFACE.

THERE are few literary tasks more delicate in conception, difficult in design, or responsible in execution, than that of composing a *parent's* life—that parent a MOTHER. Under ordinary circumstances, to portray a character distinguished for its preëminent excellence, strongly developed in some of its essential features, and remarkable for a certain idiosyncrasy which assigns to it a place in the portrait gallery peculiarly and impressively its own, would impose upon the delineator the greatest caution; lest the imagination, enamoured of its study, should be allowed unduly to control the judgment, and thereby an ideal rather than a truthful picture should be the result. But, to sketch a character which, from childhood, we have filially loved and venerated, and, in later life, have looked upon with a deepening admiration, bordering upon a feeling of religious awe;—a character, too, sanctified in an eminent degree by the grace of God, demands the possession of powers to which the writer can prefer but a feeble claim. A MOTHER! who has not felt the exquisite tenderness of her love, the magic power of her influence, the sacred reverence of her name? Has she weaknesses?—what feeling heart could unveil them?

Has she virtues?—what filial hand can paint them? And yet the holy office has been undertaken of perpetuating a mother's memory! It seemed proper that some individual should weave together the incidents of a life too interesting and instructive to be altogether lost. Who so fitted for the work, as one who had known her so long, and had known her so well? The absence of the present Memoir from the biography of the Christian church—imperfectly as its materials are compiled—the writer, with lowliness, hesitates not to say, would have been a real and serious loss. The memorial of a life so unreservedly consecrated to God,—the publication of a correspondence, so rich in Christian experience, and replete with Christion comfort, must, with God's blessing, be greatly and extensively useful. To retain and perpetuate, therefore, something of that bright spirit that has passed away, and which itself could not be retained,—to catch the mantle as it fell in its celestial flight, and pass it down, a sacred and precious heir-loom, to the Christian church, were a solemn and imperious duty, from which no conviction of inability or sense of unworthiness should be allowed to shrink.

There were difficulties in the accomplishment of the work, other than those inseparable from its peculiar nature. It was found impossible to give that fulness to the biography, that was desired, without involving allusion to the living. Personal references to some who survive,—increasingly to feel how irreparable is their loss,—have already insinuated themselves into the volume to a greater extent and more prominently than either the judgment or taste of the compiler approved. They were, however, so closely interlaced with her writings as to render a separation difficult, if not impossible, without essentially impairing their beauty and effect.

The destruction, by her own hands, of one of her earliest and most important private journals, together with a large mass of letters of a deeply interesting and circumstantial character, deprives the work of that completeness of consecutive and incidental history which the editor would like to have preserved. The habit, too, of not dating many of her letters, and jottings in her diary, would greatly have embarrassed the chronological arrangement of the matter, (and may possibly have done so to some slight extent,) but or the events themselves, which have formed tolerably correct landmarks, guiding our course along the stream of her life.

Painfully trying to his feelings, and physically exhausting, as the work has been, it is not without some regret that his task is concluded. Not only has he counted it an honour—the least in his father's house—to have been intrusted with an office so responsible and sacred, but the prosecution of his work has conferred a happiness hallowed and indescribable. It has been to him, in many a still hour of night, like a prolongation of personal communion with her pure and glorified spirit, thus "preventing the feeling of entire disruption, and forming a kind of intermediate stage between her society in this world and the everlasting union of heaven."

Acknowledgments are due to those of her correspondents who have kindly furnished for the Memoir letters in their possession. It has been, necessarily, but to a limited extent that the compiler has been able to avail himself of these invaluable treasures. He hopes, however, to follow the present volume with a second one, composed entirely of selections from his mother's unpublished remains, in which many of these letters will appear.

The work—already and solemnly dedicated to the TRIUNE GOD—is now humbly laid at the feet of Christ's ONE church, with the fervent prayer, that the example which it presents of a LIVING FAITH, and of a CATHOLIC CHRISTIANITY may instruct, comfort, and animate many saints in their Christian course; and thus bring honour and praise to HIM whom, living, it was her supreme delight to serve; and whom, though dead, through these memorials, she still may glorify.

> "Oh, cherish'd and revered! fond memory well
> On thee with sacred, sad delight may dwell!
> So pure, so blest thy life, that death alone
> Could make more perfect happiness thine own.
> He came; thy cup of joy, serenely bright,
> Full to the last, still flow'd in cloudless light;
> He came—an angel, bearing from on high
> The all it wanted,—Immortality!"—MRS. HEMANS.

Leamington, England.

CONTENTS.

CHAPTER I.

PAGE

Christianity a Spiritual Life—The Believer a Living Soul—The Prevalence of Religious Formalism—Archbishop Leighton—The Moral Incentive of a High Standard — Birth—Ancestry—Early Training—A Mother's Influence — Mrs. Forbes—Providential Preservations—First Prayer—Marriage—The Pilgrim Fathers—Military Life— . . . . 11—21

CHAPTER II.

The Day-dawn of Grace—First Convictions of Sin—"The Whole Duty of Man"—Residence at Romford—Removal to London—St. James's Chapel, Pentonville—Rev. Thomas Sheppard—Spiritual Distress—Night of Weeping—Morning of Joy—Full Conversion—Writings of Rev. John Newton—Interesting Stranger—Spiritual Conflicts—Restored Peace—Letter to her Mother—Foreshadowings of Trial . . . . 22—31

CHAPTER III.

The Practical Character of her Religion—Family Worship—Letter to her Mother—Bermuda, its Salubrity, Inhabitants, Spiritual Condition—Asylum of the Puritans—Andrew Marvel—Whitfield visits Bermuda—His successful Labours—Dr. George Forbes—Her Exertions to secure a Minister for Bermuda—Rev. George Burder—Rev. H. H. Cross—Chapel opened in St. George's—Remarkable Providence—Rev. Duncan Dunbar—Colonial Slavery—Rescue of a Slave Family—Manumits her Slaves—Providential Escape—Illness of her Husband—Dr. Hamilton—Influence of Christian Physicians—Religious Anniversaries—William Wilberforce, Esq.—Her Young Family . . . . 32—54

CHAPTER IV.

God's Adjustment of His People to their Position—Her Illness—Captain Winslow's Retirement from the Army—Loss of Property—Her Removal to America—

(7)

CONTENTS.

PAGE

Colonel Bayard—Divie Bethune—Her Opinion of the United States—Death of her Infant — Death of her Husband—Letters to her Son—Inconsolable Grief—Light in Darkness—A Remarkable Dream—An Especial Promise—Her Baptism—Walks of Usefulness—A Pious Idiot—Conflict of Faith—Letter to her Son—Memorial to the King—William Wilberforce—Her Communion with God . . . . 55—79

CHAPTER V.

Revisits England—Former Scenes — Return to America — Residence at Mount Pleasant—Letter to her Mother—Removal to New York—The Mothers' Meeting—American Revivals—President Edwards—The Pilgrim Fathers—Outpouring of the Spirit on her Family—Letters to her Children—Remarks on the Baptism of the Holy Ghost—On Faith and Prayer—Résumé of her History—Touching Letter to her Son . . . . 80—89

CHAPTER VI.

Her Second Visit to England—Earnest Letter to her Children—Extracts from her Diary—Rev. James Harington Evans—A Remarkable Providence—Heart-searchings—Death of George IV.—Reflection on Christmas—Letter to her Mother—Letter to her Son R.—Letter to her Son H.—Rev. Mr. Evans' Preaching—Thoughts in Pentonville Chapel—Interesting Discovery—Letter to her Son—Spiritual Fluctuations—Her Birthday—The Necessity of Trials—Ministerial Encouragements—Qualifications of a Minister's Wife . . 90—125

CHAPTER VII.

Her Fitness for Counsel and Comfort—Illness and Death of Mrs. Evans—Visit to Cambridge—Haslingfield—Letter to her Pastor—Rev. Mr. Carus—Diary—Rev. Mr. Melville—Letter to her Son Rev. I. D. W.—Her last Visit to America —Ordination of her Son—Diary—Revival in New York—Return to England—Death of her Mother—Tugby—Village Scenes—Her Prayers for the Queen—Anecdote of the Queen—Avoidance of Debt—Rev. R. Cecil—Memoir of Rev. Dr. Payson—Letter to her Son Rev. I. D. W., on Ministerial Work—Heart-searchings—Letter to her Son Rev. G. E. W., on Ministerial Responsibility—Missionary Memoir of Mrs. Harriet Winslow—A Jewel in Mrs. Harriet Winslow's Crown . . . . 126—163

CHAPTER VIII.

Her Thoughts on Spiritual Subjects—Communion with God—Dr. Love—Letter to her Son H. J. W.—Letter to her Son R. F. W.—Her Thoughts on Prophetic Truth—The Second Coming of the Lord—Signs of the Times—Puseyism—Clouds Breaking—Parable of the Pearl of Great Price—God's Dealings in His Leadings—Grateful Recollections—Spiritual Joy—The Christian Journey—Godly Sincerity—On Unholy Jealousy—The Unity of the Spirit—Growth in

CONTENTS. 9

Grace—Rev. C. G. Finney—On the Conduct of a Minister's Wife—Parental Indulgence—Death of her Daughter-in-law—Nearness to God—Feelings at the Lord's Supper—To her Son in Trial—To her Son R. F. W.—Visit to Napton 164—190

CHAPTER IX.

The Christian's Chequered Life—Death of her Son H.—Letters on her Bereavement—Diary—Letter to her Daughter—Taplow—Reflections on Visiting Windsor Castle—Maternal Associations—Address to Mothers—Letter to John-street Maternal Association—Visit to Brighton—Letter to her Son . . 191—209

CHAPTER X.

Her Passion for Souls—Incident of Rev. Charles Simeon—Faithfulness of an American Pastor—Letter to the Duke of ——— —Letter to Lord ——— —Letter to the Archbishop of ———, on Baptismal Regeneration—Letter to A. G., Esq., of New York—Letter to E. T. C., Esq.—Letter to I. W., Esq., Boston, U. S.—Letter to J. T., Esq.—Her Love of Union and of Truth—The Evangelical Alliance—Diary—Anti-State-Church Movement—Letter to Miss C.—Letter to the Hon. and Rev. B. W. N.—Letter to a Missionary, on the American Anti-Slavery Society—Letter to her Niece, Mrs. G.—On Public Reading and Prayer—On Ministerial Watchfulness—On Intercourse with God—Her Faith in the Resurrection of Christ—Looking unto Jesus—Conversion of her Grandchildren—Extracts from her Diary . . . . . . 210—239

CHAPTER XI.

Her Peculiar Talent—The Philosophy of Sympathy—Abercrombie on the Moral Feelings—Letters of Consolation : To a beloved Friend—To Miss L. O., on the Death of her Mother—To Mrs. F., on the Illness of her Husband—To Mrs. E. B., on the Death of her Infant—To Mrs. C., on her Illness—To the same, on the Death of her Sister—To Mrs. C., on her Affliction—To Miss L. O., on behalf of a Distressed Clergyman—To her Son, on the Death of his Child—To Mrs. G., on the Death of her Husband—To Mr. W., on the Death of his Wife—To Rev. J. H. E., on his Illness—To Mrs. H., on the Death of her Husband—To Miss E. W., in Trial—To Rev. B. P. in Domestic Affliction—"Must I my Brother Keep?"—Extracts from her Diary—"There is a Voice, it comes to me" . . . . 240—261

CHAPTER XII.

Remarks on Christian Experience—Diary—Letters on Experimental Religion—Letter to Lady B., on the Sealing of the Spirit—To a Beloved Friend, on Looking to Christ for Evidences—To Lady L., on Anticipation of Heaven—To Miss M., on Advancement in the Divine Life—To Mrs. T., on Christ's Presence in Sickness—To Mrs. A., on the Confession of Sin—To Mrs. W., on Entering Fully into

CONTENTS.

Christ—To Rev. J. H. E., a Word in Season to a Sick Pastor—To Mrs. Lieutenant-Col. P. B., on an open Heart with God—To the Hon. F. T., on making Sure of Salvation—To Lady L., on the Holy Spirit—To Miss S., on the Christian Race—To Lady Mary F., on Waiting for the Lord—To Mrs. C., Heaven an Incentive to Religious Perseverance—To Mrs. C., on the Intercession of Christ—To Mrs. C. G., on the Death of her Child—To her Son—To Miss I——, in her Illness—To E. S., on Telling Jesus—To W. D. L., in Darkness of Mind—Mrs. Alers Hankey . . . . 262—319

CHAPTER XIII.

Fruit in Old Age—Diary—Rev. Dr. Stone, Brooklyn—Prayer in Suffering—Death of Dr. Chalmers—Burden Cast upon God—Her Lameness—Remarkable Recovery—Napton Vicarage—Death of her Daughter-in-law—Visit to the Grave—Anticipations of Heaven—Bridge on Faith—Her Prayer for the Evangelical Alliance—Letter to her Daughter—Death of the Rev. James Harrington Evans—Sympathy with Anxious Inquirers—Letter to Lady A. de Capel B.—Letters to H. and E. S.—Alarming Illness—Dr. Golding Bird—Letters to her Grandchildren—Rev. David Fenton Jarman—General Correspondence . 320—395

CHAPTER XIV.

Last Epoch of the Christian's Life—Growing Heavenliness—Longing to Depart—Devotional Meditations—The Sight of the Dying—Religion the Business of Life—Faith in the Posthumous Answers to Prayer—Exclusive Dealings with God—" Beyond the Smiling and the Weeping "—Broken-hearted Communion—Longing for Revival—The One Church, the Bride of Christ—Recognitions in Heaven—Last Sabbath in the Sanctuary—Failing Strength—Holy Counsels—The Sick Room—The Gate of Heaven—Dying Sayings—The Closing Scene—Her Triumphant Death—Concluding Remarks . . . . . 396—426

MEMOIR.

CHAPTER I.

THE real believer in the Lord Jesus Christ is truly and emphatically a 'a living soul.' Christianity with him is more than a creed, a symbol, or a name; it is a vital and a vitalizing principle, an incorporate of his moral being: in a word, it is a *spiritual life*. In his experience the 'glorious gospel of the blessed God is not a myth,' but a Divine verity; and the truths it reveals are not fictions but attested facts, not dreams but solemn realities. He has passed from death unto life, is a new creature in Christ, has his 'fruit unto holiness and the end everlasting life.' And while multitudes are thronging the mere vestibule of the temple, offering their *dead* sacrifices to a *living* God; he, approaching by the 'new and living way,' has penetrated within the inner shrine, and, enveloped with the incense-cloud of the great Atoning Sacrifice, is holding 'fellowship with the Father, and with His Son Christ Jesus.' The highest element of his being is to glorify God here; and the consummation of his hope hereafter will be the enjoyment of God for ever. Thus experimentally taught of the Spirit, he is led to disbelieve as a fable, and to reject as an impertinence, every dogma and vanity that would supplant the true gospel of Christ, or that offers itself as a substitute for a real heartfelt experience of the truth. To sanctify and adorn this lower world with such 'living temples' of the Spirit, and to replenish the world to come with their wonder and praise, was the great purpose of God in the gracious mission of His Son to our race. "I am

come that they might have life." "The water that I shall
give you shall be in you a well of water springing up into
everlasting life." " Know ye not that ye are the temple of
God, and that the Spirit of God dwelleth in you?"

In an age when religious formalism—the bane of the Christian church—is so prevalent; and when even in Christ's
quickened body the pulse of spiritual life in many throbs but
languidly, it is refreshing to meet with an instance of real,
earnest religion, exhibiting in its governing principles, and reflecting in its daily habit, the power and lustre of a heaven-descending and a heaven-alluring Christianity. Such an
example now invites the study of the spiritual mind. And
to a spiritual mind only will it possess any degree of interest
or attraction. The sentimentalist, whose piety sublimates into
dreamy mysticism,—the formalist, whose religion evaporates
into ritual observance,—or the romantic, whose ideal of Christianity is the vastness and splendour of heroic achievement,
will be conscious of a feeling of disappointment as the eye
rolls over these pages. The history they detail, and the
character they portray, derives nothing of its incident or its
charm from sources equivocal as these. And yet it is no
imaginary or inimitable Christian we are about to contemplate. There was nothing in her principles or example—
nothing in the grace which made her what she was, and to
which she owed all her hope for eternity—to which the most
humble saint may not aspire, and to which the feeblest might
not attain. "If none go to heaven but such a man as this,
what will become of me?" was the desponding exclamation
of one who witnessed with admiration, yet dismay, the pre-
eminently godly conversation of the seraphic Leighton. We
anticipate, however, no such feeling of despair as the result
of the perusal of this volume. We trust that the life we are
about to trace, heavenly and holy though it was, will so exhibit the fullness and preciousness of Christ, so illustrate the
power and sufficiency of divine grace, and so unfold the loving, winning character of God, as to stimulate and encourage
the lowliest heart that admires its beauty, and would fain
transcribe its excellence. "Nevertheless, it is of incalculable
advantage to have before us some bright examples of saints
who have outstripped their competitors, and gained the summit of the hill up which the train of feeble pilgrims is still
painfully toiling. Such extraordinary proficients in the life

and power of godliness are the salt of the earth to keep it from corruption. They rebuke the slackness of those half-hearted, home-sick mariners who stand off and on, wistfully eying the shore from which they have voluntarily parted, instead of launching into the deep, and making sail for a better country."* Such a 'proficient in the life and power of godliness' we are about to present; and although a filial hand tremblingly attempts the portrait, it yet will be his single aim so truthfully to delineate each feature of her character as to present her as she really was; and yet so carefully to veil the glory of the creature as shall constrain all who look upon the picture to magnify the grace of God in her.

MRS. WINSLOW was born in St. George's, Bermuda, on the 28th of February, 1774. On the paternal side she was of Scotch descent. Her grandfather, Dr. George Forbes,† was a native of Scotland, but resided in Bermuda; and was united in marriage to the eldest daughter of Thomas Jones, Esq., President of the Council, and during two temporary vacancies in the administration, acting Governor of the colony. Robert Forbes, the youngest son of this marriage, adopting the profession of his father, pursued his studies in Edinburgh; and on taking his degree, returned to the island, and afterwards married Mary, the only daughter of Alexander Rush, Esq. MARY FORBES, the subject of this Memoir, was the single issue of this union.

An only child, and the sole representative of his family, her father's affections and hopes concentrated upon her with no ordinary intensity, and his anxiety to fit her for her future position in life was proportionably great. No means, therefore, which a cultivated mind could suggest, or ample resources command, were spared in placing within her reach the highest literary advantages. After giving, with his own hands the first form and development to her mind and character, a competent tutor was procured from Scotland, to whose educational care the interesting charge was now confided.

But while her mental training, under her father's supervision, was thus successfully advancing, another and not less potent influence was silently at work, aiding the formation of a character which, for its natural impressibility and strength,

* Pearson's Life of Archbishop Leighton.
† Dr. Forbes belonged to a younger branch of the fifteenth Lord Forbes, of Putechie Castle, Aberdeenshire.

rendered all the more necessary the skilful moulding of a mother's plastic hand. Possessing a remarkably matured judgment, great force of character, and gentleness of disposition, few women were better fitted for the task than Mrs. Forbes. Faithfulness, however, compels us to notice an essential deficiency in her early education, which no intellectual advantages, however great, or parental anxiety, however intense, could supply—we refer to the absence of the *Christian element.* Religion, indeed, was not entirely excluded, but it was the religion of form rather than of power. It was not until she had reached the culminating point of life, that Mrs. Forbes became a subject of Divine grace. Up to that period of her history she had been basing her hope of heaven upon a mere ethical religion. Those winning traits of disposition and munificent acts of benevolence which invested her character with so great a charm, and which won for her such universal love, were made to take the place of the weightier matters of faith in Christ and love to God. The perusal of Hervey's works, (aided by the letters of her daughter,) in which that deep-thinking writer exposes, by a process of reasoning the most scriptural and convincing, though in a style somewhat florid and diffuse, the fallacy of every hope of justification but by the imputed righteousness of Christ, was the first means, in the hands of the Holy Spirit, of bringing home to her mind a conviction of her lost condition as a sinner, and of unveiling to her eye the sufficiency and beauty of the Lord Jesus as a Saviour. From the moment that she exchanged her own righteousness for the righteousness of Christ, she devoted herself to the service and glory of her Redeemer with a self-sacrificing zeal and singleness of purpose which never swerved nor faltered to the moment that she finished her Christian career, and peacefully rested from her labours in the eighty-sixth year of her age.

As the chief interest of this Memoir is derived from the *religious* character of its subject, we cannot too soon introduce the reader to that period of her history which marks the first inspiration of spiritual life; prefacing it, however, with a brief record of some of those remarkable providential circumstances in her early and unconverted years, which may be regarded as the foreshadowings of God's purposes of love and grace towards her. We quote from a narrative penned by herself, and addressed to her family:—

"I have often promised to relate to you some of God's most gracious dealings towards me in my early life, showing how manifestly His people are *preserved in Christ Jesus, and called.* With Paul I may say, I have been *in deaths oft* by land and sea, by fire and water. The first remarkable event of my life was a sudden recovery from illness when about five years of age, after I had been given over by my father to die. But a more striking providence followed. Soon after my almost miraculous restoration as from the grave, I accompanied my parents· during the French war on a visit to England. Our vessel was a light barque, carrying a few guns, and but ill furnished for severe conflict with the enemy. On entering the Channel, and midway between the English and French coasts, a ship of war hove in sight. It was towards night, and as she appeared to bear down upon us, our captain prepared for action. My mother and I were hurried from the cabin to what was thought a place of greater safety below. My father remained on deck. All was confusion above us. while I was astonished at being thus suddenly removed from my comfortable berth to the dismal quarters beneath the decks. We had not been long there, when I observed a boy come occasionally to the place of our imprisonment, and with a large horn in his hand take something from out of a barrel, having first fixed a lighted candle upon its edge and leaving it there. Observing, as I sat upon my mother's lap—who was too absorbed in anxiety to notice the circumstance—that the piece of candle was nearly burnt to the edge, I got down, put out my hand and took it away, saying 'Mamma, this will burn the barrel.' It was a cask of gunpowder! Had I not removed it at that moment, or, in removing it, had a spark fallen from the lengthened wick, the vessel and all on board must instantly have been blown to atoms. What a wonderful preservation from instantaneous and eternal destruction ; for it is not supposed that there was a single person on board who knew the Lord!"

As night grew on, concealed by its darkness, the man-of-war passed their little vessel unobserved, and thus, through the good hand of God upon them, they were preserved from captivity on the one hand, and from immediate death on the other. They arrived safely in England, and after remaining until the health of Dr. Forbes was restored, they returned to Bermuda, by way of the West Indies. They touched at Antigua for a few days, and accepted an invitation to dine and spend the night at the house of a distinguished resident of the island, who asked a large party of the inhabitants to meet them. They retired late, but not many hours had passed when the door of their room was burst open, and a voice of alarm roused them from their sleep with the terrific cry that the house was on fire, urging their immediate escape. Not a moment was to be lost. Her mother, wrapping a portion of the bedclothes round herself and child, rushed from the room, while her father, seizing what valuable things he could, prepared to follow. In a few moments the flames bursting from every part, had completely enveloped the house; the roof fell in with a tremendous crash, and in a short time the beautiful mansion, which a few hours before had been the brilliant scene of festive hospitality, was now a mass of smouldering ruins. Had they not been aroused at the moment they were, so rapid was the conflagration, they must inevitably have perished. Thus was the life of God's chosen one again redeemed from destruction—still *preserved in Christ Jesus.*

Yet another remarkable interposition of God's providence, as occurring in early life, may be given. After a short passage from New York to Bermuda, accompanied by her aunt, they arrived on a beautiful morning in sight of the island. Everything looked promising, and all were rejoicing in the prospect of soon landing amidst the welcomings of relatives and friends. The prospect, as they neared the cluster of islands, was surprisingly lovely. The blue hills in the distance—the tall cedars—the coral shore stretching into a transparent ocean—the gentle breeze blowing from the land laden with a thousand perfumes—the blue sky above—and the whole panorama bathed in the warm beams of a southern sun, gave to the entire scene the enchantment of a fairy land. All were prepared for going on shore, waiting but the pilot to come off and conduct them in. But ere an hour had passed, the sky grew dark, storm-clouds gathered, a fearful hurricane, common in these latitudes, suddenly arose, and the vessel, driven out again to sea, threatened every moment to founder. All was now confusion and dismay. In a few moments the masts were cut away, and the deck, washed by the mountain waves, was swept of everything but the caboose. It was an appalling spectacle. Every face gathered paleness, and despair seized every heart. Vessels making for the same port were seen to go down into the yawning billows with all sail standing. As the sea made a complete breach over the vessel, the officers and crew were compelled to take refuge in the cabin, waiting their expected and almost certain doom. The helm was lashed, and the dismantled hulk, which a few hours before was gallantly steering for her port, was now tossed like a log upon the ocean. The first long dreary night was one of horror. In this helpless condition they drifted about for several days, when—the gale having somewhat subsided—coming up to a deserted wreck, which like themselves had suffered in the storm, they took from her the masts and rigging, which lay dangling at her side; and refitting, as best they could, their disabled vessel, once more made their way to the island, which they reached in safety, and were received by their friends as those whom the sea had given back from the dead. It was a singular providence, that on opening the caboose for the purpose of preparing some food, the goat, which had taken refuge there in the storm, sprang out; and thus, in the absence of the supply of water, which the sea had swept from the decks, afforded a little timely nourishment during the remainder of the passage. In narrating this remarkable deliverance, she adds, " But what of God? Was there one grateful heart there? I am sure mine was not. Oh, the wonders of His love! Oh, the marvellous goodness and long-suffering of our God! How much has He borne with my manners in the wilderness!"

On the 6th of September, 1791, Miss Forbes was married in St. George's, Bermuda, to Thomas Winslow, Esq., who, with a detachment of his regiment, was at the time quartered in the island. A lineal descendant of Edward Winslow, one of the earliest of the Pilgrim Fathers, and Governor of Plymouth colony, Captain Winslow was ennobled in his ancestry. The history of the Pilgrims will ever form one of the most entrancing and instructive chapters in the annals of the Christian church. Although many long years have passed since the "May-flower" sailed out of the waters of Delft Haven, and revolution has succeeded revolution, and school has followed school in church and state, the memory of the Pilgrims still lives in undimmed, undying interest, more precious and fragrant now than ever. It would seem as if it were especially awarded to the intelligence and piety of the present age to exhibit the principles, to vindicate the character, and to embalm the memory of those distinguished confessors. Certainly no preceding age has presented a light more favourable to the calm, accurate study of their history than the present. Historians, differing from them in ecclesiastical views, yet unblinded by prejudice, have delighted to glorify the grace of God in those holy men and women—who, for conscience' sake, for truth's sake, and for Christ's sake, expatriated themselves from the land of their birth, braved the storms of a winter's voyage, and sought amidst the unbroken and inhospitable wilds of New England the religious liberty denied them at home. Linked by her marriage with this "noble army of martyrs," was now the subject of our Memoir. Nor did she prove an unworthy graft of a stem so honoured. In the evangelical principles which she maintained, in the strong faith she exhibited, in the patience in suffering and the fortitude in adversity which she exemplified, the spirit of the Pilgrims would seem to have revived in her.

It would, perhaps, be unnecessary, under ordinary circumstances, to venture more than a passing allusion to the history of her marriage; but, as this event wears somewhat of a religious aspect, it being connected with the first real prayer she is supposed ever to have offered, a more circumstantial detail may be expected.

Entered upon at an age of extreme youth and warm impulse, with but a slight knowledge of the world, and deprived of a father's gentle but firm control, we conceal not that the step as taken by her involved a degree of responsibility and hazard too serious for ordinary prudence to justify. That it was in every respect a suitable alliance, yielding to its latest hour unmingled happiness, must be traced to something beyond the sagacity and forethought of a warm-hearted and confiding girl, of but eighteen bright summers. Referring to it in after years, she remarks, "I acted wrong; but God most wonderfully and mercifully directed the whole, and overruled the evil for our good and for His own glory." The 'evil' to which she here so ingenuously refers was the impetuosity which led her to act, in so momentous a matter, independently of authority. Adverse to her marrying in the army, as necessarily involving a wide separation from her child, her mother had discouraged several military suitors for her daughter's hand, and had as decidedly opposed the attentions of Lieut. Winslow. But her heart's young affections were secretly and irrevocably surrendered, not only to the most admired and beloved officer in his regiment, but to one whose station in life and whose personal excellence were worthy of her confidence. That with a step involving so much excited natural feeling there should be blended a sentiment so thoughtful and sacred as that which we are about to record is, doubtless, the most remarkable and instructive feature in the narrative. Her own pen the most appropriately and beautifully pursues the story.

"Now nearly eighteen, gay, thoughtless, full of life and vivacity, I felt my freedom and enjoyed it. Three companies of the 47th Regiment arrived at Bermuda from New Providence. The new comers soon obtained introduction to the leading families of the island, and greatly increased its gaieties. It was more than a year before I became sensible of the attractions and attentions of one of the officers. These attentions grew more marked. My mother became alarmed. I was immediately sent from home, and placed under the care of an aunt residing several miles from town. One day a gentleman came out to dinner. In the course of the conversation he casually mentioned that orders had come from New Providence for Lieut. Winslow to join the regiment there. This intelligence went like a dagger to my heart. In vain I strove to disguise my feelings,—bursting into tears, I left the table. Then was I convinced that my heart was not my own. I retired to my room to reflect upon my course. I knew the Governor could not interpose, nor had the Colonel in command power to detain an officer under orders from head-quarters. My happiness was at stake. Great was my distress, intense my agony of mind. Who could prevent his going? The thought suddenly occurred to me,—GOD *can!* In a moment I arose, locked my door, and fell upon my knees before Him. It was my *first prayer!* In the simplest form of words imaginable, I earnestly pleaded with the Lord not only to prevent his going, but to give him to me as my husband. The prayer was offered—the request was made,—and I arose from my knees with a spirit as light as a feather. My sadness and anxiety all were gone. Was not this of God? Was not this faith in the power of God? What brought such instantaneous and perfect relief to my distressed heart? Was it not that God gave me the power to believe that He would grant me my request? The next day, with the permission of my aunt, I mounted my horse, and attended by a servant, rode into town. To my astonishment my mother received me affectionately, and uttered not a word of rebuke at my return. The Lord had turned her heart. That evening I met the object of my affections. The proposal of a private marriage was made, and, after some trembling hesitation, was acceded to. The next morning—a licence having been procured—we met at the house of my friend, Judge L——, and from thence, accompanied by two of the officers and the wife of one of them, we went to the house of the clergyman of the parish,* where I was united in the bonds of holy wedlock to the man of my choice, the beloved of my heart. The first emotion of my mother, when the intelligence was broken to her, was distress; the second was love. I was received and forgiven. Never had she reason to regret my choice. She loved my husband as her own son, and an affectionate son he proved. Thus was my prayer answered three days only after I had offered it up to that God with whom all things are possible. From the moment I uttered that prayer, every obstacle which before seemed insurmountable was removed. Was there not faith in that prayer—faith in the power of God? Surely there was; and yet how many years did it lie beneath the rubbish of the fall! Still I was His, and my precious husband was His, and we were to be the honoured parents of many that should be His, some to preach His blessed Gospel, and all, I trust, to be united together in one band of love at His right hand through an endless eternity."

In throwing back a glance upon the preceding narrative, fidelity as a Christian biographer, yet blended with the most sacred filial reverence, would seem to demand from the pen that records it, an observation in reference to the principle of action which she herself, in moments of calm reflection, and when true religion had become enthroned upon her heart, so honestly and emphatically deprecated. There were two points in her marriage which render the self-responsible course she adopted such as no reasoning could commend, and the *imitations* of which, no results, however overruled by God, could justify. The one was,—the too excited feelings which were allowed to control the judgment, and the other,—the acting in opposition to a parent's wishes. It is true, there does not appear to have been any express command or positive injunction; but surely it was enough to know that her mother disapproved

---

* It was then the custom to celebrate marriages in private houses.

of the step, to have dictated a more reflective course. "Honour thy father and thy mother," is a divine precept of such importance in God's sight, as to be annexed to the promise, " that thy days may be long in the land which the Lord thy God giveth thee." In no step in life (and for the youthful reader of these pages we especially venture upon the remark)—for none involves consequences of such moment—is a child more imperiously and solemnly bound to recognize parental authority than that which Miss Forbes now took. We are not prepared to say that in *all* similar cases a parent's judgment may be the best—for it may be warped by prejudice, or be controlled by unworthy influence,—yet no circumstances whatever can justify an entire abnegation, on the part of the child, of that sacred relation which God has made a beautiful type of His own, and which imparts to the domestic constitution its dignity and strength.

And yet that *first* prayer! Ah! who can adequately describe its preciousness and importance? It is the first breath of God—the first pulse of spiritual life—the first dawn of endless glory in the soul. How many an earnest pastor, how many a pious parent, how many a fond friend anxiously waits the blessed announcement—"Behold, he prayeth!" That faint scintillation of spiritual life may retire, as if quenched in utter darkness, and long and dreary may be the night that enshrouds it; but at some future day it will reappear—for it was imperishable—and realize, in its fulness of blessing, the hope its first pale gleam had inspired. Blessed truth! the little seed of grace, once dropped into the soul, will germinate, 'take root downward and bear fruit upward' unto life eternal.

Passing over several years subsequent to her marriage— years spent in military life, and, although not devoid of much that was interesting and eventful, yet supplying in their history but little material in keeping with the grave character of this volume—we proceed to record that momentous event which gave to all her future life its reality, sanctity, and charm.

CHAPTER II.

To a mind in sympathy with the beautiful in nature, there are few spectacles more exquisitely enjoyable than the day-dawn in spring. To watch the gradual dissolving of night's deep shadows into grey twilight,—the twilight blushing into the rose-hue of morning—to catch the first new-born ray trembling in the eastern sky, all nature starting from its slumber, and hymning its early praise to the Creator, who "maketh the outgoings of the morning and the evening to rejoice"—is a scene of intense interest and beauty. But to a mind sensible of moral beauty, transcendently more lovely is the day-dawn of grace in the soul. To trace the first faint glimmer of spiritual light struggling with the darkness of the mind—to behold that mind gradually emerging from its night of gloom into the calm sunshine of a new spiritual creation, and to watch its progress as it "shineth more and more unto the perfect day," is a spectacle of yet surpassing grandeur. Such a picture, as sketched by her own pen, we are about to contemplate:

"From the age of ten years I have been in the habit of reading to my mother, every night, the 'Whole Duty of Man.' This book, I believe, brought me under a law-work of soul. After my marriage, I discontinued reading it, but still what I had read was impressed upon my mind and memory. Often would the thought come over me, 'How can such a one as I get to heaven? Heaven is a good place, and only the good go there. Oh, if I could but cease from sin and keep the Commandments.' Sometimes I shut myself up, and with the the 'Whole Duty of Man' or the Prayer Book in my hand, upon my knees I have solemnly promised I would keep all the Commandments, and while doing this have felt greatly relieved of my burden, as if the work were done that was to fit me for heaven. But ere the day was over, my goodness had passed away, and I felt as unfit as ever for the abodes of the holy and the good. At other times I thought I was not worse than most people, and that God was too good to condemn the whole world. During this period I never hinted my feelings to my husband: I was afraid he would think from my distress of mind that I had committed some dreadful sin, nor could I explain my views to him. I heard no gospel, though a constant attendant at church. Once I ventured to go to the Lord's Table, and recollect shedding tears at hearing of the sufferings of Christ. But soon after I relapsed into the ways of the world and forgot my vows. A young creature, the wife of one of the officers, died at a place where our regiment was quartered. Her death greatly shocked me, as I feared she was not good enough, any more than myself, to go to heaven. I was in the room when she died; but as we were under orders for Bermuda, I soon, in the bustle and excitement of preparing for the voyage, forgot the serious impression her death made upon me; but still an earnest desire more or less followed me to try and commend myself to God, and make myself fit for heaven. I often hoped I might die of a lingering disease, as that would afford me more time for repentance.

"Soon after my marriage I was at a ball; I was then a bride, receiving much attention, and my pride was gratified. I had married the man I loved, and who loved me in return. My mother was more than reconciled to the step I had taken —she was pleased. I had everything my carnal heart could desire, not a wish was ungratified. I was at the very zenith of earthly happiness. On returning from the ball, I took a hasty review of the evening I had passed as I lay sleepless upon my pillow. The glitter—the music—the dance—the excitement—the attention—the pleasure, all passed before me. But oh, I felt a want I could not describe. I sighed, and whispered to myself these expressive words: 'Is *this* all?' I felt at the moment that if this were all the happiness the world could bestow, then was there a lack I knew not how to supply, and a void I could not fill. I had reached the very summit of earthly bliss, and found it to fall short of what my heart craved, and my soul required. From this time I grew more fond of retirement, and less inclined to mingle with the gay world. I felt that what I had been pursuing in the early part of my life was not happiness. I turned from it with a sensation of loathing, and sought in solitude what I had never found in the brilliant and crowded walks of life. I thought that there must be a state where real happiness was to be found. In this condition of mind I continued for years, striving to keep the law, and to shape my course by the 'Whole Duty of Man.' I endeavoured to walk so as to please God, but again and again my best resolutions were broken. These feelings I concealed from all around me, for I would not for the world have breathed a hint that I was unhappy to the dearest friend. I saw every one around me apparently happy in the possession of the world which had lost its charm for me. I now sought peace of mind in domestic enjoyment. I was encircled by my children, possessed a husband who anticipated my fondest wish, and my heart could sigh for nothing of earthly bliss which I did not possess—and still I was *unhappy*. I was a *sinner*,—and this secret conviction beclouded every prospect, and embittered every cup."

Such were the mental exercises—sad, yet hopeful—which foreshadowed the day-spring from on high in her heart. It was now the twilight of grace in her soul. The dark clouds which had so long enshrouded her were breaking, and this dreary night of weeping was fast retiring before the dawning splendour of a morning of joy. After living a military life for some years, Captain Winslow was induced to retire to an ancestral estate near Romford, in Essex. But change of place and diversity of scene supply no real relief to a mind burdened with sin. Referring to her removal, she remarks:

"While here I was conscious—though surrounded by every earthly comfort, and by all I loved, and had more time for reading and reflection—of the same lack I had felt years before. My mind was restless. My soul wanted what earth could not supply. And yet I could not describe to any one what I needed, nor what I felt. I was unhappy—at times miserable; my weary soul thirsting for what it had not, and yet I could not answer myself, and say what that one thing was."

It was no longer possible to conceal from her husband a sadness which, like the spoiler, wrapped itself within the folds of every flower of earthly good. The quick eye of affection detected a lurking sorrow, the cause of which baffled his ingenuity to discover. He marked the pallor of her cheek, the stifled sigh, and the vain attempt at cheerfulness. It was enough, however, to know that she was unhappy; attributing it to the solitude of their residence, he instantly resolved upon an expedient for its relief. On returning home one day, he informed her that he had taken a house in town, and proposed an immediate removal. The idea of a change was pleasing, and in a short time they were fully established in their new abode. In all this God's hand was signally moving. He was leading her blind steps by a way she knew not, but it was to bring her soul, panting for the "living water," to the spring whence it flowed. It does not appear that the ministry of the parish church in which her new residence was situate was of a character calculated to meet the exigencies of such a case. There was the absence of that evangelical element which could alone constitute it a message of "life and spirit" to its hearers. Referring to it, she says, "There was nothing to satisfy my soul." The first event marking God's overruling providence in this change of residence was the appointment, just at this juncture, of the Rev. THOMAS SHEPPARD to the perpetual curacy of St. James's Episcopal Chapel, Pentonville, and who, seven years afterwards, succeeded to the rectory of Clerkenwell. "How beautiful are the feet of them that preach the gospel of peace, and bring glad tidings of good things!" Never did these expressive words of the evangelical prophet receive a more striking illustration than now. Mr. Sheppard was a decided man of God, and an able minister of the New Testament. His ministry, sound in doctrine, and richly experimental in its character, was accompanied by an earnestness of spirit, and a persuasiveness of address, which at once met the peculiar state of mind it was designed to relieve. Thus two individuals under the especial guidance of God entered the parish of Pentonville almost simultaneously. The one was a soul bowed down with grief for sin, and who could in nowise lift up herself—the other was a messenger of peace, whose ministry of grace was to loosen her bonds, and set her captive spirit free. For her sake his feet were guided thither, little divining, doubtless, for what especial intent his Master had thus brought him. But the narrative is best and more fully told by herself:

"The change of residence was pleasant to me. I was thrown more amongst my friends, and for awhile my mind was diverted from its gloom. We were near the Chapel of Ease. I went, but there was nothing to satisfy my soul. The minister had been preaching here for twenty-one years, but now it was the Lord's time that he should be removed, and that a real shepherd should take his place. I went, and heard from the new minister, *for the first time in my life*, the precious GOSPEL OF PEACE. This was what I had wanted to know for many years, that Jesus Christ had come into the world to save poor sinners. I was a sinner, and wanted to be saved. Oh, how eagerly I listened, and drank in every word! I had been in vain trying to work out my salvation, but my work always fell short, and left me as poor and miserable as ever. Now was held out to me the hope that I might be saved by the work of another—the work of Jesus Christ. With one observation of Mr. Sheppard I was much impressed. Describing my spiritual state of mind on one occasion he most solemnly said, 'If there is such an individual present, I will pledge my soul for it that that individual is in the way to Christ.' With this remark I was deeply struck. I thought the free invitation of the gospel he was presenting must be true, since this godly man was willing to *risk his soul* upon the truth of what he was asserting. Oh, if this were true, I might after all be saved! My heart and mind were now at work. I repaired to my Bible, and searched it again and again. *By grace are ye saved through faith, and that not of yourselves, it is the gift of God*, was a passage that arrested my attention. I found that in the Epistle of James we were justified by works, and my heart sank within me. I had no works, and could do none pleasing and acceptable to God. In the Epistles of Paul I read that we were justified by faith. There seemed a contradiction. My anxious mind could find no rest, but still I felt a ray of hope dawn upon my benighted soul, and continued to hear the precious truth as one hungering and thirsting for divine knowledge. One night, watching alone by the side of a sick child, I took my Bible and searched the Scriptures. The question how the sinner could be justified, pressed heavily upon my mind. If I could be saved by faith in the righteousness of another, then I felt that there was hope for me; but if there was anything for me to do towards meriting this salvation, I saw I must be forever lost. I read first one epistle and then another, when as I read, the words were brought to my mind, *Ask, and ye shall receive*. I reasoned, who is it that says this? It is God. Can God lie? It is impossible. He must do what he has said. He has commanded, *Ask, and ye shall receive*. I will ask. I fell upon my knees and pleaded the promise. My petition was offered in the simple language of an untutored child. I knew nothing of Christian experience, had heard the gospel but a few times, and the only thing that had fastened itself upon my mind was the truth that a poor sinner could be saved. Thus I went to God and pleaded the promise, asking him how such a wretched sinner as I was could be saved. I did not wrestle so much for my salvation as to know *how* I could be saved as a helpless sinner that could do nothing. I arose from my knees, and again took my Bible. I read and compared scripture with scripture, but the one part appeared to contradict the other, and my mind was left in darkness and perplexity. Again I carried the promise to the throne of grace, and again wrestled with the Lord. I returned to my Bible, but it was yet a sealed book. The third time I ventured near the Lord, still pleading this one gracious promise, *Ask, and ye shall receive.* In an instant light broke in upon my soul. Jesus stood before me and spoke these blessed words,— I AM THY SALVATION! I hailed the glad tidings—my heart and soul responded—Jesus was with me—He had himself spoken—I had seen the Lord—had heard His voice—my soul was saved—my burden was gone—the grave-clothes in which I had been so long confined fell off—my spirit was free, and I seemed to soar towards heaven in the sweetest, richest enjoyment—my heart filled with a joy unspeakable. I arose from my knees to adore, and praise, and bless His holy name. Oh, what a night was that, never, never, to be forgotten! I had seen Jesus. It was no vision of the bodily senses that I saw; but I had no more doubt that I was a redeemed and pardoned sinner, that I had seen Christ, and held communion with Him who died that I might live, than I had of my own existence. It was with difficulty I could refrain from calling up the whole house to hear what the Lord had done for my soul. I thought all would believe and rejoice too, so ignorant was I. As soon as it was morning I informed my husband of what the Lord had done for me. He looked amazed at what I said, and feared I should lose my senses. I was grieved that he did not believe and could not understand, and urged him, by every argument I could employ, to seek for the same blessing, which I was sure the Lord would give him.

"It has since been evident to myself, that when the Holy Ghost gave me the promise to plead, He also gave me a measure of faith to credit God for its fulfilment, and in answering the prayer of simple faith, Christ came into my soul with a full and free salvation. *I am thy salvation!* This was good news indeed, fresh from heaven. Christ was mine, heaven was mine,—all care and sorrow had vanished, and I was as happy as I could be in the body. I had found what I had long sought. I had been in search of real happiness for years, and in one night I found it all in Jesus. God's richest treasury had been thrown open to my view, and in Him I found all I wanted for time and eternity. In this happy frame I continued many weeks, imploring all I knew and loved to come to Christ, but none understood me. I began to think that no one knew Jesus Christ but dear Mr. Sheppard and myself, and often felt that if I had met a chimney sweep in the street that knew and loved Christ, I could embrace him as a brother."

Such is the simple, glowing narrative of one upon whose soul the Sun of Righteousness had just arisen. In the *earnestness* of religious feeling breathing through these genuine utterances of the heart, the reader may trace the leading characteristic of her subsequent Christian life. That at this early period of her new birth there was much holy zeal, as yet unaccompanied with deep Christian experience, she always meekly acknowledged. She thought every mind would believe her simple story, and that every heart would sympathize with her holy joy. She needed the helping hand of an advanced Christian. It would appear, however, that in the absence of personal intercourse with living saints, she met with the works of that eminent man of God, the Rev. John Newton, Rector of Olney, whose richly experimental writings, clothed in beautiful simplicity of style, were admirably adapted to her state of mind, and were richly owned of God in deepening her Christian knowledge and experience. To the latest period of her life she referred with gratitude to the benefit she had derived from his writings, and one of the books found in her room after death was a volume of her favourite author, John Newton. The foregoing remarks are thus borne out in her continued biography:—

"Some months after this Satan was permitted to try my young faith, and to cast a cloud over my mind. Unbelief began to work. I feared I might be mistaken, as I could meet with none among all my friends who either understood what I said, or knew what I had experienced. Had I then a matured Christian to whom I could have opened my heart, it would have been a great comfort. And yet it was well it was so, that I might flee, not to an arm of flesh, but to the living God. My mind was brought into darkness. The sensible presence of Christ was withdrawn, and sadness filled my heart. I sought Him but found Him not; I prayed, but received no comfort. Pacing my room one day under this dark dispensation, and fearing I never again should enjoy what I once had, I threw myself upon my knees, and cried to the Lord to come and bless me if I had not deceived myself. In a moment, in condescending love, the same precious Jesus stood before me as He did at the first, saying, *O thou of little faith, wherefore didst thou doubt?* I well recollect my answer. Clasping my hands in ecstacy, I exclaimed, 'My Lord, and my God! I cannot and will not doubt; forgive my base ingratitude.' Overwhelmed with that blessed interview, I thought I never, no, never would doubt again. Satan fled from the presence of the Lord, and I was left alone with God,—*my* God, my *own* God. I could not tell my joy, and no one understood my feelings. At this time I became acquainted with the writings of the Rev. John Newton. I read them with great delight, and if he had been alive, I would have walked miles to have conversed with him."

It was not long before the providence of God guided to her door the steps of a deeply-taught, aged Christian in humble life. To him she opened her heart, and found a warm response. He kindly took her by the hand, and in lowliness of mind she yielded herself to his instructions. In a letter to her mother she thus refers to this auspicious circumstance:—

"I enclose you a note from a poor man addressed to me. He is poor in this world's goods, but rich in faith. He watches over me as a father would a child, and I believe loves me as much. He visits me often, comforts and reproves, and endeavours to build me up in my most holy faith; and when he cannot come, he writes to me. He is a most pious, excellent Christian. His thoughts and whole heart are continually in heaven. Oh, that I were but more like him!

It is an interesting fact, that on her return from abroad some years afterwards, she sought out her early Christian instructor, found him much advanced in years, in ill-health, and the occupant of an alms-house. Thither she frequently repaired, bearing with her some little temporal comfort, and often receiving in return a word of spiritual blessing. She occasionally invited him to her house, and administered to his necessities, until the venerable pilgrim exchanged his lowly abode on earth for the many-mansioned home of his Father in Heaven.

The following letter addressed to her mother at Bermuda, with which we close this chapter, whilst it confirms the pleasing fact of her parent's spiritual change, evidences at the same time the remarkable clearness and growth of her own views of divine truth; and in the illness of her husband, to which it refers, foreshadows those trying dispensations which afterwards gave such maturity to her Christianity, and rendered her so extensively useful in comforting others with the comfort with which she herself had been comforted of God:—

"My dearest Mother,   October 22, 1810.

" . . . Thank God you are all well; but above all things, I desire to thank and bless His holy name that you and Bella are so wonderfully brought to know yourselves, and to know Him whom to know is life everlasting. Blessed be God, who passes by so many, and who has deigned to look upon us who were lying as others, dead in sin. Infinite in sovereignty, infinite in goodness, infinite in power! why He passes by some and calls others, is only known to Himself; but there is a time coming when we shall know even as we are known, and be enabled to see that He acts consistently with his goodness and mercy. All we have to do in this vale of tears is to press forward to the glorious prize He has placed in our view, looking continually to Jesus, trusting not to our own strength, but waiting in humble dependence upon Him for all our sufficiency to carry us on, and to enable us to hold out unto the end. He that has promised is true and faithful to His word. Oh, that we may be found like His beloved handmaiden of old, sitting at His feet. His eye is ever upon His dear, dependent flock; He knows all our need, and has promised to supply it. But for these things He will be inquired of. It is at a throne of grace Jesus makes Himself known to His saints, comforts them, revives their drooping spirits with a view of those blessings He has in store for them. This world is not our home—we look for a better. His people are pilgrims here on earth, and generally are a poor and afflicted people. They have not their portion here as thousands have,—their portion is to come. Their names are written in the book of life, and were written before the foundation of the world. They are as dear to Him as the apple of His eye. Then what have we to fear? nothing; but everything to hope. Blessed be God who sent His only Son to pay our debt, to rescue us from the power of Satan, to cleanse us from all our guilt, to clothe our souls with His righteousness, and thereby give us a rightful claim to a crown of glory. Blessed be that dear Son who condescended to come amongst us, to assume our nature, and to do for us what we had no power to do for ourselves. And blessed be the Holy Spirit, who in infinite mercy forms and prepares us for the heavenly kingdom. I am delighted to find dear B—— has such clear views of the doctrine of the Atonement. And oh, that they may reach her heart, and influence all her thoughts, words, and actions. My last letter will have informed you that the children's illness was occasioned by the measles, and my precious husband's from a rupture of a blood-vessel in the lungs. These things altogether, have been a severe trial to mind and body, but I have been in a most wonderful manner supported under them. I have gone through enough to kill a dozen women stronger than myself; but the Lord has fulfilled the promise, and given me strength according to my day.

"On Monday evening I heard a very popular minister, who was to preach at a chapel in Lincoln's Inn Fields. I waited some time until the doors were opened, and then obtained a seat near the pulpit. But although the place was large, every part was densely crowded, and people standing in the aisles. The preacher was Alexander Fletcher, from Scotland, a young man of about twenty-two. But oh, how zealous, fervent, and inexpressibly great and sweet in explaining the glad tidings of salvation! His discourse was addressed to children particularly, and he has such uncommon power in directing and fixing the attention of both old and young, that I do not believe the eyes of either were off him during the whole service. This good steward of Jesus preaches almost every evening in some part or other of London. Oh, when I see such servants of the Lord spending their strength, their lives, their all for God, and counting it nothing so that they might win Christ, I look at myself and mourn over my unprofitableness, and desire to lie low in the dust. This good, zealous man of God, though followed by crowds, appears humble and lowly, like his blessed Master. Oh, my dear mamma, how I long to have you with me, where you may hear the blessed gospel preached in a thousand places. How precious it is in the ear of the redeemed! It is the soul's food, and we grow lean and lukewarm without it. May every covenant blessing attend you, is the prayer of your affectionate daughter, M. W."

CHAPTER III.

The earnest and practical character of her religion soon became apparent. The yearning of her heart for the spiritual well-being of others, which now appeared, was not less the natural outflow of her new-born feelings than the forecastings of her future devotedness. The fervent zeal to which her Christianity gave birth, and which was but now in the first pantings of its inspiration, she retained in all its bloom until death. It was natural that those of her own house should occupy her first thoughts, and share her deepest sympathies. As a follower of Christ, she stood alone in her family. She felt her responsibility and resolved to act. Her first step in carrying out this her solemn resolution to serve the Lord was the erection, of what until now had no place in her domestic circle —a family altar to God. The accomplishment of her purpose demanded no little moral courage, wisdom, and firmness. The proposal was submitted to her husband, and though kindly, was yet strongly opposed. But the conviction of duty was too deep to be overcome. The energy of will, and the remarkable grace which in after years confronted and vanquished difficulties in the way of duty more formidable, and which bore her through trials yet more severe, crowned this her first work and testimony for God with the most pleasing success. Consent was at length given; the effort was made in God's strength, and God blessed it. The family and household were convened for what to them was a novel yet impressive service. Her husband, at first declining to be present, was there. She conducted the service, read a portion of God's word, and then all but *one* of that circle knelt while she offered solemn prayer,— the father of that worshipping family alone stood. But when again they assembled, that heart was subdued, its hostility disarmed, and side by side with his wife and little ones he bent the knee before their Father in heaven. From this moment the fire enkindled on that domestic altar never went out. Whether at home or abroad, journeying on the land, or voyaging upon the sea, family prayer was never omitted. "As for me and my house, we will serve the Lord," was a holy resolve with which no other engagements ever were allowed to interfere. From the commencement of her Christian course until its close, her grand and single aim was to live for God. To Him her first thoughts, first time, first duties were given. All other and secondary calls, duties, and claims were held in stern abeyance. "Seek ye *first* the kingdom of God and His righteousness," was the precept in which she undeviatingly walked, leaving God to fulfil as most faithfully he did, the promise with which it is annexed, "and all things else shall be added unto you." Happy if her holy example—the example of one ever conscious of her own weakness, yet knowing wherein her great strength lay—shall confirm the wavering purpose, or encourage the hesitating heart of some feeble, timid witness for the Lord. Alas! how many professedly Christian households are there without a family altar, simply because there are no hands in that circle strong enough in faith to rear it, and no hearts fervent enough in love to light its sacred fires. But how grievous the twofold sin,—first, the neglect of a sacred and binding duty; and then to limit, in its performance, the promised grace and strength of the Holy One of Israel! The believer should ever remember, that God has enjoined no precept unaccompanied by a promise; and that it is only as we are found walking in filial, unreserved obedience to the one, that he is found faithfully and fully performing the other. Christ enjoins upon His disciples no yoke, and imposes no burden—calls to no service, and sends no trial—for which He does not vouchsafe all requisite aid. "My grace is sufficient for thee," is a promise which embraces in its illimitable range every member, and all the circumstances of each member, of the household of faith. Looking, then, to Him, "Let the weak say I am strong:" let the timid "glory in their infirmities;" and let those who are cast down exclaim, "In the Lord have I righteousness and strength." Apposite to these remarks is the following extract from one of her letters to her mother:—

"Do you, my dearest mamma, have family prayer? I hope you do. B—— and you are of one mind, and when only two or three meet together to worship God, He has promised to be amongst them. He has not said to the seeking seed of Israel, Seek ye my face in vain. How pleasing it is to the Lord when we are enabled, in spite of an ensnaring world, to erect an altar to Him in our house, and say with Joshua, *As for me and my house, we will serve the Lord.* Call the servants together, read a portion of Scripture, and go to prayer. If you have not yet been able to do this, I hope you will do it. Let the wicked laugh; let them call you by what names they may; be not afraid, for *more are they who are for you, than those who are against you.* You have all the saints on earth, and all the saints in glory, and all the angels in heaven, and best of all, God Himself on your side. And if God be for you, who can be against you? You fight under a good Captain, the Captain of your salvation, who will make you more than conqueror. I would earnestly recommend to you extempore prayer. Lay aside your forms of prayer, and the Lord Himself will teach you to pray from the heart. The blessed Spirit has promised to help our infirmities in prayer."

Among the first general objects which enlisted her Christian sympathies and efforts, was the spiritual condition of her own native isle. In St. George, the metropolis of the Bermudas—a beautiful group of islands bestudding the bosom of the Atlantic ocean—there still resided her mother, and a wide circle of kindred and friends. God had done much, in point of natural scenery and salubrity of climate, for the Bermudas. Few spots in this beautiful, though fallen creation, concentrate so much varied loveliness, and of so high a tone, as do these isles of the sea. Poetry, in some of her sweetest, if not her most truthful strains, has often sung their praises; while history, with perhaps more stern fidelity, has awarded them an honourable page in its no less interesting annals. Nor to poetry and history alone are the Bermudas indebted for their fame. Invalids from distant climes, attenuated by disease, and abandoned by hope, who have repaired to these islands, seeking but to eke out an enfeebled existence yet a little longer, and to meet death with mitigated suffering, have, beneath their soft skies, and fanned by their balmy breezes, been restored to perfect health; and lived, either to settle permanently in the island, or to return to the homes they expected to have quitted for ever. Nor were the Bermudas less renowned for the generous kindness and boundless hospitality of their native inhabitants, than for the romantic loveliness of their scenery. No consumptive ever landed upon their shores in quest of health —no tourist ever came to explore their beauties—no wayfaring mariner was ever stranded upon their rocks, who met not here a friend, and found not here a home. The only rivalry that existed was,—who should show most kindness to the stranger.*

But lovely and fertile as these fairy islands were, and still more attractive the native character of their inhabitants, the early history of the Bermudas does not appear to furnish any clear or authentic evidence that evangelical religion had ever very extensively prevailed. And yet, if we may credit Andrew Marvel, of the Commonweath—one of the greatest wits and statesmen of his age, and a Christian poet, too, of no mean worth—it would seem that the Bermuda islands afforded an asylum to some of the Puritans from the tyranny which drove so many to seek in other lands the liberty of conscience denied them in their own.† But, if this be true, the piety which

---

* Waller, in his "Summer Islands," a poem of exquisite beauty, thus portrays this salubrious clime:—

"For the kind spring (which but salutes us here)
Inhabits these, and courts them all the year;
Ripe fruits and blossoms on the same trees live,
At once they promise, and at once they give.
So sweet the air, so moderate the clime,
None sickly lives, or dies before his time.
Heaven sure has kept this spot of earth uncursed,
To show how all things were created first."

† This historical fact is embodied in the following poem, entitled "Bermudas," composed by Andrew Marvel, and published about the year 1661. It is supposed to be a chant of the Puritans who fled to these islands:—

"Where the remote Bermudas ride
In the ocean's bosom, unespied,
From a small boat that rowed along,
The list'ning winds received this song:

"'What should we do but sing His praise,
That led us through the wat'ry maze,
Unto an isle so long unknown,
And yet far kinder than our own?
Where He the huge sea-monsters wracks,
That lift the deep upon their backs,
He lands us on a grassy stage,
Safe from the storm's and prelates' rage;
He gave us this eternal spring,
Which here enamels everything;

these holy refugees enkindled, in course of time, either expired altogether, or lived only in the smouldering embers which faintly glowed beneath the cold, deadening forms of a prevalent but lifeless religion. Yet God had purposes of mercy towards these islands, which He was about now to unfold.

It was on the 15th of March, 1748, that the Rev. GEORGE

> And sends the fowls to us in care,
> On daily visits through the air;
> He hangs in shades the orange bright,
> Like golden lamps in a green night;
> And does in the pomegranate close
> Jewels more rich than Ormus shows.
> He makes the figs our mouths to meet,
> And throws the melons at our feet:
> But apple plants of such a price,
> No tree could ever bear them twice.
> With cedars, chosen by His hand,
> From Lebanon, he stores the land,
> And makes the hollow seas that roar,
> Proclaim the ambergrease on shore.
> He cast (of which we rather boast)
> The gospel's pearl upon this coast,
> And in their rocks for us did frame
> A temple where to sound His name.
> Oh! let our voice His praise exalt,
> Till it arise at heaven's vault,
> Which, then (perhaps) rebounding, may
> Echo beyond the Mexique Bay.'
>
> "Thus sang they in the English boat,
> An holy and a cheerful note;
> And all the way, to guide their chime,
> With falling oars they kept the time."
>
> *Works of Andrew Marvel, by Captain Edmund Thompson,*
> 3 *vols.* 1776.

There is, perhaps, no man whose name deserves to be held in more sacred veneration, by those to whom the memory of the Puritans is dear, than ANDREW MARVEL. He occupied an illustrious niche in the history of his times. His father was a clergyman of great learning and of high repute. He met an affecting and untimely death. Crossing a river with a bridal party, for whom he was about to officiate, a sudden squall arose, and the entire group, including the young and beautiful bride, perished. The son, Andrew, who appeared to inherit much of his father's gifts, was educated at Cambridge, and afterwards represented Forkington-upon-Hull in Parliament, was secretary to the English Embassy at Constantinople, and Assistant Latin Secretary to Milton, under Cromwell. To him the blind bard was indebted for the early popularity of his sublime poem. Finding "Paradise Lost," the copyright of which Milton

WHITFIELD, the great apostle of his age, landed in Bermuda. He had arrived from New York, with impaired health, borne down with anxiety and toil, seeking amidst the loveliness and tranquillity of these enchanting isles a few weeks' bodily and mental rest from his exhausting labours. An entire stranger, ill, and depressed, his reception was worthy of the people, and soothing to his lone feelings; it was kind, sympathizing, and hospitable. Whitfield was pleased with the beauties of the place, and charmed with the simplicity and friendship of the inhabitants. A rapid survey of the spiritual condition of the population was sufficient to convince this zealous minister of Christ that an extended field of evangelical labour, white to the harvest, was spread out before him. Enfeebled by illness, and oppressed by care, though he was, his mighty soul was stirred within him, and he yearned to proclaim throughout that lovely group the unsearchable riches of Christ. Scarcely allowing himself a week's repose, he commenced his mission. The pulpits of the parish churches being closed against him by a law of the island, which required a license from home, and which the Governor would fain have relaxed in his favour, he preached to large, attentive, and affected auditors in the Presbyterian pulpit, in the Town-house of St. George's, in private dwellings, and in the open air. The immediate result was what might have been anticipated from the ministry of Whitfield. Everywhere from the highest to the lowest,—from the Executive to the most ignorant slave in the island,—society was moved to its centre, as by one mighty impulse, on the subject of religion. A general and powerful awakening transpired. Crowds were attracted to his ministry—his word was with power—and multitudes were profoundly impressed, and not a few hopefully converted. Such an outpouring of God's Spirit, such a revival of evangelical religion, those

had just sold for fifteen pounds, remained unhonoured and unknown, Marvel wrote a complimentary poem on its publication, which at once unveiled its beauties to the undiscerning eye of the public, and brought it into notice. He was a man of great integrity of principle, and of extraordinary moral courage. Of him it was said by an historian of his day, " He had the courage to attack arbitrary government in the reign of a tyrant, and to attempt to defend the Protestant church when the head of it died a Papist." Some poet thus refers to two of the greatest men of his day:

" 'Tis Marvel braves the wicked acts of kings ;
But what the Muses dictate—Milton sings."

islands had, perhaps, never before witnessed. Amongst the first to welcome Mr. Whitfield to Bermuda, and to offer the hospitality of his house, was Dr. GEORGE FORBES, the grandfather of the subject of this memoir. He received the interesting stranger to his home, paid him the most courteous attention, and employed his influence in obtaining the Council Chamber for his use, in which the Governor, several of the council, the clergymen of the parish, and a number of the townspeople assembled in the most devout order to hear the message of salvation from his lips. The reader will gather a better idea of the remarkable success of Mr. Whitfield's labours in Bermuda, during which he preached generally twice a day for a month, from the extracts given below, selected from his own private journal.*

* "Wednesday, April 6. After sermon Dr. FORBES and Mr. P——, the Collector, desired me to favour them and the gentlemen of the town with my company to dine with them. I accepted the invitation. The Governor, the President, and Judge Bascombe were there. All wondered at my speaking so freely and fluently without notes. At table his Excellency introduced something of religion, by asking me the meaning of the word 'hades.' Several other things were started about free will, Adam's fall, predestination, &c., to all which God enabled me to answer so pertinently, and taught me to mix the *utile* and *dulce* so together, that all at table seemed highly pleased, shook me by the hand, and invited me to their respective houses. The Governor, in particular, asked me to dine with him on the morrow; and Dr. Forbes, one of his particular intimates, invited me to drink tea in the afternoon. I thanked all, returned proper respects, and went to my lodgings with some degree of thankfulness for the assistance afforded me, but awed before God at the consideration of my unspeakable unworthiness. In the afternoon, about five o'clock, I expounded the parable of the prodigal son to many people at a private house, and in the evening had liberty to speak freely and closely to those that supped with me. Oh, that this may be the beginning of good gospel times to the inhabitants of this town! Lord, teach me to deal prudently with them, and cause them to melt under Thy word.

"Sunday, 17. God still magnifies His power and goodness more and more. This morning we had a pleasing sight in Mr. Paul's meetinghouse. I began to preach, and the people to be affected as in days of old at home. Indeed, the prospect is encouraging. 'Praise the Lord, O my soul.'

"May 7. In my conversation, these two days, with some of my friends, I was diverted much in hearing several things that passed among the poor negroes since my preaching to them last Sunday.

"One of the number, it seems, said, 'that if the book I preached out of was the best book that was ever bought, and came out of London, she was sure it had never all that in it which I spoke to the negroes.' The

"Laden with abundance of prayers and blessings," to use his own words, Whitfield bade farewell to Bermuda and its generous inhabitants, bearing with him, as the expression of their grateful love, ample provisions for his voyage, and up-

old man who spoke out last Sunday and said, 'Yes, Sir,' when I asked them whether all the negroes would not go to heaven, being questioned by somebody why he spoke out so, answered, 'that the gentleman put the question once or twice to them, and the other fools had not the manners to make me any answer, till at last I seemed to point at him, and he was ashamed that nobody should answer me, and therefore he did.' Another, wondering why I said negroes had black hearts, was answered by his black brother thus; 'Ah! thou fool, dost not thou understand it? he means black with sin.' From all which I infer that the Bermuda negroes are more knowing than I supposed; that their consciences are awake, and consequently prepared, in a good measure, for hearing the gospel preached unto them.

"Sunday, May 15. 'Praise the Lord, O my soul, and all that is within me praise His holy name!' This morning I preached my farewell sermon at Mr. Paul's meeting-house; it was quite full, and as the President said, above a hundred and fifty whites, besides blacks, were round the house. Attention sat on every face; and when I came to take my leave, oh, what a sweet unaffected weeping was there to be seen everywhere. I believe there were few dry eyes. The negroes, likewise, without doors, I heard, wept plentifully. My own heart was affected, and though I have parted from friends so often, yet I find every fresh parting almost unmans me, and very much affects my heart! Surely a great work is begun in some souls at Bermuda! Carry it on, O Lord, and if it be thy will, send me to those dear people again. Even so, Lord Jesus. Amen.

"Sunday, May 22. Blessed be God! the little leaven thrown into the three measures of meal begins to ferment, and work almost every day for the week past. I have conversed with souls loaded with a sense of their sins, and as far as I can judge, really pricked to their heart. I preached only three times, but to almost three larger auditories than usual. Indeed the fields are white, ready unto harvest. God has been pleased to bless private visits. Go where I will, upon the least notice, houses are crowded, and the poor souls that follow are soon drenched in tears. This day I took, as it were, another farewell. As the ship did not sail, I preached at Somerset in the morning, to a large congregation in the fields, and expounded in the evening to as large a one at Mr. Harvey's house, round which stood many hundreds of people. But in the morning and evening how did the poor souls weep! The Lord seemed to be with me in a peculiar manner. After the service, when I lay down on the bed to rest, many came weeping bitterly round me, and took their last farewell. Though my body was very weak, yet my soul was full of comfort. I magnified the Lord, and my spirit rejoiced in God my Saviour. Abundance of prayers and blessings were put up for my safe passage to England, and speedy return to Bermuda again. May they enter into the ears of the Lord of Sabaoth!"—*Whitfield's Journal.*

wards of one hundred pounds for his Orphan House, the spontaneous contributions of several parishes where he had preached the word. The traces of his labours existed for many years afterwards; and although, in process of time, this powerful revival was succeeded by a sad relapse into religious formalism, both in the pulpit and amongst the people, yet the seed then sown by this prince of preachers still bore fruit. Amongst the converts of his ministry appears to have been an aunt of Mrs. Winslow, a family tradition of whom still existed, that her favourite and frequent exclamation was, "Oh, for more grace!" Alas! that a declension so melancholy should have followed a spiritual awakening so gracious. But God had not left Himself without a witness. There still existed a little remnant who preserved the coal unquenched. The occasional visit of a gospel minister in quest of health, or in the providence of God, driven upon the island by stress of weather, helped to keep alive the smouldering embers of vital religion. This feeble band, who may be regarded as the conservators of evangelical piety in Bermuda, were wont to assemble statedly for public worship, one of their number generally reading a discourse from "Burder's Village Sermons." It was to meet this spiritual destitution that the thoughts of Mrs. Winslow, as expressed in the following letters to her mother, were directed:—

"August, 1813. I am trying very hard to send you a dear gospel minister to be settled in St. George's; and I do earnestly entreat that you all will endeavour, if I succeed in obtaining one, to procure him a place to preach in until he is enabled to build a chapel. The Lord has blessed me, and I think I am called in duty to lay out what He has given me for His glory. I think I can spare fifty pounds a year to aid the minister until he is sufficiently established, and draws around him a congregation who will be able to afford him a proper maintenance. I have employed several dear ministers to inquire for one who may be made a blessing to you all. Now, I wish to hear from you, just to know whether you can obtain a place for him to preach in, and whether you can raise a subscription to pay its expenses until I am enabled to build a chapel; for I mean to build one myself, in God's good time; and I trust some of my own children will stand up in it, preaching, from heartfelt experience, the unsearchable riches of Christ, when you and I, my precious mother, will be admiring and adoring the same Jesus in eternity. All things are possible with our God; and great are my expectations from Him. He has put large desires in my heart, and has promised in His own word to fulfil them. You must give me a part of the garden, if you think proper; or, if that cannot be, I must purchase a piece of ground in the town. A chapel must be built where my God will be glorified and souls won to Christ. Oh, that you knew how He blesses my soul, and how much He reveals His tender love to me, so that there are moments when I am lifted above the world and feel next door to heaven!

"My dear Mother,—I cannot express to you, though I hope you feel it also, the comfort and consolation I derive from seeing my eternal interest in Christ and in the love of God as my Covenant Father. How great, how unspeakably great are our privileges, and how glorious the prospect we have before us! Jesus will never leave nor forsake those who put their trust in Him. I have been praying much for you all lately, with respect to your spiritual welfare, that the Lord would fill your hearts with peace and joy in believing, and lift you above this poor, fleeting, perishing world. I am doing my utmost to get you a minister, but none are willing to leave their native land." At a later date she adds:—

"I am doing my best to procure a minister to send to you, but I find it more difficult than I expected, as those who are good prefer remaining at home, and I will not send you an indifferent one. However, let us trust the Lord, and in His own good time He will provide one."

The following note, addressed to Mrs. Winslow, from the late excellent and venerable Rev. GEORGE BURDER, author of the "Village Sermons," just alluded to, manifests the interest he felt in this missionary effort.

"MY DEAR FRIEND,— "London, May, 1814.

"I have not been unmindful of Bermuda. I mentioned it at a meeting where many ministers were present, and begged to be informed if they could hear of any. There is no person so likely to speak to as Mr. Thomas Wilson, of Islington. But, indeed, all the academies are jealous of transferring their students from their original destination, being supported by the public. I will still make inquiry, and hope, sooner or later, we shall succeed. I will call upon you if I can, but my hands are more than full—I cannot do half my business.

"I am, Madam, yours in the Lord, GEORGE BURDER."

From among a large number of candidates who had presented themselves, one at length was deemed suitable for the appointment, and was accepted. The Rev. H. H. CROSS and his wife embarked on this interesting mission, and arrived safe at Bermuda, amid the cordial and affectionate greetings of the little Christian band of whom he was to assume the pastoral oversight. The chapel was completed, and dedicated to the worship of God, in connexion with a remarkable and thrilling incident, strikingly illustrative of His gracious and all-governing Providence. The interesting narrative to which we refer, will be found below, in a letter from the Rev. Mr. Cross, addressed to the Rev. John Arundel, of the London Missionary Society.*

* "*St. George's, Bermuda, June* 20, 1821."

"I am happy to inform you, my dear brother, that our chapel was opened on the 13th of April, under peculiar circumstances of gratitude and delight towards Him who conducts all things after the counsel of His own will.

"Previous to its opening, my mind was a great deal exercised respecting the service of that important day. I had no brother to whom I could say, 'Come and help me:' I stood alone; and my feelings often overwhelmed me. My fears, however, were very singularly dispersed by our kind and ever gracious God. On Saturday, previous to the 13th, a ship appeared in sight off the island, hoisting signals of distress : and a report was soon circulated, ' that she was full of passengers and several Methodist parsons, in a state of starvation; six months from Liverpool, bound for New York.' I immediately thought on Mr. Ward; and by referring to the Magazine, found that the time of his sailing from Liverpool to the United States exactly corresponded. I went up the signal hill, where all vessels are seen, and looked with an anxious eye towards the ship, hoping and fearing that Mr. Ward might be on board. On my return, however, I found from a friend who had just heard from New York, that Mr. W. had been there, and was then about to return to England. On Sabbath afternoon, the ship, with great difficulty, came within anchorage off the island. Some of my friends went with provisions on board, and found the passengers in great distress, yet filled with consolation, and many of them with 'joy and peace in believing.' As the passengers were no strangers to the language of Canaan, my friends were soon introduced to the Rev. Duncan Dunbar, a Baptist minister, his wife and four children; Rev. Mr. Grey, a Presbyterian minister, and his interesting wife (to us particularly so, because we soon learnt that she had been brought to the saving knowledge of the truth from the circumstances of the voyage); and Mr. West, a teacher, a very pious young man, and son to Rev. Mr. West, of Dublin. They stated, in brief, the distressing circumstance to my friends, who could not then listen to their 'Tale of woe' before they came for some fresh supplies (circumstances prevented the missionaries from landing on the Sabbath, and my duties from seeing them that evening). It appeared they had

CHAPEL OPENED IN ST. GEORGE'S. 43

The subject of *colonial slavery* has happily ceased to rouse those feelings of horror and indignation, which at one time stirred the English mind to its centre, by the universal and

been at sea nearly six months : for four months they had been on the allowance of five potatoes per day, and for three weeks the Missionaries had scarcely a drop of water in their mouths: such were the cries of many children on board, that they were obliged to deny themselves what they could only obtain from the clouds, to satisfy the thirst of the little ones. They were, however, in good health ; and were constrained to say, 'Though we have had nothing, we have possessed all things.'

"'The Divine presence had evidently blessed the labours of these devoted servants of Jesus to the hopeful conversion of several.

" Early on Monday morning I went off with several of my friends to the ship, and was soon in the midst of this interesting Mission family. I found them perfectly happy, yea, rejoicing in the prospect of meeting some Christian friends in a strange country.

" During their stay with us, we had our new chapel opened. Mr. Dunbar preached in the morning, from Gen. xxviii. 17, and Mr. Grey in the evening, from Zech. xiv. 16. 17, to a very crowded and attentive congregation. The collection amounted to eighty dollars. Our friends remained with us nearly three weeks, and their circumstances and labours made a deep impression on many. One evening after Mr. D. had delivered an excellent and faithful sermon from Acts, vii. 34, the Collector of the Customs went to one of my friends, and begged that his name might be put down for —— doubloons, (£21 6s. 8d currency,) for the general catastrophe, which, he observed, has been so gratefully remembered by the stranger this evening. In the morning we waited on him to return our thanks, and to say, that as the government had given orders that the passengers should all be taken care of, and forwarded to New York by the first vessel, we begged to decline his kind offer. On stating, however, the great object of Mr. D.'s mission, and showing him his case which was strongly recommended by most of the ministers in Edinburgh, Glasgow and Liverpool, and particularly by a written recommendation from Dr. Chalmers, (whom the Collector knows,) he very generously presented Mr. D. with the sum for the object of his mission, adding, ' When you arrive at New Brunswick, show your case to several gentlemen (whose names he gave Mr. D.) ; and give my respects to them, and tell them to look at your book ; and say, I hope to hear from you that they have followed my example. God bless you, and give you success.' We obtained also, from other friends, subscriptions to the amount of £40, besides clothing and necessaries for the voyage. Every day rendered them more endearing to the friends of Jesus in this place. Fain could we have said, ' Abide with us, for there is room ;' and glad would they have been to say, ' We will continue with you ;' but the piercing cry of the red men of the woods, ' No white man teach red man ' had penetrated their hearts. ' For these,' said they, ' we have left all : and for these we must leave you.' They left us on Good Friday, and we are daily expecting to hear of their arrival."

entire extinction of the monstrous evil. In the Bermudas, as in all the West-India Islands, slavery of course existed. By a legislative law of the islands, however, the importation of slaves was strictly prohibited. To this enactment, as also to the benevolent feelings for which Bermudian society was proverbial, may be attributed the mitigated and mild form which slavery in this colony assumed.

If in any place involuntary servitude appeared divested of its more repulsive features, it was here. But prune and moderate the evil as you may—lighten its yoke, and gild its chain—lessen its toil, and call it by mild and gentle names,— "Slavery, thou art a bitter draught!" It is a system contrary to all the tender instincts of our nature, is at war with the genius of Christianity, and is opposed by every sentiment and feeling of true religion and virtue. Familiar as Mrs. Winslow was, from childhood, with this species of servitude, she yet never was wholly reconciled to the monstrous principle of holding property in man. On reaching her majority, she found herself the owner of two domestic slaves; but although lapsing to her by inheritance, it will appear that she was ill at ease in her possession; in this sentiment she was strengthened by the best feelings and efforts of her husband. An illustration of this may here be given:—A poor free negro man hastened one day to Captain Winslow, in the greatest distress, and informed him that his wife and children, who were slaves, were on the eve of being sold to another master, with the prospect of their removal from the island, and in all probability their separation from him for ever. He came to request his sympathy and aid in rescuing them from so distressing a fate. His appeal met with a cordial and instantaneous response. Not a moment was to be lost. Seizing his sword, and adjusting it as he passed through the streets, accompanied by the anxious negro, Captain Winslow hastened to the auction mart. The sale had commenced. There stood the poor trembling woman and her children, for whom a large sum had already been offered. Captain Winslow instantly became a competitor. The contest grew warm. Observing his determination to purchase, the price rose to an enormous sum. At this juncture, the terror-stricken father approached him, and said, "O Massa, do not bid any more; I shall never be able to repay you, Massa." "Never mind, Ben," was the answer. At length victory decided in his favour, and he bore away in triumph the slave-wife, mother, and little ones, restoring them FREE to the delighted and grateful husband and parent. "I shall never be able to repay you, Massa," was the exclamation of the poor negro. "No matter if you cannot," was all the reply of one, whose heart had already found its full reward in the generous impulse it had cherished, and in the pure happiness it had conferred. Mrs. Winslow's views on this subject may be gathered from the following letter to her mother:—

"I wish, my dear mamma, to give my two negroes, Ben and John, their freedom. I cannot bear the idea of having slaves. But if you think it most for their good to keep them in my service, I will have their freedom made out, so that at my death they may not be liable to be sold or made slaves. I sometimes think, that to give such a poor creature as John his freedom now, (in other words to cast him off,) he would soon go to ruin. But still I would desire so to manage things as to make him free whenever he can maintain himself, and to secure his freedom now in case I should be called home."

It is almost needless to add that her directions were immediately and fully complied with. And yet it was one of her bitterest self-accusations, as from the close of her pilgrimage she looked upon its past, that she had ever been the involuntary possessor of a slave. It is true, they were inherited and not purchased—were kindly treated, justly remunerated, and ultimately freed; yet, as the shadows of eternity deepened around her, this solemn background of human life brought out in bolder relief the circumstances and events of bygone years, and she was known to weep and humble herself before God, for her past participation in an evil which now appeared in a light so sinful, and in a character so abhorrent.

The spiritual mind will sympathize with the exercises detailed in the following letter.

To her Mother.—"Oh that I could commit, with my soul, all my temporal concerns into the hands of my covenant God, and feel that He who has the hearts of all men at His command will give me all things, and do all things necessary for me! for Jesus will 'do all things well.' Pray, my precious mother, that He would increase my faith, for I need it every hour and every moment of the day. I often go to Him with the intention of casting all my cares upon Him, but as often bring them away again. Oh, how far, how very far do I fall short of what a true Christian ought to be! I grieve and lament my shortcomings, and long to evince myself, by practice as well as by profession, a lowly follower of Jesus Christ; and He, I trust, with whom all things are possible, will enable me to overcome and be more than conqueror. All my hope is in Him, my eye is up to Him; and He has promised that he will in nowise cast out. Pray for me."

In the extract which follows, we trace the early workings of that simple, yet strong faith—a faith all the stronger because so childlike—for which her whole Christian life was so remarkable. It records, too, one of those providential interpositions which so frequently appear in her history. Her eldest son had recently left her, on a visit to Bermuda, and she thus writes to her mother:—

"I long to hear from my precious child, but still I am not so uneasy about him as you and others would imagine; for I know who commands the winds and the waves, and I know also who has said, *If you ask anything in my name, it shall be granted you.* So you see the Lord calls me to walk by faith, and He gives me faith to trust Him, to His own praise and glory. I awoke last night and discovered my room on fire— three of my children were with me. I had prayed that the Lord would watch over me and mine, and not forgetting you and B——, and keep us from danger. He heard my petition. I awoke just in time to save myself and family from being burnt. It was occasioned by a spark falling from the rushlight upon the dressing-table, which set fire to the wainscot and the table, which were burning when I awoke. I extinguished the fire, opened the door to let the smoke escape—for both rooms were filled—without alarming the family, and retired to bed again to meditate on the goodness of God to such an unworthy creature. Has He not said that His angels encamp round about His people; and have I not reason to believe Him and bless Him for all His mercies? So you see, my beloved mother, that you have no occasion to be uneasy about me, for I am in very precious hands. I only grieve that I make no greater progress in the Divine life. But what a mercy to be in the way to heaven; and sure I am that He who has put me in that way will keep me there until the time comes to call me to partake of those blessings He has purchased for me with the precious price of His own blood."

But a dark cloud was now gathering over her domestic happiness. The remarkable grace we have seen developing itself in the infancy of her Christian life, was about to pass through the crucible. The precious faith, so richly bestowed, was now to be tried as by fire. And, perhaps, from this period of her history may be dated the commencement of those disciplinary dealings of her Heavenly Father, which gave such a decided impress and complexion to her future life; and to the salutary influence of which may be attributed that completeness and mellowness of Christian character, for which she afterwards became so eminent. The affliction to which we now refer, was the renewed and alarming illness of her husband, the circumstances of which, and the exercises of her mind on the occasion, she thus details:—

"MY DEAREST MAMMA,— London, Aug. 22, 1813.

"I know it will distress you to hear that my beloved husband is again laid on a bed of sickness, perhaps the bed of death. He was getting better, and was looking as well as ever he did; but I thought the Lord would bring him low to save his soul. The world and worldly people were alluring him from all his good resolutions. On Tuesday evening I took a short walk with him, and then left him in good health, to go to the House of God. On my return, I was told that he had retired. I had stopped to visit a dying saint, and thus made it late before I returned. As soon as he heard me, he called me from the head of the stairs, to come to him. I found him pale and trembling, for just as he was stepping into bed, he coughed and raised blood. I sent for the physician, and endeavoured to tranquillize his mind. The doctor came, but said it was so little he would not bleed him, and after taking something prescribed, he composed himself to sleep. The next morning he appeared as well as usual, and came down stairs. But about twelve o'clock the dreadful hæmorrhage returned rapidly. I sent off for another physician, a Christian man. They took nearly a quart of blood from his arm. The hæmorrhage then abated for about an hour, when it returned again, and continued off and on until five o'clock. My dearest mother, how you would have felt to have witnessed the agony of his distressed mind. He said there was no hope for him—that he had neglected the day of salvation, and the Lord would have no mercy on his soul. He implored me to pray for him continually. I did pray. I spoke to him of the love of Jesus, and entreated him to call upon Him who had promised that those who came to Him he would in nowise cast out. He hung upon every word I said, and repeated, 'Oh, that I had but taken your advice!' He could not speak much, but I continued to repeat to him every precious promise as well as I was able. He now lies between life and death. But while there is life there is hope. The doctors have some hopes to-night that he may recover. The sight of the children threw him into great agitation. Two hours ago he exclaimed, 'Jesus, O blessed Jesus! manifest Thyself to me!' It was the first prayer I ever heard him utter; and I doubt not but Jesus has heard it, too. The physician spoke sweetly to him, and implored him to continue to call upon the Lord until He answered him. Mr. Stewart has also been with him, and endeavoured to lead him to Jesus. We have just been at prayer by his bed-side, and I am now writing close by him.

"This, my precious mother, has been, and is, a trying time to me; but the Lord, ever faithful to His promise, is with me, and gives me strength according to my day. Fear not for me; God is my Father; He watches over me, and will not afflict me beyond what he will give me strength to bear; and I trust, if it is the Lord's will, He will again restore him. I have entreated him not to think of me or of his children, but only to think of his own soul. I read and pray, and watch over him, and am scarcely a moment from his side. He says, if he is but spared, how differently will he live. Oh, that Jesus may hear my prayer, and cause his soul to rejoice.

"*Friday night*, 23.—My precious Winslow has had a good night, and has continued so throughout the day. The bleeding has not returned, but the physician says he is not out of danger. He says nothing, for he is not allowed to speak; but I trust he thinks the more. We have just been at prayer by his side. Good Mr. Baker engaged in prayer, and all the family, as usual, attended. May the Lord in mercy hear our prayers! My spirits, which for two days and nights have been wonderfully supported, to-night a little flagged, and a trifling thing threw me into tears. I have everything to be thankful for; but my mind has been on the full stretch, and weeping now is a relief. But I am, thank God, well, and have no fear but for the salvation of my precious husband's immortal soul. Oh, may he be led, in this affliction, to seek Jesus with all his heart!

"24.—Thank God, he is better to-day. Oh, may this warn

him to flee from the wrath to come! but I am afraid it will not suffice. His distress is not occasioned, I fear, by sin committed against a holy, good, and righteous God, but from a fear of death. However, the Lord knows best how to work upon the sinner's heart, and I trust He will save his soul.

"*Saturday afternoon.*—The physician has seen Winslow, and says he thinks he will do well. He implored him to pray to the Physician of souls, who knew his heart, and could read there his desires. I am rejoiced you have Miss M—— with you: I doubt not, from what Mr. S. tells me, she is a child of God, and knows what it is to be born again. May she prove a real blessing to you. Tell her I love her, because she belongs to the fold of Jesus, and for her attachment to you. May the Lord, whom we serve, strengthen your heart to persevere in the blessed cause, and to show to all about you what great things he has wrought in your soul! Broad is the road to destruction, and many go therein; narrow is the road that leads to glory, and there are few, comparatively, who find it—happy few! And, oh, what a mercy that he has guided *our* feet there! Our souls and bodies ought to be devoted to Him, to glorify Him for His distinguishing grace; for what are we more than others, that He should fix His everlasting love upon us while we were dead in trespasses and in sins? But He will have mercy upon whom He will have mercy. Blessed, for ever blessed, be His adored name. Oh, for grace to serve Him better, and to love Him more! *We love Him, because He first loved us.* Our love is the effect, and not the cause, of His love to us.

"*Sept. 3.*—I know it will please you to have a line, especially as I can tell you my dearest Winslow is mending as fast as I could wish. May grace be as thriving in his soul as health is in his body! I am strong, and in good spirits; for my Friend above reigneth, and He has enabled me to cast every weight of care upon Him. I have everything to praise Him for; for goodness and loving-kindness follow me all my days. Mrs. —— said to me the other day, "What a blessing it is, situated as you are, that you are religious!' She might have said, 'What a blessing it is that God is your Friend!' Oh, the sweets of religion! To know the Lord Jesus is our Friend, surpasses every earthly good, and is better than the possession of a thousand worlds. To have Him to go to,—to lay before Him all our wants, to express our fears, to plead his promises, and to expect that because He has promised He will fulfil,—is worth more than all the world can give. His ear is ever open to the prayer of his people, and,

> 'Though hell and death obstruct the way,
> The weakest saint shall win the day.'

"My precious husband begins to understand and to love the truth. He who has begun a good work, will complete it in him. He loves and admires Mr. Sheppard, our worthy clergyman, who regularly visits us once a fortnight; and although Winslow does not say much, he listens with the profoundest attention to everything of a serious nature when we have any religious friends with us."

Thus, the dark cloud, enshrouding her domestic happiness, and which for a while wore an aspect so threatening, was in a measure removed. The pious physician, to whom allusion is made in the preceding extracts, merits a passing notice. The gentleman referred to, was the late Dr. James Hamilton, a name as sacred to religion as it was dear to science. The peculiar and salutary influence of the Christian physician was, perhaps, never more strikingly illustrated than in the case of Dr. Hamilton. Everywhere, and on all occasions, he was the man of God; but nowhere did his Christianity shine with so rich a lustre as by the side of the sick bed. On one occasion, when allusion was made to the happy results of a prescription, with lowliness he remarked, that he "never prescribed a remedy unaccompanied with a prayer for the Divine blessing upon its use." It was frequently his habit, extensive as was his practice, to spend five minutes in prayer, before retiring from the sick room, thus leaving upon the mind of his patient a most soothing, healthful influence.* What an incalculable blessing may such an individual be! The Christian physician

---

* A marble tablet, erected to his memory in the City Road Chapel, thus truthfully records his many Christian virtues: "His religion was exhibited in his medical profession, in his family, in his general intercourse with society, in the sweetness and amiability of his temper, in the habitual composure and happiness of his life, and pre-eminently in his Catholic spirit, which led him to love all who feared God, without any distinction of sect or party. He ascribed his eminent success in his professional efforts to the power of God in answer to prayer: and he lived and died with the abiding conviction of his own unworthiness as a sinner, and of the sufficiency of a Saviour's righteousness, at the good old age of eighty-six."

is begirt with opportunities of usefulness, to which the gospel minister can scarcely aspire. The clergyman is, in most instances, the last attendant of a sick room thought of, the last summoned, and often when too late to be of any essential avail—the patient, perhaps, worn by fever, racked with agony, or stupified by anodynes. But the Christian physician is the constant attendant; he possesses the ear, the confidence, and the grateful regard of the sick person. Without awaking a needless suspicion of danger, and thereby producing undue excitement, he can direct the languid eye to the good and great Physician of the soul, and tell of His blood, the only remedy for the mind's malady. Thus, like his divine Master, whom of all others he most closely resembles, he may travel from ward to ward in this vast hospital, "healing all manner of diseases, and preaching the gospel of the kingdom." Who, as he accompanies Dr. Hamilton to the bedside of the sinking and alarmed patient, and marks his affectionate fidelity and Christian concern for the higher interests of the soul, feels not a desire that a vocation so ennobled as a science, and so purely benevolent as a profession, might be universally sanctified and consecrated by religion?

Mrs. Winslow's ecclesiastical views at this period may be gathered from the following letter to her mother:—

" We are going on as usual, so that there is nothing important to tell you. My religious pursuits are my greatest delight; and I can truly say, religion's ways are to me ways of pleasantness, and all its paths are peace. I had a long conversation with Mr. —— the other day on this subject; but as I am not a member of his communion, and dislike much I see in it, and as he is very bigoted to his own views, we, of course, cannot in many things agree. But, lest you should wonder wherein we differ, it will be necessary to say it is only on church government and ordinances; and as he sees not with the Church of England, while I remain in it, he thinks I act wrong. But as I see so many errors in his, I will remain where I am until I find a purer and more perfect branch of Christ's church. I hear the gospel in its greatest purity and excellence, and next to communion with God, it is my greatest comfort and joy to wait upon the preaching of the word. Hardly any weather keeps me at home."

Warmly attached, however, as she was to the Established Church, to which she then belonged, her soul, panting for the living water, could slake its thirst at any channel through which it flowed. She delighted, therefore, to attend the weekly ministration of ministers of Christ, other than those of her own church; and regularly once a-week she walked a mile to Islington Chapel, where her soul was often refreshed by its services. The eminent provincial ministers, who at this period supplied in rotation the pulpits of Tottenham Court Road Chapel, and the Tabernacle, Moorfields, frequently allured her to these "wells of salvation," from which, in seasons of trial and spiritual dejection, she often returned invigorated and comforted. She manifested, at this stage of her Christian course, a deep interest in the spread of the gospel through all lands; and thus refers, in a letter to her mother, to the religious anniversaries then transpiring :—

"I am just going into the City, to attend the Missionary Meeting, and will write to you on my return. *Evening.*—I did not return from the meeting until five o'clock, and then only had time to take a cup of coffee, and hurry off to the evening service. I have indeed been animated to-day, at seeing so many of God's dear people exerting their powers to the utmost for the spread of the everlasting gospel. T—— and I set out, as soon as I arranged my family matters for the day, and we were fortunately at the London Tavern in time to obtain sittings; for many ladies stood the whole service. The speaking lasted from two o'clock until five. All was animation and zeal. My favourite, Mr. Wilberforce, was most excellent. The eloquence of the orator, the elegance of the gentleman, and the piety of the Christian, were all blended in him, and in all he said. The crowd was very great, and the applause at the different speeches so loud and so long that my head ached while my heart rejoiced. Lord Gambier was in the chair, and what little he said showed that his heart and soul were devoted to Jesus. I never saw such an assemblage of gospel ministers in one place before, and such a number of ladies, whose countenances beamed with delight, and whose tears bespoke their love to the cause of Christ. This is a busy week for the church militant. Missionary meetings and sermons in all directions, and by the Church of England, Independents, and Baptists; for here they all sweetly *unite* in sending the blessed gospel to the poor heathen. Besides this, there is a society formed for instructing the Jews, and bringing God's ancient people (or rather using the means, with His blessing, for bringing them) to bow their knee to our Immanuel. This meeting also takes place this week, and I am invited, as a member of the society, to attend, at which I shall, please God, have the happiness of seeing many Jews baptized in the name of Jesus. How I shall rejoice, when it pleases God to bring you to us, to go with you to such places; for I know it will gladden your heart. May the Captain of our salvation keep us steady and persevering! And when I see the many temptations all around me, and feel my own weakness, I indeed work out my own salvation with fear and trembling. What a glorious animating prospect we have before us! A crown of glory—*an inheritance incorruptible, undefiled, and that fadeth not away;* and this is reserved in heaven for God's people, and they are kept for it by the mighty power of God. *Fear not, little flock,* says Jesus; *it is your Father's good pleasure to give you the kingdom.* Good-night."

The following familiar letter is introduced as being the only one in the volume which affords anything like a particular reference to her young family; thus supplying a link in the narrative, which, perhaps, would otherwise be missed:—

"MY DEAREST MOTHER,— Twickenham Common.

"Yours was forwarded to me at this place, where I am for a week, with my dear little suffering O——, in the hope, with God's blessing, the change of air may be of service. The Lord only knows whether I shall ever rear him. The physician in town pronounces him in a decline, but that the change of air may be of service. He is very dear and precious to me; but I desire to resign him into His hand, who is able to rescue him even from the grave; and if it be His blessed will to take him, I have a humble hope that He will give me grace to say, *Thy will be done!* But oh, my dear mother, you know my heart is wrapped up in my children; and this sweet little sufferer is particularly dear to me, because he has been almost all his life afflicted; and I believe, if every hair of his head were numbered, I have had a tear, a sigh, a groan for each one. I am often afraid the Lord is chastening me for my too anxious concern about my children. But I know that all He does will eventually be for my good and His glory.

"I have a little cottage on Twickenham Common for a month, where the air is fine, and all the other children seem much benefited by it. I have with me the five younger children. I—— and E——, with a young friend of theirs, come down to me on Saturday, as they then break up for the Midsummer. Dear little F—— is one of the loveliest boys, perhaps, you ever saw. R—— grows a fine fellow, and often talks of you and his little wife. He is a good-looking boy, nearly as tall as G——, who is as wild as possible, and as lazy as T——. I received a letter from him yesterday, at Cadiz, but there is no prospect at present of his coming home.*. . . . God is my Shepherd, and all my concerns are in His hands. Blessed, forever blessed, be His dear and holy name, who has looked with everlasting mercy on such a poor, vile sinner as me, and encouraged me with such sweet manifestations of His love, to trust my soul and all my interests in His hands; and if God is for me, who can prevail against me? If Mrs. —— comes home, I will endeavour to see her for your sake; but I rather decline much intercourse with worldly people; for if one can do them no good, they are sure to do you some harm. May the Lord bless you in your soul, and enable you to follow after the one thing needful, and induce you to make that the chief concern of your life! Religion is a personal thing; we must not leave our salvation to an uncertainty, and merely consider Jesus as the Saviour of sinners; but we are to know that He is *our* Saviour; and the Scriptures encourage us to press forward until we do ascertain this; and God has never promised what he does not mean to perform. The ever-blessed Jesus has encouraged us to ask and implore, and we must take no denial, but, like the importunate widow, never rest until He blesses us, and assures us by the witness of the Spirit, that He is ours, and that we are His blood-bought children. May He give His blessing to these imperfect words, is the earnest prayer, my dearest mamma, of your affectionate daughter."

* Her eldest son, then a midshipman in the Royal Navy.

CHAPTER IV.

PROBABLY, in no part of God's dealings with His people is the perfection of His work more apparent—His wisdom, love, and power more clearly seen—than in fitting them for the exact niche in life He had pre-ordained them to fill. And it is no slight mercy for the Christian to have a clear, unmistakable perception of the Lord's mind concerning this matter; and then, be his mission lowly or exalted, his post of duty one of honour or humiliation, to have grace vouchsafed cheerfully to acquiesce, and promptly to obey. Thus had God remarkably fitted the subject of our Memoir for the position in life in which she was now, and for so many years, in sad and lonely widowhood, to glorify Him. The path she was henceforth to tread, demanded a character of no ordinary energy, fortitude, and strength; but more than this—and apart from which the mightiest powers of nature must have succumbed—a large degree of the Saviour's grace, so freely promised, and so richly bestowed upon all who humbly seek it. But, great as was the occasion which now summoned into action the best powers of her mind, by the help of Him who perfects His strength in human weakness, she proved herself equal to the emergency. And we will glorify God in her.

The retirement of Captain Winslow from the army has already been mentioned. The circumstances which led to this step it may be interesting to the reader more minutely to relate. It was at a critical period of her life—when dangerously ill in Ireland—that the 47th Regiment was under orders to embark for India. The troops had left Cork for Portsmouth, and were prepared to sail at a moment's notice; the wind was unfavourable, and the transports were detained. It was a moment of intense anxiety to Captain Winslow. Unwilling to leave his wife under such circumstances, and with no prospect of hearing from her for many months to come, he resolved, without a moment's hesitation, to retire. Permission to sell was asked from the Duke of York—the Commander-in-Chief. Mrs. Winslow's illness increased—the Duke hesitated—a slight variation of the wind would decide the question. The suspense was agonizing. At length the Colonel of the regiment handed him a letter from head-quarters, containing the Duke's consent. In less than an hour afterwards the wind veered, and the transports sailed; and Captain Winslow relinquished a commission in the army he had held from early life, with equal honour to himself and fidelity to his sovereign. Thus, often do the most signal events of our history—those upon which all the future turns as on a pivot—transpire as in a moment, and by a power manifestly beyond ourselves. This were a phenomenon utterly inexplicable, but for the doctrine of a particular Providence, guiding and shaping the minutest as the most important events of our life. Nothing could have been further from his thoughts than the position in which Captain Winslow now suddenly found himself. A few hours before, he could not have conceived that he should be walking on the ramparts of Portsmouth, gazing upon the transports as they spread their canvas to the fair breeze, and stretched away to the ocean. This sudden and decisive step was, upon first reflection, a cause of much disappointment and regret to Mrs. Winslow, who had looked forward to the army—for which, from habit, she had now imbibed a strong liking—as the future profession of her sons. She lived, however, to acknowledge God's hand in this apparently adverse movement, and gratefully to acquiesce in a circumstance which threatened to blight so much hope, but which, in reality, resulted in so much good. And although her interest in military affairs never entirely ceased, yet as her Christianity deepened, she desired, and sought for her children other and more peaceful, yet not less honorable and useful vocations.

Some years after Captain Winslow's retirement from the army, his ample fortune became seriously impaired through ill-advised and disastrous investments. It was this circumstance—an important link in the chain of events, evolving God's purposes of love—that suggested a removal to the United States of America, as offering wider scope for a family composed almost entirely of boys, and a place of residence more favourable to resources now sadly crippled. Accordingly, at the close of the Peninsular war, the subject of this Memoir, accompanied by a family of ten children and several of her attached household, embarked for New York. Her husband —whom she was desirous of preceding, with a view of welcoming him, on his arrival, to a new and pleasant home—was to follow her in a few months. It was a novel and a serious undertaking for a female, lone and unaided,—her eldest son yet a minor, and her youngest child an infant at the breast. Writers of taste have been wont to expatiate with great eloquence and feeling upon the sublimity presented in the spectacle of a woman educated amidst the elegancies and indulgences of prosperous life, meeting the sudden reverses of fortune with fortitude, and proving the comforter and the support of her husband when bowed beneath the stern blast of adversity. "As the vine, which has long twined its graceful foliage about the oak, and been lifted by it into sunshine, will, when the hardy plant is rifted by the thunderbolt, cling round it with its caressing tendrils, and bind up its shattered boughs; so it is beautifully ordained by Providence, that woman, who is the mere dependent and ornament of man in their happier hours, shall be his stay and solace when smitten with sudden calamity; winding herself into the rugged recesses of his nature, tenderly supporting the drooping head, and binding up the broken heart."* At no period of Mrs. Winslow's life did her mental force and decision of character appear more transcendent than now. The reverse of fortune, which well-nigh crushed the spirits of her husband, but served to nerve and animate her own. The calamity which despondingly depressed him, gave intrepidity and elevation to her. She struck upon an expedient and resolved upon its execution. Few individuals, yet fewer of her gentle sex, could have braced themselves to responsibilities so great, or would have submitted to sacrifices so costly. To expatriate herself from a land of such endeared associations—voluntarily to relinquish a home of such luxurious comforts, and a circle of friendships so choice—to adjust herself with such grace to altered circumstances—to confront with firmness new difficulties, and enter cheerfully upon unknown trials, called into play no ordinary powers, and fully realized the exquisite picture of woman in adversity, as sketched with so much elegance and truth by the American writer we have quoted, and for which, so accurate in the resemblance, she might have sat as the original.

* Washington Irving.

It was in the month of June, 1815, accompanied by her responsible charge, she embarked from Gravesend for New York. The Divine precept, "Seek ye first the kingdom of God and His righteousness," was still her guiding star. Having engaged for her large party of ten children and her servants, the entire cabin of the vessel, she was not long in consecrating it to the service of God. As soon as possible, the family altar was again reared, and throughout the voyage she was enabled to maintain morning and evening worship; and during the day to carry out her little plans of domestic instruction and usefulness, with the same regularity and zeal as at home. In this God remarkably aided her. For when the voice of praise and prayer first ascended to the deck, the captain, on ascertaining the cause, immediately gave the strictest orders that all interruption should cease during the service; and he was frequently observed quietly to descend the companion-way, take off his hat, and kneel outside the cabin during the prayer. He was subsequently invited, with a few others, who requested the favour, regularly to unite in the family devotions. Thus did God honour one who, in her conscious weakness but godly sincerity, everywhere sought to honour Him. It was a favourite maxim of hers, which many readers of this volume will recognise, "Walk in the *precept*, and God will fulfil the *promise*." In the intermediate part of the ship she discovered a young lady, far advanced in a decline, and who, with her little son, was on her way to rejoin her husband. She immediately had her removed to her own cabin, that she might administer to her temporal comfort, and that the invalid migh tenjoy the daily religious privileges of the family. Thus, one who was destined to expire with the first breath she inhaled of the land air—for she died as the ship dropped her anchor in the placid waters of the Hudson, and before she met her husband—was permitted, ere she entered the eternal world, to hear frequently explained, and affectionately enforced, the grand theme of the gospel—that Christ Jesus came into the world to save the chief of sinners.

Mrs. Winslow found, in the land of her adoption, a home and a sanctuary. Furnished with introductions to some of the leading families of New York, amongst whom were Colonel Bayard, formerly of the British Consulate, and Divie Bethune, the son-in-law and biographer of Mrs. Isabella Graham, she was solaced with the reflection that, though an exile, and in adversity, she was not without that sympathy and kindness which to none is more welcome and soothing than to the lone heart of the stranger. And, as the circle of her friendships widened, enriched by some of the most eminent for Christian influence and worth, she soon discovered the continent that had attracted her to its friendly coasts to be in hospitality and courtesy, as in language and religion, the affectionate daughter of the land she had left. And when, in after years, she quitted its shores, to spend the evening of her life, and die, amid earlier scenes and older friendships, the recollection of the land that had afforded her a pleasant asylum in adversity, she still warmly and gratefully cherished. America was hallowed ground to her. The history of her sojourn upon its soil had engraven its name more deeply and ineffaceably on her heart than "France" was said to have been on the heart of Mary Queen of Scots. Her interest in its prosperity never decreased. Its religious literature, the histories of its churches, and, especially, the biographies of its saints, beguiled, happily, many an hour of her closing pilgrimage. She contemplated it with a kind of prophetic interest. Its vast territory, its exhaustless capabilities, and its glorious revivals, impressed her with the conviction that America was destined to be the future home of the church, the Mount Ararat, where the Ark would repose from the storms and convulsions of the Old World, the hemisphere upon which would dawn the first light of the millennial glory. There was but one dark spot in its history, over which she wept; and many a fervent petition she sent up to heaven for its removal. *That* spot effaced, America would stand forth peerless amongst the nations of the earth. Give her entire population equal rights and liberty—civil and religious—and she will soar in national greatness and in moral influence, like her own symbolic eagle, to the sun.

And yet it was in this land that she was made to drink most deeply of the waters of adversity. She had scarcely become settled in her new and pleasant home ere death invaded it. The infant daughter she had borne across the Atlantic sickened and died. This was the first draught from sorrow's cup. That cup was now to be brimmed. While the corpse of her babe lay yet unentombed, the woeful intelligence reached her that she was a *widow!* "Deep calleth unto deep at the noise of thy waterspouts; all thy waves and thy billows are gone over me." Such was now her mournful experience. He letters written at this sad period of her history, a few of which only are preserved, will best depict the deep and varied exercises of her mind under this overwhelming calamity. Addressing her eldest son, then in Bermuda, who, on receiving the tidings of his father's death, hastened to England, she thus writes:—

"MY PRECIOUS CHILD,— New York, 1816.

"Your dear mother is under the chastening hand of God. My dear suffering infant lies a corpse: and the letter containing the intelligence of your dear father's and my beloved husband's death, was this day put into my hands. I am humbled under the mighty hand of God. My soul is bowed down. The death of my child was almost overwhelming; but the death of my dear, my precious, my ever-to-be-lamented husband, is the heaviest affliction I have ever met with. I trust the Lord will yet enable me to say, *Thy will, O God, not mine, be done!* I wish you could have been there. Oh, that you had been in time to have closed his eyes! I need comfort. I am in a strange place. The Lord help me and increase my faith! The Lord have mercy upon me, for I am in trouble. I trust his soul and the dear departed spirit of my infant are now rejoicing together in glory. That is my only comfort. I am too much afflicted to write more. May God bless you, my child, prays your truly afflicted, widowed mother."

But overwhelming as was this affliction, God, whose chastenings are always tempered with mercy, left her not without strong consolation. It was not in unmitigated and hopeless grief that she wept. The last illness and closing scene of Captain Winslow's life afforded satisfactory evidence that he had sought and found the Saviour. His conviction of sin was deep, and his believing reliance upon the atoning merits of the Redeemer earnest and childlike. He died in the assured hope of an humble penitent, a sincere believer, "looking for the mercy of our Lord Jesus Christ unto eternal life." Such was the inexpressible comfort provided by Him whose hand had now slain her fondest earthly treasure. She now saw the fruit of her long travail of soul. Her prayers were answered, though as by fire. "Thou calledst in trouble, and I delivered thee; I answered thee in the secret place of thunder: I proved thee at the waters of Meribah." The long-sought mercy came—her husband was saved; but the blessing was draped in woe. 'By terrible things in righteousness' God had answered her, and her 'song was of mercy and judgment.' The blow fell, however, with crushing effect. Her mental distress seemed to baffle the kindest efforts of her pastor and her friends to soothe. Her soul refused to be comforted. To the deep sorrow of bereavement was now added the yet deeper anguish of spiritual darkness and despondency. Satan was permitted to buffet her, and, for a time, the dark waters went over her soul. Thus the calamity that at once withered her lovely flower, and broke the 'strong staff and the beautiful rod,' was augmented by a momentary suspension of the Divine presence. It was at this juncture the following hymn of her favourite author, Newton, read casually to her by her son E——, spoke the first consolation to her sad heart.

> " I ask'd the Lord that I might grow
>   In faith, and love, and every grace,
> Might more of his salvation know,
>   And seek more earnestly his face.
>
> " 'Twas he who taught me thus to pray,
>   And he, I trust, has answered prayer;
> But it has been in such a way
>   As almost drove me to despair.
>
> " I hoped that in some favour'd hour
>   At once he'd answer my request,
> And by his love's constraining power
>   Subdue my sins, and give me rest.
>
> " Instead of this, he made me feel
>   The hidden evils of my heart,
> And let the angry powers of hell
>   Assault my soul in every part.
>
> " Yea, more ; with his own hand he seem'd
>   Intent to aggravate my woe,—
> Cross'd all the fair designs I schemed,
>   Blasted my gourds, and laid me low.
>
> " ' Lord ! why is this ?' I trembling cried :
>   ' Wilt thou pursue thy worm to death ?'
> ' 'Tis in this way,' the Lord replied,
>   ' I answer prayer for grace and faith.
>
> " ' These inward trials I employ,
>   From self and pride to set thee free ;
> And break thy schemes of earthly joy,
>   That thou may'st seek thy all in me.' "

How well calculated were these richly experimental breathings to pour the oil of soothing over the broken waters now surging her soul! Bereaved Christian, the same fount of consolation is yours. Approach, and drink abundantly. Your pleasant picture is, perhaps, destroyed, your beauteous flower has faded, your sheltering arm is withered; but Jesus is yours, your deathless Friend, the Brother born for your adversity, and you have in Him all, and infinitely more, that was lovely and loving, tender and protective, in the treasure you have lost. This is but the Lord's all-wise and righteous mode of drawing you into a greater nearness to Himself.

We continue a few of the letters addressed to her eldest son at this period of her grief. What a beauteous bow appears in the dark cloud of her afflictions! Blessed discipline that results in such weanedness!

"My dearest Child,— New York, Feb. 7, 1816.

"I have but little spirits to write, but as I know you will be anxious to hear from me, I have struggled with my feelings to gratify you. The Lord has indeed laid His chastening hand upon your afflicted mother. My precious, my beloved husband I shall see no more in the flesh. But, oh, what a comfort to my soul that I shall meet him at the right hand of God! I grieve at his sufferings, and in imagination I am ever hovering round his bed. My soul has been bowed down, and I was afraid I should at first sink under so heavy an affliction. Wave upon wave, bitter upon bitter. But the Lord has said, *As thy day, so shall thy strength be;* and He has been faithful to His promise. E—— has proved himself a dear child; he has been everything to me, at this trying time, that I could wish. How gracious is the Lord to me! It is my Father that has chastened me, and it shall be for my good and His glory. Now, my precious child, you are my most anxious concern. You will need wisdom from above to direct, and grace to uphold you every moment. Keep close to a throne of grace, and doubt not the God of all grace will give you both. Give my love to ——. It soothed my sorrow to know that I possessed the love and friendship of some of God's dearest, choicest people. Tell dear Miss M—— I feel very grateful for her letter; for though it cost me many tears, yet it was by far the most satisfactory one I have had, and my heart has thanked her for it a thousand times. Oh, that I could have sat by his bedside as she did! Mysterious are the ways of God! This bereaving providence has done more to wean me from the world, and show me the importance of eternal things, than you can imagine. Blessed be God for all His dispensations, the evil as well as the good.

* * * * * *

"I am at times miserable indeed beyond conception. Past scenes crowd upon my mind, and unavailing regrets seem to overwhelm my better feelings. I have truly been laid low in the dust, and abhor myself as the chief of sinners. For some days Satan desired to have me, to sift me as wheat; darkness overpowered my mind; doubts and fears respecting my everlasting safety crowded upon me. This, too, was after I had thought myself resigned to the will of God, and began to be interested in my family concerns. I see it was the enemy. Oh, that I had never left your precious father. See Mr. Shepherd, and beg he will relate to you exactly every word that passed between him and my dear husband before he died. My severe trials have awakened a general sympathy among the dear people of God, who have visited and endeavoured to comfort me; but vain is the help of man; God alone can comfort. Dr. Stamford, an excellent minister, called upon me, and preached afterwards a sermon on the occasion of my bereavement, from the words,—*Show me wherefore thou contendest with me;* but I could not hear it, though I am told it was excellent."

While it is painful to trace the bitter and unjust self-accusations contained in the following letter, it is at the same time delightful to observe how richly the 'rod' 'blossomed' with the holy fruits of her deeply-sanctified grief.

"MY BELOVED CHILD,— New York, May 28, 1816.

"I have received your letter to-day, for which I have been just thanking my God and your God, the Father to the fatherless and the widow's God. I am thankful that He has supported you under the severest trial you have been called to meet with since you entered the vale of tears—the loss of your dear, your precious father. Neither you nor I knew half his worth. The Lord gave us a treasure, but we knew not its value until too late. I hope this has been a sifting time with you, as it has been with your poor mother. How great a backslider have I been! How did I let my vile heart go out after covetousness, and wander from the path of duty, when I left my beloved husband! Oh, my dear child, this thought had well-nigh drove me to despair. But, blessed be the rock of my salvation, that, though in some measure He has suffered me to be sifted as wheat, and the enemy to come like a flood, the Spirit helped my infirmities, and I was through Him enabled to keep a fast hold on the *covenant which is ordered in all things and sure.* My Father has chastened me, but his lovingkindness he has not taken from me, nor suffered his faithfulness to fail. It has been good for me that I have been afflicted. Oh, my child, self-righteousness, self-will, and a covetous spirit have led me far astray; but the Lord has overruled even these hated sins for my good, and the salvation of the precious soul of your dear beloved father. All is well. Soon we shall meet again; and this is my great consolation. We are in a strange land; but the God of Jacob is my God, and the God of my fatherless ones. England is highly privileged for the precious means of grace; but we have here the simple truths of the gospel, and much sterling piety amongst professors. . . . Lord, have mercy upon me, and let me see Thy hand in this! Lead my mind to contemplate him where he now is. For millions of worlds would he not return. But still my widowed heart aches, and will ache while I live; and yet I trust the Lord has reconciled, or will reconcile me to His blessed will. But I have touched a chord that unfits me almost for everything.

"May the Lord watch over you, and bring you in safety to me. I have so many mercies for which I desire to be thankful, but I am full of misgivings and unbelief, often ready to exclaim, *All these things are against me!* The Lord has supported me under a heavy and deep affliction; what more lies before me, He only knows *who worketh all things after the counsel of His own will.* My mind is often greatly exercised, but the Lord has said, *Leave thy fatherless children; I will preserve them alive.* To Him do I desire to look, and in Him will I trust. The promise is, *Seek ye first the kingdom of God and His righteousness, and all things else shall be added unto you.* Did I not hope to see the salvation of the Lord in the land of the living, I should sink in despair. Oh, your dear father! I mourn. It is no sin to weep: Jesus wept at the grave of Lazarus; Mary and Martha wept; and may not I also weep? I wish you would go to the vault where your dear father lies,

and see if there is room for your poor unworthy mother too—
I wish to lay my bones by him; if you can do this without
too much distressing your own feelings. I cannot account for
it, but it has been the constant desire of my heart, (as I cannot see it myself,) that you should see the coffin that contains
his beloved body. I shall see that body again, shining more
gloriously than the brightest angel in heaven."

We will not longer detain the reader on this mournful part
of her history, than to quote a short extract from one of her
letters to her eldest son, which blends a cheering light with
the dark shadows in this picture of woe. It is instructive, and
to the afflicted believer encouraging, to behold the sparklings
of the gold amidst the 'fires' of the furnace.

"At times my spirits are low, but I know it is for my good
that I have been afflicted; and I see plainly why it has been
permitted, and have to acknowledge that the Lord, even in
this, has not chastened me according to my backslidings. I
see love and mercy directing this stroke, and I trust it will be
abundantly sanctified to my soul. Your dear father is now
rejoicing amongst the redeemed, and it will not be long before
we shall meet again to part no more for ever. I have indeed
been humbled to the very dust, and my mind brought into
greater darkness and distress than I ever experienced before,
in addition to my great loss. I often sat upon the floor, and
wept aloud in an agony of mind impossible to describe; but
the Lord has put the enemy to flight, and again blest me with
a sense of His loving-kindness; so that my mind, upon the
whole, is comfortable and stayed upon my God. Tribulation
must be felt, or it would not be tribulation; and it is needful.
I think I have learnt more of my dreadfully wicked heart, and
the preciousness of Jesus, during this trial, than I ever learnt
before. It has been a bitter discipline, but I hope, with God's
blessing, it will bring forth the *peaceable fruits of righteousness;*
tending to wean me from the world and from self, and causing
me to know where my great strength lieth. Let us go to the
Lord, who knows best, for direction; taking care not to lay
down a plan for ourselves, before we ask His counsel, lest He
leave us to smart for our folly. Thank Mrs. H——, and tell
her I shall never forget her kindness to my dear husband. It
was like a Christian, and may the Lord bless her a thousand
times for it. My heart is full, and I am weeping while I
write."

The most touching review of this part of her history, written many years after, is from a narrative addressed to her family. We have no strong predilection in favour of dreams, nor did the subject of this Memoir regard them with superstitious reverence; and yet of old the Lord did sometimes make known His will by dreams, and even appointed individuals especially to interpret them. It was in a dream that the mystic ladder appeared to Jacob; it was by a dream that prophetic revelations were made to Joseph; and, under the New Testament dispensation, it was still by a dream that the angel of the Lord appeared to Joseph, the husband of Mary, on several occasions. And among the signs of the universal spread of the Gospel, we are prophetically told this shall be one. "It shall come to pass, that I will pour out my Spirit upon all flesh; your sons and your daughters shall prophesy; your old men shall dream dreams; your young men shall see visions."* We would be cautious therefore, of speaking lightly of this mode of producing sacred impressions on the mind. "In thoughts, from the visions of the night, when deep sleep falleth on man,"† we know not what communications God may make, what truths He may illustrate, or what lessons He may teach. We should keep in mind, however, that the revealed word of God is our only and sure 'word of prophecy, to which we do well that we take heed as unto a light that shineth in a dark place.' It is thus Mrs. Winslow narrates her mental exercises at this time:—

"Soon after I was brought to the feet of Jesus, I had a remarkable dream; and although I place but little confidence in dreams in general, I think this did mean something. I thought I was in the cabin of a ship in the midst of the ocean. There were others with me. We appeared to face the windows of the cabin, from which alone we had light. I appeared with others, struggling to get nearer to the light, but some invisible being seemed to draw us back at every step we advanced towards the window. And still the struggle continued. My eyes were towards the light, but I could make no progress. Presently the roof of the cabin disappeared, and I saw one like an angel coming down from heaven. He approached nearer and nearer, and fixing his eyes upon me, with such a countenance of compassion and love I cannot describe, said, 'I am

* Joel ii. 28. † Job iv. 13.

with thee.' I exclaimed aloud, 'It is the Son of God!' He then ascended, and became like a bird in the air, but not out of sight. Then the tormentors commenced again, and the struggle to get disengaged from them was renewed. Once more the same blessed Being descended, and with the same benignant look repeated the words, 'I am with thee.' While He spake all was quiet, but as soon as He ascended as before, the battle with our invisible enemies continued. The third time He came down, when He said, 'I will be with thee even unto the end.' Every object instantly disappeared. He took me in His arms, and appeared to go under the waves. I was tranquil, and felt no fear, but weary, rested my head upon His bosom. How long we were under the water I know not, but it appeared not a moment ere He arose with me, still in His arms, and ascended towards heaven; and then my joy, my ecstasy, was so overwhelming, my bosom heaved, and I awoke. The impression left upon my mind by this 'vision of the night,' I have never lost. What appeared but a dream has since become a reality. How has the Lord upheld me in the deep, dark waters, not suffering them to overwhelm me quite. He has kept my head above them, so that I sank not in their midst. In the dark night of my weeping He was near; His eye, His loving eye, was upon me. God's children came to me, but my sorrow seemed too deep for their sympathy to reach: they endeavoured to comfort me, but vain was their effort. One day, when alone, my heart overwhelmed within me, a man of God, 'a son of consolation,' was sent to me. He drew me out to disclose all my feelings, my doubts, and misgivings of God's love. I opened my heart to him in perfect confidence, and the Spirit enabled him to open his mouth for God. He unfolded God's eternal and unchangeable love to His children, and proved from every part of the Sacred Volume, that it was not because I was *not* His child, He had chastened me; but because I *was* His child. Long and faithful was his conversation, and oh, how comforting! I felt all that he said. Every word brought conviction to my mind and comfort to my heart. 'Then,' I exclaimed, lifting my eyes to heaven, and clasping my hands, 'God is still my Father, my reconciled Father.' Light broke into my benighted soul, my heart opened to receive the message the Lord had sent by His dear servant, the enemy fled from me, and I was comforted. To know I was still His, and that His love was unchanged, strengthened me to look up to Him from whence my help came. I was comforted, too, by a letter your dear father wrote to me during his illness. I believe the Lord took me from him that he might not lean upon an arm of flesh for comfort, but upon Himself alone. He did so. He fled to Jesus, and was saved. The Lord had taken him from the evil to come; and now I was to gird my mind to bear the burden alone, He supported me."

We are henceforth to contemplate Mrs. Winslow as occupying a new and untried position in life, involving responsibilities and cares of no ordinary character. She was now a widow, with a large family of sons dependent upon her for their training and settlement in life. "She that is a widow indeed, and desolate, trusteth in God." Such was her present condition. The surges of grief now yielded to a calm, intelligent survey of her position. She threw herself upon God. The covenant she made with him when a wife, she now and more solemnly renewed as a widow,—that the Lord should be her God. It was at this important crisis of her history that the following touching incident in her experience occurred:—

"I had sent one of my sons, a youth of ten years old, accompanied by a servant, across the river on a matter of business. The appointed time for his return arrived, but he did not appear. Hour after hour passed away, and nightfall drew on, but he came not. The last steamboat touched the pier, but he was not on board. I walked my room for hours in prayer, and in great agitation of mind. Keenly did I then feel my lonely, helpless widowhood. Again and again I sought the Lord. After passing hours in this state of mental anxiety, I sent a brother in search, and soon after, all made their appearance. He had missed his way. The Lord heard a mother's prayer, and brought him in safety to me. After all had retired for the night, I was left alone with God. My mind and heart had been greatly exercised throughout the day. I felt deeply my helplessness and responsible situation. I thought, 'How can I, a helpless woman, care for, and train up, these children to manhood?' I felt I should sink beneath the overwhelming conviction of my weakness and insufficiency. I paced my room in prayer, tried to take hold of a promise; but all was dark, the present and the future, as midnight. It was late before I retired to rest. In vain I endeavoured to compose myself; sleep had forsaken me. Again I lifted up my heart in prayer. I tried to cease from thinking, and to close my eyelids, but in vain. All night I continued in prayer, until just before the dawn of the day these words were spoken to my ear and heart, as if an audible voice had uttered them: 'I WILL BE A FATHER TO THY FATHERLESS CHILDREN.' I knew this voice, and could make no mistake. So powerful was it, I instantly replied aloud, 'O Lord, *be* thou the Father of my fatherless, O my God!' Oh, the solemnity of that hour! I felt God was with me, and my soul was filled with joy and holy reverence. He had condescended to visit my lone room, and fill it with His presence. He had come to comfort his widowed child, and I *was* comforted. My soul poured out its grateful acknowledgments. I could adore, and praise, and bless His holy name. A solemn, sacred influence pervaded the place. God was with me, of a truth. Fatigued with the anxieties of the day, and exhausted with the mental exercises through which I had passed that night, I composed myself to rest. The Lord withdrew, and my weary eyes were closed in refreshing sleep. Years have passed since then, and the Lord has not for one moment forgotten His promise. But I take the promise to extend beyond this poor dying world. Had the Lord given each of my children a world, and they should lose their souls, what would it profit them? I believe He designs to be their Father to all eternity, and that I shall meet all, *all* my children in heaven. How often have I gone and pleaded this promise before Him, and have always found my faith increased. And still my faith holds out; *for He is faithful that has promised.*"

From the moment God sealed upon her sorrowing heart this especial and remarkable promise, causing her to rest in His own veracity as the pledge of its fulfilment, she became animated as by a new and mighty impulse. Her natural spirits, unstrung by grief, and her mental powers, paralyzed by anxiety, now acquired fresh tone and energy. An overwhelming pressure of despondency and care seemed suddenly and entirely to be lifted from off her mind. Strengthened with might in the inner man, she cast her care on God; and girding herself anew for the arduous duties to which he now summoned her, with a calmness of judgment, a firmness of resolution, and a reliance of faith, equal to the dignity of her position, she cheerfully met and vigorously discharged all its claims. The promise thus given proved as a sheet-anchor to her soul in many a subsequent hour of storm and cloud. And when at times—for such there were—the sentence of death seemed written upon it, her faith in God never faltered; giving to that promise, as she herself tells us, its widest range of meaning, she rose above the temporal blessing it involved, and claimed, as the only limit of its fulfilment, a divine heritage, a spiritual birthright, an eternal home for her orphan ones. She knew that she had to do with a Being, all whose resources of power, wisdom and love were as boundless as His own infinity; who was not only a prayer-hearing, and a prayer-answering, but also a prayer-exceeding God; and who, in the bestowment of His blessings upon His people, never gave less, but always *more* than He had promised, or than they had asked. She reasoned—and it was the logical reasoning of true faith—that if God, in the lone hours of that night of weeping and of prayer, had engaged to be a Father to her fatherless children, that engagement bound Him to them as their Heavenly Father. To this broad interpretation of the pledge, she held Him with a grasp which never for an instant relaxed. And when she died, it was in the firm, unfaltering faith of that promise. Not having received its complete fulfilment, but viewing it afar off, she was persuaded of it, embraced it, and closed her eyes with an undimmed, unshaken assurance, that it would be even as God had said, and that she would meet again all the children He had given her—AN UNDIVIDED FAMILY IN HEAVEN.

And yet it must not be inferred from this that her path henceforth was never beclouded by the shadows of a fluctuating faith, or that she was no more of an anxious and a doubtful mind. Far from this. Where are the evidences of grace in the absence of infirmity? And where the victories of faith in the non-resistance of unbelief? There were seasons—many indeed—when she was cast down with anxious care and painful foreboding. Alone, and with but the wreck of former affluence, she was called to meet the growing demands of a family of nine sons, fast advancing into manhood. It was only by a careful husbanding and wise expenditure of her crippled resources that she was enabled to educate them for professional life; but with God's blessing upon her judicious, self-sacrificing efforts it was accomplished; and "her children rise up to call her blessed." As her sons advanced in years, she parted from them, one by one, with a view to the completion of their education at home. There, beneath the eye of her elder son, who now merged the relationship of an elder brother in the higher one of a foster-father, they were trained for their future positions in life. It was on one of these occasions that she penned the following letter to one of her sons, then a youth, on his way home to pursue his professional studies, and now usefully engaged as a clergyman of the Church of England:—

"MY PRECIOUS GEORGE,— New York, 1818.

"I hope before this comes to hand you are with your dear brother* and sister. This is the fourth day since you left me, and my prayers have been offered up for you morning, noon, and night; and often has my heart ascended on your behalf, when I have been otherwise engaged. When my weeping eyes followed you, I felt an inexpressible sweetness and comfort in offering up this short prayer,—'Now, Father, I commit this child into Thy hands. Follow him with thy blessing, shield him from every evil, carry him in safety where he is going, and let him be Thine for time and for eternity. Fulfil Thy promise, on which Thou hast caused Thine handmaid to hope, and be Thou a Father to her fatherless children.' From that moment my heart was comforted, though I felt the separation. The night was wet and gloomy, and I followed you in imagination to your lonely berth, ill, and wishing yourself by our comfortable fireside at home. I have thought of you almost continually, my dear boy; for you are now without a friend or relative. But God is with you, and that comforts me. Your dear brothers tried to look cheerful when they returned to me, but I could see they were much affected. While I am writing, you are at this moment on the mighty deep: but, as Mrs. Isabella Graham says, 'it is God's ocean,'—*my* God's.

"20th.—My dear G——, when we all gather round the evening fireside, I find myself looking, every now and then, at the door, expecting to see you enter; and once or twice, when we have been going to read the Bible, I have waited a moment or two, looking round for an absent one, who I then recollected was far, very far away from me. How often have I carried you in the arms of faith to a throne of grace, beseeching the Lord to put His hand upon you and bless you. Oh, my child, if you but knew the blessedness of the religion

* Her eldest son T., then recently married and settled in England.

of Jesus, its sweetness, rich enjoyment, and reality, you would not rest a moment until you could call the Lord your own."

To her eldest son she thus writes:—

"I felt so distressed through the whole day and night, at not hearing from you on the arrival of the packet, that to change the scene, and give a turn to my thoughts, I set out on a visit to my sweet E——, at Mrs. B——'s.* I should tell you, however, that I had heard through Captain —— that G—— was well, though he had not reached you. For this, I failed not to thank my God, and to implore His aid to strengthen me, and enable me to bear up under this and every other disappointment and trial, through what His infinite wisdom should see fit I should pass while on my pilgrimage through this wilderness. I felt sensible I was aiming in my own strength to be resigned to His will and to trust Him; and knowing how impossible it was for me to do this, went to His footstool and confessed my weakness and total inability to do anything without Him. And oh! how graciously does He at all times deal with His unworthy child, His ungrateful, unbelieving child. B—— is in affliction, and I am obliged to remind her of the faithfulness of our God, His promises, His boundless love towards His children; His power and goodness enabling Him to perform them all; and in doing so, my own spirits are revived, my own faith and confidence increased by the recital; and I am helped thereby to go on from day to day with a cheerfulness, under circumstances which I should have thought, formerly, would have made me lose my reason or break my heart. I speak not of want; for, blessed be His holy name, He has never suffered me to want any good thing that was absolutely necessary for me; for I am certain, that what I have thought I wanted, it were better I should want; for had it not been so, infinite love would have given it me."

"December 26th.—My soul longs for the privilege of again hearing a full gospel. I feel my poverty, and my need of Christ, more and more. . . . . But I do believe these exercises of soul, which I often have in consequence of this low state of spiritual enjoyment, will ultimately prove to my advantage, and for the glory of God. My choicest seat is at the foot of the cross. When I can but view His bleeding wounds, and obtain one glance by faith of His gracious countenance, it

---

* The boarding-school at which her daughter was placed.

is worth a thousand worlds to me. Nothing else can give me joy and comfort. I have had not a few battles with Satan, as it respects past experience, and have been put to my wits' end; but I find it is the safest to keep close to Jesus; and as I came at first, so I come again and again; in this way the foe is defeated, and my soul is melted with love, while He lifts upon me His heavenly countenance."

If there were one feature in the religious character of Mrs. Winslow more distinct and palpable than any other, and which, as her Christianity ripened, became a yet more strongly developed, firmly rooted, and all-controlling principle of her life, it was the profound homage with which her whole soul bowed to the supreme authority of God's revealed word. To her enlightened view, no doctrine was propounded in the Bible, the belief of which was a matter of indifference; and no precept was enjoined, the observance of which was a question of choice. As a child of God, to obey instantly and unquestioningly, she regarded as an imperious duty; and as a Christian disciple, to mould her walk according to the example of the Saviour, she counted her sweetest privilege. With her, human opinion, worldly interest, self-ease, were as the fine dust in the balance weighed in the scale with her Lord's solemn and comprehensive injunction—"Teaching them to observe all things whatsoever I have commanded you." Influenced by this principle—a principle which governed the lowliest actions of her life—and in compliance with what she interpreted as a divine and positive injunction, we find her avowing her faith in Christ, and dedicating herself anew to the Lord, in the solemn rite of believers' baptism.

The spiritual reader, who may not see eye to eye with her on this subject—and there will be many such—cannot yet fail to approve the principle which governed her, and to reverence the conscienciousness which dictated the step. Addressing her mother from New York, she writes:—

"I trust you will, by God's blessing, be able to come to us in the spring. I had intended to have written to you with respect to my baptism, but the subject requires a clearer head and a mind less agitated than mine is at present. But, my beloved mamma, I saw it to be a plain and positive command of Christ, and I am called to obey Him, as far as He gives me light so to do. I have for years been impressed with the importance of the subject. I read in my Bible that only those who *believed*, or had true faith, were the scriptural subjects of baptism; *whosoever believeth and is baptized*. Infants cannot believe, and consequently baptism, in their case, loses its significance. Nor could I, in all my examination, find a solitary passage or example in the New Testament, that will lead me to the conclusion for a moment, that children were baptized in the early church. But in the time of the apostles, as soon as sinners, or adults, were called through grace to believe, they were baptized and added to the church. I shall some time hence write more fully to you on the subject. I have not heard from T—— since he sailed for England; but the Lord is my help, and in every trial and trouble my soul looks to and and leans upon Him, and I am comforted."

In the midst of her personal sorrow and domestic duties she found time for walks of practical Christian usefulness. In one of these rambles she met with the following remarkable instance of the grace of God in a poor idiot girl: "The entrance of Thy word giveth light; it giveth understanding unto the simple." Such was the case with poor Ellen, who had been brought to a knowledge of the truth through the instrumentality of the Rev. Archibald Maclay, the then esteemed pastor of Mrs. Winslow. On every other subject but the love of Christ to her, the mind of the poor idiot was a perfect blank. But on this, the deepest and sublimest of all themes, she spake with a sincerity and earnestness of feeling which the most eloquent language could not express. In one of her letters, Mrs. Winslow details an interesting visit to this pious imbecile:—

"I entered the little room. It was clean and tidy, with a bed in one corner farthest from the fire, by the side of which, in an old arm chair, sat an idiot girl about seventeen years of age. She was dressed neatly, and looked happy, though ill. Her mother, a respectable-looking woman, was by her side. I took an offered chair, and drawing near the girl, asked her how she was. She replied, 'Sick.' 'And what have you in your lap?' pointing to a book which lay there. She opened it, and with an expression of delight I shall not soon forget, reached it to me. It was the New Testament. 'Do you love the Lord, my dear child?' 'Oh, yes,' she replied, though with great difficulty; 'Jesus is good.' 'He is good, my poor child; what a mercy for you that He has enabled you to know it.' 'Oh, yes,' she repeated again, 'Jesus is good. Mr. Maclay good man; Mr. Maclay tell poor Ellen of Jesus.' I turned inquiringly to her mother, who told me her simple, affecting story. She had a year or two back been convinced that she was a sinner, and her distress of mind in consequence was so great, that it brought on the illness (paralysis) with which she is now affected. Her intellect, feeble from her birth, is now nearly gone, and she is unable to understand little else but that 'Jesus is good, and loves poor Ellen,' and this is her constant cry. She is always reading her New Testament, which, with a hymn-book, is her constant companion. She was very attentive to all I said of the Lord, and listened with great eagerness. I read to her a hymn she gave me, and then, looking earnestly in my face, she said, pausing between each word, *In—my—Father's—house—are—many—mansions.* As she could with difficulty speak, I repeated to her the following verses. But, oh, what an expression of joy and delight did she manifest! Her whole body was convulsed, and her ecstasy seemed too much for her poor shattered frame to bear. She spread both her hands before her face, while tears of joy stood in her eyes. As soon as she could speak, 'Jesus is good; Jesus loves poor Ellen,' were the words which seemed most fully to express her whole heart. So great was her agitation, and so incessantly and rapidly were these words repeated, I was compelled to lay my hands gently upon her, and soothe her to silence. When I left her humble abode, I thought, 'There dwells an heir of glory, a joint heir with Christ Jesus, in a cellar kitchen, rich in faith.' Oh, how true the precious word of God: *God hath chosen the foolish things of the world, and weak things of the world, and base things of the world, and things which are despised, and things which are not, that no flesh should glory in his presence.*"

She was not without her severe conflicts of faith; yet we always trace in her experience the irrepressible energy of this mighty grace under circumstances of its deepest trial. Addressing her children from New York, she says:

". . . . I have nothing new myself to communicate to you, but I feel a desire to say to you all this evening, 'How are you?' 'Is it well with you?' 'Is it well with your children?' It will be a long time before I can get an answer. But my God is your God; and though a vast ocean divides us, He is present with us both, and has engaged that it shall be well; yea, that it *is* well with his people. What a mercy that a throne of grace is accessible to us both, and at the same time where we meet in Christ, and under the influence of the same Spirit commend each other to the tender care of our dear Redeemer, who has undertaken to manage all our concerns. Oh that I could at all times take the comfort of this precious truth, and be careful for nothing, but with prayer and thanksgiving make all my requests known to the Lord. My faith is but small at present; sometimes I stand in doubt whether I have any at all; and there have been seasons when I have been tempted to think I never had known the grace of God in truth. For some months past I have had sharp conflicts with my corrupt nature and the old adversary; and when I have cried out in agony of soul, 'Lord, have mercy! Lord, hear! can I be thine? can I be thy child?' this passage of Scripture has invariably presented itself to my mind, *Cast not away your confidence, which hath great recompense of reward.* I thought it strange that this passage was ever on my mind, so that I could repeat it aloud as I walked the streets. Nevertheless, I am still called to follow as under a cloud. I feel my vileness, my unprofitableness, my woful shortcomings, and am thankful if I can but only creep to the foot of the cross, and there repose my weary soul refreshed by one look at Jesus, who, I do trust, died for my sins. But oh, I want to be more conformable to His lovely image, to be sanctified, body, soul, and spirit, and to have every power of my mind under the constant influence of the Holy Spirit. You, too, have in some degree been in the furnace, but I trust it has been sanctified to you both. You have gone on so prosperously that it was time for the Lord to try your grace. The faith that is not tried is doubtful. Trials and crosses test the Christian's faith and Christ's faithfulness, and these things bring rich experience to the believer's soul which otherwise he would never have had.

The following family incident will interest the reader, only so far as affording an illustration of Mrs. Winslow's energy of character, and the deep religious sentiment which pervaded and sanctified all her secular engagements. There is a passing allusion to one of the most catholic Christians, able statesmen, and distinguished philanthropists of his age. With WILLIAM WILBERFORCE it was her privilege to be on terms of sacred friendship. His "Practical View of Christianity" was one of her favourite works; and in the early stages of her religious experience, contributed materially to mould and establish her opinions. To the latest period of life, she cherished, for the memory of this illustrious man, feelings of the most profound veneration. The writer, then a little boy, has a vivid recollection of accompanying her on a morning visit to him at Kensington Gore, and of receiving some confectionery, offered with the most winning kindness, from those hands which, more than all others, had laboured to wrench the shackles from the slave. The extract that follows refers to a presentation, through Mr. Wilberforce, of claims supposed to exist upon the British Government for the confiscation of large family estates in the North American colonies, when those colonies separated from the Crown. A short time before the revolution, the Provincial Council, which, until about the year 1765, was always the aristocratic branch of the Legislature, and, of course, composed of the most distinguished individuals in the country, had, for the most part, become attached to the popular party, and hence, in opposition to the Governor.* In consequence of this, commissions were granted by mandamus to distinguish loyalists, of whom the father of Captain Winslow was one. It is supposed, however, that he never acted under this commission. The appointment was in opposition to the general sentiments of the people, which soon afterwards terminated in the revolution and ultimate separation of the colonies from the mother country. The consequence of the acceptance of this office, however, was the relinquishment and subsequent confiscation of a large family property in Boston, U. S., and for the indemnification for such a sacrifice, it was thought, just claims existed upon the Government at home. Writing to her son, she says:—

"I must now tell you I have petitioned the King with respect to your dear father's claims. You may remember how often he intended to prefer those claims himself, on account of his father's services and his own, but never lived to put his intentions into execution. I have, therefore, written to Mr. Wilberforce, and also to Lord Dundas, under cover of my petition, urging them to exert themselves on my behalf. I know that I shall get nothing without the Lord's blessing attends it; but the hearts of Kings and Princes are in His hands; to Him I have committed the thing, and hope I shall be satisfied, whatever be the result. Your grandfather Winslow was one

* Hutchinson.

of the King's mandamus Counsellors in Boston; and during the Revolution he quitted it, and all his vast property, to follow the army, but died before he reached home. In consequence of this, your father lost the fortune that would have been his on coming of age. Your father entered the British service at seventeen, serving both at home and abroad. These are the outlines of my claims upon Government, and I mention them to you, as you may be questioned upon the subject. I thought it would be worth while for you to call on Mr. Wilberforce, at Kensington Gore, and ascertain if there is any likelihood of the claims being recognized. I have referred him to Judge Leonard, who knew your grandfather, and also to Colonel Backhouse, under whom your father served for many years. But all my concerns are in the best hands. However, make every prudent inquiry about it; and may He who is the widow's God give you all the wisdom that you may need, and follow your attempt to serve your mother with His best blessing. You remember when the widow, whose son Elijah had restored to life, cried to the king for her lands, the prophet's servant stood by and pointed her out to him. The Lord opened the king's heart, and her request was granted, even more than she asked. That same God is my God, and still *worketh all things after the council of His own will. Be not faithless but believing.*"

Powerful as was the interest with which this memorial was sustained, it failed to secure a response to the prayer, in consequence of the length of time that had elapsed in preferring the claim. But higher concerns now engaged her thoughts, as will appear from the following extracts from correspondence with her family:—

"Your grandmamma seems quite young again. How graciously the Lord has in all things dealt with his aged handmaid! She has outlived nearly all her relatives and early friends; they are passed into eternity, while she has been spared, and blessed to her old age with a knowledge of the truth, and with a stable peace and reliance upon her Saviour for all that is needful for time and for eternity. Her frame and feelings are seldom very lively, but her faith steady, and her peace unceasing. Her spiritual joy is not great, but she goes on her way relying on God, and looking forward without a fear to the moment when she will be called to pass the dreary valley of the shadow of death. While I have my changes, sometimes rejoicing in my Saviour, and triumphing over all that opposes my way; at other times cast down, feeling my unworthiness, and afraid of deceiving myself, she is passing on her way like the sun without a cloud. But our God is wise in all His dispensations towards His people, and all my exercises are needful.

"Oct. 21st.—Oh what a mercy is a throne of grace! I think I never knew the value of prayer so much as of late. Since I have parted with so many of my children, I feel I have so much more to do with God. I have so many more petitions to present for you all, that it seems to me a more constant intercourse is kept up between my soul and Jesus, and thereby enables me to discover such a fulness, such a sufficiency, such goodness, and boundless, matchless love, that at times I can but kneel and weep. My mind is led from earthly things to longing desires after conformity to His holy likeness. Oh, to be holy! How beautiful does holiness appear to be! To be holy is to be happy. May the Lord sanctify us! A little while and we shall be done with those things that but too often encumber us, and then, oh, what glory awaits the believing soul!

"January 17.—The cold is intense. Last night, while interceding with the Lord to have pity upon the poor and needy, and supply their wants during this trying season, I recollected a widow woman had called on me for help a week ago, but from various causes I had done nothing in her case. I felt humbled before a heart-searching God for my neglect, and this morning I set off and found out her abode, above the Vauxhall Gardens. Her little stock of fuel was out; and finding it a worthy case, I gave her a note to the Widows' Society, and no doubt she will be supplied with a load of wood. I then called on a young woman in a consumption. She says she has no hope for eternity. I directed her to Jesus, and then left her."

CHAPTER V.

A RESIDENCE of nearly five years in a new, and, to an European constitution, somewhat trying climate, had greatly impaired her health, and rendered essential to its recovery a sea voyage and a season of entire repose. Accordingly, in 1820, accompanied by one of her sons, she recrossed the Atlantic, and spent four or five months with the elder branches of her family. Her first return to England since her sore bereavement, it were not difficult to imagine what would be the intensity of her thoughts and feelings on revisiting once more the scenes of former prosperity and happiness. Landing at Deal, she travelled all night, and arrived in London in the grey light of morning, while yet the vast metropolis was wrapped in profound stillness, presenting all the appearance of a great city of the dead. But the sombre and grave-like aspect of the town harmonized with the feelings of her lone and saddened heart. Her course from the place where she alighted brought her in view of endeared and sacred spots—the pleasant home which had been the scene of so many years of domestic happiness—the hallowed sanctuary, within whose walls she had first heard the gospel of Christ, and beneath whose shadow reposed the beloved remains of the husband of her youth. "Overpowered by my feelings," she writes, "I allowed but a glance at scenes so painfully dear, and was soon welcomed by the affectionate greetings of my children. Blessed be God, the God of all my comforts, for His goodness and mercy to the most unworthy of all His creatures. Assist me to bless and praise His Holy name." Soothed by social intercourse with the family of her eldest son, whose generous and affectionate consideration left nothing to desire that could contribute to her comfort, and renovated in health by travel through different parts of England and Scotland, after above four months' pleasant sojourn she recrossed the Atlantic, and arrived at New York under happier and brighter auspices than those with which she first landed a saddened stranger upon its shores.

On her return to the United States she retired to a small estate, which she rented, on the banks of the majestic Hudson. Here, favoured with an evangelical ministry, and in the enjoyment of the communion of saints, she spent four years of congenial repose, revelling amidst the rich beauties of nature, for which she possessed so exquisite a taste, and indulging in those rural pursuits in which she always took particular delight. Of the many interesting letters dated from this romantic spot, we can afford space but for one, as indicating the supreme ascendancy which spiritual concerns still maintained in her heart; and as containing 'pleasant words' for those who are sincerely and honestly inquiring for the truth as it is in Jesus.

"MY DEAREST MAMMA,— Mount Pleasant, 1823.

". . . Glad was I to get dear ——'s letter; and though I grieve he is not rejoicing in the Lord, I am far from being discouraged. He has life. A *dead* sinner never feels that he is ungrateful to the best of Beings, that he is in the 'gall of bitterness,' or is afraid of being a hypocrite. The Lord himself has commenced the work in his soul, and He will carry it on; not, perhaps, in our way, but in His own wisdom, until He accomplishes the thing He has put His hand to. I would rather see him diving to the bottom of truth, for the truth, than to take it up, as many do, on the *ipse dixit* of their fellow-men; and fancy they believe the gospel because others do whose opinions they respect, and in consequence of which they are harassed with doubts and misgivings, and their usefulness impaired, all their journey through. If our gracious Lord designs that —— should be called to labour in the dear Redeemer's kingdom (a real, not a *feather-bed* soldier), He will bring him to plough deep for the truth, and perhaps bring him through painful exercises too. Blessed be His adored name, for the hope he causes my heart to feel on this subject. I have had to pray, 'Anything, or any way, dearest Lord, so that thou wilt convert his soul and bring him into thy blessed service.' Thomas thought it was all imagination as it respected the resurrection of Jesus, although his brethren declared they had seen Him, till compelled by a view of Christ himself to exclaim, *My Lord and my God!* Paul, too, hated the name of Jesus, and thought it a made up story to deceive, until Jesus met him in the way. And I have often remarked that some of the most eminently useful ministers of the cross have been extricated, by the all-powerful arm of the Redeemer, from the very hotbed of unbelief. I do not expect that this work in his soul will be done in a few days, or weeks, or perhaps years; but that it will be done, I have little doubt, and bless the Lord for his abundant goodness to him and to me. If you see Mr. ——, inquire how the revival at New Haven proceeds, and how Mr. Bethune's son holds out."

The return of Mrs. Winslow to America, and her removal from the banks of the Hudson to a permanent residence in New York, formed one of the most interesting epochs in the history of her sojourn in that land. We refer to an especial and remarkable season of Divine grace with which God visited her domestic circle, imparting a quickened impulse to her own spiritual feelings, and resulting in the accession of three of her children to the ranks and service of Christ. The existence of that striking peculiarity in the history of the transatlantic churches,—Religious Revival,—is now a fact generally well known. There are few intelligent Christians of any clime, who have not heard, and, perhaps, it might be added, to whom in some degree the influence has not extended, of those especial and remarkable baptisms of the Spirit with which the Great Head of the church from time to time visits the churches in America. It comes not within the scope of the present volume to explain the theory of this wonderful phenomenon; all that we can allow ourselves to do is to bear a lowly testimony to the fact of its existence. The ecclesiastical historian, as he traces at some future period—when their nature is better understood, and their influence better known—the origin, progress, and results of these extraordinary seasons of religious excitement, will probably date their commencement from the first settlement of the Pilgrim Fathers on those western shores. It was not, therefore, remarkable, that New England should have been the birthplace and the cradle of the first religious awakening on that vast continent. The most remarkable displays of Divine power, however, appeared in the times and under the awakening ministry of the elder Edwards—a man of colossal intellect, of seraphic piety, and of childlike simplicity. From that period, embracing the labours of Whitfield, the Tennants, Davies, Brainard, and other eminent and holy divines, to the present time, America has been the theatre of some of the most signal displays of the presence and power of the Holy Ghost the church of God has ever witnessed. We pause not to ask why it should be so. This would lead us into too wide a range of inquiry—but so it is. We may, however, venture upon the remark, that the social principle in America—though this may not elucidate the origin of these sovereign manifestations of Divine grace—has been found peculiarly favourable to the promotion of religious revivals. Commencing with an individual, the sacred influence has extended to a family, from thence to an entire congregation; the impulse thus given to religious feeling has widened until a village, a town, and even a city, has been moved to its centre on the stupendous concerns of eternity. Such have often been the progress and the happy results of American revivals. We turn our attention now to an illustration of these interesting phenomena, more circumscribed, but not less marked.

The domestic revival to which the following extracts refer was preceded by the devotional meetings of an association of Christian mothers, representing different branches of the church of Christ, who convened weekly for the purpose of especial and united prayer for the Divine blessing upon their families. Mrs. Winslow has often described those seasons as hallowed by an extraordinary degree of the presence and anointing of the Holy Ghost. Frequently has she been seen to return from them with tearful eyes and a glowing countenance, to diffuse around her home-circle the influence of her own solemn and heavenly communings. The wrestling intercessions of this band of holy women, of praying mothers—mighty in their weakness—soon brought the blessing for which they pleaded. Over one family, especially, the mercy-cloud gathered, unveiling its heaven-sent treasure. Commencing with herself, the blessing extended to one and another, and yet another of her circle, until there was not a room in her dwelling that resounded not with the voice of prayer and praise. In the following extracts from her family correspondence, written from New York, and at different intervals in the progress of the revival, she thus narrates this good and wondrous work:—

"In the commencement of this year, before a revival even was thought of, the Lord met with my soul, after some months of comparative darkness and desertion, during which time I felt like wrestling Israel; for my spirit was in heaviness, and I earnestly sought and felt after my absent Lord. At last He appeared, and filled my heart with unspeakable joy. Like Mary, I arose from the sepulchre, and hastened to tell the disciples that the Lord had risen upon me as the *Sun of Righteousness.* My heart was enlarged, and my mouth was open to speak good of His holy name; not only in my own family, but to others, exhorting them to ask and to expect great things, for the Lord was at hand. I entreated them to arise out of the spiritual lethargy they appeared to be in, and Jesus would bless them as He had blessed me."

* * * *

"In what language can I express my gratitude to God for all His abundant goodness to me and mine? I am at a loss. My cup, at times, overflows. Praise Him on my behalf, my dear children, who know the value of this great salvation. My children here are walking in the narrow road, and are sweetly united in the tenderest bonds of Christian love. Not one unconverted soul is under my roof. All, *all* love the Saviour. My house is a house of prayer."

* * * *

"The good work is still progressing. During this revival my soul has felt its refreshing influence, and still continues to experience a most precious unfolding of Christ's love. For many years I have not felt anything like it. I see a fulness in Jesus I hardly ever saw before. Bless the Lord, O my soul! Several churches have partaken of this heavenly shower, and I trust it will increase more and more. Many who love the Lord are upon their watch-tower looking out for His approach. Oh, it is a refreshing season! My own soul can testify that Jesus is among us of a truth. It seems as if new strength had been imparted to gird up the loins of my mind, and to set out afresh to run the heavenly race. I can look back and see with concern how I have loitered on my way."

* * * *

"This precious revival is still advancing. The Lord is pouring out His Spirit in a way I never before saw or felt. And what I now see and feel has tended to confirm my soul more than ever in the reality of the religion of Jesus, and of that eternal world to which we are fast approaching. There is nothing like enthusiasm. I am quite inadequate to give you any just idea of this most solemn and gracious work of God. It is to me something like the day of Pentecost."

* * * *

"Everything under my roof seems to wear another aspect. Old things have passed away, and all things have become new. I can say of my children, 'Behold, Lord, they pray!' The things of God open upon them with deep interest. The ways of wisdom are pleasant, and everything not connected therewith, tasteless. Oh, what has God, my God, wrought for His unworthy handmaid! Had He given me an earthly crown it had been dross in comparison. It appears to me that the Lord is about to do great things for our wicked world. He will pour out His Spirit upon *all* flesh, as He has promised. Oh, that you may feel that he is drawing nigh in your part of the world! Ask, and expect great things from Him. You cannot ask too much when you ask in Jesus' name, and God cannot give too much when He gives for Jesus' sake. How near He has been to us! You will hardly think I can speak too much on this interesting subject, when it is said, the angels in heaven rejoice over one sinner that repenteth. And here are three to whom Jesus has given repentance and life under my roof. If the angels rejoice in heaven, well may I rejoice on earth."

* * * *

"And now my heart is going out after you all. The Lord's arm of grace is not shortened but that it can extend across the Atlantic. Who can tell but at this moment it has commenced among you all? I must pray on. Elisha was wroth against the king of Israel because he smote on the ground thrice, and stayed; declaring that if he had smitten five or six times, his enemies should have fallen before him. May I be enabled to carry my unconverted children in the arms of faith to Jesus, until He put His hand upon them and bless them. The revival is still going on, not only here (New York), but also in every part of America. In Philadelphia, and in many other places, numbers, I am told, are inquiring their way to Zion. It appears almost like the millennial day. Unitarianism, like a pernicious weed, is spreading in Boston; but lately they have had a more extensive revival than we have had here. This has been a year of wonders; thousands have been born into the kingdom of our Lord and Saviour, Jesus Christ. These are glorious manifestations that Jesus lives, and is accomplishing all His gracious purposes, and will bring His people into a wealthy place at last. How has my faith been strengthened, and my soul established in the truth, from what

I have seen of His power and grace beneath my own roof, and from what I have experienced in my own soul! Oh, may He extend His arm of mercy to you all!' I *do* look for it, and am ready to say, 'I cannot let Thee go until Thou bless me in the conversion of all, *all*.' As it respects myself, my joy is settled down into a stable peace, and increasing confidence in the dear Redeemer. I feel a throne of grace very precious, and the name of the Lord a tower of strength. It appears to me that I was to have travail of soul for these children, and a deeper work in my own. I am still utter weakness in myself, but am enabled to keep a more steadfast eye upon Jesus."

Such is the prevailing power with God of a praying and believing mother. Let the Christian parent, anxious and earnest for the spiritual and eternal wellbeing of her children, take encouragement from the preceding narrative, and give herself to prayer for the outpouring of the Spirit upon her family. Taking hold of His word, let her remind God of His promise,—" I will pour my Spirit upon thy seed, and my blessing upon thine offspring;" and thus travailing in birth a second time in the energy of faith, and in the wrestling of prayer, it will be the joy of her heart to behold Christ formed within them the hope of glory.

And why are not Revivals of religion more frequent in this land? Why have we not those special baptisms of the Spirit, for which the churches in America are so distinguished? That we are not entirely without manifest tokens of the Spirit's presence, we thankfully acknowledge. In the absence of the *showers*, we have the continual *dew* of the Spirit. But are we not justified in expecting more than this—even the *outpouring* of the Spirit? Is not the Spirit the property of the universal church? Is not the present emphatically the dispensation of the Spirit? Have we not the prediction and the promise of His large bestowment in these last days? And is not Christ enthroned in heaven, having received the promise of the Father, prepared to rain down righteousness upon His church? Why, then, have we not the blessing? Some observations of Mrs. Winslow, on the power of prayer and faith, gleaned from "Thoughts" recorded in her Journal, may probably supply an answer:—

"O Lord, revive us in the midst of the years! How is it that we have no precious revivals here, and that the all-important subject lies with so little weight upon our hearts? It is because we do not *believe* the matter-of-fact, although God has promised, and declared the truth. When Christ had risen, and some were eye-witnesses of the fact, yet when they declared the blessed truth to the rest, they were as those that mocked. We testify that these things are so, for we have seen and felt them ourselves. Our hearts have burned within us, and our souls have been refreshed as with new wine from the kingdom. The doors have been shut about us, and Jesus has been in our midst within, blessing, reviving, and refreshing us — giving life to the dead, and speaking comforting words to His saints. It has been the mighty work of an Almighty God, manifesting His power, and displaying His love.

"Oh, the mighty power of prayer! Even the best of Christians know but little what it really is. The apostle felt the truth, when he exhorted the saints to *pray without ceasing.* Christian, are you in trouble?—call upon the name of the Lord, and He will deliver. *This poor man cried, and the Lord heard him, and saved him out of all his troubles.* His ear is ever open to the cry of His people, and His arm outstretched on their behalf. His aim is ever to make you happy in Himself, and happy throughout eternity. Make Him your confidant; entrust Him with all your secrets. Let Christ be your friend, and you need no other. All hearts are at his disposal; *and if a man's ways please the Lord He maketh even his enemies to be at peace with him.* Are you poor and needy? Go to Christ for all you need. Satan may suggest that these are carnal things. But did not the Lord send His servant to the widow, to be fed for many days? and did the barrel of meal waste, or the cruse of oil fail? Did He not send a celestial messenger to prepare Elijah's breakfast while he slept? And is He not the same now? Go, then, to Christ for *all* you need.

"Faith is the gift of God, and it is a working agent in the soul of the believer. It has to do with God, and with Him only. It takes hold of His faithfulness, who cannot deny Himself. Simple faith honours God, and God honours simple faith. True faith works in the dark as in the light. It cannot fail, but will always come off triumphant. And what is faith? It is simply believing what God has said—taking Him at His word. Faith tries God, and God tries the faith He gives. Little faith brings home but little. *Be it unto you according to your faith.* Seek much for this Divine grace. It is for you treasured up in Christ. Look not for it in yourself. It grows in its native soil. It is in Christ Jesus' rich treasure-house. It is of heavenly origin, and leads the soul to the source from whence it came. Only believe. Trust Him, ye tried and empty saints, and you shall rejoice in the goodness and tender mercies of your faithful and unchanging God. I may also remark, that nothing tests or strengthens faith so much as the trying dispensations of God towards His people. The furnace destroys everything but the pure gold. Nothing but real faith can endure the heat of the fiery crucible, and, what is strange, it grows in the fire."

Coupling, then, these cognate graces,—prayer and faith,—let the churches of Christ prove God now herewith, if He will not open the windows of Heaven, and pour out a blessing, that there shall not be room enough to receive it.

The following touching reminiscences, from her own pen, of a period in her history, thus rapidly traversed, may form a befitting close to this chapter of the work. As a personal communication, and unveiling thoughts and feelings most sacred to a mother's heart, some hesitation has been felt in introducing it; but the conviction that it beautifully illustrates her character as a Christian parent, while it bears a noble testimony to the faithfulness of a prayer-hearing God, has pleaded against private feelings. It is addressed to one of her sons:—

"Before I rose this morning, I was led to take a review of the Lord's dealings with you and me. I could not but see and feel that you have been a child of many prayers, and that God has turned a listening ear to the voice of my supplications for you. A few months before your birth, the Lord met with my soul, and most blessedly drew me to Himself, making Himself known to me as my Saviour and my God. I bore you during this sweet season of my espousal to Christ. It was the time of my '*first love.*' The first spark of divine life I then received. After your birth, I was brought to the verge of eternity; for nearly twenty-four hours there was hardly a hair's-breadth between me and death. The physicians concealed my danger; but God did for me what no human skill could do, and I was spared,—snatched as from the grave. When you were about five years old, I took you into the country for your health; and there, through the mistake of the nurse, who brought me a wrong medicine, I administered to you a powder, 'sufficient,' the doctors said, 'to have killed ten men.' At the moment of the dreadful discovery, these words of a beautiful hymn were brought to my mind—

> 'In all thy troubles sharp and strong,
> My soul, to Jesus fly.'

I did so. He heard my prayer. The physicians said that you must die. The Lord said, 'He shall not die, but live.' He answered prayer, and gave you back to me. They afterwards said it was a miracle. During the time of that gracious revival, how did I pray that He would meet with your soul. He did so. He knows, and He only, how I wrestled for your full conversion. I wanted a clear proof of a new birth in Christ. He answered my prayer, and gave you once more to me as from the dead,—a living child, born again of the Spirit. . . . Oh, it is good to look back, and trace His dealings and His wondrous works to the children of men! Taking thus a review of these gracious things, under the teaching of the Eternal Spirit, so far from being puffed up, they will lay us low in the dust under a sense of our base ingratitude towards Him, and the wretched returns we have made for such distinguishing mercies. Oh, that He might keep you humble, and give you such views of your own heart as will cause you to feel as well as confess, that you are *less than the least of all saints.* This is my prayer for you, and myself too. A mother's prayers have been your swaddling-clothes from your birth. Do you pray for me? I am sure you do."

CHAPTER VI.

In 1828, a few months following the interesting events recorded in the preceding chapter, again prostrated in strength by the excessive heat of an almost tropical climate, and, perhaps, scarcely less so by the extreme mental excitement through which she had just passed, she found it necessary to make a second voyage to England, for the purpose of recruiting her health. In contemplating this step, she thus writes to her family:—

"I am not quite certain but that, with God's blessing, you may see me in the autumn. If I come, you must be prepared to find me much altered in appearance. I suppose you will hardly know your weather-beaten mother. But I think the change of climate would soon recruit my health, with the Lord's blessing. But I am growing old, and nothing can repair the ravages of years. I do earnestly pray, if the Lord do not go with me, He will not suffer me to go hence. I long to see all my children, but I desire to wait patiently the Lord's time. *My times are in His hands.* Oh, that He may direct my steps!"

After a perilous passage, but marked by especial mercy, she arrived at Liverpool in safety; spent a few months with her eldest son in the country, and thence took up her residence in London. Anxious for the holy walk, and growth in the divine life, of those of her family she had left in America, she had scarcely touched the shores of England when she addressed to them the following earnest epistle. We have no heart to abridge a document so strikingly illustrative of the spirituality of her mind and the practical character of her Christianity, and so replete with useful sentiments:—

"My dearest Children,—   July, 1828.

". . . . And now that I have given you an account of the goodness of God in bringing me through so many dangers, and in the midst of my dear family on this side of the water, let me turn to your best interests. I have left you, my beloved children, (still more beloved, because you belong to Christ,) in the place of your spiritual birth. *I have left you, but God is with you.* Keep close to Jesus. Forget not my old exhortation, *Pray without ceasing.* Go to Him for all you need; lean upon Him. There is a fulness in Christ, treasured up for you, that the highest angel in heaven cannot fathom. Tell Him all that is in your heart. Lay your case before Him as if He did not already know it. This is the sweet simplicity of faith that Christ loves. You cannot come too often. Bring to Him your little cares as well as your great ones. If anything is a trouble to you, however small it may be, you are warranted, nay, commanded, to take it to Him, and thereby you glorify His name. *I will also leave in the midst of thee an afflicted and poor people, and they shall trust in the name of the Lord.* Pray much for a tender conscience, a conscience susceptible of the least sin,—as susceptible as the eye to the touch; and never rest if you feel guilt there, however small, until it is removed by a fresh application of the precious blood of Christ. *If we confess our sins, He is faithful and just to forgive us our sins, and to cleanse us from all unrighteousness.* Wherever you are, at home or by the wayside, lift up your heart to that precious Saviour who has manifested so much love to your souls. Never be afraid to come to Him. Satan will tempt you here; but beware of his suggestions. He would keep you from Christ; but Christ is as needful for you, every step you take to glory, as when you were overwhelmed with sorrow, under a sense of your awful state as a sinner before God. Never look within for comfort; you will find nothing there but what is calculated to humble you. But look to Jesus. There is everything in Him to encourage you in your warfare. And yet it is needful that you examine your own hearts from day to day, that you may be well acquainted with all your spiritual diseases, and forget not that Christ is your Physician. He has undertaken for your cure, and to fit you, by the indwelling of His Spirit, for the inheritance He has prepared for you. Oh, live upon Him out of yourselves. You need fear nothing but sin, nor even that with a slavish fear, but with a godly, filial fear. Avoid trifling, lukewarm professors. They are the bane of the church of Christ. If you can do them no good, they will do you much harm. One thing I would especially remind you of; in all your difficulties and trials, (for many you will have,) go not first to an arm of flesh, nor sit and ponder what you shall do; but go directly to your dear Saviour, and ask earnestly for wisdom and grace to guide you through them; watch the leadings and openings of His gracious providence, and follow on as He leads the way, and He will make even these things to work for your good. If you feel your want of faith, ask this of Him, that you may come in faith; for this is as much His gift, as the blessing you want. . . . Your wives are professors of the same blessed hope. But, *the husband is the head of the wife, even as Christ is the head of the church;* and they will look to you for an example. Walk before them circumspectly; pray with them, and pray for them, and allow nothing to interrupt family worship. May God give you wisdom in all things. I thought, when you were brought to the knowledge of the truth, my care for you would be over; but I feel as anxious now that you should walk worthy of His blessed name, as I was before that your souls might be saved. Remember that your strength is perfect weakness, and yet with Christ's strength you can do all things. Again, I repeat, live upon Him. Aim to glorify Him in all things, and to possess an abiding sense of the indwelling of the Holy Spirit, that your thoughts, desires, and affections may soar to heavenly and eternal objects. If you lose this, you cannot walk comfortably. Cast your cares, as they arise, upon Him who careth for you. Do not covet riches: pray against this more or less easily besetting sin of many of God's people. Forget not the exhortation, *Be content with such things as ye have.* Keep close to Jesus; for if you walk at a distance, you have need to fear the rod: nevertheless, His loving-kindness He will not take from you. He loves while He chastens. A few more years, and we shall have done with all things here below, and eternity, with all its glorious realities, will burst upon your view. Oh, then, live for eternity. Think much of your blessed inheritance there, and let the glory of God be dearer to you than your own lives. Follow on to know more of Him. Be very thankful for what he has already done, but press on for more. Be not satisfied with a little, when He has such immense riches to bestow. *Open thy mouth wide, and I will fill it.* Above all, before I close,—and do bear with me, for my heart is very full, and you are doubly dear to me, since you belong to Christ, my beloved children—never, never omit *secret* prayer. I take shame to myself that I have not spoken of this before. Remember, the first departures from Christ begin at the closet, or rather in the heart; and then private prayer is either hurried over, becomes a mere form, or is entirely neglected. My dear children, grieve not the Spirit; and whenever you feel a desire to pray, that moment lift up your heart to Him who is always near you. I can truly say,

'Sweet the moments, rich in blessing,
Which before the cross I spend.'

How often do I leave the family circle, when one or the other of you is pressing on my mind—passing, perhaps, through some trial, or beguiled by some temptation; I retire to my room, close the door, and fall upon my knees, plead for you with many tears, and commend you again and again to Him who has promised to *carry the lambs in his arms.* I wish to caution you against a great evil in many churches; I allude to gossiping professors, who, when they meet, instead of talking of Christ, talk about almost everything else,—'busy bodies,' who go from house to house, speaking things which they ought not. Oh, what a dishonour are such to the cause of the dear Redeemer! Rebuke such in gentleness of spirit, and withdraw from them. Pray that your own minds might be duly solemnized with the weight and importance of eternal things, and that your conversation might have a savour of the gospel at all times, for your own comfort, and for the edification of others. *As ye have received Christ Jesus the Lord, so walk ye in Him.* Pray and watch against a light and trifling spirit in yourselves, and go nowhere where it is likely to be called forth. Remember that God has to do with the heart. *To this man will I look, even to him that is poor and of a contrite spirit.* Humility is one of the sweetest graces of God's Spirit. Earnestly seek to know as much of your own hearts as will keep you sitting at the foot of the cross; and at the same time to know as much of Christ's heart as will enable you to rejoice in the fulness and sufficiency there is in Him. May God keep you, guide and instruct you, in every good word and work, and carry you in His tender bosom, are my unceasing prayers, night and day."

It may be proper that we should now introduce the reader to the more private and sacred records of her hidden life. The journals from which we quote were visible to no other eye than her own; and were kept by her but as way-marks of her religious progress, and as memorials of God's gracious and providential dealings in her personal history. Her lowly spirit cannot now be wounded by their publication; while their embodiment in this work will, perhaps, more than anything else, illustrate the close transactions of her soul with God. The essence of real religion is intimacy with God. The divine life in the soul will ascend to the source from whence it came. And that record, which reveals to us the sacred mysteries of this holy life, which throws a ray upon its intricacies, and shows us how, like Enoch and Noah, we too may "walk with God," must be of inestimable value to the Christian church. In the extracts we are about to make, we trace the experience of one who dealt faithfully with her own soul, and honestly with God. She set the Lord always before her. With an eye intent upon her path, yet ever looking to, and resting upon Him, she sought so to shape her course as to please God in all things. She lived as constantly "beholding the Invisible," and felt that she had alone to do with Him.

In the course of her diary, a name frequently occurs, embalmed in the memory of many who will read these pages. It was a kind Providence that gently led her steps, soon after her arrival in England, to the chapel of the late Rev. James Harington Evans. But recently returned from the hallowed scenes her letters have so glowingly described, her heart was fully prepared warmly to sympathize with a ministry, the peculiar excellence and winning charm of which was the power of the Holy Ghost, with which the Saviour was exalted. On the first occasion of her appearance within this sanctuary, the Lord especially met with her soul,—first in the spiritual, fervent prayer, and then, more manifestly, through the powerful message of His truth.

We now introduce the reader to the more private experience of the subject of this Memoir, as recorded from time to time during 1828 and 1829 :—

"London, July 10th, 1828.—Had nearness to God this morning, and an earnest desire to resign myself, my children, and all, into His blessed hands, and to know no will but His. We are reading regularly through the Bible. The 12th of Exodus was the chapter of the day. Oh, that I and all my household might feed continually upon the precious Lamb of God · and with the bitter herbs of unfeigned repentance may we eat thereof, with our loins girded about with truth, and our hearts and faces towards the heavenly Canaan ! Prayed. Oh, for more of the spirit of prayer! Lord, pour it down upon us, for Jesus' sake ! Poor old Mrs. D. came. I must obtain a pension for her soon, or she will be removed, before she gets it, to a better pension above.* She appears ill, but contented, though in a workhouse. God has, I trust, prepared her for a home not made with hands, eternal in the heavens. How many such hidden ones has our dear Jesus in this vale of tears! Although overlooked by the rich and mighty, His eye sees them, His heart pities them, and He is meetening them, by all His dispensations, for the glorious inheritance He has prepared for them above. What a change, from a body of sin and death—from the privations of a workhouse—to the heavenly abode and presence of Jesus!"

"12th.—Read this morning the 14th of Exodus, detailing the many trials of faith in the history of Israel of old. They were commanded to 'stand still, and see the salvation of the Lord.' Hedged in on every side, what could they do but stand still, until the Lord opened a way for them? My way, too, is hedged up just now. May I be able to trust in the Lord, and never be left to murmur or repine, but to wait and see the salvation of my God! Lord, let me see the pillar of cloud by day, and the pillar of fire by night. Not one step can I take without Thee. My soul is much exercised. Undertake, O Lord, for thy widowed handmaid! I can truly say, To whom can I go but unto Thee? I never fail to find, that trials drive me closer to Christ, and quicken me in the exercise of prayer. Oh, how is it that I do so constantly need the rod?"

"13th.—I awoke in the night, and a care, something like a trial in prospect, presented itself to my mind. I could not sleep until I laid it before the Lord ; for, to whom can I go in all my troubles and difficulties, but to Him who is a Father to the fatherless, and the widow's God? Almost directly afterwards I fell asleep. I had unburdened myself to Him who has all hearts in his hands; and my mind was at peace. Oh, what a privilege is this! How remarkably precious is a throne of grace to a tried, tempted Christian at all times! Had a sweet opportunity this morning, and much liberty.

---

* This pension was secured.

Could unhesitatingly say, 'Abba, Father!' and lay before Him all that was in my heart, believing he heard me."

"14th.—Intended to have gone to Hampstead, but the rain prevented. I desire to acknowledge the hand of God even in a shower of rain. I was not to go. Felt a wandering of mind while engaged in prayer for a moment, and in the whole exercise a want of fervour. It was not a heart-searching, melting season, such as I am sometimes favoured with. Oh, how good is God to permit such a one to approach Him!"

"15th.—The Lord orders all things. I desire to keep a steadfast eye upon Him. How much I felt to-day, my prayers needed to be prayed over and to be repented of. What need have we of a merciful High Priest, who can be touched with a feeling sense of our infirmities! Precious Jesus! let me feel my dependence upon Thee more and more."

"20th. Sabbath.—Illness has kept me from the house of God to-day. I have felt very insensible, although I have so much cause for thankfulness and gratitude. The Lord has heard my prayer, and graciously answered my petition, in spite of unbelief and ingratitude on my part. He has turned away the evil I feared, and made this hard thing easy, and this crooked path straight. Blessed be His ever-adored name. In those things that troubled me, I sought the Lord. My petitions were graciously answered. May I never forget the least of His benefits! I am surrounded with innumerable blessings. My children round me, the sweet privilege of the gospel at hand, when able to attend, and no bodily pain of any consequence. Bless the Lord, O my soul!"

"23rd.—Had a most comfortable assurance, both last night and this morning, of my interest in a crucified, risen Saviour, and found I could tell Him all that was in my heart. I am a poor, wanting creature; always coming for a fresh supply. But oh, what cause for thankfulness it is an ever-flowing, overflowing fountain to which I come! I have much comfort in commending my children, the dear lambs of Christ's flock, to the especial care of the dear Shepherd. Lord, keep them as the apple of Thine eye; and may those who are waiting for, and expecting their halting, be ashamed and confounded when they see that Christ is in them of a truth."

"26th.—Awoke with distressing thoughts of ———. As soon as I was up, I dropped upon my knees before the Lord;

and without preparing my mind for prayer, as some are enabled to do, I brought my want directly before Him. My heart was troubled, and I told it to the Lord. I did plead with many tears, that as He had given me His Son to die for me, He would not withhold the lesser blessing, and impart to —— all that grace he so much needed to preserve him from the ten thousand snares Satan would lay for his unguarded feet. This is the only way I can get on. When trials press upon my mind, I must arise and carry them to God. To whom else can I go? I would not often tell the dearest friend in the world what passes in my mind; but I can disclose it all to Jesus! I can and do unbosom myself to Him whose compassions fail not, and who remembers I am but dust; yet pities and loves me better than I love myself. Had much more comfort and openness in prayer in the family last night. Felt the Lord very near, and eternal things all-important."

"August 2nd.—Yesterday was dear ——'s birthday. I felt happy at the birth of my son, but that happiness was trifling, although all that a fond mother could feel, in comparison of what my heart experienced at the hour of his spiritual birth. I truly did travail with him a second time, that Christ might be revealed within him the hope of glory. Oh, the gladness of that interesting moment! Angels united in a mother's joy. The church below, the church above,—all, all rejoiced; and Christ was well pleased to see the travail of His soul. May He who then made Himself known to him as his Redeemer, be graciously pleased to pour into his heart the rich blessing of His grace, and fit and qualify him for great usefulness in His blessed cause. Give him, O Lord, humbleness of spirit, and stamp Thine image deep within his inmost soul."

"I increasingly feel that this is not my rest; it is polluted. Go where he may, rest where he will, trials and crosses await the Christian. Oh for faith—a constant, abiding faith, that keeps a steady eye within the veil, where our tempted, tried, and afflicted Saviour, *now* triumphant Conqueror, is seated, and ever lives to make intercession for His dear people, who are following his footsteps! What a sore trial is the working of pride within the heart! I have had to conflict with this enemy of late, which I had almost thought was quite gone. Heard an excellent sermon from the Lord's sent servant, Mr. Evans, from the words, *Tell me, O thou whom my soul loveth, where thou feedest,* &c. He was, as usual, most sweetly experimental. It was chiefly to the church, though he forgot not to address sinners."

"Have had much exercise of mind, and deep searchings of heart. Some new lesson in the school of Christ is daily, nay, hourly, to be learned; some hidden evil to be felt; some new enemy to be encountered; some fresh, precious views of Jesus to be obtained. Oh, how lovely, how good—exceeding good —is Jesus Christ to unworthy me! He is enough to satisfy my soul. When disappointed in the creature, and I turn with a sickening feeling from the world to Christ, I find here no disappointment; here is fulness of joy, an ocean of love, a heart to feel and sympathize, an eye to pity, and a power, an infinite power, to supply all my wants, to comfort my drooping spirits, to refresh my fainting heart, and fill me with joy and peace in believing. Jesus is an all-satisfying portion, and He is thy portion, O my soul."

"Had an interview yesterday with Mr. Evans. I pray the Lord to bless it. In the evening went where I need not have gone, and found the conversation of some professing Christians a great snare to my soul. Have need to pray, O Lord, not only lead me not into temptation, but hedge up my way, though with thorns and briers, that I go not into it. Oh, the sad levity and trifling of some, even of the ministers of Christ! I am aware of the same evil in myself, and by these things lay up material for bitter repentance. On my return home, had to go to the Lord for fresh pardon, humbled in the dust. But for ever blessed and adored be His name, to me He is love. I feel to-day a sweet tenderness of spirit; and while reading in the family, my heart was drawn out by faith to Christ, and could not but speak of Him to my children."

"Mr. ——, a professed minister of the gospel, has been here, and has just left with —— to see ——. I wonder what business a man, declaring himself sent of God to lead poor sinners to Christ, has to do with the sights and shows of this perishing world! How can he exhort his flock to live above the world and all its vanities, while he himself is going after them? As good Mr. —— says, it is our duty to have our eyes shut and our ears stopped to everything that is not a step in that ladder that reaches from earth to heaven. I cannot understand some Christians, and they do not understand me. I may be wrong; but when I read, *Come out from among them, and be ye separate; Love not the world, nor the things that are in the world*, and many other such solemn exhortations, with so many exceeding great and precious promises to the overcoming Christian, I am satisfied of the way a believer in Christ should walk, and have only to regret I so often wander from it myself. Dear Saviour, keep me near, very near, thy blessed self. Shelter me under thine almighty, protecting wing, till the storm of life is past. And oh, in infinite mercy remember the dear lambs of the flock, and suffer them not to wander from Thee. Let them feel their own weakness, and take hold of Thy strength."

"Feeble in body, but very happy in the Lord, a sweet, contented, childlike spirit, looking upward and *feeling*, as well as knowing, God is good. His name to my soul is Love. Had a delightful open view, as it were, while engaged in family prayer, of the glorious work of the all-sufficient atonement and sacrifice of the Son of God. Tears flowed while I thanked my God, and my children's God, for this most precious covenant of grace, for my interest in it, and the sweet assurance I have that some of them are also interested therein. Blessed, for ever blessed, be His most precious name. I am not well, and this tabernacle seems daily to decay. Be it so; it shall be raised again at the last day, fashioned like unto His glorious body. Christ's own resurrection is the earnest given, and I know that my Redeemer liveth to fulfil His engagement. My soul rejoiceth in Christ my Saviour. Often the enemy whispers to me, when I feel a holy nearness to Jesus, and my soul is very happy, that some trial is near at hand. Lord, I desire to trust in Thee, in whom is all my hope and my salvation. My children are Thy children. Blessed be Thy name for that. Help me to say, 'Thy will, not mine, be done.' I cannot do this without the especial influence of Thy Spirit."

"Sept. 1st.—Took possession of my pew yesterday at John-street. May the Lord, in His rich mercy, make this step a blessing to me and to my children. *The steps of a good man are ordered by the Lord.* Had to contend, while in the house of God, with a wandering spirit; felt it impossible to keep my mind stayed upon the precious truths I heard, or attempted to hear. Oh, how the world, with all its cares, crowds upon the poor pilgrim, even in his most solemn moments! He would fain say, *Abide thee here, and I will go yonder and worship.* What a mercy that we have a faithful High Priest at the right hand of the Majesty on high, to make intercession for all—*all* our manifold short-comings, sins and transgressions."

"Rev. Mr. W—— called this morning, and mentioned that after an unsuccessful attempt to obtain a curacy, he received a letter from his wife, saying, that she had discovered that a confidential servant had robbed them, and that she had determined to dismiss her. Mr. W—— wrote to say that she had better keep her for the present, as his circumstances were too straitened to pay her the wages due to her. A few days after, he returned home, and found his family much tried by the girl, who had refused to remain, and had gone to a neighbour's, alleging as a reason for her leaving, that she would not be paid for her services. In addition to this trial, a bill from a tradesman was sent in, demanding immediate payment. They had no money. Mr. W—— felt his character as a minister was at stake in a village, where everything was soon known from house to house. In this dilemma and distress, they knelt down and laid their case before the Lord. In the morning the postman brought a letter. On opening it, it was found to contain a ten-pound note in a blank cover. This paid all demands, and left a surplus on hand. Oh, that men would praise the Lord for his goodness to the children of men! He came to relate to me this remarkable providence. My heart felt refreshed, and my faith strengthened, by this sweet manifestation of God's kind remembrance of His poor servant. It is good to walk by faith; to feel dependent for all, and to come to Him as little children for all we need."

"Sept. 5th.—Find that many of my difficulties and trials—I dare not call them afflictions—arise from quarters where one least expected them. O Lord, help me more and more to cease from man, whose breath is in his nostrils, and to expect nothing but evil from an evil world! But these are but little trials after all. They do not wring the heart; they may grieve and wound, but nothing more. I think I know what afflictions are—yea, the deep waters of affliction too. Bereaving providences—the joy of my heart, the companion of my youth, the father of my children, cut down as with a stroke! Dwelling in a strange land, surrounded by a helpless young family, bereft of fortune when most wanted—the enemy suffered to buffet my almost defenceless soul, the very foundations of my faith trembling beneath this flood of tribulation—*these* are afflictions! I was in the furnace, but the Lord stood by.

Since then I have been enabled, upon my knees, amidst floods of grateful tears, to thank Him for those very afflictions that I then thought would bring me to nothing."

"8th.—Have much cause to be humbled. Why does every little disappointment affect me so much? I feel truly I am a sinful creature, unable of myself to think a good thought. Never, never did sin appear so hateful, and my own nothingness so great, as yesterday at the table of the Lord. Felt something of a broken heart. I wept much, but still my hope was in the Lord, and did look up, like the wounded Israelites, to the cross of Christ. Lord, my help is alone from Thee. Strengthen me with might in the inner man, and let not my enemies prevail against me. Oh, the hidden evil of the heart, unknown and unfelt, until the Spirit of Christ sees fit to reveal the depths of iniquity that are there. It is a sickening view; and were it not that Christ Jesus came into the world to save sinners, I should lie down in utter despair."

"18th.—How has my heart been pained to-day from what it has felt of evil within! How much I often discover contrary to the Holy Spirit of Christ! To-day has been one of sore conflict—the spirit lusting against the flesh, and the flesh lusting against the spirit; so that I have been obliged again and again to cry to the Lord for help from on high. Nothing but the precious blood of Christ can wash this guilt away. How soon was I ruffled to-day; and now could weep, yea, and do weep, and shall weep for it. Lord, forgive me, for Jesus' sake. Oh, for a sanctified heart! Lord, undertake for thy unworthy creature, and come not into judgment with me! Look upon me in the face of thy dear Son, and when thou lookest, forgive."

"27th.—Found much sweetness in drawing near to God in family worship—a blessed sense of the reality of eternal things. Oh, that I might be kept through this day with a steady eye upon Christ! Read for our morning's portion part of the interesting life of Gideon. How true it is—*Not by might, nor by power, but my Spirit, saith the Lord.* There is an inexpressible sweetness in the thought, that salvation is not of works; and that our full and complete acceptance is not in our wretched selves. It is all, all of grace."

"Nov. 7th.—A little more than twelve months ago the Lord led me up into the mount, and showed me in a small measure His glory, and caused His goodness to pass before me. My soul was happy, oh, how happy. Felt I was with God, and that God was with me. Was permitted to talk with Him—as a friend talketh with his friend. Perceived in Christ a fulness I had no conception of, and it was but—*Ask, and ye shall receive.* My dear children were wonderfully brought to the foot of the cross, and one after another translated out of Satan's dark kingdom into the kingdom of God's dear Son. Shall I ever forget that most precious season of Divine love? Oh, never, *never* may it be blotted out of my mind for one moment. But how is it now with thee, oh, my soul? What has thy God been showing to thee of late? He has been showing me more of the hidden evil of my heart, and calling me to sore conflicts with the world, the flesh, and the devil. With this threefold troop I have had much to do lately. But, thanks be to God, my Saviour is not out of sight, and he has engaged to bring me off more than conqueror."

"20th.—I think it wrong to be always living in anticipation of affliction, just because it is written, *Through much tribulation ye must enter the kingdom. Sufficient to the day is the evil thereof.* It is very discouraging to hear ministers say, especially to young Christians, 'Pray for faith, but remember, in so doing, you pray for afflictions.' Christ says, *Ask anything in my name; ask, that your* JOY *might be full.* I know that the apostle speaks of *rejoicing in tribulation.* Howbeit, I do think by constantly poring over anticipated troubles, we lose the sweet enjoyment of present mercies in the expectation of future evil. I pray to be enabled to praise Him for the present, and trust His love for all that is to come. Lord, increase my faith, and let my joy be full."

"Dec. 10th.—This day is set apart by the churches of the Baptist denomination for prayer and fasting, for the outpouring of the Holy Spirit. May God give His especial blessing, and hear their prayers! The gracious Revivals in New York have stirred up the Lord's people on this side of the Atlantic. May it be for the glory of His own name."

"This evening attended a prayer-meeting in John-street, for the outpouring of the Holy Spirit. It was full. The fault I generally perceive with most prayer-meetings occurred again to-night. The prayers were too long, and not to the point. Everything was touched upon but the one thing we had agreed to meet and pray for, except by one dear brother, and that but slightly. I do wish there were less *preaching* in prayer, and more *beseeching*, as poor needy sinners, for what we want. On my return home I assembled the domestics, who all profess to know the Lord, and suggested that we should join our supplications as a household, for the great blessing that thousands to-night were looking up for. I read the second of the Acts. We then sang an appropriate hymn, when each— all except the housemaid—prayed, following each other without rising from our knees. We had four short, sweet, and simple prayers, and it was a time of refreshing, for which God be praised. Oh, that the Holy Spirit may be poured out from on high upon all our souls, and upon the churches."

"20th.—Still travelling on, I humbly trust, through this waste howling wilderness, to my heavenly home. Want to look more to Jesus, that I may be strengthened for this continual warfare, for so it is with me. But am too often looking to some broken cistern still; but afterwards can say, when enabled to turn and take a fresh view of Christ, I do prefer Him, with all my trials and cares, to all that the world calls good."

"Jan. 21st, 1829.—What a mercy, of more value than a thousand worlds, to walk in the fear of the Lord all the day long; to be enabled to live above the smiles or frowns of this world, and to find the love of Christ all-satisfying to our souls; to feel all creature-love swallowed up in Christ, and to know that he loves us better than we love ourselves. Have felt these few days very comfortable, stayed upon the Lord; and to-day, sweet peace and joy, arising from a believing view of the ever-blessed gospel of the Son of God. As soon as I take my eye from Jesus, and look for anything like comfort from this world, or look within for something to rest upon, I begin to be in trouble, and have again to run into the name of the Lord, which is a strong tower to my soul at all times."

"Have been conflicting more or less, for some time, with vain thoughts. But yet I can say, *In the multitude of my thoughts within me, thy comforts delight my soul.* But yet what grief it is that my thoughts are not always on the Saviour, and that there is such proneness to attempt to draw comfort from the creature, and to sorrow when we find it all vanity and vexation of spirit. Oh, why look to creature-love when the love of Christ is always the same?"

"March 8th.—How many mercies have I had to recount since I last wrote in this journal! How much of God's gracious dealings with my soul have I omitted to record—and I regret it; for it is good to look back and see, from time to time, how wonderfully and mercifully He leads His people forward through a host of enemies to that happy place He has prepared for them. I find Mr. Evans's ministry as rich pasture to my soul, and the fellowship of the church very sweet and encouraging. 'How sweet to my soul is communion with saints!' I can truly say so."

"April 13th.—Had, to-day, a most sweet and endearing view of God, as my Father in Christ. Felt as if the Lord were again about to pour out His Spirit, and revive His work in our hearts. Went this morning to see West's picture gallery. A view of 'Death on the Pale Horse,' and 'Christ Rejected,' was very interesting. But who can portray, in any painting, the extent of misery and woe sin has brought into our world; or the sufferings of that holy, spotless soul, that was once on Calvary made an offering for sin? Upon the whole, it is not an outward exhibition of these important truths to the natural eye, but the application of them to the heart by the power of the Holy Ghost, that can alone convince, humble, and lead the soul to Christ. May I be led more and more to cling to Jesus, and feel increasingly the power of His resurrection in my soul: the Spirit bearing testimony within that He still lives to do all He has promised for me and mine, and all who come unto Him."

"Answered Mr. W——'s letter of inquiry, respecting the revivals in America. In his acknowledgment, he seems delighted with having an account from one who had been so blest in such a season of especial love, and who could bear a personal testimony to the truth of them. Received from him a kind invitation to visit N——; but cannot go so far from home, unless the Lord had something for me to do there. *I am his.* Blessed be His name! if it were His will to send me to the farthest corner of the globe, to bear my evidence to that most blessed truth, I would most willingly go. God does pour out His Spirit in a most especial manner upon His church. At such times of 'refreshing from the presence of the Lord,' sinners are converted to God, and saints are awakened out of their slumbers, and set out with fresh vigour and zeal to run the heavenly race. Thanks be to God for such seasons!"

"When the first Adam fell, God cursed the ground for man's sake, and said, *Thorns also and thistles shall it bring forth to thee.* When Christ, the Second Adam, came to be made a curse for us, He was crowned with those very thorns with which the earth was cursed, thereby removing the curse far from us. How wretchedly poor are my best conceptions of this most glorious work! Dear Lord, enlighten my understanding, that I may more and more see the infinite value of this wondrous work of everlasting love; and may my base ingratitude and unbelief never be thorns to wound Thee afresh. Give me more of that precious faith that purifies the heart and works by love."

"I have been ill, and was much reduced in strength, but the Lord has heard prayer. At a time when my disorder was peculiarly distressing, and was pronounced likely to be fatal, a word of rich comfort was brought to my mind, and I was supported. This was the passage of Scripture my mind was stayed upon: *With God all things are possible.* Then, thought I, it is possible He can relieve me from this sore disease; and I know something of his tender mercies, and that His ear is ever open to the cry of His people. My pain was removed, and my strength is gradually returning. Oh, how precious is a throne of grace, and a God of grace to go to!"

"Last week, dined with the poor of the church, nearly sixty in number. The rich waited upon the poor, and they seemed happy. The dinner was provided by our dear pastor, who also waited upon them. It was a delightful day—not soon to be forgotten. We had much Christian experience and profitable conversation, and did not separate until near nine o'clock. Want more life in my soul—more of the Spirit's influence—a closer walk with God."

"How often has an unkind look or word proved a blessing to my soul! It has made me flee to Christ; and there I have found no unkindness. He has appeared, at such times, more than to make up for the want of all creature-love and created good."

"The King of England is very ill, and perhaps will shortly be called to lay aside all his earthly honours and royal apparel, and feel his crown of nothing worth. What a change! What are kings better than the poorest beggar, when they are about to die? One drop of the precious blood that cleanseth from all sin, and applied by the power of the Holy Ghost, is of more worth to a dying sinner than millions of kingdoms. How does our poor King feel at this present moment? God be merciful to his soul!"

"The Lord has housed my dear H——'s eldest girl before she had tasted much of the bitter weeds growing in this waste, howling wilderness. He took her to Himself; and she is safe from the windy storm and tempest. Oh, for grace to improve all His dispensations, and to remember, that *all things work together for good to them that love God, to them who are called according to His purpose.* I desire to keep a steadfast eye upon Christ, come what may—desiring no will but His!"

"The King of England now lies in his splendid palace, closed in his leaden coffin from the sight of every one. Nearly his last words were, 'O God, I am dying!' And a few moments before he expired, looking wistfully around upon his attendants, he exclaimed, 'This is death!' But oh, what is the death of the body in comparison of the death of the soul! Mrs. P—— is also taken away in a moment. She was preparing mourning for the king; but they have met in eternity. The curtain has fallen, and we cannot tell what is passing there. Oh, how needful to be ready! Precious Jesus! bind the gospel to my heart, and let it be dearer to me than ever."

"Dec. 26.—Was ill yesterday, and was obliged to keep my bed. The family had a happy day together. It was pleasant to them to meet so many, and I am sure my kind-hearted T—— was as happy as a prince. After all I could not but reflect on the way in which Christmas-day is generally kept. It is the birth-day of our blessed Lord. In general, when the world celebrates the birth-day of a highly distinguished individual, they speak much of his character, ways, and exploits. But on this day of carnal delight, Christ's name [in the social circle] is seldom mentioned. He is kept out of sight, or if any allusion should be made to him, it would be received with grave looks and sullen indifference. Oh, what a God of long-suffering is ours! How He bears with, and how much He has to bear with, even in his children. May He keep us from the evil of the world! '*I pray not that thou shouldest take them out of the world, but that thou shouldest keep them from the evil!*'"

From her diary we turn again to her correspondence, which affords a further insight into the activities of her Christianity. Truly, like her Lord and Master, she "went about doing good." And here it may be appropriate to advert to a feature in Mrs. Winslow's Christianity, thus far almost entirely veiled from sight. The simple design with which we set out was to exhibit more her inner and hidden, than her outward and visible life. The careful reader will not fail to infer from the preceding pages, and will still more so from those which follow, that her Christianity was eminently *practical*. Her whole religious life was an embodiment of the great principle—" No man liveth to himself." From the moment that she felt the power of vital godliness in her own soul, the grand, all-absorbing aim of her life was the bringing of souls to Christ. She sought to accomplish this in that way for which God had peculiarly fitted her. Other Christians, equally devoted and zealous, may have possessed more taste and aptitude for Committee work; and others might be more frequently seen moving amidst the whirl and din of the great machinery of Christian benevolence. But while in the earlier stages of her religious course, when health and time were more at her command, she took a prominent and active part in the various religious societies of the day, yet as years grew on, and life became more mellowed and contemplative, she sought to promote the same object from more concealed and sequestered points of observation. It would therefore be unjust to the subject of our Memoir to infer, that because we especially restrict ourselves to the more important feature of her Christian character—HER WALK WITH GOD— that therefore it was deficient in that outward and corresponding life of Christian activity—that 'looking not upon our own things, but also upon the things of others'—which, more or less, is essential to the harmony and symmetry of Christian character. If ever an individual laboured for the conversion of sinners, it was she. But she laboured, as we have remarked, in that way for which God had peculiarly and eminently qualified her. He had given her the "pen of a ready writer." This gift—a rare and a powerful one—she wholly and constantly consecrated to God. It is believed she seldom wrote a note, however brief, in which there was not something to lead the thoughts to eternity. But not to this instrumentality of doing good was she wholly restricted. For several years she had her district, which she faithfully and systematically visited. And when too advanced in life for so active an employment, she would often steal away to some scene of sickness and sorrow amongst the abodes of the poor, especially to those who were of the 'household of faith,' to administer spiritual instruction and comfort, and on her way home she would frequently make purchases for their temporal necessities. Truly, like her Lord and Master she "went about doing good."

TO HER MOTHER.

"I have just returned from visiting the poor and wretched in the lanes and alleys of this great town. I have but little time to write as I formerly did. I often have thought that the Lord had nothing more for me to do; but He seems to have called me to my old work again, and it is one I always had, and still have, great delight in. May He bless it to me and to the poor to whom I am sent. Mr. —— and I go arm and arm with our Bibles from house to house, and from attic to attic. He always gets a little behind when I am leaving and tells them to be sure and 'say their prayers.' He is a high churchman, but I believe he is laying it aside every day. There is no doubt in my own mind of his conversion. He is the Lord's, and He is teaching him."

"If dear —— is, through God's blessing, with you, my dearest mamma, you will find enough in the journal addressed to him to interest you as far as details go. I do feel very anxious about you all at this unhealthy season of the year. May God preserve you all! How very necessary to have our witness within quite clear, that when he says, 'Come up hither,' we might be able to reply, 'Lo, Lord, with joy I come!' Oh, to look upon this world continually as one we have nothing to do with but to pass through it to the glory of Him who has prepared a better for us! The road through it was designed to be a thorny one, that we should not set our affections here; and as it is our dear Lord's will that we should have tribulation, what a mercy for us that He chooses all our trials, and arranges them in proper order in His infinite love and wisdom to suit our soul's best interests. Let us look oftener to our mercies, and less to our trials, and then see what cause—oh, what cause—we have for thankfulness. I feel at present very low, but am trying to look to Jesus. The cares of my children, though not beneath my roof, and under my eye, are ever mine in a measure. Who can tell what a mother's heart feels, but a mother? You and I know; but what is best of all, our God knows. Let us think a little of our home—our pleasant home. A precious Jesus waiting to welcome his weary pilgrims there. A sweet home indeed—a Father's home—and a happy meeting with all who are dear to us and to Christ. No more sea to separate us—no more sickness, no more sin, nor more labour—but one endless scene of love and happiness."

LETTERS TO HER CHILDREN.

TO HER SON R——.

"MY DEAREST R——,

"How is it that you do not write more often? It grieves me much when I do not hear. I have heard that your little R. was ill; and as no letters have come to hand, I begin to fear some evil, and my spirit seems to rest upon you, my precious child. Oh, that God might keep you from all evil; above all, keep you from ever sinning against Him, or grieving His Holy Spirit, by whom you are sealed unto the day of redemption. I do pray that the glory of God might be dearer to you than your own life. Oh, be very jealous of it, and watchful over yourself. Think what a God, God has been to me. How He has led me continually to look to Him in all my difficulties, and delivered me out of all my troubles. Oh, it is sweet to live a life of holy dependence upon the Saviour! I find it more and more so every day. May he save you from trusting your own heart, or leaning to your own understanding in anything. I feel I as much need His faithful hand at every step *now* as when I first started in the divine life, and so will you. Oh, try Him. The more you try Him, the more you will find Him *a Brother born for adversity.* Make use of His precious promises. He will accept them, and make full payment, and you shall have to praise and bless His holy name. Oh, that God might be pleased in mercy to keep us all from ever bringing a disrepute upon His holy cause. It were better to die. I think —— is still seeking, but he certainly has not found Him yet, whom we love and desire to love more and more. Oh, how precious is Jesus to a poor seeking sinner! His name is as ointment poured forth. What a mercy that when we sin we have in Him an Advocate, and a fountain still open to wash away our sin, and always welcome to come; never so welcome to Christ as when we feel our misery and poverty, our nothingness and unworthiness. He it is who gives the broken and contrite heart that He delights to look upon. The enemy would fain keep us from Christ when we feel our vileness; but it was for *sinners* Jesus died. May the Lord bless you, and keep you moment by moment, is the daily prayer of your affectionate mother."

TO HER SON H——.

"MY DEAREST H——,

" . . . . What should we do were it not for a throne of grace to go to? In all my troubles and difficulties I flee to

Christ, for none can help me but Him. Do you the same. You need not carry your own burdens, when Christ has commanded you to cast them on Him. Learn, in the earlier stages of your Christian pilgrimage, to go constantly to Jesus. Live upon Him for all you need for both soul and body, for He has redeemed and will take care of both. In doing this you honour Christ, and glorify your Father who is in heaven. Another thing I would wish to impress upon you is, never to keep guilt upon your conscience. As soon as you are sensible of having sinned, go that moment to Jesus, confess it, and ask His cleansing blood to be applied, and the guilt removed. Do not be tempted to put it off to a more convenient hour. Here Satan will endeavour to foil you by persuading you that it is time enough to confess that sin at night, when you retire for prayer; but go at that moment to Christ, and this will enable you always to rejoice in Him, and enable you to retain a tender conscience, which is a great blessing. . . . We have no revivals here, but still there is a great deal of sterling Christianity found."

TO HER SON O———.

". . . . Oh, what a God do you serve? How infinitely condescending in all His steps towards you, and how deeply indebted are you to give yourself entirely to Him! Dear Mr. Evans was showing on Tuesday evening the various ways in which a believer first declined from God. One was in making light of little sins. He remarked the Holy Spirit might be grieved even by a look—a lie in the heart which did not escape the lips—a word—a thing which might be lawful in itself, but might wound the tender conscience. The Spirit consequently withdraws His heavenly influence, and the soul is left barren and cold: and this state grows more and more, until the Lord again appears, restores the soul, and heals the poor backslider. There is a backsliding in heart which only God can discern. Oh, let us beware of that. Beware of trifling conversation; it grieves the Spirit. One way to be assured that we are not *going back* in the divine life is to *go forward*. This is an observation of Mr. Evans yesterday, and which he says he got from good Mr. Adams, of whom he speaks in the highest terms as a minister and a Christian. He preaches at Cowes."

TO HER MOTHER.

" . . . . To-morrow we shall have our dear pastor again. Oh, what a precious gospel we hear; doctrinal, practical, and experimental religion, beautifully blended. He preaches the gospel, lives and walks in it. We all love him. He is truly a man of God, highly gifted, yet humble as a little child. I never knew a man who seemed to find his way to one's affections as Mr Evans does in his preaching. He arrests your attention, instructs your mind, and captivates your heart. While he is preaching, you never see a wandering eye. Oh, for many more such labourers! . . . . I have had a minister from —— on a visit; but his conversation has been unprofitable. He is too light and trifling. My soul was grieved; but remembering that a sparrow falls not to the ground without my Lord, I thought he was sent here by Him. I asked the Lord if He had not sent him, to remove him; or that, if He had, to change his spirit and sanctify his sojourn under my roof. The Lord heard me. This man is changed for the better, and confesses he feels as different as a man could feel from what he did before he came. He attended Mr. Evans's ministry, which was greatly blest to him; and he is now humble as a little child, and his conversation serious and proper. He remarked to me, 'I believe in Revivals now, for I can truly say I feel a revival in my own soul since I came to town.' So you see how good is God to all who trust in Him.

TO HER SON O——.

" Sabbath.—Heard Mr. Evans from the words, *Bear ye one another's burdens, and so fulfil the law of Christ.* How deep are the riches of the love of Christ. The Lord does wonderfully open His heart to this His beloved servant. In the afternoon the newly-appointed deacons were set apart. It was a most delightful season. Mr. Evans so humble and excellent in his address to them, particularly in his allusion to their care for, and their kindness and tenderness towards the poor—their poor brethren. Saw beloved Mr. Whitmore; he gave me a loving look for you, I know. It was just such a look as he used to give you, so you can fancy it.

" Well, I have been to prayer for you. What a comfort we can meet at a throne of grace, although so far apart: and that Jesus can answer our petitions for each other at the very moment they are presented! God be praised for this glorious plan of salvation, and this method of access to Him, so suited to our condition. No other way would have done. I see, dear child, by the papers, you are delivering a course of sermons on the Second Advent of Christ. I pray you may be kept within the strictest bounds of Scripture, for it is critical ground upon which you are treading, and the imagination may be made a handle of by the enemy of souls to lead you into vain speculations, as it has done many others. Keep close to the word of God. Do not wear yourself out.

"I miss your arm when I go to the house of God, and the little chat when we return. But I think of you as I go, and remember Jesus has said, *I will never leave thee nor forsake thee.* Heaven would be no heaven to me if I did not find my Saviour there—He who loved me in prosperity, loved me in adversity, and will love me even unto death. This evening I received your interesting letter. It did me good, but I was grieved to hear your spirits were depressed. My precious child, when you accepted the pastoral office, you commenced a life of trial both from saint and from sinner. Oh, do not be surprised at all you meet with. Look to Jesus. Do not let difficulties dirtress you. The cause is Christ's, and all you have to do is to take them to Him."

"16th.—Since I last wrote, the Lord has turned my heart to praise, and has most blessedly drawn my soul nearer to Himself, and blessed me with a clearer view of Jesus seated at His right hand—risen indeed; risen for me, and risen for you. These words have been a sweet portion to my soul:— *This Jesus has God raised up, of whom we all are witnesses.* And you all are witnesses too, my dear children; for surely God did bow the heavens, and pour out His Holy Spirit upon you as a witness that He that was dead was alive, and liveth for evermore. Oh, witness for Him! let your preaching witness for Him, let your lives witness for Him, let your hearts witness for Him, abounding in love towards Him, and towards all who bear His image."

TO HER SON H——.

" . . . . I have just heard of the loss of your dear little M. E.—I feel more for you than for the dear child; for she, I know, is happy beyond description; but you, the dear parients, will feel it keenly. I trust the Lord who has wounded will heal and sanctify. We ought to hold our comforts with a loose hand. This is a little scion severed from the parent stem, and transplanted to the garden of glory above. We ought to rejoice while we mourn, that she is taken from the evil to come, and so soon made happy. Keep your eye upon Christ. He loves you as you loved your little one, but He loved her far more, and so took her to the enjoyment of Himself. May He preserve you both, and keep you near Himself." . . . .

TO HER MOTHER.

" . . . . I am as sure as I have got this pen in my hand that a life of constant employment is the best for the Christian; and, on the contrary, a life of worldly ease and prosperity is a time of temptation to the soul, and great grace is needed to keep us from falling into it. Trials and difficulties lead to God, and the soul is kept lively and active. When external things flourish, inward things droop. When the world frowns, Christ is welcome, and we flee to Him; and this is one of the reasons that our Heavenly Father so often appears to chide, for His love is always the same, even when Providence frowns. I do not know whether I told you of a little circumstance that took place a few days ago. I was called to visit the case of a poor widow with seven children, living in a miserable alley, and in great distress and want. After some conversation with her, which did not entirely satisfy me that she was altogether a Christian, I left her some assistance, pointing her, at the same time, to the widow's best Friend. On visiting her again, after some conversation not at all satisfactory, I went to prayer, bringing her and myself to God, not as saints, but as two poor sinners. My heart was much drawn out to plead for her; so much so, that I wept as I prayed. On resuming my seat, the poor woman made some allusion to her husband's ordination. 'Was your husband a minister?' I asked. 'Yes, ma'am, he was; and he preached the truth, for which he was persecuted. His name was ———.' 'Was he ever in America?' 'Yes, in New York.' Did he ever preach in London?' 'Yes, and came to this house to die.' I was deeply affected to find I was in the lowly cottage where the Rev. Mr. ———, whom I had often heard with interest, breathed his last. I said, 'I knew your husband in New York.' She eagerly fixed her eyes, swimming in tears, on my face, and said, 'Oh, ma'am, tell me your name.' On being informed, she said, 'Ah! I have heard my poor husband mention that name; and only think that you should be brought here, in such a place, to visit me!' I felt very much affected; and, as you may suppose, more interested in her case than ever. Good-night. The watchman is crying the hour of nine o'clock."

TO HER SON O——.

"October 9th.—On Sunday evening I worshipped in Pentonville Chapel, and heard Mr. Sheppard. As soon as I was seated, I felt such an inexpressible love to God for His great and wonderful goodness to me in all my weary pilgrimage, from the time I used to worship there with your dear father and all you little ones, that I wept. I took a review of all the way He had led me, the troubles and difficulties through which He had brought me, His long-suffering patience and unmerited goodness and love in following, upholding, and comforting me, and at last bringing me back where my eyes again saw my teacher in the sanctuary where I first heard of a precious salvation and a crucified Saviour. He caused all His goodness to pass before me, and my heart overflowed with penitence and love. I felt, too, near the body of my dear husband, whose spirit, I trust, is rejoicing in glory with Christ. Dear Mr. Sheppard preached an interesting sermon on prayer, illustrated by Samson, when he pulled down the pillars, and destroyed both himself and the Philistines. But there was too much of Samson, and too little of Christ."

"13th.—Heard Mr. Evans from Hebrews iv. 14; *Seeing then that we have a great High Priest, that is passed into the heavens, Jesus the Son of God, let us hold fast our profession.* He dwelt a great deal upon the real professor holding fast his profession, in which he advanced much to encourage; while he addressed nominal professors very awfully, and half-hearted professors very closely. While the Doxology was being sung, I thought I would raise my voice in praise, which, as soon as I did, the Lord broke sweetly into my soul, and filled my heart with joy and peace,—the peace which the world knows nothing of."

Oh for this love let rocks and hills
Their lasting silence break."

"Monday.—I was yesterday enabled to attend the prayer-meeting in John-street before the service, which is always very sweet to my soul. Afterwards, Mr. Evans preached from the words, *Thy gentleness hath made me great.* In the evening we sat round the table of our dying Lord. I had not that clear view of my Beloved I am sometimes favoured with. The subject of the discourse was the command of Joshua to the Israelites to go in and possess the land. Mr. E. dwelt much on the freshness of the gift, and the fulness of the good land; and showed how many stood but on its borders, and did not enter in. He spoke of Canaan being a type of the kingdom of God in this world; that there were not two kingdoms, but one, part on earth and part in heaven, as Christ says, *The kingdom of God is within you.* At the new birth the believer enters into this kingdom, and becomes a subject. He was very full and sweet in encouraging the timid Christian to go fully into this good land, and enjoy the rich blessings that are for him."

"Another sabbath is passed. I could only attend one service. The text was from Genesis xxiv. 53: *Wilt thou go with this man? And she said, I will go.* He was very excellent; but as Mr. Whitmore said, he did not open the casket enough, and speak quite so much of Christ as he might have done. On Tuesday morning I heard Mr. Wilkinson at the Bank. Genesis xxi. 3. It was full of Christ, and so refreshing and encouraging. Remember, my dear O——, the more your sermons are filled with Christ, from first to last, the more will Christ honour your ministry. There is no preaching like it. Never be afraid of not finding something new to say of Him. The Holy Ghost will supply you with matter as you go on. Never doubt it, never fear. The whole Bible points to Christ, and you must make it all bear upon the same subject—Christ the sum and substance of the whole. In Him, God and the sinner meet, and they can meet nowhere else. All the promises are in Christ Jesus, and we must get into Christ before we can get at the promises; and then they are all *yea and amen* to us."

TO HER MOTHER.

". . . . I often think how mysterious are the ways of God. It is our mercy, however, to know at all times that He is directing our steps, and that not a circumstance in our lives but is included in the everlasting covenant that is ordered in all things and sure. I feel your society would add much to my happiness, I often have so much to say to you. But oh, what a mercy that we both have Jesus to open our hearts to! It is a great thing to be helped to be satisfied with God's dealings and ways, and not to dictate to Him, even in our minds, what we conceive would be better for us. It is not change of place or circumstances, but Christ alone that can make us truly happy here and hereafter. God would have us cease from these things, and live upon Him alone for our enjoyments. Mr. —— is fast declining, and seems to have to make a fresh acquaintance with Jesus. A cold, intellectual faith, a mere assent to the gospel, will not stand in a dying hour. We want something more."

"Yesterday I heard a precious sermon from Mr. Evans, from Rev. i. 8, showing, throughout the whole, that Jesus Christ is the omnipotent God, 'the Almighty.' It was grand, it was sublime. I trust I felt something of the convincing power of the truth, that this omnipotent Being was my precious Jesus, in whom I trust, and on whom I daily depend for all I need for time and for eternity."

TO HER CHILDREN.

". . . . I look upon —— more in the light of a backslider, and have a more favourable opinion of him than his family have, although he is in a most miserable state for a Christian to be in. But *let him that thinketh he standeth, take heed lest he fall*, is an admonition that should cause us to look narrowly to our own way, and not cast the first stone at a fallen brother, but rather pray for such a one. Beware, my dear, dear children, of the first declension from Christ. Examine your hearts, and bring them daily, yea hourly, to Jesus, with all that you find evil there; and He will subdue it, and give you the victory. Never sit down to reason with your own heart, for it is deceitful; but fly to your true, your tried Friend, and He will never disappoint nor deceive you. Never neglect private prayer; and plead hard with Jesus for a constant and abiding spirit of prayer, so that you can lift up your heart to Him wherever you are, or in whatever you may be engaged. Plead much for the promised indwelling of the Holy Ghost. Be cautious of grieving this most blessed Guest of your souls; and when you do, go immediately to Christ, and He will wash it all away. Avoid light, trifling professors of religion; their influence will be as poison to your souls. Be very cautious to whom you open your heart. Make no one your confidant but Jesus. Oh, commune with Him of all that is in your heart. If you are wounded, go and tell Christ. If you are in need, go and tell Christ,—the silver and the gold are His. If you are in trouble, go and tell Christ, and He will deliver you out of it, and you shall glorify Him. Live upon Him as little children would live upon a dear, kind, and tender father. Oh, how happily will you then pass on your way! If at any time you are in perplexity or difficulty, through your own imprudence or otherwise, go not to an arm of flesh, nor sit down to consider how you are to obtain deliverance; but go directly to Jesus, and tell Him all, *all;* and He will appear for you, and bring you out of all, by suggesting to your minds the right means to be used, and following them with His blessing. Oh, I beseech you to do this, and may the Lord incline you to do so for His name's sake! Amen and amen."

TO ONE OF HER SONS.

"How is it with your soul and body to-day, my dear child? I trust you feel Christ very near and increasingly precious. I felt much comfort to-day while pleading with many tears for you. I believe the Lord heard, and will graciously answer. I seldom lift up my heart to God, but you are present to my mind, morning, noon, and night. May He hold you continually in the hollow of His hand, and make you a rich blessing whenever He calls you to stand up in His name."

Elevated as were at times her spiritual feelings, it will appear from the following that she was subject to those changes and depressions which more or less mark the experience of all the Lord's people. And yet it was a characteristic of her faith, that in her gloomiest depressions, and in her deepest trials, she never lost sight of her interest in the unchangeable covenant. That covenant was her sheet-anchor in every storm. She knew that God might vary His dispensations, but could not change in His love. She learned to judge of Him, not by His providence, but by His word; by what He said rather than by what He did; and this kept her soul confiding and serene amidst the fluctuations of hope and the waves of sorrow. One trait, however, of her Christianity we must not overlook. She was never satisfied to remain in a sluggish state of soul, or to walk beneath the veilings of the divine presence. She arose and "went about the city, in the streets and in the broadways, seeking Him whom her soul loved," nor rested until she found Him. The following extracts, illustrating this, are from letters addressed to one of her sons:—

"29th.—I feel very low in my soul, and need a plunge in the divine life. I have not, since that precious revival, felt so barren and so listless as of late. But God knows my heart, how I long after Him, and how far I am from being happy or satisfied in such a frame. How miserable it is to walk without the sun! But in the darkest hour the Christian has, he may safely rely on the faithfulness of Him with whom is *no shadow of turning.* This is my comfort—Jesus is still the same. But I want to walk closer to Him, and to enjoy the smiles of His blessed face. What is the world, or ten thousand worlds, to me, if He withdraw His heavenly countenance? Nothing under heaven can compensate for the loss of this. True, we are to walk by faith; but I always fear something is wrong in us when Christ retires, even for a day or an hour. I have been trying to examine myself, and can see nothing but evil; therefore I must turn afresh to Christ, and one believing glance of that all-sufficient Atonement will dispel every cloud, and fill my soul with joy and comfort. How I covet the broken heart and the contrite spirit! I would rather seek my Saviour, sorrowing every step I take, than feel a dull, hard, insensible heart. Jesus has died—Jesus is risen—and Jesus is in very deed at the right hand of God exalted, and there ever lives to plead the cause of His poor, tried, tempted followers. I have been thinking of the worldling's happiness. It never satisfies—affords no real enjoyment—it does not reach the soul. Ten thousand worlds could not satisfy me, now that I have tasted the unspeakably precious love of Christ. Well, then, let us hold fast our confidence, and still look upward; and when we cannot run, let us walk; and when we cannot walk, let us creep after him—but still, *go forward.* Better to follow Him as a Mary did, weeping, than be satisfied without Him. Oh, that we may press on, remembering Jesus' eye is ever upon us, although we may not always be able to discern Him."

"I am convinced that much intercourse with lukewarm professors does great injury to the believer, for which reason I longed to return home once more. Oh, avoid such! Light and trifling conversation acts as a poison to the life of God in the soul. It grieves the Spirit, and He withdraws His sensible influence. May the Lord keep us from evil, that it grieve us not, and restore constantly to us the joys of His salvation."

"I felt refreshed on Tuesday evening at the lecture. How needful are the means of grace, if we wish to thrive. I hope you will encourage meetings for prayer, my beloved child. May God give you wisdom in all things, and grace to do His most holy will! Let me entreat you to look to him continually, for counsel to direct in little as well as in great matters. Great things often spring out of little things. I perceive you have forgotten 'Rutherford's Letters.' I wish you had taken them. Keep to the old divines. Modern divinity is very shallow—has very little of Christ and experience. May God give you a spiritual appetite and deep experience in the things pertaining to His kingdom! Oh, that we might both be led to sit more constantly at the feet of Jesus, looking up, like little children, into His face to catch His smile and watch His eye—to see what He would have us to do, seeking nowhere else for comfort and guidance but in Him. In a short period, and we shall have done with everything but God; and oh, that we may have chiefly to do with Him now."

"How sweet to feel that all the kindness and tenderness of the creature flow first from Christ. If this be so, the creature may change, but Jesus never. In all your perplexities, *rest in the Lord, and wait patiently for him.* It is in a patient waiting for Him and not in an impatient dictating to Him, that He blesses. Does the burthen of your work press heavily upon you? Try and think it not a burthen—Christ has borne a heavier one for you. Count it an honour; and be assured that this is a trial of your faith, and to lead you to know more of your own heart and more of the heart of Jesus. The religion of Christ I more and more see to be a divine, a glorious reality. It is no cunningly-devised fable; it is truth—confirmed, settled, grounded in the heart and soul by the power of the Holy Ghost. Let us not, then, be faint and weary because of the way. It is the Lord's way. Thorny and steep though may be the ascent, when we reach the summit we shall be well repaid for all our labour."

"Your dear letter has been a source of much comfort to me, and this morning particularly was much blessed to my soul. As you say, 'What a blessing it is to realize the *Being of God.*' I feel that He is, and that He is all around us—closer to us than we are to ourselves; for *in Him we live, and move, and have our being.* I often awake in the morning with strong unbelief, attended with such a feeling of despondency as throws a gloominess over all my prospects. How dishonouring is this to God! I fall upon my knees, and in a moment it is gone. I see the face of Christ, and his loving, compassionate look disperses the cloud, and all is peace. This morning, your sweet view of God refreshed me while in prayer, and drew forth my soul towards Him in adoring gratitude."

"Last evening, at the church-meeting, in relating the experience of a child of God, Mr. Evans spoke of the individual's earnest wish to be *honest with God.* Oh, I thought, that God would make me honest with Him; that He would give me a holy, upright, honest dealing—having no concealments, no reservations! A thorough cleansing from all hypocrisy, vain-glory, and hated emulation—a wanting to be thought something, when we are less than nothing! What a chamber of iniquity is the heart, all hidden and unknown, until God in mercy shows it to us, as we are able to bear the disclosure! This is ploughing up the fallow ground afresh."

"I have never felt God the Father so dear and endearing as of late. To say, 'My father,'—to come to Him as to a father who loves and pities you, and can and will do all needful good,—how sweet! But while He sends the trial until it accomplishes the end for which it was designed, yet he will give all-sufficient grace while it lasts. I would gladly have you with me, if it were the Lord's will; but our happiness depends not upon change of circumstances or of place, but upon a submission of our wills to the will of God—a complete surrender of every desire and wish to Him who is acquainted with what is best for us."

"Feb. 27th.—This is my birthday. This morning, before rising, I had such a precious manifestation of love poured into my soul by the God of love, that my heart was broken with deep contrition and repentance, accompanied with a holy longing to be more swallowed up in God—to be more like Him—more wholly and devotedly His, than I have ever been. My heart seemed opened to God, and His heart opened to me. I felt such a spirit of praise as I could scarcely contain. What shall I say to these things? I am Christ's and Christ is mine. He causes me to know it; I feel it to be so without a doubt, or even the shadow of a doubt. And yet this very thing it is that humbles me in the dust before Him. I weep that I am such a sinner, while I stand in wonder and astonishment that God can love, and does love, such a one as I; and having loved me in time, will love me through eternity. Oh, help me to praise Him! Jesus is mine—Jesus is yours; and we shall live together to praise Him and cast our crowns at His feet."

"I opened my Bible this morning, and my eye rested upon Nehemiah, i. 11: *O Lord, I beseech thee, let now thine ear be attentive to the prayer of thy servant, and to the prayer of thy servants, who desire to fear thy name; and prosper, I pray thee, thy servant this day, and grant him mercy in the sight of this man.* It was quite a season of reviving to my soul, and my heart was made glad, for Nehemiah's God is my God, and your God, too, beloved; and His ear is ever open to our cry. And yet, when the Lord was about to answer Nehemiah's prayer, he was afraid through unbelief. What a good and gracious God He is, to bear with us as He does! Our wicked, soul-destroying, God-dishonouring unbelief, keeps us grovelling in the dust, when we ought to be soaring on the eagle-wing of gratitude and love."

"How needful it is to have a Guide who knows the end from the beginning, and if we ask counsel from Him, He will give it, only watching our deceitful hearts, that we do not make up our minds, and then go to God for counsel. I believe there are many Christians who are walking in a smooth path, and have nothing outwardly to contend with, who would be thankful to be tried; for they feel that if they have faith it has never been tested, and are sometimes doubting, because they have never been afflicted as God's people usually are. They have never been led to feel deeply the abounding iniquity of their own hearts; and while they read, *If ye be without chastisement, whereof all are partakers, then are ye bastards and not sons,* they tremble lest they should only have a name to live, while they will be found wanting in the last day. Oh, that God would make us grateful that it is as well with us as it is; and that the little trials we have may be so sanctified as to draw us near to Christ, and make Him more precious than ever!"

"The difficulties and trials connected with your holy office as a minister of the everlasting gospel, give me many errands to the throne of grace, where I lay your case before the Lord, and plead with many tears on your behalf. But I pray to be kept, at the same time, from a spirit of dictation. Our heavenly Father knows better how to control and direct our concerns than we know ourselves. Oh, to be among the number who *wholly* trust in the Lord! What a perpetual warfare is the Christian's course! Many of God's saints talk to me as if I had got above these things; but oh, they little know that I am as poor as poverty itself, and am obliged to draw all my supplies from the same source with themselves, and that without Christ I can do nothing. Indwelling sin is my daily cross, compared with which every other appears light."

"Nothing but the power of the Holy Ghost can convert the soul. The word, and the preaching of the word, pass for nothing, unless accompanied by the Holy Spirit. It is like attempting to shoot a bird from a gun charged only with powder. This should give the trembling, doubting believer much comfort, and also the more assured one; for if God has begun His work in the soul, God will complete it, and all sin cannot destroy it. A sinner converted by the Holy Ghost cannot destroy himself. He may destroy his comfort and peace, and impair his spirituality, but his soul he cannot destroy, for Christ has redeemed and sanctified it by His blood. How poor and contemptible is all the wisdom and talent of man when left to itself! Salvation, from first to last, is of God. God begins it, God carries it on, and God will finish it for ever. Blessed be His holy name!"

"January 28th.—I perceive by your letters that you are often depressed. This is natural, from the many trials and difficulties connected with your office. But you must remember that you are called to endure hardship as a good soldier of Jesus Christ; and must expect to be tried and buffeted if you would be an *experimental* minister of the cross. And do not forget He is infinite in wisdom, who selects and orders all your trials as those best suited to your case, and most qualified to prepare you for your work. Be assured no other would have done. May we be more sanctified by what we suffer! I am yet a learner, and seem as if I always required my Father's discipline. Oh, for a more subdued and weaned heart from all but God!"

"The more I know of the utter impossibility of the Christian, after he is a Christian, to keep himself for one hour, yea, for one moment, the more deeply anxious I feel for myself, and for all who profess the name of Christ. Those may be ready to say, who are but little acquainted with the deceitfulness of their own hearts, *Is thy servant a dog that he should do this?* but the longer we are in this warfare the more jealous we should be of ourselves. It was the prayer of David, *Hold thou me up and I shall be safe.* Tender love to dear ——. Tell her I have never been so firmly convinced as of late of the absolute necessity of the holy, wise walk of a minister's wife. It is my constant prayer that God will fully qualify her for her high and solemn position. One consideration is of importance. A minister's wife should never allow her husband's mind to be harassed with the anxieties and perplexities of domestic concerns. Every little difficulty and annoyance of that kind should be kept quite from his knowledge. Not long since, I was much pained, when on a visit to a dear man of God, while listening to his many conflicts, his wife, a Christian woman, too, entered, and commenced a tedious detail of a difficulty she had had with one of the domestics. Poor man! he sighed, and that sigh conveyed a volume of meaning to my mind."

"Unbelief is the strongest enemy we have to contend with. How it tries and harasses the believer every step of his eventful journey! It engenders in him often the basest ingratitude, and causes him to mourn when it is his duty and privilege to rejoice. How much too it curtails all his mercies; for it is now, as in the days of Christ, *Be it unto you according to your faith*—so that little faith secures but little comfort, and less enjoyment. Oh, for a stronger confidence in God!"

As a means of embodying and giving practical effect to the holy sympathy of Christian mothers, perhaps no institution has been found more suitable, or has been more honoured with the Divine blessing, than the "Maternal Association." The influence of pious mothers, silent, yet mighty, has become almost proverbial. How few training for the Christian ministry in the schools of the prophets, or as settled pastors are cultivating successfully the vineyards at home, or on heathen shores are honoured missionaries of the cross, would be found, on inquiry, who had not been blest with godly mothers! And of these how fewer still the number who would not testify that it was that mother's hand that first guided their infant footsteps to the Saviour! It was here, in the bosom of the Christian family, the tiny seed was sown which, in long after years, and when, perhaps, the hand that dropped it was mouldering in the grave, struck deep its roots, and extended wide its branches, blessing the world with its fruit, and beautifying the church with its comeliness. It was here, in the pious home, the latent desire to be a Christian was inspired, the first thought of being a minister was conceived, and the purpose of a life for God was formed. Oh, let Christian parents awake to a conviction of their mighty, almost creative power! Few were more sensible of this than Mrs. Winslow, and few more honoured than she in the right direction of her influence. Compelled by her removal from town, to withdraw from attendance at the meetings of the John-street Chapel Maternal Association, yet cherishing for its object an undiminished and prayerful interest, she addressed the following letter, designed to encourage her in this good work, to the former wife of her pastor:—

". . . And so you are discouraged. Trials and difficulties many, faith tried, and only three met! Did you expect to undertake a work for Christ and get on smoothly, while there is everything within and without to oppose it? Did you expect faith would not be tried in this matter? Faith takes hold of the strength and power of God, and looks alone to Him. You were looking to your little feeble band of three, although you were within the number Christ has promised to bless. In a country place in America, a few Christian females engaged to meet to pray for a blessing on their families; but after a while it declined, and continued to do so until only two came. "Shall we give up?' was the question. They thought of God's faithfulness to His promise, of His power and goodness, and resolved to go on. They met. these two only, again and again. They pleaded the promise, and encouraged each other by their prayers. At last *the answer came.* God tried their faith, Jesus interceded, and it had not failed. Some who had left them returned, others followed; the place of prayer was soon filled. The Lord poured out His Spirit on them, and they prayed in earnest until the blessing was given. The church felt the holy influence; their children at home began to inquire what they must do to be saved; the mothers directed them to Jesus, and prayed on. God in very deed bowed the heavens, and came down in their midst to bless them. Many of their unconverted children and husbands were led to submit to Christ, and the whole church shared in this remarkable revival. Dear sister, take courage and look up. God loves to hear your prayers. Did the mothers in John-street Chapel but see their children standing on the edge of an awful precipice, and know that none but God could prevent their destruction, would they not cry day and night to Him? But what can be compared to the eternal death that awaits them, if they die unconverted? And will they not meet together for united prayer, that their dear children may escape from the wrath to come? *Again I say unto you, if two of you shall agree on earth as touching anything that they shall ask, it shall be done for them of my Father which is in heaven.* Matt. xviii. 19. This is a promise worth millions of gold and silver, and this promise you have to plead. May God help us to give full credence to His word, and deal with Him as one who cannot but do all He has promised, *because He is God!* In proportion as we feel the infinite value of the immortal soul, we shall feel anxious for its salvation. Now, beloved, expect difficulties, expect opposition, even from your own heart; but you have the Lord on your side. Jesus is waiting to be gracious. The Holy Spirit is waiting to do all that He has engaged to do; and angels are waiting to rejoice over unconverted sinners, in answer to your prayers. We shall never fully know, until we get to heaven, the mighty power of importunate prayer with God. If I knew your time of convening, I would unite my poor prayers with yours. I am earnest on this subject, knowing the great blessings that have attended such efforts. Go forward in the strength and power of Jehovah-Jesus, and God must and will bless you."

CHAPTER VII.

Mrs. Winslow was never more at home, and, we might add, never happier—for her happiness and her Lord's glory were one and inseparable—than when administering counsel to the perplexed, or comfort to the afflicted. Her own naturally strong judgment early brought into exercise, and schooled for the greater part of her life in adversity, she was thus eminently fitted, from the rich stores of her own experience, to administer to the exigencies of others—advising those whose path was intricate, and comforting those who were in any sorrow, by the comforts with which she herself had been comforted of God. Hence so many of the letters which appear in this volume are addressed to persons in circumstances of trial and affliction.

The bereavement of her pastor, by the removal of his wife, under circumstances of such painful interest, would naturally call forth the expression of her deepest and most tender sympathy. During the week which intervened between the sudden attack and its fatal termination she was scarcely absent from the scene of anxiety; and one whole night was spent in prayer with Mr. Evans, in the vestry, over which lay the suffering object of their long midnight wrestlings. We find in her journal the following references to this mournful event.

"May 5th, 1831.—Since I last wrote, the Lord has taken my dear friend, Mrs. Evans, after little more than a week's illness. His presence was with her, and He most graciously manifested His love towards her in carrying her through the dark valley. She died in the triumph of faith. Her dear husband was almost overwhelmed by the suddenness of the stroke, and staggered under his irreparable loss. But the Lord who spake such sweet peace to his wife, supported the bereaved husband, and enabled him to say, *Thy will be done!* It was a shock almost sufficient to overcome nature; but God is all-sufficient at all times for His saints."

"The last time I saw our dear departed sister, Mrs. Evans, was on the day she died. When I entered the room, she held out her hand, and, taking mine, said some most affectionate things; for her whole heart seemed dissolved into love. I never saw such a death. Her countenance was full of holy, joyful anticipation. Her soul seemed filled with Christ. She said, with uncommon energy of manner, 'See, dear sister, how good is the Lord! Jesus is most precious. Christ has so blessedly manifested Himself to me. He has been with me through all the operations;' and then looking earnestly into my face, said: 'I have known more of Christ *in this week* than I have known in all my whole life put together. And now,' she continued, with such a sweet smile, 'I am going to Him, He has prepared a place for me.' 'Yes,' I replied, 'and He will come and receive you to himself, according to His own word.' After a few words of prayer, I left her, with a sweet hope of meeting her at the right hand of God. Death, in her case, was divested of its sting and the grave of its victory, and Jesus enabled her most blessedly to triumph over both."

In one of her letters to her family, she refers to the grace which sustained her afflicted pastor:—

"Dear Mr. Evans will be again in his pulpit on Tuesday evening. He is now in the country. I dined at Hampstead the Friday before we went; he was very much supported, but still greatly afflicted. He came to me on the Sunday night before the funeral. I heard his voice below, and ran down to meet him. Finding I was alone, he dismissed the carriage and came up. He sat down, and gave vent to his feelings. We had much conversation, and God did bless it to the comfort of his dear servant. I said, 'God will restore peace to your soul.' He replied, '*He has done it,* and within this house.' He left me, composed and comfortable. He told me since, that he shall never forget that spot, to the day of his death."

Soon after this event, she visited her eldest son, who was then resident at Cambridge. From thence she writes:—

"I had a pleasant journey to this place, with only two ladies inside. We had some agreeable and, I hope, profitable conversation, although they were both, I could see, but moralists, depending upon their doing and their not doing. Yet they listened very attentively while I endeavoured to show them the cobweb garment of such a profession. They gave me their respectful attention, but I could clearly perceive they did not at all understand me; so I left them as I found them. Perhaps they may think more about it some time hence. On arriving at the house, dear E—— met me in the parlour, and instantly after Mrs. C——, with her good husband, in his gig, at a little distance. And now I am seated in the sweet little drawing-room, surrounded with shrubbery, and everything looking delightfully refreshing to the eye. You might fancy yourself twenty miles in the country, it is so encircled with trees. In a short time T—— made his appearance, in cap and gown, looking very well. We all went, in the evening, to hear good Mr. Simeon, and my soul was sweetly refreshed with the simple, but precious truths of the gospel. G—— took me to some of the colleges; but although they are very fine, I have but little taste for these things. Miss M—— and Mrs. F—— called yesterday. To-morrow I go to Haslingfield. Dear Mrs. C—— insists that my visit to Cambridge is to her."

Of the letters written during her visit to Haslingfield, where she met much that was congenial with her taste—a picturesque village, and spiritual and affectionate intercourse—only one can be found. It is addressed to her bereaved pastor;—

"Haslingfield Vicarage, Cambridge, May 24th, 1831.

" . . . . I long to know how your mind is, and if the Lord is keeping you resting in the bosom of His love, comforting and refreshing your soul by continual draughts from the overflowing fountain of living waters. Oh, how sweet it is to be kept in such a position! Pray that I may be kept in it. I have had some taste, and that makes me long for more. I am staying a little while with those who truly love the Lord, and whose works proclaim their love sincere. I see godliness brought into daily practice, without ostentation. These dear friends do the will of God from the heart, and it is their meat and drink so to do. May God bless them more and more! Mrs. C—— is a real labourer in the cause of Christ, and Mr. C—— one of the kindest-hearted and most benevolent beings I ever met with. . . . Oh, what a mercy to have a throne of grace, and a tender, compassionate, loving Christ to go to at all times, and under all circumstances! A large welcome; no frown to fear; no distant look. Oh, that we all might LIVE upon Him, moment by moment! For this reason, He takes away our props, that we might lean altogether upon Himself; and that is why He has dealt with you, my dear brother in affliction. God knows, I have loved you better since the Lord placed you in the same furnace with myself. My heart can feel all you felt. You will at some time or other see, as I have seen, that that was the very thing you needed, and wonder at the Lord's goodness in delaying it so long. Blessed be His name, that He has in a measure comforted you! and be assured He will fill the void He has made, with Himself. He took your dear wife away to make room for Himself; and the place that was prepared was quite ready for her, and she was quite ready for it; so that all we have to do is to bow to His most blessed will, and fill up the little span that now remains for us here, in doing the work He has assigned us, and be ready to go home at a moment's warning. . . . You have a double claim upon Him now; make good use of it, for He loves to have us argue the point with Him. We need not fear being too familiar or too troublesome. The oftener we come, the more welcome. Now I do thank God, who has blessed you with His own Spirit, or you could not permit such a poor one as I am, who have need to be taught of you, to talk to you in this way. I am persuaded you know all this, and oh, how much more! But God does often speak a word of comfort through his poor and despised ones, and sends a message of love by the mouth of a young child to an elder one; and the elder will be glad to receive it, too. May Jesus comfort your heart, and give you much of His sensible presence. Love to dear C——."

It was during her visit to Cambridge that the touching incident in her Christian feelings, mentioned in the following extract, took place:—

"I wrote to you yesterday; but as I was just now reading dear Mr. Simeon's Memoir, I felt such a gush of holy love, even the love of Christ, filling my heart, that it brought afresh to my mind a circumstance, which, if you see Mr. Carus, I wish him to know. I went to hear Mr. Carus one evening when at Cambridge. My heart during the day had been cold and barren. I took my seat in the pew, in this wretched state of soul. Dear Mr. C. announced his text: *I sat down under His shadow with great delight, and his fruit was sweet to my taste.*—Song of Solomon ii. 3. His first observation was, 'These words refer to Jesus.' In a moment my soul was melted, my heart overflowed with love: I wept. His name was as ointment poured forth. I coiled myself up in one corner of the pew, and had the most blessed season of communion through the whole service. What he said of whom my soul loved was sweet and refreshing. From that time I have never seen nor heard Mr. Carus, but the Lord did, through him, send a rich blessing to my soul. Give my love to him. We shall soon meet where we shall be all of one mind, in a brighter, happier world, surrounding the throne of Him we love. Blessed be God for this prospect! It often causes the dark cloud to withdraw, and the weary soul to take fresh courage, and press onward, and look upward. Blessed is the hope of the Christian! Many may be the trials of his faith; but I believe the most tried Christian knows the most loving heart of the Saviour. He is a *tried stone*. Tried by the hand of His Father; tried by the hand of justice; tried by the wicked, and tried by His saints. He tries the faith He gives. Had He not tried me in the furnace of affliction, my loss would have been immense. I thank Him for my deep, deep cup of sorrow. Whatever draws or drives us to Christ is a blessing. We then breathe a holy, heavenly atmosphere, and see the poverty of all other things to make us happy here or hereafter."

From her Diary.—" Returned from Cambridge. The Lord carried me out, and brought be home in safety. I have had many things to exercise my mind, and some very important ones to decide upon. May God add His blessing, and mercifully forgive my manifold infirmities and shortcomings. I have to praise His holy name for a comfortable assurance of my adoption in His family. I can come to Him as my Father, and find it good to draw near to Him at all times. His loving-kindness He does not take from me, nor suffer His faithfulness to fail. Blessed be God for His goodness to dear G——! From a letter received from him, it appears Christ has mercifully at last shone in upon his soul. I rejoice over him, and pray he may be kept still going forward, until he obtains a clearer view of the loveliness of his dear Redeemer."

"April 17th.—I have just returned from Islington church, where I heard Mr. Melville. I wished much to hear him preach on the second advent of Christ, but was disappointed, as he did not touch upon the subject; but he was very great and powerful. The text was, *I am the Lord. I change not; therefore ye sons of Jacob are not consumed.* He was very excellent upon the immutability of God. I never heard a more powerful preacher, and one so completely full on every point he touched. I thought, however, there was not enough of Christ; but he was more on the attributes of God, particularly on His unchangeable nature, and the impossibility of being otherwise than what he had declared Himself to be—an unchanging God."

TO HER SON, REV. I. D. W——.

"June 15th.— . . The Lord has wonderfully upheld me in ——'s illness, and under great fatigue and anxiety. *As thy day is, so shall thy strength be*, is a promise fulfilled afresh, as it has been a thousand times over in my experience. I have been thinking of —— entering upon his new sphere of labour, and it recalled to my recollection, as illustrating the uncertainty of life's brightest prospects, the Lord's mysterious dealings with two ministers, with whose cases I became acquainted in New York. The one was that of the Rev. George Duffie, minister of St. Thomas's Episcopal church; and the other, that of the Rev. M. Bruen, minister of the Bleeker-street Presbyterian church. Their attached congregations erected for them new and beautiful sanctuaries, with handsome dwellings adjacent. Their prospects for the future were bright and promising, but soon after these edifices were completed, and they had taken possession of them, both, after a few days' illness, were brought to the grave. The circumstances made a deep impression on my mind at the time, and which I have not yet lost. I have written to —— to remind him of this, and to implore him to turn in upon his own heart, and see how matters stand between his soul and God. It is an easy thing to preach to others, and to do many things: but it is quite another matter to appear naked before a holy God, and to render an account of every idle word. True, His children are already justified, and stand complete in Christ; but even here we may be taken by surprise, and what is yet more awful, may make a fatal mistake. Therefore it is that the Lord warns us to watch for His coming. Oh, that we may go to Jesus for a fresh anointing of His Spirit! The Lord has, I hear, suddenly removed one that was committed to your charge. Did you ever examine her as to the state of her soul? Did you personally warn her of her woful condition as a sinner? It is easy for you to warn sinners from the pulpit; but to go to them, examine their hope, and to deal faithfully, honestly, yet affectionately with them as in the sight of God, is the solemn duty of every one who stands up professedly in the name of Christ. Whatever God has given you to do, do it faithfully as in His sight, whose eye is watching all you do and all you do not. Oh, that you might feel the infinite value of one lost soul, and the responsibility that rests upon you as a professing minister of Christ! You may reply, that people will resist this personal examination. They may say so at first, and yet they may have to thank you for it to all eternity. It is not talking about religion, or assenting to all you say, that accomplishes the great object; it is a close personal investigation of the real condition of their never-dying soul. It is not their constant attendance at church, and taking the sacrament, and saying prayers, that will save them; you have been taught differently from this, and therefore more will be required at your hands."

"I was glad to hear from you, and trust you are in your new habitation by this time. Be thankful for it, and look fully to the Lord, and He will *supply all your need, according to His riches in glory by Jesus Christ.* Only think of such an encouraging promise made to us! Why need we want any good, when the Lord has said, *No good thing will He withhold from them that walk uprightly?* And again, *I, the Lord, search the heart, to give to every man according as his work shall be.* Thus the Lord deals with us according to the working of the heart. How jealous, then, ought we to be over our hearts; and when we find a traitor there, how earnest should we be to bring him directly to the Saviour, that He might enable us to place our foot upon its neck, while He himself subdues the evil that He hates. How many, alas! there are, who deem a life of external decency and order alone sufficient; who think, if they scrupulously attend religious duties, visit the poor, &c., God is well pleased, and all is well. But God has to do with the heart, and all these external things might be done, and yet everything be wrong there. He looks at the spring of all we do, not at the action only, but at the motive from whence it springs. The apostle speaks of the *constraining love of Christ.* Love to God, and love to His people because they are His, should be the ruling principle urging on to every good word and work. The Lord is blessing ——'s ministry. Leamington is highly blest with the Gospel. Mr. Craig is faithful to sinners, and so is dear Dr. Marsh. Lord —— has got the **honour** he sought, but oh, what a bubble! Oh, that we might always endeavour in all things, in thought, word, and deed, to please God; setting aside everything which is not connected with His glory, and contemplate all things and all events more in the light of eternity! My dear children, I see myself more and more, every hour, a poor sinner, unworthy of the least crumb that falleth from the Master's table. But I see, at the same time, Jesus a great Saviour, divinely able, and most lovingly willing, to save the chief of sinners, even me; and no one can tell how this thought fills my heart with contrition, and my eyes with tears. I have never wept so much for sin as I have done lately. Often have I put up the prayer, *Search me, O God.* The Lord has heard and answered it; and oh, if it had not been that the fountain was still open, I should have sunk into unutterable despair. He has ploughed up the fallow ground afresh of my poor heart, and the view presented has prostrated me in the dust; and if ever I felt what a broken heart and contrite spirit was, I have of late. Oh, the evil that is there covered over by the rank weeds of self-love, self-complacency, or self in some hideous form or other, that it is not discernible until the Holy Spirit makes it known. And yet how little do we know of it even by this divine teaching! But if God is pleased to show us enough to make us cling closer to the cross, to make Jesus more precious, sin more hateful, and our prayers more of a wrestling character for the special, sanctifying, life-giving power of the Holy Ghost, shall we not have cause to praise and bless His holy name for ever and ever? But while I have thus been led of late to mourn so much for sin, I have never felt *pardon* so abundantly manifested. God be praised for a free-grace gospel! Oh, keep close to the cross! Look well to your own vineyard, and then will you be able to take care of the vineyards of others. Know nothing among men save Christ Jesus crucified. Take Him for an example in all things; aim to have a single eye to His glory; and that God may bless you and give you abundance of grace here, and a plenitude of glory hereafter, are the prayers of yours, &c."

It was in 1833 that Mrs. Winslow paid a final visit to the United States. It was at a somewhat advanced period of life that she took this step; but she was constrained to do so with the view of meeting, for the last time on earth, her aged parent, and her children who were residing there. Accompanied by her daughter she again embarked upon the ocean.

Her outward passage was attended with much personal suffering and relative anxiety. But God sustained and bore her through it all, and granted her a happy re-union with those she loved. After twelve months of sacred enjoyment, she parted from them, to meet no more until they assembled again "without fault before the throne of God and the Lamb." The following interesting letter to her pastor, Rev. J. H. Evans, and extracts from her private journal, touchingly describe her exercises during this visit; while they present her as still maintaining the same elevated tone of spirituality, child-like trust in God, and singleness of heart in His service, which characterized her in all places and under all circumstances:—

"BELOVED BROTHER,— New York, June 22d, 1833.

"How I have wished to write to you since my arrival, but hitherto I have not been permitted. The Lord has carried me through many trials and sorrows since I saw you, and He has also given me to see much of His goodness, faithfulness, and unchanging love, towards the unworthiest of all His saints —the weakest of the weak and the vilest of the vile; but so it is, and on such he loves to bestow His choicest mercies. For ever blessed be His name, my soul can adore Him; and it is my heart's desire to trust him to the end. I left England with a heavy heart. The parting with my dear children on the deck of the vessel, on a wet, dark, and dreary night, was dismal. When they left me, I retired to my cabin, to commit them and myself to God. [Here follow details of the severe illness of her daughter and herself.] But God was with me; and, as soon as I was recovered, I lifted up my heart to Him who alone could help me in this my great time of need. I felt persuaded my dear child might in a moment be in eternity. Oh, it was a trying season. I clung to Christ—pleaded the promise that He once had made over to me, that He would be a Father to my fatherless children, and implored Him, in the dear name of Jesus, to spare her until she knew him as her reconciled Father in Christ Jesus. It was a trial of faith— naked faith, resting entirely on the faithfulness of God. The Lord heard my petition; and, although she continued more or less ill, she gradually recovered. The weather was stormy and most unpleasant during the greater part of the passage— but He brought us through all; and on the 7th of May I had the comfort, nay the joy, of seeing my three sons shedding many tears of gratitude over me, on that very spot upon the deck where my heart had been agonized with sorrow, and from whence I had sent up so many fervent petitions. E—— was alive and better; R——, H——, and O—— were clustering around me, in joyful gratitude to God for bringing me once more to them. I felt happy; but oh, my dear brother, none but God himself could bear with such as we are. Did my thank-offerings go up with as much fervour as my earnest wrestlings for help? Ah me! This has been my grief, and has often laid me low before God. I abhor myself in dust and ashes on this very account. It is my greatest comfort that Jesus lives, and is at the right hand of God, and His precious blood cleanseth from all sin."

"Last evening dear O—— was ordained. It was a most interesting service. You may suppose what I felt when I saw my son kneeling, while the hands of the Presbytery were laid upon his head, and prayer was offered that God would fit him for the great work to which he was solemnly being set apart. When I saw the hands of the ministers resting upon him, my prayer was, 'Now, Lord, lay *Thy* hand, Thy blessed hand upon him, and fill him with the Holy Ghost, that he may do Thy work from the heart, and be kept humbly sitting at Thy feet.' My paper is drawing to a close, and I have not said half that is in my heart. We both said, that evening, 'Oh, that dear Mr. Evans had been in that pulpit! We love you; and never can be sufficiently thankful to God for the rich blessing He has made your ministry to us both. Pray for us. I do value your prayers; for often have they led me nearer to Christ. Dear friend, farewell."

From her diary at sea.—"May 1st, 1833.—Left England on the 1st of April, from Portsmouth. We are now nearly four hundred miles from New York, with a light wind. Our passage thus far has been most unpleasant. The first ten days E—— was so ill I thought she would have died. I cried to the Lord and He heard me, and has been better to me than my fears on her account. We have had unpleasant passengers, which has added much to the discomforts of a sea-voyage. My health has greatly suffered, from fatigue of mind and body. Oh, that the Lord may be gracious to me, and overrule all for our good and His own glory! He has been my Helper hitherto, and will he not be my Helper still? In Him is all my trust. The weather is now fine, and all on deck are enjoying it. May the Lord, who has preserved us through so many storms and dangers, carry us in safety, and give me to see my children's face with joy, and not with grief, and lay His cause upon all our hearts; so that we may, as with one heart, enter upon the work with a single eye to His glory, and find it our sweetest meat and drink to do His will."

" *New York*, 8*th*.—The Lord has again brought me to this distant land, after passing through much sickness and anxiety on the passage, and caused me to see the faces of my three children with joy; and has, within a few days, brought dear G―― from Bermuda to join our family circle. For ever blessed be his dear name, for so many instances of His wondrous love to unworthy me."

"19th.—I have had the comfort of seeing my three children engaged in the service of Christ, on that very spot where, seven years ago, He translated them out of Satan's kingdom into the kingdom of His dear Son. Precious Jesus! fit them all for great usefulness, and cherish this infant church in Thy tender bosom. Carry the pastor and the flock near Thy compassionate heart, and greatly bless with the gifts and graces of Thy Holy Spirit. My dear mother, too, in her 84th year, has arrived, accompanied by B―― from Cincinnati. She is confined to her room from lameness. Her memory fails her much; but, although the earthly tabernacle seems by little and little to be dissolving, she still retains the same kind and tender feeling towards all around her. Her faith seems firm in Christ; and when she can fix her mind, she appears to rejoice in the hope set before her in the gospel. May her last days be her happiest and brightest!"

"Have had of late increasing reason to know that God's ear is ever open to the cry of His children, and that He will send down answers of peace. I was ill,—my pain very great for some hours,—nothing appeared to give me relief. At last I fled to my stronghold: I cried unto the Lord, and He heard me. The pain abated, and in about fifteen minutes I fell asleep, and awoke in the morning, feeling only weak, and gradually recovered. Oh, that I did but always at once look up to Christ! But what a lamentable proneness to go everywhere else before we flee into the name of the Lord, which is a strong tower to the righteous. Have been helped to rejoice in His goodness of late, and feel my confidence increase while at a throne of grace. It seems, while there, as if I could not doubt. I can realize the mighty blessings of the everlasting gospel as mine, and my mind sweetly rests on the Divine faithfulness. I seldom rise from my knees without weeping; my whole heart melted with contrition in view of the wonderful love of God to one so poor and vile as I. Oh, how near does He sometimes draw me to Himself! And when I look around, and see so many mercies, so many blessings, such tender care in providing for all my wants, no good things withheld,—although my base heart has distrusted Him in the very midst of countless proofs of His love,—I abhor myself in dust and in ashes. God has forgiven, and does forgive me, but I cannot forgive myself."

"25th.—How is it with thee, O my soul? How is it between thee and God? This is a question I often need put to myself as I journey onward. I require to pause and think what I am, and what I am doing, and whether I really am going forward or not. I have been thinking with what a delusion Satan continually aims to blind the minds of men as to the brevity and uncertainty of human life. How often does he prevail, even with the real Christian! On looking back upon the past sixty years of my life, and forward to the little point that remains, what a dream! How like a vision does it appear! Oh, how little of it, if any at all, has been spent to the real glory of Him who gave it. I cannot trace a single thing I ever did in my whole life, that affords me any real pleasure to look back upon. Oh, if I had nothing more to comfort me, I should be a wretched creature indeed! And now I know and feel at times what a believer in Christ should be who is a candidate for a crown of glory, and a disciple of Him who was not of this world; but how far short do I come! Sometimes, when at a throne of grace, I can see and feel forcibly the littleness of everything around me; and when I have a glimpse of God as He is in Himself, as well as what He is to my soul, I sink in all my nothingness, melted into love at His feet. What should I do but for Jesus? Precious Jesus! I do love Thee. Thou art the chief among ten thousand. I am wearied with the creature, for disappointment is written upon the dearest object here below. But in Thee there is no disappointment, thou blessed, dearest one. Oh, that I could love Thee as I wish to do, and serve Thee with all the powers of my mind and body! Let not my heart wander from Thee: keep me under the shadow of Thy wing till the storm of life be past."

"Oct. 15th, 1833.—New York.—My dear mother sailed on this day for Bermuda. I felt I never loved her so well before as I have since she left us. When I fancy her, aged, feeble, and, perhaps, ill, on a tempestuous ocean, and exposed to all the discomforts of a voyage, I can but weep and pray. Pray for her I do, and that is my only comfort. I believe the Lord loves her better than I do, and to His care I constantly commit her. She was determined to go, as she said, to lay her bones in her own native place. I urged her to remain with me, but it was her wish and decided determination; and if the Lord takes her in safety, she will escape the cold winter here, and may live a few years longer for it. May God in His mercy carry her in safety!"

It was again her privilege during this brief and final visit to the United States to participate in one of those showers of spiritual blessing to which reference is made in the earlier part of this volume. The following letter, addressed to her pastor, will convey some idea of the themes and the style of the pulpit addresses which generally prevail on these interesting occasions, and the mode of meeting the numerous cases of awakening which occur:—

"BELOVED BRO. IN THE LORD,—   N. Y., Jan. 24th, 1833.

"The Lord seems to have awakened his servants here to a sense of their duty, and the vast responsibility attached to them as His ministers. 'Protracted meetings' are now held in almost all the churches, and some of them are of a most interesting character. I have been for some days attending one; it is in a Presbyterian church, and the ministers who conduct it seem men of God, and preach as with the great white throne full in view. The grand aim in their preaching and addresses is, to rouse the sinner—to follow him in all his refuges of lies—to knock from beneath him every false prop, and to show him that if he perishes, the fault is not God's, but his own. Next to this, their endeavour is to awaken the church itself to activity and earnestness in the cause of God. The whole day, from six o'clock in the morning until half-past nine o'clock in the evening, with intervals, is devoted to prayer and preaching. After the sermon, all who feel themselves lost and undone sinners are invited to come forward and occupy pews in front of the pulpit. The praying part of the assembly then cluster round them, and petitions are offered on their behalf. This would be a new and strange thing in England, but God sees fit to own this to the salvation of many souls. Last evening I felt it peculiarly solemn. I felt *God was there.* Seventeen individuals advanced, many young, some elderly men, deeply concerned. Oh, how my heart was drawn out towards God on their behalf! There was no excitement—no noise or enthusiasm. The feeling was deep, silent, solemn as eternity. All knelt and followed in prayer, which consisted of eight or nine short, earnest, wrestling petitions to God for their salvation. The church was earnestly exhorted to lay aside their earthly concerns for a season, and give themselves wholly up to the Lord and to His work. While some are engaged in the prayer-meetings, others go out in the lanes and alleys to persuade men and women to come and hear the sound of the gospel. The minister visits, and receives visits at home after the meetings for prayer. I feel my heart a little revived already, and bless God for it. . . . . I should remark, that while the church is stirred up to plead earnestly for sinners, the Lord the Spirit causes them to feel their own lack, and brings them to God in humble confession of their coldness and unbelief. Unbelief, unbelief, oh, this is our great crime before God! We will not take Him at His word, fully believing all that He has promised. Did we really believe that sinners will be cast into hell, should we not be more earnest both with them and with God, although we do know that salvation is of God, and that He alone can save a sinner? Oh yes, we should. But our faith is so small, and what we have we do not exercise sufficiently to obtain more. Is it not often but a mere form of words, when we pray, *Lord, increase our faith?* It is a cold, formal duty, and we go away, and think no more of it, and so God does not grant the boon we so little value. May the Lord renew His precious work in our souls! If the religion of Christ is not *the* business of our whole life, it is nothing, and we are nothing, and shall be found as nothing, or worse than nothing, when He comes to judge the world."

"25th.—The Lord is doing a great work here, my dear brother, and my soul rejoices in God and in the prospects of His church. . . . . Whole families have, in the last two weeks, been translated out of the kingdom of Satan into the kingdom of God's dear Son. The addresses yesterday were chiefly to urge Christians to increased activity and earnestness in prayer, showing their great responsibility, especially at such a season. It was solemn, heart-searching truth. Oh, if we did but fully believe that God will condemn the impenitent sinner to eternal perdition, we should act very differently. But we do not believe it, although Jehovah is as much bound to fulfil that promise as any other. How He bears with His redeemed ones! Why are not our children converted? Because, humanly speaking, we care so little about it. We pray for them, it is true; but it is with formality and coldness; and so we wrap it up, while they are rapidly travelling to the regions of eternal woe. Last evening, the 'anxious seats' were filled with those who earnestly desired the prayers of God's people. Many have been reconciled to God through the peace-speaking blood of Christ, and many more are inquiring what they shall do to be saved. I am glad to be where Jesus is passing by. I just get a glimpse of His face now and then, and can plead with Him as a man pleadeth with his friend. Help me to praise Him. When I cannot find words, I sit and weep before Him. His name is Love. That my soul knoweth right well. Oh, that *all* our children might rise up and call Him blessed! A young lady in the bloom of youth and beauty, living in all the gaiety of the world, was brought under the appalling conviction of her awful state before a holy God. The world she so much loved was at once dressed in sable to her view. She was miserable, and everything else looked so. For nights she knew not scarcely what it was to sleep. Some time after this she thought she had obtained a hope in Christ, but it was soon gone, and she was left in darkness. But in a few days, while she was in prayer, and while prayer was being made for her by the church, the Lord revealed Himself to her soul, and filled it with unspeakable joy. Her eyes were now opened, and everything appeared changed. She was happy in the Lord, and her countenance was radiant. When her minister entered the parlour, and extended his hand, he said, 'I need not ask how it is with you; I see you have been with Jesus.' I must add that this young convert, in all the fervour of her first love, went from house to house, amongst her kinsfolk and friends, imploring them to come and hear the gospel."

"29th.—Never did I feel my mind more solemn, and my heart more drawn out for the salvation of sinners, than at the present time. As I sat last evening in the sanctuary, and saw twenty or thirty, old and young, go forward for the prayers of God's people, thus acknowledging that they felt their need of Christ, I raised my heart to my Father, and prayed Him, for Jesus' sake, to have mercy upon them. Dear brother, the Lord is with us, doing a mighty work. The Baptists are much engaged. A cloud of mercy is hovering over this city, and the prayers of God's people will pierce it, and bring down showers of blessing. My children are earnestly engaged in bringing sinners where the Holy Ghost is displaying His mighty power. They visit from house to house, dealing faithfully with all they meet who know not God. My own soul is greatly refreshed and drawn near to the Lord. For ever blessed be His name for this renewed token of His kind remembrance to one so unworthy of the least of His mercies."

" 30th.—There is not a country in the world where religion and religious intelligence are so constantly and prominently brought before the attention as in this. In fact, it is, at least at the present time, one continued, interesting topic of conversation. Every one is talking about it and engaged in it some way or other. This is a delightful state of things. Our own prayer meetings are taking a deeper tone, and the members of the church are engaged each in visiting from house to house, endeavoring to induce some poor sinner to come and hear the gospel. This evening is to be spent chiefly in prayer and exhortation. The Lord is indeed doing a great work, and all seem alive to its importance, except a few who are endeavouring to justify their coldness and supineness under the plea of God's sovereignty, and so sit still while others are reaping this rich harvest of souls to the glory of God. I think I never heard before such fervent appeals to the consciences of men, so completely divesting them of all their refuges of lies, as I have this last week. How I do love old-fashioned conversions, where sinners are brought to feel they are sinners, crying out under the conviction ' What must I do to be saved?' and are then led by the self-same Spirit to look to Jesus, and are at once enabled to believe and rejoice. I cannot understand this long process of months and years seeking, and seeking, and never finding, until, perhaps, at a dying hour. God is the same now that he was in the New Testament times—Christ is the same—the Spirit is the same—and the sinner is the same. Well, then, there must be a woful lack of the Spirit's holy influence, owing to our unbelief. I will continue to give you, as the Lord will help me, an account of His most gracious dealings with His churches on this side of the water. Oh, that the Lord might visit you in your part of the vineyard, and so revive His work that sinners may be converted, and the saints sealed and set apart under the fresh anointings of the Holy Ghost. I love poor perishing sinners more than I can express. I have been very narrow-hearted and selfish, and I hate and abhor myself because of it. I have been looking for salvation too exclusively for my own family, and the little circle about me, and have wanted more of that expansive love that brought Christ from heaven to save sinners. Dear brother, endeavour to show them their awful condition; scatter their vain excuses, and tell them they must repent and believe the gospel, or they are lost for ever. They need not be told that they have no power to repent and believe. They will soon find they are *powerless*, and begin to cry for mercy to Him who will give repentance, and power to believe too. Forgive me for saying so much on this subject to you, who are so much better qualified to judge than I; but I feel more than ever the absolute necessity of awakening the sinner to see his lost condition; for Satan has ten thousand ways of deluding; and shall we not, under God, do all we can, if by any means we may save some by plucking them out of the fire? Salvation is of God, but the means are ours, and we cheerfully leave Him to give the blessing. My love to the church in John Street."

After spending a year in happy and useful intercourse with her children, in reviving the cherished friendships of other days, and in seeing her aged parent once more, and for the last time in the flesh, she re-embarked for England. Her homeward voyage and arrival are thus noted in her journal:

"May 24th, 1834.—*On board the packet ship Philadelphia*, I am once more upon the mighty ocean, on my return to dear England, with E. and J. R. under my care. The weather is delightful, the wind fair, and everything comfortable as I could possibly expect on board ship. It was a severe trial, parting with my dear children. My mind was greatly exercised, as usual, to know the path of duty. So far the Lord has prospered our voyage. I do pray He may be pleased to continue His tender mercies towards us, and grant me to see the face of my dear children, to whom I am going, with comfort, and preserve those I have been obliged to leave behind. The Lord is good, and my soul desires to praise His holy name."

"In sight of the Lizard and of dear old England once more, after a prosperous voyage of eighteen days from New York. The Lord has wonderfully appeared for me, and many have been the prayers offered up on my behalf, and which He has in condescending mercy deigned to answer. A pleasant captain and a fine ship."

"Landed in Portsmouth in good health, and left the next day for London, where I arrived at nine o'clock in the evening, and found all well and happy to see me again. The Lord has been merciful indeed to me. His name is 'Love.' For ever blessed be His holy name, for all His dealings towards me. My hope is in Him for all things here and hereafter. God be praised!"

The mother of Mrs. Winslow has already been introduced to the reader. The time arrived when her long and steady course should be finished, and she should enter into the joy of her Lord. Full of years, rich in grace, and ripe for glory, this venerable and beloved lady breathed her last in her own native isle, and was buried in the sepulchre of her fathers. In her diary Mrs. Winslow thus briefly but touchingly records this event :—

"Heard of the death of my beloved and ever-precious mother, the oldest and dearest friend I had in this world of sorrow. She has gone, I trust, to glory, and is now rejoicing with Christ and the many dear friends who have gone before her. Who can tell the glory that surrounds the saints on their entrance into that abode of bliss? How strange that we do not more long to be there! Dearest mamma, you are now freed from a body of sin and death, and a life of pain and suffering. I sorrow, but not as those who have no hope. I do have a hope of her that gladdens my heart, and I trust to see her again at the right hand of Christ, and to spend a happy eternity with her, and go no more out for ever. Oh, that I may be helped to keep my garments unspotted from the world, and to be ready when the summons comes."

On the appointment of her son, the Rev. G. E. Winslow, to the vicarage of Tugby, Leicestershire, she spent a few months there, from whence the following extracts are dated. Possessing, as we have already remarked, an exquisite taste for landscape beauty, and charmed with the simplicity of rural life, a picturesque country village—its ivy-mantled church and pretty vicarage, its rude hamlets and honest villagers, its simplicity and repose would harmonize with her feelings, and supply her with rich material for reflection of an interesting and varied character. And when to her fondness for the country we add the spiritual eye with which she would contemplate the works of God—seeing, enjoying, and glorifying Him in all—we are prepared to find her pouring forth such pious thoughts and poetic feelings, and sketching, with her holy and graphic pen, such interesting village scenes as are contained in the following extract from letters:—

TO HER SON.

"*Tugby Vicarage, July,* 1837.—How lovely is all nature. As I sit at my window with the casement open, the beautiful lawn in front, the fine tall trees surrounding it, the hawthorn hedges, the green fields stretching beyond, with the bright sun and refreshing breeze imparting life and healthfulness to the whole, truly do I feel that there is nothing like the works of God. I have just been walking round the lawn, inhaling the fragrance of the sweet roses which hang in rich clusters from the house, thrusting their heads into the parlour window. This is a sweet place. But every place where Jesus is, and which He blesses with His presence, is sweet. He can transform a dungeon into a palace, and His presence can turn darkness into light. G—— has just gone to Norton to preach. I have been praying for him, that while he is preaching to others God might, through the Eternal Spirit, preach to him. And I have been praying for you too. And oh, that God might make you a real blessing, anoint you afresh for your all-important work, and keep you sitting low in a low place at the feet of Jesus. My heart is often drawn out on your behalf, that you may be more and more deeply taught of the Holy Ghost, may preach and act only to please God, losing sight of self and of everything but Christ, in a full view of the great white throne, and under a deep sense of the vast responsibility that rests upon you as a minister of Christ. I sometimes think I should have wearied out all the host of heaven with my many thousand prayers and petitions for you all, and for myself; but God is love, and His love is never wearied with hearing."

"At the entrance of the village is the cottage of a poor aged widow, who can with difficulty move upon her crutches from chair to chair; but she knows and loves the Lord. Her Bible, 'Fox's Book of Martyrs,' a volume of sermons by an old divine, and the 'Pilgrim's Progress,' have been her chief means of instruction, and God has blessed them to her soul. She is greatly afflicted with bodily infirmity, but patient, submissive, and thankful. I often leave the vicarage, and bend my steps to this lonely pilgrim, where, seated in an old broken chair by her little fire of dried sticks, we talk of Christ and what he has done for us both, and of our happy prospects, till my heart is soothed and refreshed, and the dear redeemed old saint unites her praises with mine.

"The church is romantically situated on a rising ground, which looks down on the village below, and commands a beautiful prospect of the surrounding country. It is skirted with large and beautiful trees, which overshadow the graves of the many dead who sleep here until the resurrection day. It is a pleasant retreat for contemplation. I often sit here, and turn my eyes from the dead lying at my feet, to the various rural occupations of the living beyond, and some are seen milking the cows, feeding the lambs, or mowing the grass; others, in the distance, are gathering in and stacking the hay, while the sun setting in rich splendour, imparts animation and loveliness to the whole. Oh, that men would praise the Lord for His goodness! And oh, that these things did more elevate my heart to Him, the Giver of all good! And yet, after all, this is not my rest, blessed be God.

"I have just returned from a visit to my poor pilgrim. I walked softly in, and found her with her glasses on, attentively reading a book she had upon her lap. 'What are you reading?' I inquired. 'The Shepherd, ma'am; the Shepherd who laid down his life for the sheep,' looking up into my face with an expression of sweet peace and content. I replied, 'Yes, and for you and for me too, if we are His sheep.' It was one of the sermons of the good old divine I mentioned, and the dear aged saint was feasting upon the precious, sterling truths it contained. I found another excellent work in her *rich* library: 'Boston's Four-fold State.' I said, 'Have you dined?' 'Yes.' 'What have you had?' 'Boiled milk.' This, I found, was her chief diet; and oh, how happy she is! She says she is happier than the rich or the mighty in their palaces, and from my heart I believe it. The squire is kind to her, and has lent her a little garden in a field, which her attentive and dutiful son cultivates for her."

"I went last evening to see another aged pilgrim; but mark

the difference. This good woman (for I have little doubt but that she is one) is abounding with all the comforts of life. She is a widow, with two industrious sons, and one kind daughter. She has a nice house, comfortable farm, and everything to make her happy. But she is far from being so. For although I believe her to be a child of God, she is constantly harassed with the idea that she has grieved away the Spirit, and will be lost for ever. This, I believe, has arisen from bad teaching and disease of body. I have endeavoured to cheer her up by leading her to look more fully to Christ than to herself. I sat with her last evening for nearly an hour, and found it refreshing to my soul to speak of Jesus."

" E—— writes me that he has had two boroughs offered to him, but I have urged him not to stand. The country is in a state of ferment at present. The new accession to the throne involves a new Parliament, and the Tories are straining every point to secure as many Conservatives as possible. In the evening G—— drove me in his phaeton to Alexton Hall, where we took tea with Mrs. W——, who was alone. We had a long conversation on religion and Christian experience, and stayed until a late hour. What a mercy that Jesus is everything to me! Truly in Him I live, and move, and have my being. He is around about my path by day and by night, and my soul rejoices in God my Saviour. The sun is just setting, and looks beautiful as it casts its fading beams upon the tall trees and green fields ere it bids us good-night. The birds, too, are chirping their evening song before they fold their little heads beneath their wing for rest.

'The ploughman homeward plods his weary way,
And leaves the world to darkness and to me.'

So I learned in younger days at school. Nearly a dozen have just passed the garden gate, each with a bundle of sticks upon his shoulders, to kindle a cheerful blaze when he gets home, ere he lays his jaded limbs to rest. *The sleep of a labouring man is sweet.*

" Here and there I find a humble soul in a thatched cottage, who but few know, but who are the lowly and hidden followers of the meek and despised Saviour. I rode on horseback the other day to the adjoining village; and while G—— went on some miles further, I alighted at a good man's dwelling, the front of which was covered with roses trailed up against the wall, and went in, and passed two or three hours with him and his aged wife very happily. They offered me the best their house afforded, which was a glass of cowslip wine. I seated myself on their sofa in a nice little parlour, where everything indicated neatness and industry, with a wide window in front, of small panes of glass, but tastefully ornamented with clusters of fresh-blown roses on the outside. Here I sat and talked of Christ, while the dear old man (his eyes filled with tears) echoed to his wife, who was deaf, what I had said to him from time to time. I had much profitable conversation with them. The good man said at parting, 'Oh, ma'am, you do not know how comforting this visit has been to me.' When G—— returned, I mounted my horse, promising to see them again, and galloped home to the vicarage."

"Yesterday was the Sabbath. G—— preached an excellent discourse. He took for his subject the anxiety of Zaccheus to see Jesus as he passed by. He drew some excellent ideas from it, and the application was good. Dear E—— has been greatly blessed in her labours in the school. Her thorough and effective method of discipline, blended with so much winning softness, has produced a complete revolution for the better. You can form no idea how promptly the children obey, and yet how tenderly they love her. She has, with the aid of the mistress, made the mode of instruction so interesting, that the parents could not, if they were so inclined, detain their children at home. Yesterday they were brought to the vicarage, and underwent a private examination previous to the public one, which takes place next week. G—— examined them on two chapters of the Bible; and it was pleasing to hear how well they answered, while his observations were instructive and solemn. They then sung their hymns, accompanied by E—— on the piano. The chapters on which they were questioned were the 18th and 19th of the Gospel of John: and as I sat in an adjoining room, listening to the sufferings of the Redeemer, and the unheard-of ignominy heaped upon the matchless Son of God, the effect on my mind was such that I could not recover my spirits the whole evening."

"G——'s ministry seems much blessed. There is in his preaching a rich savour of the Divinity of Christ. He insists constantly and earnestly upon the Godhead of Jesus, as the 'everlasting Father,' as 'the mighty God;' and this imparts such strength and consolation to the soul, that my heart has often been refreshed in a way that I little expected "

"'How sweet,' as dear Mrs. Winslow* says, 'to receive expressions of love from strangers, who show them, not for our sakes, but for Christ's sake.' It emanates from the fulness of His love. All the affection of Christian friends is the result of His overflowing heart—just as the beams which scatter light and warmth around us flow from the sun, the great centre. He inclines them to love us, and do us good for His sake. I have felt to-day much blessedness in viewing the Lord as my own and only Friend on earth and in heaven; and making a renewed surrender of my whole heart to Him, desiring above all earthly good that it should be moulded according to His will, and made conformable to His likeness. I feel much of the blessedness of one who is emptied of all confidence in himself, feeling there is nothing in him of his own, but what he hates, who yet in the midst of all this poverty finds he has a store of incalculable riches in another, and that one is God in our nature—the God-man. Christ is everything to me—I could not live without Him, I could not die without Him, and heaven would be no heaven to me, if my Beloved were not there."

"Dear ——, I think your trials have been sanctified to me, as well as to yourself; for they have kept me in close contact with God, and have brought me into more of His real character, not only as to what He is to His redeemed, but also as to what He is in Himself. Is He a good God? He is *goodness*. Is His name love? He is *love*. Is He faithful? He is *faithfulness*. Is He the true God? He is *truth*, and therefore cannot lie."

After spending thus happily and profitably some months at Tugby, she left amidst the general and affectionate regrets of the kind-hearted villagers. One of her letters thus pictures the parting scene:—

"We left Tugby, followed by a weeping tribe of the children and cottagers. You would have supposed they were parting with the dearest friend on earth. The school was let out sooner than usual, to bid us good-bye at the Vicarage; and although most of them were forbidden to follow, when we reached the turnpike-gate they were there, and E—— was surrounded with tears from the young, and with blessings from the old. There we left the girls; but at the

---

* Mrs. Harriet Winslow, of the American Mission in Ceylon.

end of the field there was another cluster waiting to say good-bye, and the boys ran after the carriage as far as they could. I have never before seen such an exhibition of tender feeling and affection from people who but a few months ago were perfect strangers."

On her return to town, she was seized with the prevailing epidemic which carried off so many hundreds, but in mercy her valuable life was spared, God having yet a work to accomplish in and by her.

"Since I last wrote I have been very near eternity, but the Lord rebuked the fever, and I am able to sit up for a few minutes at a time. It was the influenza in its most powerful form. The Lord, out of His own kind heart, put kindness in all around me. My mind, during those few days and nights of suffering, was in a very peculiar state. I could not pray, or even think. I could only say, and at intervals, 'Lord, have mercy upon me, and heal me.' The whole power of mind seemed prostrated at once. I thought, Oh, if I had left the salvation of my soul to this moment, I should have been lost. Good Mr. D. once ventured to inquire the state of my mind. I recollect saying, 'It is in a cloud, but my hope does not depend upon my feelings, but upon Christ, upon God.'

"While I sit writing, I see opposite to me two mutes standing at a door. It is the funeral of an individual who died of the same disease from which a gracious God has raised me up. He was a healthy man, but death had a commission, and he has appeared before the judgment-seat of Christ. I, like the barren fig-tree, have been spared a little longer, through the intercession of a precious Saviour, that I may bring forth more fruit to His glory. I have just sent a note of inquiry to dear Mrs. R——, for I feel anxious to know how they are. Every day will appear a year to them as the time draws near for their return to Brooklyn. God grant they may find all well at home, and then it will be a happy time indeed. I think it is good sometimes to leave those we love, that we may taste the sweetness of meeting again. How many of these happy meetings have I had in my time! It is almost all over now. But, oh! the meeting in heaven! *that* will be the best of all. Oh, may God, in His rich mercy, grant that I may meet all, *all* that He has given me, and all I love on earth, at His right hand at that great day. I know you will say, Amen and amen!"

How heart-searching and solemn, yet how true and precious, are the following thoughts:—

"I have often thought that, although God did so convince you of sin as to make you flee into the very bosom of Christ, yet you have never been led much into the depth of the hidden evil. You have still to be led into the great chamber of imagery. Oh, the aboundings of sin there which no eye discerneth but God's until He, by increasing light, declares it to us little by little! How have I to mourn and weep before Him, while He shows me to myself—poor, wretched, sinful, and yet washed and justified from all things! What can I say to these things? Love abounding,—grace subduing,—blood-cleansing,—Jesus pardoning,—the Spirit renewing,—God reconciled; and all this mighty work for one so vile, so worthless, so hell-deserving! Dear ——, watch, as with a jealous eye for God's glory, every hidden spring of action. Look to your thoughts and motives; and while you do this, keep your eye upon the cross of Christ, and you need not fear to see yourself *as you are*. This is the Spirit's work alone, and this only will make us go softly all our days."

The tender and prayerful interest with which she viewed the accession of the present Sovereign to the throne, was in beautiful keeping with the benevolent feelings of her spiritual and enlarged mind. Called, in the providence of God, to a position of great responsibility, and at an age so tender, the young Queen became an object of her liveliest and holiest sympathies. Frequently has she been known to pour forth the most fervent intercessions on her behalf, especially praying that, next to her own personal interest in the salvation of God, she might have grace vouchsafed faithfully to maintain the true Protestantism of this land. She also formed one of a little circle of Christian ladies who, in different places, and at a given time, met in concert to pray for their Queen. In one of her letters, she relates this touching incident of the youthful Sovereign:—

"Just as the Princess Victoria came of age, the King was suddenly taken ill, and a few weeks after died. I heard an interesting anecdote of the young Queen. The first death-warrant that Lord Melbourne presented for her signature, she said, 'And *must* I sign it?' and burst into tears. He replied, 'Your Majesty has the power of mitigating the sentence to transportation for life.' She instantly exclaimed, 'Oh, then, let it be; and transport him.' This looked lovely."

Her Christianity was highly perceptive, and her religious character, consequently, singularly practical. It was the testimony of David, when referring to his own experience, "I esteem all thy precepts to be right." Such, in truth, might have been her language of whom we speak. With an enlarged heart, she ran the way of God's commandments, finding in their keeping great reward. But there was especially one divine precept by whose clear and holy light she conscientiously and undeviatingly walked; the apostolic injunction, "*Owe no man anything,*" was the precept to which we refer. It was her principle *never to incur debt*, upon any pretence or under any circumstances whatever. She would make no purchase which she was not prepared to meet, and was always uneasy in the recollection of the smallest claim undischarged. And when deprived of affluence, and combating with limited resources, a large and expensive family dependent upon her, she had the strength of character and the grace of heart never at any period to allow her expenditure to exceed her income. It was thus the grace of God enabled her to guide her affairs with discretion, and to provide things honestly, not only in the sight of the Lord, but also in the sight of men. By a strict, conscientious observance of this divine rule, she was not only enabled to "render unto all their due," but also to contribute liberally of her substance to the cause of God, and to the necessities of Christ's flock. She refers to this subject in the following extract:—

"28th. —— was speaking to me about purchasing a ——; but I really thought that, under existing circumstances, it had better not be. A thing like this, which one might do without, ought to be let alone. That sweet precept which God laid upon my heart in the commencement of my dreary widowhood, He has enabled me strictly to keep: *Owe no man anything, but to love one another.* If in debt, which I never allowed myself to be, I should have thought nothing was at my own disposal until I had honestly paid that debt. I have endeavoured faithfully to impress the same upon the minds of all my children, entreating them rather to live on the lowliest fare than incur claims which they have no power to meet. It is as much a command of God as any other, and woe be to us if we disobey it. God will chasten us if we do; and we shall find that what is withheld, justly due to another, He is able to take from us, and make the sweetest ingredient of our cup bitter as gall. Let us walk in this holy precept of the gospel, and there is then nothing to fear. Let us often look back upon all the way our God has led us, and trace His gracious dealings at every step; and we shall not only acknowledge that He is good, but we shall aim more and more to do everything that is right and pleasing in His sight. Oh, for more grace, more uprightness of heart, and more singleness of eye! It is *with God* we have to do, and not with man."

"Dec. 24th.—I have to recount the goodness and unfailing mercy of my good and gracious God, who has brought me thus far on my weary pilgrimage. I have to lament my unfaithfulness and backslidings of heart from Him. This has been a year full of especial mercies. Yet I do not feel my heart, as I could wish, going out towards God. I desire the renewed anointing of the Holy Ghost, and am looking up for this blessing. Nothing can satisfy me without it. An indwelling God; the water springing up into eternal life; the constant and abiding presence of Christ,—this is what I want, and for this I pray."

"Jan. 26th.—Feel much nearness to God. Can tell Him all that is in my heart,—all my wants,—and feel that Jesus hears me. I am directed to carry my small as well as great things to Christ; everything that troubles, be it what it may. Satan contends with me here, so that at times I feel almost ashamed of troubling the God of heaven with such poor trifles; but I recollect that a sparrow falls not to the ground without His notice, and I am encouraged: God gives me faith, and I conquer the arch-enemy of souls."

"The way to God has seemed to me of late so delightful, so exactly suited to a poor lost sinner,—so suited to me. A way sprinkled with atoning blood; justice and mercy as a wall of defence on either side; and this way leading to such a rich treasure-house, filled with all blessing for time and for eternity. All is in Jesus the way to God, the way of holiness, the way to glory.

> "Sweet the moments, rich in blessing,
> Which before the cross I spend;
> Life, and health, and peace possessing,
> From the sinner's dying Friend."

"16th.—The dear Redeemer continues to lift up upon me the light of his countenance. But with all this matchless love,

I have been, and still am, tried with earthly wandering thoughts. While in the body we cannot escape the world; though cloistered from it, the god of this world would still follow and harass us as much as he is permitted, in order to show us our weakness, and the long-suffering patience of our God towards us."

"Feb. 29th.—Yesterday I completed my sixty-second year. Few and evil have been the days of the years of my pilgrimage. To Jacob's words I can add this testimony,—goodness and mercy have followed me all my days, and I am longing to praise and bless His holy name, who has done great things for me and mine, although we have not returned Him according to His goodness. I look back, and sigh, and grieve, and think how many evils I could have avoided with my present experience. I think and feel more and more the exceeding sinfulness of sin, and my own weakness and inability to stand one moment without the all-upholding arm of Jehovah-Jesus. How needful are trials, and how precious then the sweet promises of the gospel!"

"It is wondrous how God, when we wander from Him,
Our fears and afflictions can double;
And then comfort impart to the sorrowful heart,
That we never could know but in trouble.

"Thus faith in the dark, is pursuing its mark
Through many sharp trials of love,
In this sorrowful waste which the Christian must pass
To the heavenly Canaan above."

"22nd.—God is love, and His mercy endureth forever: this my soul knows to be true. I would be holy, even as He is holy. My heart longs for full sanctification. I am wearied with sin; my soul loathes it, and I abhor myself in dust and in ashes. Truly, *I would not live alway.* Heaven would be greatly to be desired, were it only to have done with sin for ever. But oh, the presence of Jesus in all His glories, unveiled to our wondering eye, will make our happiness complete. O earth, earth! let my heart's best affections go, and trouble me no more. I want this heart only for Christ! It is His by the purchase of His blood; it is His by the conquest of His grace; and I covet it all for Him. Oh, that every throb may beat with love, gratitude, and adoration to Him who has saved my soul, and redeemed me from the power of the enemy! Amen and amen."

"I would not live alway—live alway below!
Oh no, I'll not linger when bidden to go.
The days of our pilgrimage granted us here
Are enough for life's woes, full enough for its cheer.
Would I shrink from the path which the prophets of God,
Apostles and Martyrs, so joyfully trod!
While brethren and friends are all hastening home,
Like a spirit unblest o'er the earth would I roam?

"I would not live alway—I ask not to stay,
Where storm after storm rises dark o'er the way;
Where, seeking for peace, we but hover around,
Like the patriarch's bird, and no resting is found;
Where hope, when she paints her gay bow in the air,
Leaves its brilliance to fade in the night of despair,
And joy's fleeting angel ne'er sheds a glad ray,
Save the gleam of the plumage that bears him away.

"I would not live alway—thus fettered by sin,
Temptation without and corruption within;
In a moment of strength, if I sever the chain,
Scarce the victory's mine ere I'm captive again.
E'en the rapture of pardon is mingled with fears,
And my cup of thanksgiving with penitent tears.
The festival trump calls for jubilant songs,
But my spirit her own *miserere* prolongs.

"I would not live alway—no, welcome the tomb!
Since Jesus hath lain there, I dread not its gloom;
Where He deign'd to sleep, I'll too bow my head;
Oh! peaceful the slumbers on that hallow'd bed.
And then the glad dawn soon to follow that night,
When the sunrise of glory shall beam on my sight,
When the full matin song, as the sleepers arise
To shout in the morning, shall peal through the skies.

"Who, who would live alway—away from his God,
Away from yon heaven, that blissful abode,
Where the rivers of pleasure flow o'er the bright plains,
And the noontide of glory eternally reigns;
Where the saints of all ages in harmony meet,
Their Saviour and brethren transported to greet;
Where the songs of salvation exultingly roll,
And the smile of the Lord is the feast of the soul;

"That heavenly music! what is it I hear?
The notes of the harpers ring sweet in the air;
And see, soft unfolding, those portals of gold!
The King, all array'd in his beauty, behold!
Oh, give me, oh, give me the wings of a dove,
Let me hasten my flight to those mansions above,
Ay, 'tis now that my soul on swift pinions would soar,
And in ecstasy bid earth adieu evermore."

Rev. Dr. Muhlenburg.

TO HER SON O——.

" . . . If you can obtain the Memoir of Mrs. Hawkes, written by Miss Cecil, do so, and read it. It is republished in America, with an Introduction, I think, by Washington Irving. Miss Cecil is a delightful Christian. I had a long interview with her after I read the book. To-day I called on her, and was introduced in the drawing-room, and sat in the very chair where good Mr. Cecil, Newton, and Simeon once sat. It is the same house which Mr. Cecil occupied for forty or fifty years, and around the walls are hung numerous portraits of good men, his and Mr. Newton's among the rest. It was a treat of no ordinary kind,—a feast of the soul. These are now before the throne in glory. Once they were like us, tried, tempted, and often sorrowing; but now they are reaping the rich reward of all their labours."

"I smiled at your idea of my arranging my thoughts on given subjects when I address my children. Why, I never know what I am going to write, until I take up my pen, and then I give full licence to my ideas as they flow; and, as it happens, the Lord seems to direct; for I believe in general,— at least so some of my correspondents say,—what I write comes just in season; but let that be as it may, it comes in season from my heart. Once formality shows its ugly phiz, away would go all I would wish to say. When I write to Christians in trial, I am often comforted with the comfort I am endeavouring to impart to others. The same in conversation. Were I a minister, perhaps this would be my favourite subject. But the Lord has not called me to that office, so you must take me just as you find me; for I am too old now to mend my ways in that respect; but I will try and bear in mind what you say when I write to ——. Pray will you choose a text for me when I next write to *you?*"

"I have been feasting upon the memoir of Dr. Payson. He seems, however, to have looked too much to frames and feelings, and as they ebbed and flowed, his faith did the same, and this caused him so much distress, and wore out his health. Sensible enjoyments are very desirable, but they are not Christ. Faith in the dark puts honour on God, and the more we know of His faithfulness, the more will our peace flow as a river that never changes its course. There is always something wrong when He hides His face; but after all, He remains the same, and we must come to Him again as poor sinners. *If we confess our sins, He is faithful and just to forgive us our sins, and to cleanse us from all unrighteousness.* Confession of sin is a holy strengthening exercise, and brings a sweet blessing to the soul. Never let us keep guilt upon the conscience. The Fountain is always open to us; and we should not leave a throne of grace until we have a sense of pardon through the fresh application of his blood. Have no concealments from God."

" 25th.—Such a sermon from Mr. Evans! His mind is gigantic, and so deeply spiritual. The world to him is nothing, and God first and everything. He lives near the Lord, and cares neither for the frown nor the smile of man. His ministry has been much blessed to me of late. He has just parted with C——, who sailed for India on last Saturday. His trial—and a great trial it was—has been sanctified to his soul; and he preaches like a man standing on the verge of eternity, and in full view of heaven. He has fled into the bosom of God for consolation, and has found it."

" 4th.—I wish you would always write on the Monday, and then I should know how the Lord dealt with you on the Sabbath. We had a feast of fat things yesterday. I think Mr. E. preaches more of late as if he looked full into eternity, and saw the great white throne. He is solemn, powerful, and often awfully true. But I must prepare for my Bible class, which I have in my room. They all seem interested, and it is quite encouraging. We are going on with the 'Pilgrim's Progress.' I trust I had sweet nearness to God this morning in family worship. I was reading the history of Asa and Jehoshaphat, and could trace the character of God in His dealings with them, as well as His general conduct with the Old Testament saints, that it seemed to establish my soul in the truth, enabling me to feel that He was all that He says He is, and the same yesterday, to-day, and forever. Oh, that we may walk uprightly before Him, and watch against the treacherous foe we carry within!"

TO HER SON, REV. I. D. W——, ON MINISTERIAL WORK.

" . . . I long to hear how you are, and whether the Lord is blessing you with His presence: without it this world is a desolate wilderness indeed. I fear you will find it lonesome where you are; but if the Lord gives you plenty of work to do for himself, He will give you a sweet reward for your labour, and a contented mind with your lot. If you feel you are put where Jesus would have you to be, how sweet will be the thought! It will repress every wish to be elsewhere. How delightful to live to please Him, and Him only, who died for you! I have been just praying for you, and the Lord blessedly drew my heart out. I have prayed that you may feel increasingly the vast responsibility that rests upon you as a messenger of the Lord of Hosts, and that you may continually have an eye to that great day when you must render up the account of your stewardship. Oh that you may hear those blessed words, *Well done good and faithful servant!* I asked the Lord, too, to speak to you, and to speak through you to the people. Remember, before you fix your mind upon a text, to go upon your knees and ask your Master for one. If He gives you one, He will speak by it to you and your flock. Oh, you know not what a blessing will always attend this childlike faith in your heavenly Father. Be much in *searching* the Scriptures, for, in so doing, you will find rich food for your own soul, and for the flock over which the Holy Ghost hath made you overseer. If you have only a dozen poor people, never let it be a temptation to be less earnest and fervent in your preaching. If you watch the wind, you will not sow; but keep your eye upon the Lord of the harvest, and do His work faithfully, and He will give you your hire. And may God bless you and make you a blessing!"

To some individuals the deep searchings of heart, in which she was wont to indulge, will appear almost painful. But those searchings marked the honesty with which she ever sought to walk before God. And yet the lowliest estimate she entertained of herself was always accompanied with the most exalted views of Christ, and the clearest apprehension of her completeness in Him. She grew downward, and *so* brought forth fruit upward. Like the banyan-tree, whose branches first strike down into the earth and then shoot up again, she sank into a deep consciousness of her helplessness and dependence, and then, as from the lowest depths of self-humiliation, she rose strong in faith, glowing with love, and clinging all the more closely to the Saviour. Such would seem to be her experience, as thus portrayed:—

"A note from ——, inviting me to meet a minister and his wife who were on a visit to them. But I do not feel in spirits to meet strangers. I need a refreshing myself, and blessed be God, He has melted my heart this morning with sweet contrition, blended with holy joy, and an increasing desire to live to Him and for Him, who is all and everything to my soul. Oh, if He were to turn from me, I am lost for ever. This world, with the dearest earthly creatures, could not satisfy my soul. And oh, to call the Creator, the Upholder of all worlds, mine—yes, *mine*, for I am His, and He is mine, and that through all eternity—is a privilege so sweet that angels might envy. And is it boasting to speak boldly of these things? And yet I have been convinced, on examination, that in what I have felt it a duty and a delight to tell of His great goodness, there was much of self—hateful self—insensibly, at the time, that has laid me low in the dust before God. For this cause I do not like to meet with strangers who have heard of me from dear friends, who themselves are willing to overlook ten thousand infirmities and imperfections, because they love me. They do not know me as I know myself, and as God knows me. And I can truly say, that it is my unspeakable comfort that He does know me altogether. I would not have one thing hidden from Him, which He in love hides from the world. Oh, the praise due to His restraining grace!

"Last evening I heard a stranger. His text was singular. *And Adam called his wife's name Eve, because she was the mother of all living.* He remarked, that as soon as Adam and his wife ate the fruit, in disobedience to God's command, they died—spiritually died. God preached the gospel to them while in this awful state, and by the light of His Spirit they were enabled to believe in the promised seed that was to bruise the serpent's head. He first showed how much all names then had a significant meaning. Thus, God changed Abram to Abraham, because he was the father of the faithful. Jacob's name was changed to Israel, because, as a friend, he had power and prevailed with God. Eve was the mother of all *living*, who, like herself, were made alive in Christ Jesus. The seed of the serpent could not have been included, as they were always dead, *dead in trespasses and in sins.* Christ was the seed of the woman, and all the members of the body, of which He was the head, were alive in him. Of these Eve was the mother, for she was the living mother of all made alive in Christ Jesus. This sermon was full of Christ throughout."

"Heard Mr. E—— on Tuesday evening. Ought I not to grow in grace, and in the knowledge of God my Saviour? But oh, how slowly I advance to what I ought! One thing I do know,—I feel increasingly my own vileness, and see increasing beauty in the gospel, and its suitableness to the wants of a poor sinner. God shows me more of my own sinful self, and more of that perfect righteousness in Christ Jesus, which is unto all and upon all them that believe."

"Have you seen 'Mammon,' by the Rev. Mr. Harris? It is excellent. The next best essay on the subject was by a policeman, who wrote it while on his rounds in the night, and by the light of the lamp. Mr. Baptist Noel has just sent out a tract on the 'Unity of the Church.' It is delightful. There has been such a demand for it, that I could not obtain a copy from the publisher to send you. How needful both to Churchman and Nonconformist is such a work just now, when the members of Christ's body are warring against each other,— brother against brother, and that before unbelievers. May God bless this work to His church, and raise up many such faithful heralds of the cross, to warn their brethren of their evil ways!"

TO HER SON, REV. G. E. W——, ON MINISTERIAL
RESPONSIBILITY.

". . . Yesterday was the Sabbath, and you, I trust, were standing up in your great Master's name, to declare the whole truth as it is in Jesus. The more I think upon it, the more I feel the vast, the weighty responsibility that rests upon the minister of Christ. I look through a series of years, short and uncertain, to the judgment-seat, and there behold him the first to render an account of his stewardship. Oh, the tremendous responsibility—the care of precious and immortal souls! And when I remember that I have three now standing in this all-important position, I feel a trembling lest any of you should come short at last. 'Be faithful unto death.' Beware lest you speak peace when God has not spoken peace. Oh, think of a poor, deceived soul, going into eternity, fancying all is well, and the minister helping on the fatal delusion from want of faithfulness and obedience to the command of his God. Shrink not from duty, however painful. Let all things be right between you and God. It would be well to make a report of each day's work to God; and although you may have failed in many things, and have come short in all you will yet find this daily exercise sweet and profitable. It will preserve tenderness of conscience, and have a sanctifying influence upon the heart. Never forget for one moment whose you are or whom you serve; and may the love of Christ constrain you to diligence and devotedness of heart."

Who does not feel, as he closes the preceding extracts from her letters to her children, how powerful and deathless is the influence of a holy mother! That influence employed in planting the first seedlings of thought, in shaping the first actions of childhood, still lives to instruct, admonish, and cheer in manhood's riper years. Honoured and privileged are they, around whose toilsome path yet lingers a spell so sacred, a power so gentle, and a charm so holy and persuasive. The sepulchre has closed in silence over her; but her inspiration, vital, and balmy as the breath of spring, still floats over life's dreary way, gladdening, moulding, and guiding. Thus is it that Christianity ennobles, sanctifies, and immortalizes all the endeared relations of life. Beneath its embalming power the parental relation never dies. The authority to which as children we bowed so submissively, in later life, when the snow-flakes of time have frosted our brow, still lives to sway; and the maternal influence which shaped our youthful step, yet holds us in its deathless enchantment.

TO HER SON O———.

"March 14th.—Lord L—— is expected in town to-morrow. He has just lost his second daughter, a most interesting and amiable girl of fifteen. She died a week ago, in Paris. I grieve and sympathize with him as a parent. He never left her bedside, and deeply feels her loss. I pray for him, and desire that his heart may be sustained, and his affliction may be sanctified. On Wednesday morning, Mr. Evans preached, in Rowland Hill's pulpit, the annual sermon for the Baptist Missionary Society. He was most excellent. Surrey Chapel was excessively crowded. His people met at six o'clock that morning, for prayer on his behalf. Previous to his undertaking this service, he had entered with much earnestness into the missionary cause, and regrets he had so long stood aloof from it; and now it occupies much of his thoughts and labours; in fact, it has enlisted his whole heart. This evening they meet in John street, to form a missionary auxiliary."

A reference in the foregoing extract suggests the remark, that it is always interesting to trace an important result to its cause. The strong sympathy with which the subject of Christian missions was now regarded by Mr. Evans, appears to have been in a great measure awakened by the perusal of the "Memoir of Mrs. Harriet Winslow," the eminent and beloved American missionary to Ceylon. Having received a copy from New York, Mrs. Winslow brought it under the notice of her pastor in the following letter, addressed to the second Mrs. E.:—

". . . My dear Friend, I want you to get the memoir of dear Mrs. Winslow, the missionary who died not long ago in India. It will do you good. She was a most devoted woman, and bright example. I have read it with deep interest. She knew your dear sister in India, and corresponded with her. Your brother's name is also mentioned. I think that, next to the Bible, the lives of God's dear people, their Christian experience, and the dealings of God with their souls, is most profitable. It stirs one up to diligence, and to press forward to great things. I have felt more than ever, since I read the labours of this dear saint, what a poor unprofitable servant I am, and have been led to cry to the Lord for more of the mighty influence of His Holy Spirit. Mrs. Winslow mentions the Maternal Association formed in India, and God's especial blessing upon it in answer to praying mothers. You will see, too, that revivals are not confined to America, but are wherever God gives a wrestling spirit for them, and His people are looking out for the fulfilment of His promise. It has very greatly delighted me to see how Christians of different denominations live and cling together when away from home, and feel they are engaged in one common cause. The Church of England, Presbyterians, Baptists, Wesleyan missionaries, all aiding each other in this blessed work and labour of love. Oh, for hearts full of the love of Christ!"

She again more distinctly refers to the happy influence of this beautiful and soul-stirring missionary biography, in a letter to her daughter-in-law:—

". . . I rejoice, my dear A———, that you are both comfortable and happy, and believe that you are where the Lord would have you be. Oh, that you may return according to His great goodness, and trace His dear hand in all His tender, gentle dealings. Walk *doubly* close to Him in the day of prosperity, and watch over your heart with a jealous eye, lest it prove a temptation and a snare. Time is short. You have much, my dear daughter, to do for God in a little space. Eternity will be quite long enough to rest. Now is the time for honouring God; and you may be a great help to your husband in the ministry of the blessed word. Oh, that God may keep you both faithful to His work. Read dear Mrs. Harriet Winslow's memoir. I am sure it will do you good. It was sent to me and I lent it to others. Mr. Evans says he cannot be thankful enough that I ever placed it in his hands. It has made him quite an ardent missionary at home. John-street is now a missionary church; and already one of their own number is going forth to carry the glad tidings of the gospel to the heathen."

Few brighter jewels will adorn Harriet Winslow's crown than this.* To have been instrumental by her holy, self-denying labours in a foreign field, long after she had passed to that

---

* Among those jewels is the following:

"A short time since, there arrived one evening in a small village in the western part of Indiana, a man in middle life, clad in the garb of a sailor. His athletic form, dark eye, and death-like paleness, together with the peculiar bearing which a sailor alone possesses, drew around him at once a peculiar interest. He had spent his youth and early manhood on the ocean, amid the toils and perils of a sailor's life. He had enjoyed, in one of the New England States, the blessings of an early education, and the instruction of a *pious mother*. But that mother had long before gone down to her grave, sorrowing over the waywardness and absence of her wandering son; while he, far away from the home of his childhood, and the influence of a *mother's* prayers, had become a reckless and ungodly sailor. He mingled among the vicious and profane. He forgot his *mother's* warnings, and became a swearer and an infidel. Broken down at length, by the excessive toils of seafaring life, and the influence of the burning climes he had traversed, and under the influence of an incurable disease, he was sinking rapidly to the grave. He had now turned his face to his own native shore, and on the evening I have mentioned above, had arrived at the house of an only sister to die.

"The neighbours and friends all flocked around him to see and hear a son of the ocean. But he was melancholy and silent. He foresaw the fate that awaited him. He knew that he was doomed soon to *die*, and to enter upon that dark uncertain future, which he had for many years tried to believe to be only a phantom of the imagination. But now he had no ungodly companions about him to laugh away his fears. His thoughts ran back to his early life. He remembered the warnings and counsels of his mother, now no more. He called to mind the tracts that had been given him, and how he had slighted the faithful admonitions he had received.

"Christian friends now gathered around his dying bedside, and en-crown, in awakening in behalf of the work to which she consecrated her youth, and in which she sacrificed her life, a deep, earnest, practical sympathy in the heart of *such* a Christian and *such* a minister, and, through him, of influencing hundreds more with a zeal for Christ, which still lives and acts, is an honour before which earth's proudest, brightest laurels pale. Such is the deathless influence and the reward of a life devoted to God!

deavoured to point him to the Redeemer of lost mankind. He lingered on for weeks, sometimes in the agony of despair, sometimes buried in the most melancholy stupor: at length, through the pardoning mercy of Christ, he found peace in believing. Then, oh, what a change came over his whole appearance. A smile of heavenly joy now lighted up his pallid features. His tongue was now unloosed, and he was constantly conversing with those around him of the preciousness of the Saviour he had found.

"He spoke, too, with mingled feelings of sorrow and interest, of the efforts that had been made for his salvation by Christian passengers on board his ship while he was a sailor. He took particular delight in speaking of the lamented HARRIET WINSLOW, and of her voyage to India, on board the 'Indus,' in which vessel he was then an officer. 'I well remember,' said he, his dying eye brightening with animation,—' I well remember that devoted missionary band, who then sailed to their field of labour in our vessel. Mrs. WINSLOW, in particular, I can *never* forget. She was so kind and faithful, so persevering and constant in her endeavours to arrest our attention, and le d us to reflect on our awful condition, that I have always wondered why I did not then become a Christian, with some others of the crew. But I stifled all my convictions, and put off the all-important concerns of my soul. Some of the tracts she gave I read, others I threw away; but I could never throw away or get rid of her faithful admonitions. They have always followed me. In the ocean storm—amid the fierce howlings of the tempest, when a yawning eternity was at my feet, her sweet, kind voice of admonition was sounding on my ear, wherever I went, among my profane associates on shipboard, or in the haunts of vice on the shore. When I consider how she had left for ever the home of her childhood, and her dear brother and friends behind, forsaking all the pleasant associations of her early life, to go and spend her days among an ignorant and barbarous people, I could not withstand such arguments against my scepticism. There must certainly be a reality in the religion of Christ. And, then, the delightful memoir of her, prepared by her husband, I have read it many times. Oh, it is all true! She *was* a Christian, and now I hope to meet her in heaven.'

"During the few last days of his life, he spoke frequently, with tears of gratitude, of Mrs. Winslow, and enjoined on all his friends to obtain and read the interesting memoir of her life. He died in the triumph of *faith* in a glorious Redeemer, whom he had, through nearly his whole life, slighted and despised.

"Dear reader, here you have an example of the wide-spread influence of Christian effort. That same good seed which was sown twenty-eight years ago on board a ship on the ocean, we find springing up in the centre of the great West."

CHAPTER VIII.

'It is a certain fact,' remarks Foster, 'that whenever a man prays aright, he forgets the philosophy of it, and feels as if his supplications *really would* make a difference in the determinations and conduct of the Deity. In this spirit are the prayers recorded in the Bible.' Mrs. Winslow, whose life was baptized in devotion, whose soul was clad with prayer as with a garment, presents a striking illustration of this beautiful thought. While ever deeply conscious of the solemnity of prayer, recognizing it to be, what it truly is, the most exalted exercise of the soul, the most elevated state of thought and feeling of which the mind is susceptible,—yet none engaged in the exercise with more simple views or with a more childlike spirit than she. Convinced that God answered prayer in a way consonant with the Divine purpose, and worthy of His own character, she yet so wrestled, and argued, and reasoned with Him, as if, in the words of the profound thinker we have just quoted, her 'supplications really could make a difference in the determination and conduct of the Deity.' And so must we approach the mercy-seat, not as philosophers, but as Christians,—not as slaves, but as children, feeling that if prayer cannot move God to us, prayer yet can move the lowly supplicant towards God. The 'Thoughts' we are about to glean from her private record and her letters, will give us a deeper insight into the interior of her inner life, and exhibit her views on some important doctrinal and experimental points of divine truth.

ON COMMUNION WITH GOD.

"How little is this understood! A cold, formal, heartless prayer often; and if not in God's own children altogether heartless, yet how little real communion,—oh, how little! No interchange of love, no confession of sin, no adoring gratitude, no emptying of the burdened heart into the loving heart of God. This is communion, and such as even the angels themselves behold with delight, while they can but imperfectly understand the happiness known only to the saints of God. How was I privileged this morning, confessing my own and my children's sins, and giving myself and them up into the Lord's hand, to do with us as seemeth Him good."

"*Taplow, July 9th.*—The Lord has been very gracious in suffering me to draw near to Him, and granting me much of his sensible presence. Dr. Love, in his 'Letters,' describes my experience better than I can myself. If ever my heart truly rejoices, it is in the view of what God is, as seen in Christ, irrespective of my personal interest, and yet not losing sight of my union to Christ. Dr. Love, whose attainments were giant-like, compared with my poor speck of knowledge, expresses this more fully; but his experience is mine. On the same ladder the Lord has placed my foot, though he is higher up by many rounds than I. When the character of God is unfolded in Christ,—His infinite greatness, overpowering goodness, and glorious perfections,—my soul is filled with inexpressible joy; I feel swallowed up in their vastness, and weep, without being able to say why I weep. Oh, if a glimpse now and then is so overpowering, what must the full vision of that glory be? The body here could not contain it. God be praised for the little view, and for the full revelation that awaits us in that better, brighter world above."

"12th.—Dr. Love remarks, 'How sweet is the bitterness of that repentance which is truly divine and gracious! The same light which opens the springs of godly sorrow, also uncovers the fountain of divine joy.' These words express my own experience, and which I had thought was peculiar to myself; and have therefore seldom advanced it to others, lest I should mislead or perplex those to whom I wish to do good. Still I think dear Dr. Love did not deal sufficiently with the manhood of Christ. He seemed to look too little to God in Jesus. What comfort or sympathy can a poor sinner desire from looking to an infinitely holy God out of Christ? When God spoke to men, He came down clothed with a cloud; and when this same God speaks to us, it is in Jesus, robed in the cloud of our sinless humanity. Thus revealing Himself, we look and live. It is then we behold Him in all the milder rays of divine light and glory, and adore, love, and bless Him who says, *Fear not, it is I.*"

TO HER SON H——.

"I received your long and interesting letter, and thank you for it. . . . When you enlisted under the banner of King Jesus, you commenced the life of a soldier, and are therefore called, as *a good soldier of Jesus Christ*, to fight manfully. Your enemies are the word, Satan, and the flesh; this last is the greatest of all; it lies down and rises up with you, and wherever you are, this enemy is always at hand. But you are exhorted to put on the whole armour of God, and to stand; and by faith in Christ you shall conquer. Keep your eye steadily upon Jesus. Be not surprised at the conflict you wage; it is an evidence that you are Christ's true disciple. If you were not a possessor of spiritual life, you would have nothing to oppose you from within. Those who are dead in sin know nothing of this warfare. A corpse floats down with the stream; but where there is living faith in the soul, it stems the tide, buffets with the waves, and makes its way through all that opposes it. Be of good courage, keep close to Jesus, and you have nothing to fear from within or without. God, who is our *Sun and shield, will give grace and glory; and no good thing will He withhold from them that walk uprightly.* Be diligent in the use of all the means of grace, and may the Lord abundantly bless your soul, and provide for all your wants."

To the same.—"I did not mean to write to you this time, but you are so good yourself in writing to me, that I could not bear to pass you by. . . . It is a mercy to be kept with our eyes, and our hearts too, up to the dear Saviour, that we may be ready when He gives the summons. This world is nothing more than a wretched, dying vanity. But the bright world to which we are travelling has substantial blessing and happiness unutterable to bestow. Oh, then, what folly to grieve here, and suffer our affections to wander from God! I am glad you attend Mr. S——'s. The prayer-meetings will revive your fainting soul. I do not recollect what first led me there, but it was the Lord who directed my steps. *The steps of a good man are ordered by the Lord.* May He meet with your soul and bless you. Many a time have I poured out my heart for you in that sanctuary, and my fervent prayers were offered up for your salvation. Those were blessed times. I often think of them now. May Jesus keep our soul going out after Him. I had rather seek Him sorrowing from morning to night, than not to seek Him at all, or feel cold and barren in my soul. Kiss the little ones for grandmamma."

TO HER SON, R. F. W——.

". . . I earnestly hope nothing will induce you to relinquish your habits of temperance. How earnestly and constantly I pray that God may keep you from everything that, by slow and insidious steps, might lead to certain and, perhaps, irremediable ruin. Anything in the form of drink, but simple water,—I mean, of course, of an intoxicating nature,—is dangerous. I have, in the course of my life witnessed such sad, such awful effects resulting from moderate drinking, that my heart sickens at the very remembrance of it. Place nothing to your lips stronger than water. No one but God can know how anxious I am that all my professing children may be kept walking in the fear of God, and in the love of the Spirit. Remember Him who loved you unto death; live to Him and for Him, and resolve rather to die than do aught dishonouring to His dear name, who, in so remarkable a manner, called you out of darkness into His marvellous light. Dear child, bear with a fond and anxious mother; for you know not how my heart goes out after you. The Lord has wonderfully kept me these twenty-eight years in His blessed way, and has never permitted me to bring dishonour upon His dear cause. And yet I feel that I as much require His upholding hand, and His restraining grace, at this moment, as I did at the first. *Let him that thinketh he standeth take heed lest he fall.* Jesus is very precious to my soul. I feel I cannot live without Him. He is my all-in all. The world, and all its glory and riches, is as dross to me in comparison of Him whom my soul loveth. And yet I find the Christian life to be one of constant warfare, and feel, at times, as though a host were encamped against me.

"Again, let me exhort you to keep close to Christ. Make Him your Counsellor and your Confidant; Him to whom you may entrust all your concerns, and into whose ear you may breathe all your wants. Keep an open heart with Christ; you need no other friend. Do all you can for His cause, and He will take care of you. Walk in uprightness before Him, in heart, lip, and life. Should you discover failures, go at once and confess them, and get your pardon sealed to you afresh by the Holy Ghost. Never keep a sense of guilt upon the conscience when it can be removed at once by the blood of Christ. There is not a more holy exercise in the Christian's life than the confession of sin to God. I mean by this, that confessing sin to God has a sanctifying influence on the heart, maintains purity, and keeps the conscience tender. You need not wait until you can retire and fall upon your knees; you can do it in a moment. The heart lifted up in silent prayer is sufficient. *I, the Lord, search the heart.* I have no greater joy than to see my children walking in the truth. Put on Christ, walk in Christ, and may God bless you and make you a blessing."

The subject of prophetic truth, doubtless the more solemnly urged upon her attention by the remarkable aspect of the times, of which she was a close and spiritual observer, began at this period to interest and occupy her thoughts. The doctrine of the Lord's second coming,—the signs which appeared to herald, and the events which probably would be ushered in by his glorious advent,—seemed to be the great truth which particularly arrested her attention. We gather her sentiments and feelings on these interesting topics of inquiry, from her diary and correspondence :—

"Awoke this morning at about six o'clock, and read 'Hugh White on the Second Advent,' and was led to lift up my heart to the Lord to direct my mind into this important truth, and enlighten what was dark in me on the subject. In the course of the day, felt much tried at my want of spirituality, my coldness and worldliness. I besought the Lord to revive in my soul every drooping grace of the Spirit, to save me from sad declension, quicken me afresh by the power of the Holy Ghost, and draw me nearer and yet nearer to himself."

"My dear O——,   Lord's day, Torrington-square.

"Have you ever read the Rev. Hugh White on the Second Advent? If you have not, obtain it, and read it. I am perusing it with deep interest, and, as far as I have gone, I can enter fully into his views. I am longing to have my eyes open to the subject more than they were. It appears to me a delightful theme for close and prayerful investigation. Do give it your attention. May the Lord unfold His own truth to your soul and mine! Mr. Evans's mind is also opening to this truth. Could I but be sure that He would indeed *soon* come, how my soul would rejoice; but of this I cannot so far see any clear evidence. Oh, for more weanedness from the world! Oh, to love Jesus more, and to have Him more in our thoughts! How soon we *may* behold Him in all His glory, coming in the clouds of heaven, with all His saints and holy angels! May the Lord keep us watching and waiting, and looking for the summons, and enable us to say, *Come, Lord Jesus, come quickly!* I grieve that I have so long neglected to search into this glorious subject; but I am only now just beginning to investigate it, with much prayer, as I read that the Lord would lead me into the truth, and keep me from all error in judgment. But as it opens upon me, I feel my soul led out in grateful praise and thanksgiving. Do get the book I have mentioned, and read it with prayerful attention."

The following unfinished letter, addressed to her pastor, on the subject of the Lord's Coming, and found among her papers, it is believed was never sent :—

"MY DEAR AND BELOVED BROTHER,

"I send you the enclosed, and hope, if you can spare the time, you will give it a perusal, and compare it with the Word. Truly it behoves us, as much as it did Daniel, to search diligently to know and understand the signs of the times. God was far from being angry with His servant at that time; and if the apostles wrote and spake so much of the coming of the Lord in their days, as it is now nearer to us than it was to them, it is assuredly of the greatest consequence to examine for ourselves. Truly I can say, for one, *Come, Lord Jesus, come quickly!* I trust you will make time to investigate this subject, and may the Lord enlighten all our minds. That some great movement is going on in the kingdom of Christ on earth, is as evident to my mind as that I live. We cannot close our eyes to what is passing all around us. The wheels of God's wonderful providence are moving onward, and I think that none who love Him but must be prayerfully anxious to watch the way He is taking with His church. My heart is at times overwhelmed with the thought of His near approach. How delightful the prospect of being with Jesus, our dearest and best friend on earth and in heaven! To *see* Him whom we have loved, communed with, confided in, gone to in every time of trouble, and found Him a present help! And then to meet with those dear to our hearts, who have got there before us to welcome us home! I long to see Jesus; He is very, very precious to my soul, and I trust He is to yours."

To one of her sons in America, who held what she considered extreme views of the Lord's coming, she thus faithfully writes :—

"...... There is no doubt but that the coming of the Lord draws nigh, but as to the *exact time* no man knows, nor can know; therefore you have been wrong in fixing a time, and running into extravagance, and causing the infidel to boast and tauntingly to ask, *Where is the promise of His coming?* The believer is so to live, that whether he goes to Christ, or Christ comes to him, he may be found with his lamp brightly burning, ready to obey the summons. While you have fixed in your mind that you shall certainly be on earth at the coming of the Lord, should death arrest you, you might in one sense be totally unprepared for the event, and probably disappointment and anguish would fill your heart. Such has been the case with some, who as fully expected the Lord as you do; and yet the Lord sent for them, and they had to pass through the dark valley of the shadow of death, that they might swell His train when He really did come. Two members of our church were sadly tried when the Lord sent for them, and for some time their minds were greatly distressed, and they met the last enemy with reluctance. Now, see the danger of fixing the time as to the designs of God towards us. I long for the coming of Jesus, and would leave the world; but as I know not the day nor the hour, let me be ready to meet Him in whatever way He might appoint. *It is not for you to know the times or the seasons which the Father hath put in His own power.*"

It has been remarked—and the reader will have gathered from these pages confirmation of its truth—that she was a close and intelligent observer of the characteristics of the times in which she lived. Events which to others might pass as trivial and meaningless, would, to her deeply spiritual and observing eye, be replete with interest and pregnant with significance. She read the journals of the day, and studied the movements of the age, with but one object,—the development of God's purpose in the progress of His truth and kingdom in the world. It is thus she records her sentiments on this subject:—

"The Lord God will sift His church, and throroughly purge His floor. He has commanded His ministering servants to separate the precious from the vile. This duty they have most awfully neglected, but now He is about to do it Himself; and what He does will be *well* done. Satan is endeavouring to overturn, but God holds him in His hand, and will overrule all his wicked designs, for the welfare of His church, the honour of His truth, and the glory of His name. So shall the precious be separated from the vile, and the world be driven out of His church. The work began in Scotland, has commenced in England, and will go on until the whole is accomplished. Then comes the Bridegroom, in the clouds of heaven, to meet His bride, purified by fire from all her dross. The time is drawing nigh. Everything indicates it. How strange that any who profess to be the disciples of Christ, should be indifferent to what is passing before their eyes at this momentous period! Surely the wise virgins are slumbering. Oh, that the church would awake and rejoice at the glorious prospect that is before her! The Lord Jesus is on His way. Puseyism is the forerunner of His second coming. It is preparing the way of the Lord. How truly can God overrule all things to accomplish his own purposes,—even Satan's device, to work His will, and do His chosen people good."

"CLOUDS BREAKING."

"The Lord is about to do a great work in the nominally professing church of Christ. He is preparing the way for His second advent. Error, in the shape of semi-popery, is spreading like wildfire, and this will finally consume the chaff, and leave the pure wheat yet more pure. Satan thinks differently; but God designs much good to His church, by permitting the abounding of this error. The church of Christ has nothing to do (in its union) with this world; but Satan has contrived to mix up the world with the church, and now a holy and jealous God has put His own hand to the work, and a complete and final separation will take place. I have long seen His blessed hand like a bright light rising in the darkness that has obscured the glory of His church. To me, it grew more distinct as the darkness grew more palpable; and while many, trembling for the ark of God, were quaking for fear, I have been enabled to keep my eye upon the little bright cloud which grew brighter to my view. And oh, how my soul has rejoiced! for I could discern the faithfulness and love of my God, in that He was not unmindful of his promise, and that His eye was upon, and His heart still toward, His church."

It was probably in its prophetic light that she was led to study the Lord's parable of "the pearl of great price," and to offer an interpretation differing entirely from the one generally received.

"I can truly say," she writes in her diary, "O Lord, come quickly, and take Thy one church—Thy bride—to the home prepared for her. This is the 'pearl of great price,' the *church*—not Christ—hidden in the field. Jesus comes down, parts with the last drop of His precious blood to purchase this 'pearl,' and also the field—the world—for the sake of the pearl which is the church. The world is now kept in existence for the sake of the church alone; and when the church is complete and brought home, the world, being of no further use, will be burnt up and destroyed. Now the matter in dispute stands thus; either the church purchases Christ, or Christ purchases the church. As the church had nothing wherewith to purchase Christ, then Christ must have purchased the church; and such was the magnitude of the price, that none save God's own Son could have bought it. In *this sense* Christ died for the whole world. He purchased the world for the sake of the treasure that was hid in the world. To sum it up in a few words,—'the pearl of great price,' and the 'treasure hidden in the field,' are identical—the elect church of God. Christ parts with all that He had, even life itself, to complete the purchase; and on the day of His public espousals with His church He will wear the pearl in His crown of rejoicing; and the world in which it was hid, and from whence it was taken, will then be consumed."

As sustaining this interpretation of the parable, she was wont to quote Toplady's beautiful and familiar lines:

> "Deathless Principle, arise!
> Soar, thou native of the skies!
> *Pearl of price, by Jesus bought,*
> To his glorious likeness wrought;
> Go, to shine before his throne,
> Deck his meditatorial crown:
> Go, his triumph to adorn;
> Made for God, to God return."

The study of God's general providence necessarily implies attention to His particular providences. The eye that is broad awake to scan with prayerful interest each new sign in the political and ecclesiastical firmament, eager to trace some indication of God's unfolding purposes towards his church, was not likely to overlook His more especial dealings in individual history. We find her, therefore, thus recording what she entitles

"GOD'S DEALINGS IN HIS LEADINGS."

"The text last evening is from the 146th Psalm, 8th verse: *The Lord raiseth them that are bowed down.* It was excellent truth, and most comforting to the tried believer. How little do we think of whose care we are under, and whose loving eye is ever guiding our way through the wilderness, causing all things we meet to work together for our good! Thus has He led me. He has brought me into the wilderness to teach me, to lead me to cling closer to Himself; to brighten every grace of the Spirit; to wean from a dying world, and to show me this was not my rest, because it was polluted. Here He gave me precious faith, and then tried the faith He gave. When bowed down, He lifted me up. He shut me out of the vain things of a poor empty world, and shut me in to Himself. He gave me my work to do, and fitted me for it. Every moment was occupied in doing His will. Whatever I needed I went to Him for, and never was denied one good thing. He proved himself the Husband to the widow, the Father to the fatherless, the home of the stranger. His name to me has been a strong tower, into which I could flee and be safe. His Spirit came upon me with all His life-giving, converting, and reconverting power; filling my dwelling with the richest blessings of heaven. Oh, what returns can I make for all His abounding goodness to me? Shall I not sing the loudest in heaven?"

"GRATEFUL RECOLLECTIONS."

"Reading a New York religious journal, I observed an account of the erection of a new place of worship in Oliver street, the former one having been destroyed by fire. This little circumstance recalled to my mind many trying yet hallowed scenes that have passed away for ever, yet cannot be forgotten. It was in that sanctuary I sometimes worshipped, the pulpit being then occupied by the late Rev. JOHN WILLIAMS. When my soul has been oppressed and desolate, finding comfort nowhere else, I have repaired thither, and have found it. Dear Mr. Williams was an eminent man of God, and a deeply experienced preacher of the gospel. The precious truths, as they fell with so much weight from his lips, were often clothed with a remarkable degree of the unction of the Spirit. And although I have gone there often with my heart overwhelmed within me, I have yet been enabled, by his ministrations, to look afresh to the Rock that was higher than I. Oh, that I could then have seen how blessedly and wisely the Lord was training me and mine for better things to come; causing me to pass under the rod, that He might bring me into the bond of the covenant!"

"THE TRUE SOURCE OF SPIRITUAL JOY."

"I believe that our joy and rejoicing in Christ Jesus depends upon our faith, that is, our believing more firmly the matter-of-fact truths revealed to us in the Bible. Do I *believe* that Jesus Christ lived, and died, and rose again from the grave, and is now *alive* in heaven, and is there for us? In proportion as we are thoroughly persuaded of this, we can and must rejoice. It is written, *In whom ye also trusted; after that ye believed, ye were sealed with the Holy Spirit of promise, which is the earnest of our inheritance.* Eph. i. 13. Therefore it follows, that in proportion to our firm belief of these divine verities, these glorious realities, we shall not only rejoice, but be transformed into the Divine image. Another mistake common to many Christians, is the habit of looking for ever *within* for some evidence of their adoption; and finding nothing there satisfactory, they do not and cannot rejoice. Now, this is a serious defect. It is not by looking within ourselves, but, on the contrary, it is by looking quite out of ourselves, and directing the eye alone to Christ,—to what Christ is, and where Christ is,—that can alone give us real consolation; and in proportion to our faith in Him, we not only rejoice, but our evidences brighten, and the Spirit within, whose office it is to glorify Christ, bears witness with our spirit that we are born of God. The life of God in the soul of man is one of the most glorious works of God. It is a greater work than that of creation. He says, *Let there be light,* and in a moment there is in the soul *the light of life.* The sinner looks to Jesus, believes, and is saved. He lives now for God and for a glorious eternity. The Holy Ghost, having full possession of the soul, carries on the great work of sanctification. He has written on the heart, *Holiness unto the Lord;* and the constant prayer of the renewed soul, as a result, will be, *Lead me in the way of uprightness.*"

"THE CHRISTIAN JOURNEY.

"Life is a journey, often a short one, and always uncertain. But there is another journey. The believer is travelling through a waste howling wilderness, to another and a glorious region, where ineffable delight and happiness await us. The road is narrow, the entrance strait, so strait that thousands miss it and perish in the wilderness; but true believers, under the teaching and convoy of the Holy Ghost, find it and walk in it. The King, in His infinite love and compassion, has made a hedge about them, separating and defending them from the many beasts of prey that lurk around them; and although they hear their howlings and behold their threatnings, they are safe from their power. But their strongest foe is within themselves,—a heart deceitful above all things and desperately wicked. From this there is no escape but by constant watchfulness, and earnest cries to their best Friend and Guide for protection. And were it not for this faithful Guide, how often, discouraged by reason of the way, would they turn back! But He watches over them by night and by day, strengthens them when weak, upholds them when falling, encourages them when cast down, defends them when attacked, provides for them when in need, leads them by living streams, and causes them there to lie down in pleasant pastures, and on sunny banks. And as they advance they obtain brighter views of the good land they are nearing, and they long to see the King in His beauty, and the land that is yet very far off, and to meet those that have already arrived on that happy shore."

"GODLY SINCERITY."

"Never pay a compliment at the expense of conscience or of truth. *Fear God.* Never say what you do not really feel. Confess those sins of heart which no eye sees but God's. Assume nothing that does not belong to you, and comes not from your heart. Beware of adopting another person's experience as your own. Let the fear of God dwell richly in you. Let your heart be right with Him. Do all with your eye upon eternity. Think little of time, except to improve every moment. Have an abiding sense of the Lord's presence with you, and do not be satisfied without it. Never suffer your politeness to carry you beyond truth. *Fear God.* Let truth dwell in your heart, and nothing but truth flow from your lips.

Pray, and look for the answer. Aim always to have the consciousness of God's ear harkening. Be not satisfied with an empty, lifeless form, nor leave the throne of grace without a recognition. Honour the Spirit, and the Spirit will honour you. Plead for His indwelling power. Grieve Him not, lest your heart grow cold, and your soul become barren. Strive to live on high, and you will live holily; and to live holily is to live happily."

"UNHOLY JEALOUSY."

'A suspicious, jealous spirit is one of the most corroding evils and uncomfortable states of mind an unhappy individual can be tormented with. It makes its subject, and all others, miserable. It impairs confidence, weakens friendship, separates the best friends, and produces incalculable mischief far and wide. It was jealousy that hurled the sinning angels from heaven. It was jealousy that caused the fall of our first parents, and drove them from paradise. It was jealousy that led to the first murder. It was jealousy that produced hatred and revenge in Esau towards Jacob. It is marked in God's word as a hateful, God-dishonouring, soul-destroying sin. Let us beware of it, watch and pray against it, and the moment we detect its workings within us, crush it at once. It is the offspring of Satan, and the destroyer of mankind. Let us also beware of engendering and encouraging dislike to any one with whom we associate. This evil unchecked, tends to corrode the whole inner man, sours the temper, and causes us to be an annoyance to every one around us. The instant we discover the hateful feeling, let us go at once to Jesus, lay the heart open before Him, unveil the festering wound to His loving eye, and He will heal, and give us the victory over ourselves."

"THE UNITY OF THE SPIRIT."

"The Spirit recognises His own image wherever He meets with it. If I have the Holy Spirit dwelling in me, (and if I have not the Spirit of Christ, I am none of His,) the same Spirit dwelling in another will acknowledge it. The Spirit is a Spirit of love as well as of holiness. And this He has made the test of our sonship. *We know we have passed from death unto life, because we love the brethren.* Not brethren only of the church at Ephesus, or of the church at Rome, but brethren in Christ having his own blessed image engraven on the renewed soul. Whenever we feel not this spirit of union, we might well doubt our spiritual life and our allegiance to the Son of God. If I meet a beggar in the street, or a poor woman at an applestall, or one of the great of the earth, and discern in that individual the Spirit of Christ, I ask not of what church he is, or to what communion he belongs; my heart goes out in love to him, and this is the one and self-same Spirit recognising His own image in another. How is it with you? Do you love Christ's image wherever and in whomsoever you meet it? Do you speak unkindly or think uncharitably of any of God's redeemed ones, because they are not of your sect? Then you may well doubt your sincerity. The love of the Spirit—the love which he inspires in the heart —is an unselfish love, a holy love, a uniting, cementing love, a bond of union to the one family of God, and to Christ the one Head. Again I repeat the unfailing test, *By this shall all men know that ye are my disciples, if ye have love one to another.*"

"GROWTH IN GRACE."

"There is such a state as growing in grace. Not that I believe, in one sense, I am a whit better now than I ever was; for *in my flesh there dwelleth no good thing.* The flesh is the same that it ever was, and will continue the same until laid in the grave. But is there not such a thing as knowing more of God, and more of the absolute certainty of the truth of the gospel? Is there not such a thing as knowing more of Christ, His excellence, preciousness, and fulness, through the teaching of the Holy Spirit? And will not this advancing knowledge confirm and establish our souls, strengthen our confidence, promote our happiness, and lead to holiness of heart, and of life? This growth in divine knowledge, this knowing more of God in Christ, is calculated to invigorate the new man, and thus to keep in subjection the evil which we feel is ever striving for the mastery. This is growing in grace, and this is grace growing in us. Then let us not grieve the Holy Spirit, this Divine Indweller of our hearts. Also to know more of our wretched, lost condition, our helplessness and unworthiness, is growing in grace; for this view of our state will cause us to value that precious blood that can alone atone for our sins, and to cleave more closely to Christ, endearing Him to the heart, and glorifying Him in the life."

8*

The writings of the Rev. C. G. Finney, an American Presbyterian clergyman of much and deserved celebrity, are extensively and favourably known in this country. Some of his theological views were not considered as strictly sound; favouring, as it was supposed, the notion of a certain degree of moral ability in the sinner. It would appear from the following quotation, found in Mrs. Winslow's journal, that his views on this point have become essentially modified; thus ranking him more decidedly amongst the orthodox, as he previously was amongst the most zealous and useful divines of his age. It is with peculiar satisfaction we transcribe the extract for the present work:—

"In a recent publication by the Rev. Mr. Finney, I met with the following statement from his pen:—'I have thought that (at least in a great many instances) sufficient stress has not been laid on the necessity of Divine influence on the hearts of Christians and sinners. I am confident that I have sometimes erred in this respect myself. In order to rouse sinners and backsliders from their self-justifying pleas and refuges, I have laid (and I doubt not others have also laid) too much stress upon the *natural ability* of sinners, to the neglect of showing the nature and extent of their dependence upon the grace of God and the influence of His Spirit. This has grieved the Spirit of God. His work not being honoured by being made sufficiently prominent, and not being able to get the glory to Himself of his own work, He has withdrawn or withheld His influence.' How much it is to be regretted that Mr. Finney did not make this discovery earlier. Much mischief might have been avoided, and much more substantial good accomplished."

ON THE CONDUCT OF A MINISTER'S WIFE.

". . . . Every time I bow my knees before God, I pray for you that you may be spared to your dear husband, and be increasingly fitted for the all-important work He has given you to do. Oh, how important the care of precious souls—souls that are destined for an endless eternity! A minister's wife is, of all others, placed in the most responsible situation in the church of God. Much of his usefulness depends upon her. She must be a helpmate to the Lord's servant, and a servant of the Lord herself. His mind is to be kept free from the little cares and annoyances that would interrupt and distract him in his studies; and, above all, his ears closed to the trifling gossip of those who talk much, but do little for the cause of a precious Saviour. I am persuaded that Satan is ever on the watch to make a handle of everything to impair the usefulness of God's ministers. Be humble, prayerful, and watchful, always feeling yourself as much called to aid the work in your way as he is in his. And may God bless you both, beloved children."

ON PARENTAL INDULGENCE.

"How necessary it is to bring up children in the nurture and fear of the Lord! Without this, even in a worldly point of view, they and others are often miserable. No children are so happy as those who have been early taught implicit and immediate obedience to a parent's wishes, or will, or commands. Would that parents more universally felt that, when they suffer their children to disobey them, they are absolutely teaching them to sin against God by breaking one of His commandments, and one to which the promise of long life is given. No wonder if God, in just displeasure, remove the child from such tuition. Remember what a solemn and instructive lesson the Holy Ghost has given in the history of Eli. There is much danger, from an amiable wish to gratify a child, of counter-ordering our own orders. If you once direct a child to do a thing, however unpleasant it may be to yourself or the child, insist in firmness upon immediate and full obedience. There should be no demur, nor delay. Prompt obedience is as lovely in a child, as its enforcement is dignified in a parent. The firm and gentle constraint of parental authority commands respect, and even inspires reverence and love in the child towards the parent. Thus, then, if you desire your children should grow up, cherishing for you profound esteem and affection, insist upon this filial duty—the duty of implicit obedience—and commence early. To begin right is the way to end right."

The death of an amiable and much-loved daughter-in-law, the wife of her son E——, whom she had fondled as an infant, and who, in later life, clave to her with an affection the most tender and inseparable, was a sore bereavement. She was never so conscious of her own weakness as when under trial; and yet, to those who knew her best, she never, in reality, more fully exhibited the strong marks of a Christ-clinging,

God-honouring faith as then. This problem will be of easy solution to the Christian. It was at the moment of felt weakness, that Christ's own strength was perfected in her, and His grace found sufficient for her need. A letter to a daughter-in-law in America describes her state of mind under this calamity.

" MY DEAR J――,   Leamington, March 19th, 1844.

"You will be grieved to hear that the Lord has seen fit to lay His heavy hand upon us, and to take to Himself, most unexpectedly, our dear, precious S――. She has gone, leaving us all to mourn her loss, which, I doubt not, is her eternal gain. The stroke has been most afflictive to every member of the family, but to none more so than myself. She was tenderly and deservedly beloved by all, and we shall miss her in a way that few can be missed. To me no daughter could have been more devoted, or more tenderly and sincerely affectionate. During intervals of her illness, her mind was taken up with eternal things, and her thoughts of Jesus were sweet. The Lord had been for some time preparing her for this event—it was a preparation for heaven, for glory, and for the full enjoyment of Himself. During the most trying period of anxiety I ever passed through, the Lord mercifully supported me. Prayer was offered for her by the whole church in John-street, I may say morning, noon, and night; and also by all who had the happiness of knowing her, who could pray. But the Lord had need of her, and He took her from the evil to come. She was an obedient wife, a devoted mother, a loving sister, and a most affectionate daughter to me. I never knew what it was to have a care, when with her. She always thought of me, and everything she imagined would contribute to my comfort, she did. Always cheerful, and never out of temper, her home was made happy for all. I never knew a more unselfish person in my life; her whole aim and study was to make all happy around her. She ever considered her husband's interests above everything else, and to please him was the first thought of her heart. He never left her, but hung over her until the last, with the most tender, heart-rending solicitude. Dear, precious saint; she has escaped from a world of trial, sin, and sorrow, and is now with Him she loved. The stroke has been almost too much for dear E――'s state of health. But after all, there is one Friend from whom death cannot separate us. In imagination I have followed her into the presence of Jesus, witnessed her adoring, sinless gratitude and love; her pure spirit recogniing those once known and dear to her, around the throne of God. My thoughts have been much in heaven, and I seem, sometimes, (so real has it been,) to wish to be there. Dear J——, live more and more for eternity. That the Lord may keep you and me, and all we love, in close readiness for the summons, come when it will, is my prayer."

From her Diary.—"March 20th, 1844.—Dear S——'s death has brought eternal things very near to me. Heaven seems always before me, and in imagination I am constantly there. I long to be gone. I much enjoy, in anticipation, the blessedness of that place where Jesus is, where He unveils His beauteous face, and we shall behold Him without a cloud between. My sweetest meditation, lying down and rising up, or waking in the night, is HEAVEN. Dear S——'s pure spirit walking in white, enjoying the unutterable bliss of perfect freedom from sin, in the presence of Jesus, her dearest, her best friend, is before me. She once heard of Him with the hearing of the ear, but now her eyes behold Him. I can scarcely realize that she has outstripped me in the race, and has reached the goal before me. *The first shall be last, and the last first.* How often have we conversed together of Him, as we walked arm-in-arm to the house of God. Now she sees Him—is at His side—adoring gratitude fills her soul, and boundless love beams in every look. Dear relations, too, meeting to part no more for ever. What do we not owe a good and gracious God for the hope of immortality beyond the dark and dreary grave! Precious S—— was mercifully preserved from all those dismal forebodings, which the thoughts of death and the grave often create in the dying believer. Before she knew her danger she was there, safely housed in the mansion prepared for her. *Thanks be unto God for His unspeakable gift!* And now, my dear Lord, my soul waits and longs for the fruit springing from this dispensation. Oh, let it not pass away without a rich and mighty blessing. It *may*, but God can speak, if not in affliction, yet in prosperity. The work is His. When He begins, none can hinder. If He speaks but the word, it shall be done."

TO A FRIEND.

" DEAR SISTER IN JESUS,— April 4th, 1844.

"Accept my thanks for your little volume; it just came

at a moment when most acceptable and most needed. My beloved daughter's death has brought heaven very near to me. It appears but a step and I am there. I have followed her departed spirit into the presence of Him whom she loved; have beheld her wondering delight, adoring gratitude, and overwhelming love, while she gazed on Him whose precious blood redeemed her soul from all sin and sorrow for ever. I have imagined the recognition of her dear relatives who had gone before her, and have fancied the holy joy of her pure spirit in meeting them again. Oh, heaven is worth living for! A life of trial and of tribulation is as nothing when compared with the mighty blessings that await the believer in Jesus, when he drops the body of sin and of death. After recovering, in some measure, from the shock of her sufferings and death, my mind turned to the bright scene above, and there my soul has been more or less regaled ever since. I have been, and still am, looking to the things that are not seen, and that are eternal. It seems to have raised me some feet above earth, and I pray that I may not only be kept there, but rise higher and still higher. Precious Bible! precious revelation of God's most gracious doings of eternal mercy to such sinners as we are! Oh, to look beyond that dark and dismal grave, and remember the word that says, *Absent from the body, present with the Lord!* My soul does rejoice at this moment in God my Saviour. Oh, He is very, very precious—none like Him on earth or in heaven. Much as I anticipate of happiness in meeting dear, very dear relatives in heaven, it would be no heaven to me if I did not see Jesus, my best, my dearest, my constant friend, who, with unceasing patience, tenderness, and mercy, has followed me through all my wanderings in this wilderness world, and has never, no, never left nor forsaken me for one single moment. To know Him aright, is a little heaven begun below. The nearer we get to Jesus here, the more we taste of the blessedness that awaits us above. Never, dear friend, be satisfied with what you know of Him now. Press on to know more and more. And what a humiliating reflection it is, that we require often trial upon trial to rouse us from our slumbers, not only to our duty, but to our sweetest, highest privileges! Dearest Jesus, help Thy pilgrims to live more like pilgrims, above a poor dying world, and more in full view of the glory that awaits them when they shall see Thee face to face. Dear friend, forgive me; but my heart is full of this one subject, and I can seldom write, speak, or think of anything else. Precious S——'s death has been in some measure new life to my soul. I thank God for it; oh, it was a mercy to her and a mercy to me. Jesus does all things well. I cease now to think of her in the grave; I see her with the eye of faith alone. Let us aim in all things to follow Him who, despising this world's show, left us an example how we should walk. The world and its nothings are often a sad snare to God's saints. Oh, that by faith we may overcome it all, and keep close to Jesus. *Ye are not of the world, even as I am not of the world.* Let us try and not attend to its gewgaws, and keep a more steadfast, unwavering eye upon Christ. He has gone a little before us, and stands beckoning us to follow. One word before I close. Live for eternity. Let go your hold upon the world. I need this exhortation myself, as much, perhaps more, than you do; but receive it from an aged pilgrim who, as she nears the solemn scenes of eternity, and more realizes the inexpressible joys that await, and the welcome that will greet us there, is anxious that all the believers who are travelling the same road, might have their hearts and minds more disentangled from earth and earthly things, and themselves unreservedly given to Christ. Have your lamp trimmed and brightly burning, for every day and every hour bring us nearer and nearer to our home."

The heart must be right with God, that can maintain a fixed, filial, and confidential intercourse with the Holy One. As the proximity of the compass to some false attraction deranges its movements, and perils the bark it steers; so the Christian's heart, brought too near some creature object, or some earthly good, flies off from God, and thus disturbs the serenity, and retards the sanctity of the soul. But how enviable the conscious nearness to God, unveiled in the following familiar epistle to her family!—

"I could not forbear telling you how graciously God is dealing with my soul. There seems no distance between the Lord and your unworthy mother. He draws nearer and still nearer day by day. I cannot describe, for language fails me, His exceeding gentleness, His tender, His almost *speaking* love to my soul. How condescending is He in all His dealings and varying dispensations! I go to Him often in perplexity, not knowing where to look; and as a babe is hushed to quietness, soothed and comforted on its mother's bosom, so the Lord calms and quiets me. *Even down to old age I will carry you,* is His promise fulfilled in my experience. I cannot describe the inconceivable enjoyment, mingled with much sorrow for sin, I have had for these many weeks. And as I cannot descriae, so I must leave it, praying that should the Lord ever cause you to feel the world, and all that you have loved, insufficient to impart one grain of real happiness, you may find in Jesus all, and more than tongue can express, of what your soul needs—an everflowing, overflowing fountain of indescribable happiness and holy enjoyment. This is my sweet experience. I lie at His feet a poor, saved sinner, in sure and certain hope of eternal life already begun—heaven foreshadowed and foretasted. May this encourage you, in a time of deep need, to apply for, and expect similar blessings. Never, never could it enter into the heart of man to conceive the rich gifts there are in the heart of Christ for His saints. But He has revealed a little to my weary spirit, and God be praised for His wondrous condescension and grace, so richly bestowed upon the chief of sinners.

The communion of the Lord's Supper has ever been regarded by the spiritual Christian as an occasion of especial nearness to Christ. It is then he seems to be brought the closest to the cross. All other objects vanish from his view, and, like the disciples on the mount, he feels himself with 'Jesus only.' This was pre-eminently Mrs. Winslow's experience. The occurrence of this institution was always a season of brokenhearted and endeared communion with Jesus. She brought nothing of her own to the Lord's table but her emptiness. Lying at this beautiful gate of the temple in all her helplessness and need, she fastened her believing eyes but upon one object, 'expecting to receive something from Him,' or 'seeking to catch something out of His mouth.' It was seldom indeed, if ever, that she was sent empty away. Happy for the church of God would it be if such scriptural and simple views of the nature and design of this ordinance more generally prevailed! She thus describes her feelings on this hallowed occasion:—

"I trust the Lord was with us last evening, at His own table to bless us. It is generally to me a feast of love, and of close communion with Christ. I then feel I am more at liberty to make any especial request at the hands of the Lord. While I am trying in my poor way to remember Him, is it likely that He will not at that moment more especially remember me, the child who is looking full in His blessed face, for an answer to her request? It is a season of remembrance on both sides. Jesus and His redeemed one meet together in close contact and sacred fellowship. It is, too, a season of melting love. The heart is softened; Christ crucified for my sins is placed before the eye; deep repentance and holy affection fill the soul."

It was to one of her family passing through a season of relative and painful anxiety that she penned the following letter so replete with comfort, and glowing with holy, elevated feeling :—

"*In the day of my trouble I will call upon Thee, for Thou wilt answer me.* The Lord has favoured me this morning with such a blessed interview, that my heart is full of His goodness, and expression fails me quite. He is the same, the very same that He ever was; and all that He says is true, blessedly true. He spake to Abraham, to Jacob, and to Moses, and to all the prophets; and He speaks to you and to me, the unworthiest of all, the poorest of the poor, and the vilest of the vile. Every new trial, and every fresh cross, drive me into the very bosom of Jesus; and it seems as if I could lie there, and feel the very throbbings of His loving heart. In the cup of trial we are called to drink, there is no wrath, all is love, though faith may be tried, and we may for a season weep. Dearest child, language fails me to tell you of the sweet condescension of my God and your God, to my waiting, wrestling soul, this morning. I could do little but weep, and my tears fall even while I write. Surely His name is love, and we shall see how needful this trial of our faith was. Whatever draws or drives us to Christ is a mighty blessing. Who can be permitted to have intercourse with God, and not find it a blessing? Can we come in close contact with Infinite Goodness and not get good? Dear child, all God has said to us in His word is true; heaven is true, and we are very near it. It is all around us. Jesus is there before us—there to welcome us. Oh, to realize it! try and realize it. Every dispensation of His loving providence is to cause us to realize all that He has said. He wants us to be more and more like Himself, and therefore we should be more anxious to derive the full benefit of the affliction, than that it should be removed. This is a time for wrestling prayer with God, our own God. How needful are these high winds and storms to cause us to cling to our heavenly Pilot, and to speed our way to our blessed harbour of eternal rest. May this season of trial be fraught with a large blessing. The Lord, I trust, after He has tried our faith and blessed the affliction, will restore dear —— to us again. He has ordered every circumstance attending it. Be fully persuaded of this. Satan often endeavours to work upon the wretched infidelity of our nature, by leading us to look at second causes. The Lord has done it, and the reason He will by-and-by reveal to us. Prayer is continually offered up here on her and your behalf, by your loving people. They have proved their love to Jesus, and to you as one given to lead them in the way to glory. I am thankful the Lord has sent dear Mr. Evans to comfort you at this time. May He make you a mutual blessing. Mr. Franklin is to preach. The post has come. The Lord be praised for the good news. May He give us grateful hearts for all His mercies"

"I received yours, and was glad to hear of your safe return home; and that the Lord not only preserved you in your journey, but was blessing your labours. He is everything to us; without Him we are wretched, and with Him we have all that can be desired. What would heaven be without Jesus! On Friday evening I had a most blessed season. The Lord drew sensibly near, filled my heart with love, and my mouth with arguments. I felt I loved Him better than the dearest object on earth, and could appeal to Him for the truth, who alone could search the heart. It was a season of mutual love and holy confidence. I pleaded for my children and for my children's children, while His loving eye was upon, and his heart towards me. I wept for sin, and wept for joy. God caused all His goodness to pass before me, and this it is that breaks the heart of a poor sinner. It was one of those special seasons I have been favoured with in my pilgrimage. I was again favoured at family worship; to my own soul it was a solemn, endearing season, while I prayed for the conversion of the whole household and all that were dear to me. The enemy has since suggested that some heavy trial was near, and that this was sent as a preparation. Well, I am His, and in His own loving hands, and can fully trust Him for all."

TO HER SON R. F. W——.

"I was glad to get your last, and am anxious to encourage you to keep up the correspondence during the little space that is now allowed your mother in this vale of tears. It is a world lying in the wicked one, and we are encompassed about with a body of sin and of death. It is a mercy that it is as well with us as it is; and above all, that our gracious and long-suffering Father has given us such a bright and good hope of a better one to come. God be praised that, vile as I am, that hope shines brighter and brighter as I draw nearer the end of my race. There is such a thing, my dear R——, as, in a measure, living with God even here. Take Him as your dearest and best Friend. Treat Him as one to whom you can fully confide your all. Never be afraid of opening your whole heart to Him, however hateful you may feel it. Did you but more know the depth of that love that is in the heart of Jesus, you would never be reluctant to go to Him for all you needed. It is to know the character of God as your Father in the person of Jesus Christ, that can alone give you confidence in Him. Dear child, a few years and you pass away to millions and millions that await you. Waste not the little space allotted you to prepare for them. I pray for you; you will never know how often until we meet above. Oh, that I might have the happiness of meeting you and all my dear children in heaven! Is it not worth living for? Is it not worth dying for? The 'signs of the times' declare that the coming of the Lord draweth nigh. All sanctified hearts seem to feel this. I seem myself, like a vessel that had weathered storm after storm, and tempest after tempest, and at last was brought within sight of my desired haven, but have not yet cast anchor. But oh, the land is in sight, and it looks delightful to the eye. Jesus is on his way. Dear H——, who was always looking for Him, will come with Him. . . . . Remember, that to walk in the precept is the way to the full enjoyment of the promise. We must not expect the comfort of the one without the observance of the other. Rather than incur debt, exercise the most rigid self-denial. Go not against God, and God will be for you. None ever disobey Him, but are sure to pay the penalty of disobedience: I speak now of His own children. The wicked are turned into hell, but His own elect are punished here. *Some men's sins go before to judgment; some men's sins follow after.* The Christian has been brought to judgment here, and acquitted. *There is, therefore, now no condemnation to them that are in Christ Jesus.* And again, *We are chastened of the Lord. that we should not be condemned with* *the world.* 1 Cor. xi. 32. Never undertake a cause* without kneeling down and asking the Lord for wisdom and grace. If Solomon felt it needful to do this, well may you. Christ says, *Without me ye can do nothing.* Be not fearful you will lose your cause by so doing; but only trust your case in the Lord's hands, and if a just one, He will prosper you. Walk in His fear, and you need fear nothing else. The account of your visit to Mount Pleasant, and of our friends there, was very interesting to me. I never lose sight of old friends, particularly those whom I hope to meet in another world."

While on a visit to her son E——, at Taplow, Bucks, she met with a slight accident, the consequences of which might have been severe, to which she thus gratefully refers:—

"*Taplow.*—Came here on the 25th, and am much recruited in strength. Mr. and Mrs. E—— called, and passed an hour. A few days ago, on returning from visiting a sick cottager, and while conversing for a few minutes in the road with the medical man, about the young woman I had just left, his horse backed the chaise; and before either of us could get out of the way, he was forced against the wall, and I was thrown down, the wheel passing over my foot. I fainted, and was carried home; but on examination, no bones were found to be broken, only a few cuts and bruises received, and so the Lord preserved me from the greater evil. Enough of this, but not enough of God's tender love in it all. Had my hip been dislocated, as my dear mother's was by a much less accident, I should have been crippled for the remainder of my life. What you said of God's adopted children was very sweet to me to-day. How often one word—a simple sentence—when applied by the Holy Ghost, gives comfort, and lifts one up! How much we need these helps all through our weary pilgrimage! We are such forgetful creatures; too often forgetting what *we* are, and what a God *He* is."

"I have often thought of the goodness, kindness, and tender sympathy of God, that though man had sinned and was at enmity with his Creator, Benefactor, and Friend, so that the ground was cursed for his sake, there should yet be so much in this world to comfort, to alleviate, and delight; so much still lingering of its pristine beauty to regale and please. And if this world is still so attractive, so lovely to the eye

---

* Her son to whom these holy admonitions were addressed was then practising at the American Bar.

and pleasing to the senses, what must that world be which infinite love has gone to prepare for the redeemed and pure spirits designed to inhabit it!"

"I want to learn to live by the day, trusting God for the daily supplies of His grace, and for the leadings of His providence; leaving the morrow in His own blessed hand, who knows how to give, and when to withhold."

From her Diary.—"This is a lovely day. Have had nearness to Jesus in prayer. Felt I loved Him above all earthly love. Could recall all His past dealings, watchful providences, unwearied care, from infancy to the present moment. I delight to trace before Him His wondrous dealings all my journey through. Oh, what a God He has been to me! and what return? often the basest. How often these thoughts bring forth tears from my aged eyes, in the remembrance of what He has been to me, and what I have been to Him. I think I love the saints above better than the saints below. Their pure spirits look so lovely to me. Oh, the purity of heaven! what attraction has it to one conflicting at every step with an unholy nature! Precious Jesus, help and strengthen Thy unworthy one in doing what is right in Thy sight. I am Thine, and thou art mine."

TO HER SON O——

"I have just been trying to sing to your tune, my dear child, that sweet hymn which we have often sung together,—

'There is a fountain fill'd with blood,
Drawn from Emmanuel's veins.'

Oh that you and I, and all we love, may be washed in that blessed Fountain. May we live more to the honour of Him whose precious blood it is. Oh, for more grace, more love, more engagedness of heart in His blessed service, more weanedness from a poor dying, disappointing world, which at best is but a cheat, promising much, but performing little. The poor King of the French, Louis-Philippe, who, a few weeks ago, sat proudly upon his throne, has just landed in England, seeking an asylum in the political storm. When the steamer that bore him and his family approached the shore, seeing a number of people assembled, he was afraid to land, thinking he should be insulted. In vain the people on board endeavoured to encourage him; he insisted upon the vessel stopping until an individual went on shore, and returned with the assurance to the dethroned monarch, that no indignity would be offered him. He then ventured to land, shook hands with several individuals, bowed to all around him, and stepped hastily into the carriage that awaited him, expressing his gratitude that he was on English ground, and that he had been received with feelings of courtesy as a stranger in distress. Oh, what a world is this! What a mercy that we have a Friend who rules over all. and who has said, *I change not.*"

CHAPTER IX.

THE believer's life is changeful and chequered. The path along which he is retracing his steps back to paradise, is paved with stones of variegated hues. And yet, painfully diversified as are often the events in his history, that very diversity is as essential to the symmetry and completeness of his Christian character as are different shades of colouring to the perfection of a picture, or as opposite notes in music are to the creation of harmony. "I will sing of *mercy* and of *judgment;* unto Thee, O Lord, will I sing." Mrs. Winslow was called to record two events in her domestic history, singularly illustrative of this thought, in which two characteristic features of her Christianity were beautifully exhibited—her unwavering faith in suffering, and her grateful spirit in joy.

The first event to which we refer was the death of her son H——. His conversion has been alluded to. From the time that he became a subject of Divine grace, during the revival already narrated, he was to her, in the highest sense, 'a dear son,' a 'pleasant child,' 'tenderly loved of his mother.' They took sweet counsel together, and walked to the house of God in company. It was often his privilege to speak a word of heart-cheer when her soul was depressed, and, by his filial affection and sympathy, to fling many a warm sunbeam upon her lone and shady path. He was in all respects worthy of the grief she thus touchingly records in her Diary of his decease :—

"April 2nd.—The Lord has again laid His chasening hand upon me, but in love. Dear Henry is gone home, and I am a bereaved mother. He sleeps in Jesus, that is my only comfort; and oh, what a comfort it is! Oh, to be with Jesus,—that is happiness. It is happiness to walk with Him here, but what happiness to see Him as He is, and to behold His glory. And now, dear, precious Henry, thou art beholding

Him in all His glory, whom thou didst long to see coming in that glory in the clouds of heaven. How highly favoured thou hast been! Oh for faith to see this, to me, painful dispensation in its true light. *Let not your heart be troubled; ye believe in God, believe also in me.* Lord, I believe; help thou my unbelief. Oh, to believe that Jesus is indeed at the right hand of God! If He is there, H——— is there too, and I shall meet him again. On the resurrection of Christ depends our eternal all. Upon that single and glorious truth hinges every other. If that be true, all that He has said, all that He has promised, and all that He has engaged to do, is true. Lord, increase my faith, and sanctify this trial to us all. Dear ——— received the mournful intelligence, and immediately left home, and came to me, to comfort me under my trouble. Dear H——— was taken to his happy rest on Saturday morning, and spent a happy Sabbath with the Lord of the Sabbath. He was fully prepared for the change, and was more fitted for heaven than for earth. The world seemed to have no charms for him. It had lost its hold for a long period. He was living in full expectation of Christ's coming, and now he is with Him whom he so ardently longed to see. Day and night he was looking for Him, as if *hastening unto the coming of the Lord;* so that Christ was in all his thoughts. Ought I not to rejoice that he has realized his wish, though not in the way he anticipated? When he had to grapple with the 'last enemy,' he feared not death; and, to use his own words, 'longed to clap his glad wings and fly to Jesus.' May God, in His tender mercy, be the Father to the fatherless, and the widow's God."

"5th.—I love to contemplate him there, to think of the welcome he has received, first from Jesus, and then from the dear ones who had gone a little before him. All is now perfect knowledge, perfect purity, perfect love. If communion with departed spirits is attainable, I have realized something of it. I have felt such a nearness to him, and such soothing from knowing that he was quite safe and happy with Christ. How sweet, how comforting is the thought that I shall see him sooner than if he had continued on earth. Heaven is nearer to me than New York.* This affliction has wafted me closer to my happy home. Oh to realize it fully even *here.*"

* "Do you think your daughter lost, when she is but sleeping in the bosom of the Almighty? Think her not absent who is in such a Friend's house. Is she lost to you, who is found to Christ? He is an ill debtor

A few extracts from one or two letters penned at this time of her affliction will still further evidence the submissive, heaven-breathing spirit with which she bowed to this chastening of love. She thus addresses the bereaved widow of her son:—

"What can I say to comfort you, my dear J——, in this heavy trial, while I feel heartbroken myself? I trust ere this the true Comforter has enabled you to cast your heavy burden upon Him, who has promised to be a Father to the fatherless, and the widow's God. The shock that I have received has brought me a little nearer to my home; and my great comfort is that I shall see my dear child much sooner than if he had remained where he was. Heaven seems nearer to me than New York, and dear Henry nearer too. It seems but a step and I am there, where there is no more sin, nor death, and where all tears are for ever wiped away. This is a vale of tears. I have been a child of sorrow, and yet not one trial too many have I had. Dear Henry was more fit for heaven than for earth. The Lord has been weaning him from things below for some time, preparing him for a better home above. He was looking for Jesus, and longing to see Him, and the Lord has given him his wish in His own way and time. We must not look at second causes. Every circumstance connected with God's children, living or dying, is ordered by Himself. He has not gone a moment sooner or a moment later than God had appointed. Chosen in Christ before the world was, so were all things connected with him here wisely and mercifully ordered. Oh, I love to think of him with Jesus, mingling with the pure spirits above, and long to join them. . . . Go to Jesus for all you need. Take Him as your true, your best, your only Friend. There is not another like Him. Take Him as your brother born for adversity. The oftener you go to Him, the more welcome you will be, and the better acquainted. You were His child before, but now you are His widowed child, and have a double claim upon Him. Put in your claim. Do not first go to an arm of flesh, and then to Christ. But go to Christ first, before you make up your mind as to the course you should take. Aim to bring up your children for eternity. May the Lord bless, comfort, and guide you, is my constant prayer."

who payeth that which he borroweth with a grudge. Prepare yourself; you are nearer your daughter this day than yesterday. It is self-love in us that maketh us mourn for them that die in the Lord."—*Rutherford*.

TO MRS. C——.

"I have not written to you for some time, although my thoughts have wandered to you. I have been in trouble. The Lord has laid His loving hand again upon me. I know it is in love to my soul, and not one unkind feeling has lurked in my heart towards Him. He has taken home to His own bosom one of my dear and justly loved sons; my dear Henry is with Jesus. He has sweetly housed my child, leaving me one the less on earth, and one more to welcome me to glory. Dear friend, in spite of all I know of His goodness, my poor heart has deeply felt this stroke, and the shock to my nerves has brought me a little nearer to the grave; but the support and consolation I have experienced under it, have amply repaid me for all I have suffered. Oh the goodness of God towards unworthy me! What can I render unto Him for all His loving-kindness and tender mercies towards me and my departed one? I have not the shadow of a doubt of his happiness at this moment. There was not one in my family, not myself excepted, who was so thoroughly prepared for this great change as he. He was brought to the feet of Jesus at nineteen, and since then has held on his way, carrying out the principles of the gospel in his life and conversation. He had much of the Spirit of Christ, manifested in all kindness and benevolence, even, as some thought, to a fault. For the last two years he has been looking for the coming of Christ, and imagined, with many others, that the time was near. So did the Lord prepare him for his inheritance. Dear as he was, I would not recall him for a thousand worlds. If there is such a thing as communion with departed spirits, I think I have felt something of its sweetness. Oh the comfort, the rich consolation and blessing, this trying dispensation has afforded me! It has enabled me to realize the unseen realities of the eternal world. . . . I long to hear how your soul prospers. You are the Lord's, His portion for ever; and He is training you and me for our happy inheritance. Oh, let us try and live up to it. What are the various sorrows of the way, compared with the glory that shall be revealed in us? May the Lord lead us into an experimental knowledge of Jesus. No other is worth having, living or dying. As I draw near the confines of eternity, how poor and contemptible is everything that has not Christ in it,—Christ first, Christ last, and Christ all through. Jesus must be all in all, or He is nothing. Oh, to be ready, *quite* ready, to obey the welcome summons, to believe all that God has promised us in His word, and to live more under the sanctifying influence of the Holy Spirit within us. We must honour the Spirit more than we do, and He will honour us, by revealing more of Christ to us, and in us the hope of glory. . . ."

From her diary.—" Received a letter from J——, announcing the death of her mother, six weeks after my dear H——. This is a severe stroke to her. May it lead her closer to Jesus. She would, perhaps, have leaned more upon her mother than upon Christ, and so He removed this prop too. He will have His people lean upon Him alone. I hope she was ready for the change. Oh, to be quite ready! O Lord, keep me mindful of my latter end. Prepare me for that great change. Confirm me in the truth of Thy precious resurrection; and when the time comes, take away all fear of death and the grave, and let me see Thy face, Thy welcome face, all through that dark valley, and give me an abundant entrance into Thy kingdom of glory above. Absent from the body, I shall be present with the Lord. To be with Thee, will be heaven. Come, Lord Jesus, come quickly."

The second event to which we refer (although not occurring at the same time) was well calculated to illustrate another feature of her religion—her praiseful spirit in joy. The conversion of her daughter to Christ, was in answer to the wrestlings which had broken the stillness of many a midnight hour, and was the precious fruit of a faith that had long and patiently travailed. Ever on the alert to win a soul to the Saviour, the decision of one for Him, so near and so justly beloved, would enkindle in her heart a joy such as none but a *mother*, a *Christian* mother, and *such* a Christian mother, could feel. Her private journal thus records this pleasing occurence:—

"April 30th.—About two months ago, the Lord most graciously answered my prayers, in bringing my dearest E—— to sit at the feet of Jesus. She is now a child of God, pardoned, justified, and adopted into His family, and walking in that narrow, blessed way that leads to life eternal. God be praised for His marvellous goodness to her and to me. Oh, he is, in very deed, a God hearing and answering prayer. I receive it as a precious earnest of greater things to come. O dearest Lord, I cannot rest until all are called, and all call Thee blessed. A dear company of believers meet several times in the week, unitedly to pray and wrestle for the outpouring of the Holy Spirit. This is what I have long been urging upon the minds of the pastor and the people, and now it has commenced. O Lord, hear! O Lord, pardon our lukewarmness, and come with all Thy glorious train, and take a full possession of every heart, and bring rebellious sinners to relinquish their enmity, and bow to Thy rightful sceptre. Let Thy kingdom come, and Thy will be done on earth, even as it is done in heaven. Amen and amen."

"May 10th.—Still feeble in body, but oh, how thankful at times! My heart overflows with love to Him who is to me an ocean of love. Eternity, *eternity* will only be sufficient for my song of praise and thanksgiving. Dear E——'s conversion has lifted me nearer to God. Jesus lives, still lives to answer prayer, and give life to the dead."

"*Lo, God hath given thee all that sail with thee.*"—Acts xxvii. 24.

"Father! who o'er time's boisterous tide
A precious bark art steering;
Mother! who anxious at his side
Each distant storm art hearing;
Bind ye the promise to your heart,
Thus by the angel spoken;
Believe ye that your circle blest
Shall gain the port unbroken.

"When stranded on the rock of woe,
Life's last faint watch-light burneth,
And shuddering toward that bourn to go
From whence no guest returneth,—
Then may each bark your love has launch'd.
Gliding with sail unriven,
Send forth a seraph soul to form
YOUR FAMILY IN HEAVEN."

"God, in the riches of His grace, grant that it may be so with my own dear ones; and I believe it will, for God has said to me, *I will be a Father to thy fatherless children.* For Jesus' sake, hear my prayer, O Lord, my God."

TO ONE OF HER SONS.

"My mind, body, and whole heart, are engaged in the blessed work of the Lord, which is now going on. Precious E——'s conversion is a pledge to me of greater blessings to come. God is a great God, and He loveth to do great things like Himself; and I come not in my own most worthless name, but in the name of a great Saviour, in whom He is well pleased, and who has said, *Ask anything in my name, and I will do it.* Here is encouragement for a poor worm of the dust, to come with large demands upon the royal bounty of the King of kings and Lord of lords. We have constant meeting for prayer for the outpouring of the Holy Spirit. The hearts of God's people are stirred up to wrestle for the blessing, and be assured we shall receive it. E——'s conversion has awakened many to inquiry, and has done much good. She is indeed a new creature. Glory to God in the highest, for this mighty blessing.

"Last evening dear Mr. Evans met his Bible class, both male and female, in the body of the chapel. It was full, and solemn as eternity. E—— returned with her mind much engaged, and rejoicing in the prospect of the blessings that would follow such a solemn and deeply interesting service."

It often seems good to Him who is "excellent in council and wonderful in working," to bring early to the proof the grace He early gives. Painful and mysterious as this may appear at the time, it is yet in after years that the reason, as the results, of such a procedure, is more apparent. When the duties of life increase, and with them, life's trials—when a matured Christian experience, a strongly-developed character, and a mellowed judgment, are demanded,—it is *then* the Christian reaps the golden harvest of his *early* training, and traces the infinite wisdom and love which in the first and gentlest evolvings of his faith marked for him a path of early suffering. Thus immense and far-reaching are the blessings which flow from sanctified sorrow. The illness of her daughter, while yet in the glow of her new-born joy, elicited from Mrs. Winslow's pen some of the most affecting expressions of her quick and tender sympathy. The following choice extracts, composed at this and at other periods, are culled from her

LETTERS TO HER DAUGHTER.

"DEAREST E——,

"I have just been praying for you, and oh, that a good and gracious God might condescend to send down answers of peace to the petitions offered in the name of Jesus, His own well-beloved Son. I cannot hear until to-morrow what Dr. Jephson says, and wishes you to do; so I must continue to look up. Oh for more precious faith; I feel I need it. May you enjoy much of the presence of Him who can make a sick room a Bethel to your soul. All places where He is, are a heaven below. That presence can make every cup of affliction sweet. May God give all needful judgment to Dr. J., and incline you strictly to adhere to his advice. I have prayed continually that wisdom might be imparted to him. Now that you are in his hands, my mind is comparatively composed."

"I have been desponding about you this morning, precious child. Oh that God, my God and your God, may answer my prayers in His rich mercy! I know that He always hears them. I believe that there is not a single petition put up by a child of His, however faintly expressed that petition may be, but He hears it. The smallest degree of faith will send it not only into the ear, but into the heart of God. The Spirit indites it, and Christ, the believer's surety and advocate, presents it, sprinkled with His own precious blood, to the Father. How can a poor believer ever fail, in his lowest state, of having the perfections of God—His power, love, and faithfulness —encircling him moment by moment? His tender heart now enters into all your weakness and pain, and all is sent in love to your precious soul, more precious in the sight of God than ten thousand worlds."

"The Lord stretch forth His healing hand, and restore you to health and strength; and may He cause your soul, above all, to prosper and be in health. Surely *our times are in His hands*, who loves us better than we love ourselves. Oh, to trust Him wholly! He careth for us. How much easier at times it seems to trust Him with our eternal all, than with the inferior concerns of a few short and uncertain years. I have just been reading the Journal of Sir A——'s Scripture Reader. Sir A——'s remarks on the iniquity of removing such men from a sphere of usefulness, on the plea that they interfere with clerical duties, are excellent. . . You are in your Father's hands, and besides, Jesus was the healer of bodily disease, when on earth, as well as spiritual. Is He less so now? By no means. Have faith in this Physician; He is able, and as willing as He is able, to do us all possible good. Simple, childlike faith, a constant coming and looking to Jesus, will do wonders. Have not I called upon him in trouble, times without number, and has He ever denied me? Never, no *never* in any one instance. Oh to know the character of God! When He imparts a glimpse even of Himself, it seems as if the heart could not contain what it feels. To behold Him in Jesus, sheds a holy mildness, gentleness, and lustre over all His great and glorious attributes. I am at a loss at times for language to express what I feel."

" I often think, how could I live without a throne of grace! It is a sure refuge, a resting-place to my soul, endeared by a thousand most tender, soul-humbling, soul-refreshing interviews with the God of heaven,—the God of love to me and mine. How sweet to draw near to Him, and hear the whispers of the still, small voice of the Spirit, reproving, counselling, and soothing the too often turbulent and excited feelings of the soul! My dear child, you need never mourn that you are fatherless, since God, the eternal God, is your own Father, better than ten thousand earthly parents. Oh, trust Him fully; open your whole heart to Him; tell Him all you wish, all you feel, all you fear. Keep nothing back. He will remove all that is wrong, set everything right, and keep you quietly resting in the embrace of His matchless love. It is a heaven below, to be passive in His hands, and know no will but His, believing that His is best."

"*Taplow.*—I could sing of the praises of the Lord by day and by night. He is the joy of my heart; yea, He is my life. So may He ever be to you. Cling to Him, nor let Him go. If He hides himself behind a cloud, it is only to make you more earnest in seeking Him. Go again and again, until you find Him. Think of a poor sinful mortal holding converse with God, the mighty God, the everlasting Father! But so it is. Be not satisfied with a commonplace Christianity. How many there are who have no certainty as to their union with Christ, are satisfied with a lifeless form, and go no further. Ah, what losers they are! No tongue can tell the blessedness, when the believer can testify at times that he is with God, and that God is with him. Give my love to dear Lady L——, and to dear C——. I feel much love to that dear child. May the Lord draw her nearer and nearer to Himself. He has given her one who fears Him, which is a sweet token to her of the love He has towards her. Let us watch the gracious hand of our God in all His eventful providences. How circumspect should we be, yet not walking in bondage, but as dear children, watched over and directed by a tender, loving Father, whose aim is to make us happy here, and eternally happy hereafter."

"Yesterday we were at Windsor Castle. It was a solemn sermon to my soul. Where are all those kings and queens, and other great ones, whose pictures and monuments cover these walls? Where are they now? They have passed away, and all the pomp and show that surrounded them here has vanished with them. Oh, how trifling does everything appear but the one thing needful! We, too, are passing away; and what a mercy if enabled to say, 'I am going to my Father's home above, my happy home, prepared by Him who laid down His life for me.'"

"May the Lord in mercy keep us in health, best of all, in soul-prosperity; for I have had to learn that the wealth and honours of this poor, dying world cannot compensate for the loss of the sweet and precious life-giving influence of the Holy Spirit within. My soul has of late been much tried, so that it has been a trial to me to open my mouth in prayer; and often, when I did, a cloud would pass that obscured every ray of divine light. My soul seemed like a bark at sea, without a helm to steer or a pilot to guide it. And yet the Lord has not been quite out of sight in private prayer. Like Mary, I have been ready to say, *They have taken away my Lord, and I know not where they have laid Him.* And yet, like her, I have stood weeping and sorrowing after Him. This may be owing to a pressure on the nerves and an over-tried mind; but this I know, when I turn within to search for the cause, I see so much reason that God should thus chasten me, that I only wonder He should ever cast a look of mercy towards me. Unprofitable, unprofitable servant I feel I have been all my life, and am compelled to lay my mouth in the dust before Him. Such have been my feelings of late, and yet, though cast down, I am not in despair, blessed be God. When he has tried me, I shall come forth as gold, I trust, and shall yet praise Him who is the health of my countenance and my God."

It was during this domestic trial—the illness of her daughter—that she received the following characteristic letter from her Pastor, the Rev. J. H. Evans, touchingly expressive of the sacred sympathy peculiar to the beloved writer.

"John Street, July 6.
"MY BELOVED FRIEND AND DEARLY-ESTEEMED SISTER IN JESUS, OUR SYMPATHIZING HEAD,—

"How much did I wish to see you yesterday before you

left for Leamington, but it was out of my power. We can do but little—nothing. Jesus has all, is all, can do all, and will put all forth in our necessities, be they ever so deep. You shall find him everything in this your need of all things—a very present help. We could never know His heart but for our troubles, never know His grace but for our worthlessness. There is a tenderness in the love of the Saviour which our miseries, I will not say draw out, but exhibit. In no other school could we learn it. Be not afraid, dear and precious sister, of the form in which His loving hand has placed you; He will come and sit by you, and should it be painful to the flesh and the spirit too, He can smooth it. One smile of his can dry up all your tears. Your dear and precious E—— is more near to Him than she is to you, dearly as you love her. Oh! leave her in His hands. He has a right to her. And whether He lend her to you for a little longer or not, yet He will have you trust her with Him. His is a tender bosom, and tenderly has He borne up your weary head in many a wearying day, and sleepless night. He said that He would, and He has done it according to His word, and He will yet do it, because He has said that He will.

"I was lately told of a dear brother who said that when he first thought of losing his only daughter—and he had but one other child—he felt that he could not part with her; but when he followed her body into the churchyard it seemed as if he was going to her wedding. This was the husband of Lady L. S. What cannot grace do? Dear and precious sister, may the all-sufficient God and precious Saviour be your sufficient help in your deep trial. He alone can. My best love to dear O—— and his wife. Thank her for her kind letter. My tender love to dear E., when she can bear to be told of it."

FROM HER JOURNAL.

"Brighton, Feb. 6.

"Came here a week ago. . . . I have just had some sweet interviews with a young Christian for whom the Lord has done great things. Surrounded by worldly connexions and worldly prosperity, yet brought to sit at the feet of Jesus, and blessedly taught by the Spirit, I was interested to find so young a creature in so short a time (only two years) with such a deep experience of spiritual things. The Lord has laid ill health at her door, so that she has her cross to carry, but it

has been most graciously sanctified to her soul's best interests.
. . . The Lord be praised for all His tender mercies and loving-kindnesses—unceasing and unwearying as His love. My continual shortcomings, and oftcoming for forgiveness again and again, does not exhaust Him. I should have wearied out the whole host of heaven before this; but Jesus is never wearied with hearing the cries of His poor tried and tempted saints. Always are they welcome, and I think the oftener I go, the more welcome I am. Not a frown upon that countenance towards one who really feels his need of Him. A smiling welcome, fraught with mighty blessings, which, while it gladdens the heart, fills the soul with a humbling sense of its own vileness,—humbled in self, exalted in Christ."

"I want to live more on high,—more above the world and all its little things. Oh, for wisdom to enable me to discharge all relative duties without being cumbered; to live in heavenly places in Christ Jesus. The Lord has strengthened me to maintain family worship; the people of the house regularly attending, and gratified in being permitted to come. The Lord helps me to speak a word now and then in His name, and gives me liberty in prayer; and yet I feel quite unequal in body and mind. I feel it a cross, but dare not withdraw. May the Lord forgive all my mistakes, my reluctance to do what I felt it was my duty to do. But oh, how good and how kind He has been to me! What a God, no one can know or tell but myself. It almost breaks my heart when I think of the wondrous love He bears towards one so utterly worthless. I am wearied to find I do not get on, except in knowing more of my wretchedness and vileness, and more of the sufficiency of Jesus, and the absolute necessity of going to Him for everything I need, and living upon Him moment by moment. But this is to be learnt out by means of much ploughing of the Holy Ghost upon the renewed heart, and this through the providence of God. God's providence acts as the handmaid to faith; and there is not a truth in God's word but what must be learnt out in the same way and by the same process. Oh, to be a real Christian! This is no easy matter. How many trials and crosses, ups and downs, are needful to fit us for the mansion Jesus has gone to prepare for us! And as soon as our education is complete, He takes us home to the full enjoyment of our inheritance above. Blessed be God for the hope He has given us in the gospel of His dear Son."

"13th.—A stormy day—the sea in a foam. Heard a sermon on *the blessedness of the man unto whom God imputed righteousness without works.* The great conflict in my soul when I first sought the Lord was, how I was to be saved without works, for I had no works to come with. How blessedly did Jesus manifest Himself to me that night, and say to me, 'I am thy salvation without thy works;'—a night to be remembered throughout eternity! Bless the Lord, O my soul! Hitherto has He blessed me, chastened, upheld, and comforted me; and even down to old age has He carried me."

"This morning, was led in prayer to ask the Lord, if it were good in His sight, to make me in some way a humble instrument in His hands of good to Lord ——'s precious, never-dying soul. It came twice, after waking from sleep, so forcibly to my mind, that I felt I must pray for him. How could I show my regard in a more suitable way than in praying that he might know what it was to possess durable riches and honours; for oh, how far do they exceed all earthly glory! Oh, to know to a certainty that God hears the prayers of His saints, and not one shall ever be disregarded. The Spirit indites them, the Son presents them in the incense of His own sacrifice, and God the Father is well pleased to honour them for Christ's sake and His own. After offering up my humble petition for Lord ——, the thought occurred to me, how utterly impossible it was for me to be of any spiritual service, circumstances like mountains preventing. But the thought again occurred, what are mountains in the way of the Lord's purposes? He can do all things, and He can do this. There I leave it. My request has been made, and if not through me, yet through some other means, may God bless him and save his soul at last."

TO HER SON O——.

"Brighton, Feb. 18th.

"E—— went to the Town Hall, at a meeting for the Jews, last night. Dr. Marsh spoke, and also his son. She says the latter spoke remarkably well and to the purpose. We have a nice circle of friends here, which makes it pleasant. As it respects myself, one or two to whom I can speak of Jesus, of Him whom my soul loveth, is quite sufficient. What a company I shall meet (if permitted to get there) in heaven! It makes me long at times to depart and be with them. I feel that all is true that is written of Him; and if so, I shall see Him and be with Him for ever. On His resurrection hangs all my hope. If He is risen, my soul is as safe as if it were there now. The whole truth of the gospel hangs on the resurrection of Christ. I am writing with the ocean full in view, and it looks beautiful and serene."

"22nd.—How continually is the Christian's experience varying, chiefly through the varying providences of God! There is a close connexion between what is passing within the believer and what is transpiring without; both engaged in furthering the work of the Lord in His kingdom of grace in the soul. There is no cessation. The Spirit unceasing in His work, and Satan as busily engaged in thwarting it, through the artful and corrupt propensities of the flesh. How heartily do I hate the flesh, and long to drop the body of sin, and be done with it for ever."

"Monday. . . . . It seems a long time to wait for the post, before I can hear how the Lord has been dealing with you on the Sabbath. Had I not Him to look to for comfort, I know not what I should do. Yesterday, again and again I lifted up my burdened heart for you; and last evening, at our feast of love (the Lord's Supper), I forgot you not. That is always an *especial* season of sweet communion between my soul and my God. Jesus sits at His table, and I am permitted to sit at His blessed feet, and many gracious tokens of love do I receive. Last evening, while thus communing, He gave me a gentle rebuke, which dissolved my heart into holy contrition, and laid me in the dust; but oh, how condescending His love, no tongue can tell! I wept—He pardoned—showed me His loving heart, and made me weep still more. My great sin was in looking to an arm of flesh, instead of the living God; that God who has said, *I will never leave thee, nor forsake thee.* This produced a murmuring spirit, and sorrow followed in its train. But I was to go to the table where Jesus sat, and obtain a full view of Him, before my sin was discovered to me; and then did I prostrate myself before Him, confessing my sin, and He forgave it all. He looked upon me as benignantly and lovingly as He did upon Peter, and this brought my ingratitude and unbelief—God-dishonouring unbelief—to mind; and I fell before Him humbled, penitent, and forgiven. Is not this just like Jesus? The text was, *Let us draw near;* and truly did a good and gracious God draw near to me, unworthy though I was; and my prayer then ascended, that He would draw near to you and bless you with strong faith in His love; for there is no love like the love of God. The faint glimmer of a rushlight, compared with the brightest noonday sun, is the love of the creature, the tenderest and the fondest, in comparison with the wondrous, boundless love of God in our nature—*God is us.*"

". . . I have nothing particularly new to tell you; but when I remember that the Lord is especially in all the events of His providence towards His people, I ought not to say I have no good news to tell you. Jesus reigns, and that is good news, though not new to you. And yet we require to be continually reminded of it, for we are prone in our worldliness to lose sight of it, and then, like the Israelites, we murmur. Jesus is alive, and at the right hand of the Majesty on high. He is at the helm, guiding our vessel skilfully and safely through all dangers and storms, ever varying and changing, through this eventful voyage; and He will most assuredly bring us at last to anchor, where all suffering, and trial, and perils are at an end for ever, in that harbour of perfect rest which remaineth for the people of God. . . . Civil affairs are just now in rather a perplexed, transition state. They cannot form a government. How wonderful the way God takes to accomplish His mighty purposes in this lower world! Who would have thought that the *potato disease* would have been the means of overthrowing the government, which but a short time ago seemed so strong and powerful? But so it is. Sir Robert Peel was for opening the ports; the Duke was not; and this broke up the Cabinet. Oh, how truly God is in all things! By the most trivial and mean things, in His allwise, wonderful providence, He performs His wonders and accomplishes His purposes. Never mistrust Him. Let us keep from unbelief, walk uprightly, and no good thing will He withhold."

"Lord's day. . . . I have prayed again and again to-day for you, remembering the vast importance of the subject on which you are to preach; and oh, may the Holy Ghost descend with all His mighty power upon preacher, saints, and sinners, that great good may be done in the name of Jesus to the glory of the Tri-une Jehovah. I was enabled, though feeling unwell, to be at the house of God this morning. The text was, *The way of life is above to the wise, that he may depart from hell beneath,* Prov. xv. 24. He was excellent, as usual, and spoke with apparent comfort; but, O Lord, I long to see a whole congregation brought under the power of the Holy Spirit. There is a constant hearing of sermons, but nothing effectually done in comparison with what ought to be done. Slumbering saints and dead sinners compose most of the congregations. Oh! for more of the power of prayer among the children of the kingdom. How my soul longs for it! How I wish I heard in those who wait upon the sanctuary more of the enjoyment of the truth in their own souls, and of the sensible presence of the Lord. How sweet it is to have the enjoyment of nearness to God; and how can we feel near to Him and not express our gratitude and love for His kind condescension? We know when we have the society of, and enjoy intercourse with, an earthly friend; how much more endearing and soul-refreshing is that of our Heavenly Friend! The defect is, we do not have His sensible presence, and this is our own fault, and not His; for the essence of His nature is love—love, free, unbounded to the poorest, the vilest, who look for it, expect it, and will not be satisfied without it. The secret is, we grow cold towards this precious Friend, and are then satisfied to do without an expression of His love. No wonder dear Mr. Evans remarked to-day that 'there were none so basely ungrateful on earth as God's own children. And so it is."

"How often does God answer prayer by terrible things in righteousness! When we are in a thick mist we can discern nothing, and are anxious to escape from its perils. But, as it rolls away, we begin to see a gleam of light, and hail it as the commencement of a fuller and brighter discovery. Now this is often the case with the objects of God's everlasting love. We pray for what we believe would promote our happiness and the comfort of others, and for the glory of God. Perhaps we do not in so many words ask for this favour; but we earnestly desire it in our hearts, and often plan in our minds how it may be brought about. God sees the heart's fond wish; presently He brings us, by His all-wise providence, to the very thing we desired; but oh! in such a different way from what we had planned in our own minds. And yet, how much more effectually has He done it than we had thought. Such is our God, and it is a mercy when we do see His blessed hand in every dispensation towards His own elect. But how few—how very few—watch the hand and the doings of God, and lacking this, they continue blind to His great goodness and His unceasing care. How many walk with a sickly Christianity, and although often tried, they seem not to profit from their trials, because they are not earnest in watching God's loving hand. For years they are under the rod, yet we see so little real advance. Oh! let us watch against an infidel Christianity, if I may so express myself; for there is so much infidelity in our fallen nature still lingering in the renewed heart, that we have reason mightily to pray against it. The believer should seek to make the most of his trials. They are disguised covenant blessings, and as such, in love are sent. We should pray over them, and pray in them, and regard them all as designed but to prepare us for an eternal glory. They are sent for an especial purpose, to accomplish an especial good."

"Thus, then, it is good to see God answering our prayer, although it be by sharp trials of faith. This tried faith glorifies God, purifies our hearts, endears Jesus as a precious Sympathizer in our sorrows, and fits us for His dwelling-place. We may not, as I have remarked, see how God is working for us in the event; for, in the language of Job, *Men see not the bright light which is in the clouds, but the wind passeth and cleanseth them*, and then the bright light is visible. I bless God again and again for His most trying dispensations; and that He has given me, even such a one as me, to see Him in all things connected with my present good and eternal happiness. What losers are some of God's children, who watch not and see not Him in every step they take through the wilderness world! Oh! it is inexpressibly sweet to walk with God full in view; to trace Him in everything—in creation, in providence, in grace, in all things on earth and in heaven. What manner of person ought we to be in all holy conversation, who have thus to do with God! Keep a steady eye upon His ways, although they may be at times wrapped in mystery. Watch the leadings of His providence; be careful not to go from Him; there is the danger. Follow after, and patiently wait with a watchful eye, and a praying heart, and a trusting mind, His doings, seeking childlike obedience to His most blessed, loving will. And when the Lord thus brings our self-willed hearts into meek submission, so that we are perfectly satisfied to have Him to do with and by us as best pleases and glorifies Him, having no choice in this or that, *then* it is God works like Himself, educes good from evil, and brings light out of darkness."

"How much of needless care and anxiety does unbelief cut

out for the tried believer in this wilderness world! Distrust, base, ungrateful distrust, seems to follow close at my side, to mar present comforts, and to dishonour Him whom, in spite of all, my soul loveth. Since four o'clock this morning, the hour at which I awoke, has this enemy had a hard contest with me. I went to the Lord and asked for that help which only He could give; but it was not until half-an-hour ago I opened my Bible, and my eye rested on the 53rd Isaiah, 4th verse: *Surely He hath borne our griefs and carried our sorrows.* At once my base ingratitude dissolved my heart into deep contrition, and tears flowed down my cheeks. Did he indeed carry my sorrows, which I must have carried through eternity? Did He bear my grief, was He striken for my transgression, for which hell must have been my portion for ever? Even for this my sin of distrust did He suffer, and shall I doubt, for one moment, of His wondrous love, unceasing and unchanging? He was indeed the Antitype of the ram caught in the thicket, and offered up in my stead, as a burnt-offering to a holy God, and by His stripes my soul is healed, and healed for ever. How marvellous is the display of electing love and sovereign grace to such a one as me! How do I abhor myself in dust and in ashes, while I remember that, unless upheld and preserved by that same love, the very next difficulty that occurs will find me as distrustful and doubting as ever. What a God is ours! He loves to pardon and delights in mercy. And yet, God forbid that we should think lightly of sin because He is so good and ready to forgive!"

TO HER SON, REV. G. E. W.——, ON HIS ILLNESS.

"Dearest G——,

"God is love, and this has been most blessedly manifested to us from first to last. He has been to us a God hearing and a God answering prayer; and yet he has not left us without a Father's chastening hand. As His children, His redeemed ones, He has caused us to pass under the rod, but it has been in such a tender, gentle way, and so blended with manifestations of love and goodness, that we have to bless and praise Him for it all. He is raising you up again, I trust, for greater usefulness, and more devotedness of heart and life. It is no small matter to be a consistent Christian, *an Israelite indeed, in whom there is no guile.* To accomplish this great end, we too often need the discipline of that covenant which is ordered in all things and sure—and we shall have it. How often and how much do we mistake the character of God! We think He is such a one as ourselves; but He must do all He has declared that He will, *because* He is God. *I, the Lord, change not.* There is no after purpose or thought with God! He sees the end from the beginning. This is a delightful subject for contemplation; and if you will give it your attention, restricting yourself to the study only of God's pure word, comparing scripture with scripture, you will find a delightful field of truth in which to roam, worthy the labour of a whole life; for out of it will grow many most precious and important truths, on other branches of the glorious gospel of our Lord and Saviour Jesus Christ. . . . I should have wished to have been with you, but it seems I was to stop here for a season, and this was without my own planning, and therefore I know it to be of the Lord. Oh how much infidelity there is in our fallen nature to contend with, all our journey through. May the Lord increase our faith! Let me hear from yourself, how you are and how you feel, I was grateful for your last, and praise God on your behalf."

" A holy familiarity between God and His redeemed children is most lovely and blessed. He feeds the lamp and keeps it burning, and the soul rests quietly in the hands of the best of Friends, and best of Fathers. I think that, in general, we do but take too superficial a view of what sin is in the sight of God, a holy God, and we do not sufficiently examine our hearts by His holy law. Such a view of what sin is would make us cling closer to the cross of Christ; it would send us oftener to the atoning blood for cleansing, and endear to us the preciousness and worth of a throne of grace. It would also keep us from being mere yea and nay Christians, or half-hearted Christians, and make us more earnest for the salvation of others. It would, too, enable us to form a better judgment of our own case, as well as more clearly discerning the case of others. A slight, imperfect knowledge of what sin is, leads to almost every evil a Christian is liable to fall in, and is dishonouring to God. Let us look more at what He inflicted upon His beloved Son for sins not His own. Oh pray to have just that insight into it as may make you cling more to Christ, and fit you for increased usefulness to souls. May the Lord lead you into all truth, keep your eye and heart towards Himself, moment by moment, and make you a faithful minister of Jesus Christ.

CHAPTER X.

Compassion for the well-being of souls is one of the most holy and spontaneous impulses of our religion. In this consists what is termed, the 'energies of Christianity.' Christianity is not a person, but an idea; and the development of this idea in the soul of those who believe and obey the truth, inspiring all its faculties, and consecrating them to God, is the power or energy of Christianity. "The expulsive power of a new affection," as Dr. Chalmers beautifully expresses it, dislodging from the heart its reigning selfishness, inspires it with the feeling and sentiment of the purest benevolence, which yearns to make others partake of its joy. When Andrew found the Messiah, moved by the impulse of a discovery so great, he went in quest of his brother Simon, and " brought him to Jesus." The impassioned exclamation of the Jewish queen, as she contemplated the threatened massacre of her nation, may befittingly express the intense and holy solicitude of a pious heart, yearning to save the objects of its love from a more certain and appalling doom, " How can I endure to see the destruction of my kindred?" And yet, while thus I write, we are far from speaking of personal faithfulness on the subject of religion as either a facile or a pleasant task. Nay, it is probably the most difficult and delicate of all Christian duties. To conquer an instinctive feeling of delicacy and reserve; to assume an appearance of superior sanctity; to chill, perhaps, affection; forfeit friendship; and to rouse a feeling, if not of hostility, yet of dislike, and yet be *faithful*, demands no ordinary grace.

We have already spoken of her passion for souls. Never was the subject absent from her mind; it entwined itself with all her thoughts, engrafted itself on all her actions, breathed in all her prayers. Her views of eternity were so realizing, her conviction of the truth of the gospel was so strong, and her sense of the preciousness of the Saviour was so great, that the interests of the soul rose before her eye with a magnitude so vast, and a solemnity so overpowering, as to lessen the comparative importance of every other object. No one crossed her path, and her pen traced no lines, without a word that spoke of a world to come. With singular appropriateness might she have embodied her deep and holy passion in the expressive language of the poet:—

> "For me, when I forget the darling theme,
> Be my tongue mute, my fancy paint no more,
> And, dead to joy, forget this heart to beat."

In illustrating the importance of a direct appeal to individuals on the subject of personal religion she would frequently quote a touching incident, related to her when at Cambridge, of the late excellent Rev. Charles Simeon. On one occasion he was summoned to the dying-bed of a brother. Entering the room, his relative extended his hand to him, and with deep emotion said, "I am dying, and you never warned me of the state I was in, and of the danger to which I was exposed from neglecting the salvation of my soul!" "Nay, my brother," replied Mr. Simeon, "I took every reasonable opportunity of bringing the subject of religion before your mind, and frequently alluded to it in my letters." "Yes," exclaimed the dying man, "you did; but that was not enough. You never came to me, closed the door, and took me by the collar of my coat, and told me that I was unconverted, and that, if I died in that state, I should be lost. And now I am dying, and, but for God's grace, I might have been for ever undone!" It is said that this affecting scene made an ineffaceable impression on Mr. Simeon's mind. To this startling fact she would add another, scarcely less affecting, authenticated by the gentleman to whom it referred. A distinguished American clergyman was especially and deeply concerned for the conversion of a member of his congregation who, from his great wealth and moral worth, occupied a position in society of considerable importance. He had for years attended the faithful ministrations of the pastor, but as yet gave no evidence of a change of heart. Regular in his attendance at the sanctuary, fascinated with the eloquence of the preacher, and generous in his expression of admiration, he yet remained immersed in the world and without the pale of the church. His minister yearned for his conversion. Calling upon him early one morning, he requested a private interview. He at once disclosed his mission. In a conversation, brief but pointed, earnest but affectionate, personal but courteous, he pressed upon his friend's serious attention the immediate consideration of his soul, the claims of eternity, and the duty of immediate submission to God. The solemn appeal was listened to with kindly respect, but with the brief, emphatic reply, " I have *no time* for these things." "Not time!" exclaimed the beseeching, faithful minister, "then, sir, you must *find* time!" With these brief but thrilling words, uttered with the profoundest solemnity, he left him. The merchant repaired to his counting-house, and was soon immersed in the world. In vain, however, he strove to give his thoughts to business; the words, "You must find time," still vibrated on his ear, and excluded every other thought from his mind. Quitting the scene of his gains, he returned to his home, bowed down under the conviction of his lost condition as a sinner. The Spirit of God was now moving, as of old, upon the dark, disordered elements of the soul, and soon a new creation was to spring forth—holy, beautiful, and deathless. In a few days the object of this holy solicitude and personal appeal became a new creature in Christ Jesus, and afterwards a distinguished and useful member of His church.

Such was the tender faithfulness to souls she was wont to urge upon all Christians, and which she herself so beautifully exemplified. *Application* of gospel truth in the pulpit, and direct *personal appeal* out of it, were points upon which she would insist with an earnestness and solemnity of manner peculiarly her own. It was no slight evidence of the sincerity and depth of her holy sympathies, that she shrunk not from the task of addressing, on all the momentous subjects of religion, individuals occupying high places of responsibility in the land. She was frequently, and with tears, heard impassionately to exclaim, "Oh, who will warn—who will entreat them?" Copies of letters thus addressed, were found among her papers, one or two of which may be given, as illustrating this noble feature of her Christian character.

"TO THE DUKE OF ——.

"Understanding that your Grace knew Colonel Mackinnon, of the Coldstream Guards, and having heard that he died a believer in the Lord Jesus—a truly converted and holy man —I have taken the liberty of sending you a copy of a small book of prayers, composed by himself, and expressing, as I trust, the true breathings of his heart. A few friends of his, I have understood, finding them among his manuscript papers, published them after his death. I should hope, however, that at a later period of his life, clearer light was vouchsafed him, as from one of the prayers, which I shall mark, it is evident he then had not. I presume that as you knew him when a young, gay, thoughtless man of the world, his conversion will not be entirely without interest to you. In the prayer to which I have referred, it is evident that he is mixing up his repentance and reformation, in some degree, with the atoning, finished work of the Saviour. Now it is clear from the gospel of Christ, that he could not be saved by any work done in him, nor for any work of merit done by him. God pardons, justifies, and saves poor sinners for Christ's sake alone. It is Christ's obedience and death which honours the law of God, and which satisfies divine justice on our behalf. The Holy Spirit works repentance, faith, and every other Christian grace in the believer, as a fruit and consequence of his free justification, not to justify him, or to fit him for being justified. As a believer he is already justified by the Atonement made on his behalf by the Lord Jesus. We are saved as sinners, not as saints; and if we come to Christ lost and undone in ourselves, having nothing to commend us to His notice, or to propitiate His favour, and seek this great mercy with our whole heart, we shall surely find Him, and He will manifest Himself unto us as He does not unto the world. The Lord grant that you may have this precious blessing before you go hence. It is a perilous and an awful thing to be satisfied with a form of godliness without the vital, saving power. *Except a man,* says Christ, *be born again, he cannot see the kingdom of heaven.* Eternity and an immortal soul, surely, are solemn realities, and not to be sported with. God, with whom we have to do, is holy as well as merciful, and righteous as well as gracious. Justice must be satisfied, and holiness must be honoured, ere mercy can reach the sinner. Jesus Christ is alone able to save you from eternal ruin; and if you have not sought Him with the whole heart, I would most affectionately and earnestly implore your Grace to lose not a moment in this all-momentous work. The mistakes of time cannot be rectified in eternity. You cannot return to make good the errors of the present. It is, therefore, of infinite moment, that you should be sure that you are building your hope of heaven upon the one, only foundation, which is, Christ Jesus. *Believe in the Lord Jesus Christ, and thou shalt be saved.* I do not thus address you because I think you are a greater sinner than myself, or than thousands who are basing their acceptance with God upon unscriptural and fatal grounds; but because the Lord has laid you much upon my mind; and situated as you are—encircled by the pomp and gilded vanities of this poor, dying world—it was not likely that the truth, the precious truth, would reach your ear. I pray God that you may be faithful to your own soul, and be led to examine yourself, and ascertain if you are prepared to stand at the bar of God. He may summon you at any moment —at midnight the cry may come, 'Prepare to meet thy God!' Come to Jesus then, just as you are. He will receive, and welcome, and save you, for He will in nowise cast out any who come to Him. Come as a poor, bankrupt sinner; come empty and self-loathing; come with a life of sin, and rebellion, and folly: only come to Jesus, and He will be gracious and and save you, *without money and without price.* This is from one who wishes to meet you at the right hand of Christ.

"TO LORD ——, ON HIS ILLNESS.

"MY LORD,—

"I have heard with regret that you are ill, seriously ill, and likely soon to stand before God. Permit me, with unfeigned respect and sincere sympathy, to approach you with the question, Are you ready? Are you prepared for the solemn change that awaits you? Eternity, with its dread realities, is before you, and you have a soul to be saved or lost for ever! What, at the present moment, can be of such importance to you as a correct knowledge of your real condition as a sinner in the sight of a holy God, who searcheth the heart? You must be sensible that you have hitherto lived in neglect of your soul, in forgetfulness of God, and in oblivion of eternity. The world with all its pomps and gaieties, its interests and honours, has had complete control of your mind, and full possession of your heart. You have lived *without God and without hope in the world.* That you may have observed the forms of godliness I admit, but God will not be mocked with a mere external work; He has to do with the *heart*. His language is, *My son, give me thy heart.* And now, my lord, you are about to appear in the presence of this holy Lord God, who is just to Himself, while He is most merciful to the sinner. Most earnestly and respectfully do I urge upon you the immediate consideration of the things that make for your eternal peace. Trifle not with your endangered and immortal soul. Even now, at the eleventh hour, you may find mercy. The fatal error in your present state may be a false security, or a reliance upon the mere mercy of God's character, not knowing that if He does not accept you in the righteousness of Christ, He is to you, and will be to all eternity, *a consuming fire.* Flee to the Saviour now as a lost, self-ruined, and helpless sinner. Listen to His own most gracious and encouraging word, *God so loved the world, that He gave His only-begotten Son, that whosoever believeth in Him should not perish, but have everlasting life.* Do not reply, 'I do believe,' if your belief is but the bare assent of the understanding to the truth of the gospel. *With the* HEART *man believeth unto righteousness.* If, with the penitent jailer, you truly believe in the Lord Jesus Christ, if your faith is a simple coming to Jesus, as a lost, undone sinner, receiving Him with your whole heart, you will experience a joy, and peace, and hope, which nothing in this poor world could ever give or take away. Cease not to wrestle with Him in prayer until He bless you. Yield your heart, if now a conviction of guilt burdens it, if now a sense of sorrow saddens it, to the gracious invitation of the Saviour, *Come unto me, all ye that labour and are heavy laden, and I will give you rest.* Seek that rest nowhere else but in Christ. The heart of Jesus overflows with love to sinners. It was to save sinners He condescended to live, and consented to die. He came *to seek and to save that which was lost.* Those who seek Him with the whole heart shall certainly find Him. Oh, lose no time! Every moment is of more value to you now than ten thousand worlds. Close your door, and exclude every object from your mind but Christ. Be importunate, and give Him no rest until you yourself find rest in His atoning work, and the Holy Ghost, in the riches of His mercy, applies to your conscience that precious blood of Christ that can alone impart peace to a poor, guilty, condemned sinner. Banish from your mind the notion of making your peace with God. It is only the Lord Jesus who can make our peace, by becoming, as He has done, a peace-offering to God for us. To Him, then, flee, who *saves to the uttermost all who come unto God by Him.*"

TO THE ARCHBISHOP OF ——, ON BAPTISMAL REGENERATION.

"MY LORD ARCHBISHOP,—

"Observing, by the papers, that the case of Mr. G—— is soon to come before you for adjudication, I presume to address you on the subject. It is as a fellow-believer in the Lord Jesus that I take this liberty, feeling that the question, that is to pass under your consideration, is closely connected with the glory of God and the honour of our Redeemer. Eternity is before us, and at the tribunal of God you and I will soon stand, pardoned, I humbly trust, by the blood and justified by the righteousness of Christ. It is with a close realization of this solemn fact I now write. The doctrine of Baptismal Regeneration,—a doctrine which, by those who hold it, is made to take the place of the renewing, quickening power of the Holy Ghost—is a dogma not found in the Word of God. That it may be taught in the writings of men I admit—and it is appalling to reflect how many souls, deluded and ensnared by this error, have gone to their account ' with a lie in their right hand,' caught in this net of Satan—but it has no place in the Bible. The Word of God is the Christian's sole rule of faith. It is from this word we are to draw the truths we believe—by this word we are to order our steps—and by this word we shall be judged in the last day. 'To the law and to the testimony.' A most solemn admonition meets us at the close of this sacred record. *If any man shall* ADD *unto these things, God shall add unto him the plagues that are written in this book.* Thus jealously has God guarded the purity of His holy word. He has spoken it, and I believe it. Baptismal Regeneration has been added by the dictum and teaching of men as a doctrine to be believed. For this He has a controversy with His church. I believe that He is sifting her, and is showing, by the existence and spread of Puseyism, the great iniquity of those who have engrafted, and would engraft, upon the revealed word an error so fatal to souls, and so dishonouring to the work of the Holy Spirit. I do most respectfully and earnestly implore you to ponder well your position. Seek counsel from the Most High. May He enable you to set aside the world's opinion, and to act with your eye fixed upon the great white throne and in view of an endless eternity. How many have passed into the eternal world fatally deceived by this error! Baptized in infancy, they were taught to view themselves as spiritually regenerated, as made the children of God; and they died, it is to be feared, with no more light and no more grace, believing they were safe. Terrible delusion! I beseech you to enter your solemn and decided protest against this insidious and spreading error. Who can tell but that God has placed you in your present eminent position, in order to deal a death-blow at this unscriptural and fatal dogma. When the Jewish nation was to be massacred, Mordecai said to the queen: *If thou altogether holdest thy peace at this time, then shall there enlargement and deliverance arise to the Jews from another quarter. . . . And who knoweth whether thou art come to the kingdom for such a time as this?* May the Lord God impart to your grace all wisdom, prudence, and faithfulness to do His will in this, and in all things connected with His glory. Soon will He come whose right it is to reign! All the devices of Satan, and all false doctrine, and erroneous teaching of men, will then vanish before Him. Oh, let us meet our God with unspotted hands! Cleansed by the blood of atonement, and sanctified by the indwelling Spirit, we shall stand complete, *not having spot or wrinkle or any such thing.* Regard me as one who prayerfully desires to see you, in your present position of responsibility and influence, act boldly for God, for His truth, and for His one church, so that His dear and blessed name be not dishonoured.

TO A—— G——, ESQ., OF NEW YORK.

"DEAR FRIEND,— May 3, 1848.

"I was much grieved to hear that your dear mother was no more. I believe she loved the Lord Jesus, and that she is now with Him who loved her, and washed her from her sins in His own most precious blood. I cannot forget her. Very dear was she to me. Many hours of happy intercourse we have had together; and the sincere, disinterested affection manifested towards me and mine has never been forgotten. I never cease to love, or can forget old friends. And oh, what a joy it is to know that, although she is gone from earth, I shall see her again, and enjoy a far more delightful intercourse with her above than ever I did below. God be praised for this good hope through grace. This, my dear

Mr. G——, was your dear mother's hope, and it is mine, and oh, may it be yours! Time is short, and eternity, with all its solemn realities, is before us. Oh, let me urge upon you to give your mind, your heart, your every power, to seek earnestly and perseveringly an interest in the Saviour of sinners! What can the world do for you at a dying hour? What could the wealth of ten thousand worlds avail you when you stand before the judgment-seat of Christ? When I last saw or heard of you, you were an unconverted man. But how is it with you now? Do you love Jesus, the sinner's Friend? Are you reconciled to God? Do you know Christ for yourself? Sincerely do I trust that God will answer your precious mother's ten thousand prayers, offered up for you, her only child and her beloved son. You were everything on earth to her. May you meet her in heaven! Shall I tell her when I meet her there (for soon my time will come), that you are on your way to glory? Write and tell me what are your views on the all-important subject of religion, and what are your hopes for eternity. Oh, flee to Jesus! He requires no work from you in order to purchase salvation. It is His own free gift of everlasting and unchanging love. Go to Him, then, as you are; He will open His arms to embrace you, more glad to receive you than you are to come. He came into the world to save sinners—poor, helpless, lost sinners—sinners that could do nothing to save themselves. To them he says, *Look unto me, and be ye saved. Him that cometh unto me, I will in nowise cast out.* I will not weary you, but will conclude, only expressing the hope that you will let me hear whether you have been brought to sit at the feet of the Son of God, that I may carry the news to your dear mother, whom ere long I hope to see, when we shall know even as we are known, and when all tears will be wiped from our eyes for ever. Believe me, heaven is worth living for, and worth dying for. It is all true. Heaven is true, and Christ is true, and God is true, and His word is true. May He bless you, dear friend, and save your never-dying soul.

TO E—— T—— C——, ESQ.

"Dear C——, June 3, 1848.

"Poor Mr. O—— is dead! Have you heard of it. If so, what was the state of his mind? Write and tell me. His poor wife, how I feel for her! Is not this a solemn call to us all? What is our life? How uncertain! and yet is it not awfully true that poor wretched man rushes heedlessly on, thoughtless of what awaits him in an endless eternity? Oh, that we who profess to have our eyes open—we who profess to know the way, the truth, and the life—did but so let our light shine around us, that others might be led to seek the same mighty blessings that await all who value their own souls! Dear friend, this is a solemn warning to you and to me. Poor O—— is gone! and we are travelling fast through this wilderness world, and soon shall pass away too. Let us, then, feel more like pilgrims and strangers here. Let us not seek our rest where our precious Jesus had no place to lay His head. Let us rejoice more in the prospect of that glorious inheritance prepared for us above, where He is who hath loved us unto the death. Oh, for ten thousand world would I not have my portion here! But I only intended when I took my pen to inquire of you any particulars of poor O——'s state of mind before he departed. He was your friend, I presume, or what the world calls a friend. Will you not go and see his poor wife? Be, in the best sense, the good Samaritan to her now. Visit her in her sorrow, and lead her mind to Jesus, the Friend of the friendless. Such has He been to me and mine, and as such I can commend Him to all. Oh, that all did but know Him, then all must and would love Him! My love to your wife. I wish I knew her better.

TO I—— W——, ESQ., BOSTON, U. S., ON THE ATONEMENT.

"DEAR FRIEND,— London, June 6, 1848.

"Although I have not written to you for some time, yet you have been much in my thoughts, and I determined, in the strength of the Lord, to address you once more, and, perhaps, for the last time on this side of eternity. You and I are hastening fast through time. At the longest period of our existence it is but short. But, oh, our spiritual existence! where and when will it end? Never, *never!* It is a solemn and awful truth, yet to the Christian delightful. As long as the existence of God Himself, so will be ours. *Because I live* (says Christ), *ye shall live also.* It is a blessed thought that the Triune God—the Father, Son, and Holy Ghost—are all engaged in the salvation of a poor sinner. The Father so loved the world as to give His only-begotten Son. The Son,

Jesus Christ, came into the world to save sinners. And it was through the Eternal Spirit He offered himself without spot unto God. The whole seventh chapter of Hebrews is full of the precious Atonement made by Christ for the redemption of the soul. *Without the shedding of blood there can be no remission.* I could wish, if possible, to be much in earnest on this subject; as it is *here*, my dear friend, I fear that we differ. If I am not saved by the Atonement made on Calvary, I am yet in my sins, and am *unsaved*. To be sound in the doctrine is needful (as you justly observe), for who can build a hope of heaven on any other foundation than that which is laid, Jesus Christ himself, the chief corner-stone? This one foundation is— God manifest in the flesh—offered and making a full and sufficient atonement for the sins of His people, laid to His account by the hands of Eternal Justice. He *was made sin for us, who knew no sin, that we might be made the righteousness of God in Him.* Without the Divine Atonement, I repeat, I am lost for ever. No mere *creature* could atone for the sins of millions of the human race. It was the Divinity of Christ that made efficacious all that he did and suffered. His resurrection was a receipt from Divine Justice that ample satisfaction had been given for the broken law of a holy God. All our righteousness is but as filthy rags, and how can we commend ourselves to God but as we stand in a better righteousness than our own? I feel my journey drawing to its close, and if I had to put my finger upon one single good action that I have ever done during my life that was not tainted and defiled by sin, as a term of my salvation, I should be eternally separated from God. Sin is mixed with every thought, and nothing but the blood of Jesus Christ can cleanse us from its defilement. If Christ is (not the *power* of God) not God Himself—God in our nature—He could not have atoned for one single soul of Adam's race. On this doctrine of the Atonement hangs our everlasting happiness. Our eternal all is at stake. Oh, let us never forget that Jesus Christ came into the world to save sinners! My only hope is in this; and I believe I shall be saved through the vicarious sacrifice made on the cross, when he exclaimed, *It is finished.* The Holy Ghost, too, the Third Person in the glorious Trinity, performs His part in this great work, in applying the atoning blood to the conscience, renewing, sanctifying, and taking possession of the soul here, and fitting it for the full enjoyment of the glory that awaits it hereafter. May the Lord the Spirit open our eye to see, and our heart to receive the truth as it is in Jesus. Love to all your circle.

TO J. T——, ESQ., ON REALIZING OUR ONENESS WITH CHRIST.

"DEAR CHRISTIAN FRIEND,—   May 30th, 1848.

"I have just received yours, and hasten to answer it. I am never better prepared to reply to a letter than when I first receive it. The memory is treacherous, and at 74 (this is, I suppose, the case with all dying mortals) particularly so. But I am wrong; the believer in Christ is, in a sense, immortal. For although the body dies, it only sleeps in Jesus, and shall be raised again at the last day. Three times in one chapter Jesus says, *I will raise it up again at the last day.* Here is comfort for you and me. Is Jesus increasingly precious to you? I gather from your letter that He is so. Bless Him for it. He is faithful to all His exceeding great and precious promises, and by them we are made partakers of the divine nature. Keep hold of your oneness with Christ. If we lose sight of that blessed truth, we are at sea in a moment. *I in you and you in me.* Think, then, that Jesus and you are one; one in time, and one in eternity; never separated, and inseparable. Oh, how this precious truth should be ever present with us on all occasions, at home and abroad, in public and in private, living or dying! Dear brother, go on to know more of the power of the resurrection of Christ in your soul, that you may thereby glorify Him who is your life, and that you may be more abundantly useful in His service. I am glad to hear that you have been able to do good in the name of your beloved Lord. Time is short—life is uncertain. Let us, then, employ the talent God has given us, that we may have more abundantly. Each believer has his or her gift, whatever that gift may be; and Christ says, *Occupy until I come.* Let us not bury our talent in earthly things, for these pass away, and we shall live for ever. We are on a journey the most eventful that ever an immortal undertook. We must press forward. There is no standing still in this journey. We are to follow on to know the Lord; to grow in grace. You have already travelled some stages in this heavenly road since I saw you; but there is much of the good land yet to be possessed. We are to go forward to know more of Christ and of our election of God; so shall we be happy in our souls and established in the truth. I am often grieved in meeting some, professing godliness, who seem to be standing still in the same place for years, and know no more of God than at the first. . . Let us, then, live near to Christ, and go oftener to Him. I find, from long experience, that confession of sin is one of the most healthful exercises of the renewed soul—constant and immediate confession. *If we confess our sins, He is faithful and just to forgive us our sins.* If I feel a corruption in my heart, dishonouring as it must be to God, what am I to do? If I sit down to reason it away, I might as well attempt to create a world. Then what am I to do? Take it at once to Jesus; tell Him all about it; and the faith that carried it to Jesus will overcome it in His name. Precious faith, with which we are to fight all our battles, and overcome in the name of Jehovah-Jesus. Oh, what mighty privileges has the follower of the Saviour! We learn to deal unceasingly with God, and God deals unweariedly with us. Let us aim in all things to glorify Him, for in a little while, *He that shall come will come, and will not tarry.* Let us keep a purified conscience by constant confession. We need not always retire to do this. In the street, in company, or anywhere, we can lift up our heart to Him; and a thought, a sigh can reach His heart, and He can manifest His forgiving love. I think, if there is a verdant spot in this wilderness world, it is where a poor believing sinner, with a contrite broken heart, sits at the feet of Jesus. The sinner confessing—Jesus pardoning—the blood applied, and the conscience cleansed—all guilt removed, and the redeemed of the Lord rising from his knees, rejoicing in the Lord his God. Such have I often experienced, and therefore I commend it to all who are followers of the Lamb. We have had trials of sickness; but the Lord often tries the faith of His saints, that they may try His faithfulness in the fulfilment of His promise. He is ever with them in all their troubles, and in all their concerns He is equally concerned. When we depart from Him He chastens, but does not lose sight of us, no, not for an instant. His glory is closely connected with all we say and all we do. *Know ye not that your bodies are the temples of the Holy Ghost?* Oh, how should this keep us watchful, lest we grieve this blessed Inmate! The Lord bless you and increase you in all spiritual knowledge, prays yours in a most precious Jesus."

It is a lesson which the church of Christ, in "these last days," has been practically learning, that the broadest spirit of Christian charity may exist in connexion with the most inflexible fidelity to Christian truth. A union that demands, as a holocaust upon its altar, the right of private judgment, freedom of conscience, and the privilege of 'speaking the truth in love,' is wanting in all the essential elements of a true and holy union. No individual ever maintained more strenuously the unity of the church of God, and at the same time bowed with profounder reverence to the supreme Headship and authority of Christ, than the subject of our memoir. To those who knew her but partially, she might have appeared, at times, exclusive in her views, and stern in her spirit. But to those who knew her long and well, that exclusiveness was but an uncompromising attachment to God's word, and that sternness but the intensity of her love to souls. As illustrating these happy features of a truly catholic Christian, we quote from her letters and journal:—

TO HER SON, REV. I. D. W———.

"I have just had a sweet visit from my own dear pastor Mr. Evans. How full of Christ is the heart of this dear man of God! Oh, that we were all more like him, or rather more like Christ. . . . Where I see the love of Christ most prevail in the heart, there I see love to the saints. *Love ye one another, even as I have loved you.* Blessed be God there are no separating walls in heaven; and of this be assured, wherever you meet with one who bears much of the image of Christ, you will find no bigotry or exclusiveness, but a prevailing love to all who are conformed to the same image. Let us beware of a spirit of sectarianism and exclusiveness, for sure I am, God is displeased with it, and will show His displeasure in due time. Let us live above all unholy, unrighteous feelings, and have little to do with those who hold them, for *evil communications corrupt good manners.* God is love. Heaven is one ocean of love, and believers are commanded to love one another, even as Christ hath loved them. The Spirit does not love to dwell where love is not the prevailing feeling. In fact where the Spirit is, there will be love; and the manifest want of this grace in any, is a proof that the Spirit of Christ is not in them."

TO ANOTHER OF HER SONS.

"If God will, I shall come to-morrow, and remain over the Lord's-day. May the Lord direct all my steps, and all my doings, and hedge up my way where I would go wrong. I shall see you, please God, soon after you receive this. I long to hear more about the sailing of that precious ship called the 'EVANGELICAL ALLIANCE.' I was fearful of a wreck on the slavery question. May the Lord, the Pilot, conduct her safely through all the dangers of her boisterous voyage. His banner over her is LOVE; and her freight is composed of precious gold, and jewels of the first water."

On a subsequent occasion she again alludes to this subject:—

"I rose early, and after a hurried breakfast, prepared to go to Exeter Hall, to the Meeting of the Evangelical Alliance. The place was filled, many standing. The meeting was not of that animated character that was exhibited at the first gathering at Liverpool; but still it was truly gratifying to see so many happy faces assembled together, to join heart to heart to aid in this alliance of Christian love and fellowship. The first speaker said a few words which, to me, were anything but encouraging. He remarked that we were not to expect much, or look for any great results at present, &c. I could hardly sit patiently, and listen to his unbelieving speech. We *are* to ask for, and expect great things, from a great God. Dr. Liefchild followed, and spoke well. Then Mr. Bickersteth, who also spoke much to the purpose. And then a hymn, and a long, a very long prayer, from a vicar. A Wesleyan minister followed, and after him Mr. Baptist Noel rose, and spoke with great energy, earnestness, and a clear head, but without excitement, for above an hour, and much to our satisfaction. Others were to speak, but, it being late, we were obliged to leave. There was, in my judgment, a deficiency. There needed more of the humble acknowledgment of sin,—the sin of disunion, want of love, &c.,—and looking to the Holy Spirit for help, which always indicates the Divine presence. There was this great lack. Nevertheless, it was cheering and pleasant to witness the union."

FROM HER DIARY.

"The love of Christ in the heart of the believer, is the cement that unites the church together as one body—Christ the Head. The Spirit of Christ in me recognises and acknowledges His own likeness in another, and goes out to that Christian in holy love. This is the sweetest of all Christian fellowship. It is thus the Lord is preparing His church on earth for the blessed place He has gone to prepare for it in heaven. He is spiritually educating and training her for her glorious inheritance above. It is ready, and the invitation from the lips of Jesus will soon be heard, *Enter into the joy of thy Lord.* And oh, the unspeakable happiness and joy of the redeemed and glorified family! With a calling so heavenly, and with a hope so glorious, what manner of persons ought we to be in all manner of holy conversation and godliness?"

> "Then let the rude tempest assail,
> The blasts of adversity blow,
> The haven, though distant, I hail,
> Beyond this rough ocean of woe.
> When safe on the beautiful strand,
> I'll smile at the billows that foam,
> Kind angels to hail me to land,
> And Jesus to welcome me home."*

TO A MINISTER—ON THE ANTI-STATE-CHURCH MOVEMENT.

"On reading your excellent remarks on the Anti-state-Church Association, I felt a union with your conciliatory spirit, and a sympathy with your views. With you, I think, as I did indeed from the first, that the movement was inexpedient and unwise. No one upon earth, calling himself a Christian, and in reality one, could more earnestly desire than myself, the severance of the Church of Christ from the world; and no one could more deeply deplore, or sincerely mourn over, such an alliance, than I. The Church of Christ upheld by the world, is contrary to Christ's express word,—*Ye are not of the world, even as I am not of the world. My kingdom is not of this world.* He who is the Head and Husband of the Church, surely is able to sustain and guide it through the wilderness, and conduct it at last to glory. It is not the puny arm of man that can accomplish this great work. From the moment that I saw the serpent head of Popery, under the disguise of Puseyism, rear itself in Oxford, from that moment I felt that God Himself was about to accomplish a great work, and by this *very thing* at which all were alarmed and which all deplored.

* Miss Taylor.

What is impossible with man is possible with Him. And when I saw, and firmly believed, that God was beginning to purify His one church, and with His fan thoroughly to sift His floor, separating the precious from the vile, I did deplore such an organization; and wondered that its promoters did not so discern 'the signs of the times' as to see God's own hand working. It appeared to me like Uzzah's attempt to steady the ark. And though I feared not like sad consequences as befel him, still the attempt seemed to me as unnecessary and feeble. I fear it has done no real good, and has but resulted in widening the separation already too much existing between the truly spiritual of God's people within the Establishment and those without its pale. At the same time I do call in question the motives of those who have embarked in the movement."

TO MISS M. C——, ON HER BAPTISM.

"Taplow, Lord's-day.

"I do rejoice to hear that the Lord is evidently in your midst, and with you, my young sister, in a particular manner, who has led you to acknowledge Him before a gainsaying world, and His church here below. Not that you are one bit more safe, or more in Christ than you were before your baptism; but you have showed your love to Him in obeying His sweet command, and casting away all confidence in what you once thought would do quite as well. You have now openly put on Christ—*buried with Him in baptism, wherein you are risen with Him through the faith of the operation of God, who hath raised Him from the dead.* So, beloved one, I trust, as in a figure, you were baptized in the likeness of His death, and your death, too, to the world, and the flesh, so you will be helped to go on your way rejoicing in Christ Jesus. Precious Jesus! how sweet to walk with Thee, taking up every cross we meet in the way, Thy love making it light and pleasant. Oh, to have faith simply to follow the Lord wherever he sees fit to lead us; to live for eternity, manifesting that we are not of the world, even as He was not of the world. So let us walk as He walked, taking His word only as our guide and directory; and I am persuaded, that if we go to Jesus and inquire of Him only, He will make our path plain before us, yea, and will travel every step of that way with us, too. We shall walk in God's company when Jesus is with us, and we walk with Him. . . . While I do wish to enforce upon all believers the great duty of obeying Jesus in *all* He commands, I do not wish to attach any undue weight to this sweet and most expressive ordinance. And yet I do think it is the duty of every believer to follow Christ, to walk as He walked; and in so doing, I believe it will add much to his comfort, consolation, and advance in the divine life. May the Lord lead us all safely and uprightly in the way, and the glory shall be to His holy name for ever and ever.

TO THE HON. AND REV. B, W. N———, ON UNITY OF JUDGMENT IN THE CHURCH OF CHRIST.

".... I am informed that you are writing a work on the church.... How important to remember that we are Christ's servants; that He hath given us all needful direction, and left us not to our own wisdom in any one thing connected with His glory, and the spiritual welfare of His one church. How necessary that in His church there should be unity of judgment in what He has taught and enjoined. The exhortation is, *Be of one mind. I beseech you, brethren, by the name of our Lord Jesus Christ, that ye all speak the same thing, and that there be no divisions among you; but that ye be perfectly joined together in the same mind and in the same judgment,* 1 Cor. i. 10.... Dear brother in Jesus, examine, in prayerful attention, the word of God. Lay the case before the Lord, and when you pray, *expect an answer.* Jesus is the very same—as full of compassion, sympathy, gentle, tender love, as when he walked the streets of Jerusalem. Oh, aim to get his listening ear. *Without me,* He says, *ye can do nothing.* It is as needful to hearken and to expect an answer, as it is to pray. The Lord does in reality bow down His ear to what His child would say. *This poor man cried, and the Lord heard him.* Dear brother, bear with an aged pilgrim who has almost got home—the pearly gates in view. Heaven seems a glorious reality, and I shall soon be there. It is all around us. Oh, to *live* for Him who *died* for us, and in constant communication with the Father, and His Son Jesus Christ. I am seldom in town, but when I am, I occupy my place in John-street, and have found it pleasant to hear and see you in that pulpit, where but a little while ago I heard my beloved friend and pastor for so many years."

To an eminent missionary, who, in his fervent and somewhat indiscriminate denunciations of slavery, had alluded in strong terms to the system in the United States, without recognizing the existence, and encouraging the labours, of those Christians in America who, amidst obloquy, self-denial, and loss, were toiling for the extinction of the evil, she addressed the following affectionate and faithful remonstrance:—

"BELOVED BROTHER IN JESUS,—

"I rejoice that the Lord has so graciously blest your work of faith and labour of love among the poor slaves in the West Indies; and may He go on to bless you. I feel it, however, a duty I owe to many dear people of God, to endeavour to correct an unintentional mistake into which you appear to have fallen, with respect to slavery in America. It is in the *Southern*, and not in the Northern States, that slavery exists; and even where it has its stronghold it is yielding to the force of public sentiment. In the non-slave-holding states there exists a noble band of Christians, who have come boldly forward to grapple with the evil, and whose labours God is blessing. You speak from hearsay, but I from personal observation. During my recent visit to New York, the first anti-slavery meeting was held by men who, in the fear of God, went forth with their lives in their hands, boldly and fearlessly protesting against the system. They took the spoiling of their goods joyfully; their dwellings were assailed—their sanctuaries were outraged—their persons were endangered; but God upheld them, and has so marvellously blest their efforts, that the little band has become a great one, continues to increase, and will increase, I doubt not, until there exists not a slave in America. These dear men are not to be overlooked, but acknowledged and affectionately encouraged, by all who love the cause of universal emancipation. I am personally acquainted with some of them, and a witness to what they endured for Christ's sake. We, in this land, can speak quietly on this matter, but it is quite another thing to confront the foe on his own ground, which these men of God do. God bless them and uphold their hands, until they shall see the blessed gospel carried through the length and breadth of the land; and not a slave in that highly-favoured country be found who shall not, in all the glory of his freedom, both from the bondage of Satan and of man, stand up to praise God for having inclined the hearts of His people to advocate their cause. May the Lord bless you, and keep you near himself, that while you are labouring for the souls of others, your own soul may be continually refreshed from the Fountain of living waters, is the sincere prayer of, yours in the dear Redeemer."

TO HER NIECE, MRS. G.———, ON COMMENCING THE DIVINE LIFE ARIGHT.

"DEAR M———, March 30.

"I have only time to write a few lines in answer to your question. Mr. E—— never did preach one thing and do another. He does not himself baptize, as his health would not admit of it; but that he has been baptized is certain, and your informer has been misinformed. . . . May the Lord direct you in every step you take in this heavenward journey. It is most important and eventful. Nothing on earth can possibly be of equal moment to you and to me. Oh, to be quite sure that we are right! Short may be our journey, as we have seen by many dear to us. They have passed away, and we are following. The scene unfolding before us is grand —it is most glorious. The prospect to me, at times, is most delightful, and soon shall I see Jesus, my best Friend, with whom I have had sweet communion here, and so many precious souls dear to me, among the millions that surround the throne. Oh, commence this journey right. Everything depends upon a right beginning. One wrong turn in setting out, and all will be wrong the whole of the way. The starting point for the saint of God is the finished work of Jesus—to know he is pardoned and accepted in the Beloved of God the Father. It is then he knows his election of God, and can say, 'I am saved!' He then can run the race with holy delight; and though he may necessarily have many enemies to contend with, both from within and from without, yet He who has once set him upon his feet and bid him go forward, will watch over him, by day and by night, guide him and correct him when needful, and assuredly enable him to hold out to the end. And then the reward!—*Come, ye blessed of my Father.* I do not say that all the children of God have equally clear and distinct evidences of their sonship; but I do say they ought to have it, and it is their own fault, and not Christ's, if they have it not. I would inquire of such, Has Christ spoken peace to your soul? Has He manifested himself to you, according to His promise? If He has not, do not rest yourself, or give Him rest, until you have that mighty blessing. It is for any poor, needy, seeking sinner. Seek it until you receive it, and be not satisfied without it. '*Ye shall find me when ye seek me* WITH YOUR WHOLE HEART.' Many who, from not setting out aright, have gone on sickly and infirm all their journey, are never truly happy in themselves, or capable of administering to the happiness of others. Jesus Christ is the same now that He ever was. He that spoke to Abraham, to Isaac, and to Jacob—who was with Moses in the wilderness, and with the Apostles in their labours—who appeared to Saul of Tarsus, and to many others, after His resurrection, is the very same now. He is not changed one bit. He is as ready now to make Himself known to His saints, and to speak sweet peace to their souls, as He ever was. Only believe, and you shall see, and your soul shall rejoice with joy unspeakable and full of glory. Oh, to have the Lord always with us, by day and by night, and not to rest without we are sensible of His precious presence! Seek for Him; for everything indicates that His coming draweth nigh. Have your lamp bright and shining—plenty of oil in your vessel."

TO ONE OF HER SONS—ON PUBLIC PRAYER AND READING.

" . . . . I have often wished to say a word on the subject of public prayer and reading. You know my dislike to *preaching in prayer;* and you also disapprove of it. And yet I think many ministers are apt to fall into the same evil, although I know some who never do. Prayer is the most holy exercise of the soul, and should be the pure breathings of the renewed heart in humble, earnest petition, as in the presence of a holy God. And when the soul feels in the presence of God, and loses sight of the worms of the dust who are listening to Him, there is no self-seeking or wish to please the ear of man, but humbly to get the blessed ear of God himself. This may be a difficult matter at times, but the more it is tried, the more the Lord, the Spirit, will aid the effort. My opinion is, that both prayer and preaching should be what the poorest might understand and feel, and also meet the warmest desires and approbation of the most cultivated intellect. How sweet is the simple, precious truth just as the Scriptures give us! May the Lord bestow every gift and grace of His Holy Spirit, and anoint most richly for His own work. Again, I have observed that in reading the Scriptures in public, there is frequently this defect. For instance, the epistles are often read in a devotional tone of voice. Now, they are merely letters to the churches, and should be read in the same tone of voice as one would read a letter, and not as if one were praying. Then, again, the gospels are mere narratives, or details of the history of the church and the apostles, and should be read in the same manner in which one would read any other history. Some of the Psalms may be read in a more solemn and devotional tone of voice, but not all. Those that David offered as prayers should be read as prayers, but no others A person with a refined taste and a cultivated ear would soon detect the inconsistencies. I think a good *reader* is almost as necessary as a good *preacher;* indeed, the one seems essential to the other."

TO HER SON, REV. G. E. W———, ON INTERCOURSE WITH GOD.

" . . . . As it respects what is generally called 'news,' I have none to tell; but as you will expect to hear from me, I can have a little chat with you; for how strange it would be if a Christian mother had nothing to say to a believing child, without adverting to this poor dying world, while professing to be striving for another and a better! Is there not enough in a precious Jesus to engage all our thoughts and all our hearts? We love to talk of an absent friend who is dear to us; and what friend is there like Him? And should He not be dearer to us than the dearest object on earth? He is that *Friend that sticketh closer than a brother*, and a *Brother born for adversity.* Let us not for a moment imagine that when things go smooth with us here, that we are no more to see tribulation, that we shall have no more time of trouble. If we forget or neglect Him in prosperity, will He hear and answer us in adversity? Oh, let this base ingratitude be far from us. Let Him be our chief joy now. Let us keep very near to Him, and let no idol come between our soul and our best, nearest, and dearest Friend. Believe me, when I have passed an hour in company with the worldling, and the precious Saviour has never been mentioned, I have felt, when upon my knees, guilty before Him, and have hid my face in shame; and more so still, when He has condescended to seal a fresh pardon through the application of His precious blood, by the power of the Holy Ghost. Oh, how dead are the unconverted to this heavenly, holy intercourse between a child of God and his Heavenly Father! Truly, *the secret of the Lord is with them that fear Him.* . . . I wish you had one day set apart at your own house, or in the church, for meeting and conversing with those who are inquiring their way to Zion. Good Mr. —— does this, and also has a particular service with the believers every week, to know the state of their souls. *Be thou diligent to know the state of thy flock. Take heed, therefore, unto yourselves, and to all the flock over which the Holy Ghost hath made you overseer, to feed the church of God, which He hath purchased with His own blood.* Oh, walk in the truth, to the glory of Him who will have you render up an account of your stewardship at that great day, for which all other days were made."

The reader will not fail to have remarked how strong a hold upon her faith and Christian feelings the doctrine of our Lord's resurrection maintained. It might almost be said to have been *the* truth which the Holy Spirit unfolded to her mind. She saw, as with the keen eye of the acutest theologian, the intimate and essential relation of this single truth to the whole Christian scheme. This one fact of the gospel verified, she knew that all other doctrines were true. Her whole Christian life was a constant dealing with the life of Jesus. In the grace that sanctified her, in the strength that supported, and in the consolations that soothed her, she was a constant witness of the fact that—*Jesus was alive.* She was never known to linger at His empty grave. Often has she been seen to weep at His cross, never at His tomb. The sufferings of Christ have been known to dissolve her whole soul into penitence; the *resurrection* of Christ to fill it with the sublimest joy. And who, with any spiritual apprehension of this truth, will charge her with exaggerating either its importance or its preciousness? The resurrection of Christ is the resurrection-life of the Christian. A living Christ dwells in him—a living Christ intercedes for him—a living Christ upholds, guides, shields, and comforts him; and when "Christ, *who is our life,* shall appear, then we also shall appear with Him in glory."

"I experienced much comfort and enjoyment this morning, in meditating on the resurrection of Christ. I felt that He was really risen; that my best and dearest Friend was truly alive and in heaven for me; there, seated at the right hand of God, loving and watching over me and mine, and that I was safe in His hands, come life, come death. I fell upon my knees, and poured out my soul in adoring gratitude, praise, and thanksgiving. I long for another fresh token of His love in the conversion of all dear to me. I thought of the stone rolled from the door of the sepulchre, while Mary was pondering in her mind how it could be accomplished. The Lord, who can do all things, can remove the stone that lieth upon the dead, and the dead shall live to praise and bless His holy name."

"The only way which a good and gracious God has pointed out to us in the Scriptures, in which we may be enabled to go on our heavenly journey is, by LOOKING UNTO JESUS, not only when we first commence, but all our journey through. In the first place, we ought to be well assured that we have really and truly been reconciled to God through the precious peace-speaking blood of His dear Son. If we have sought Him with our whole heart, we have found Him; and if we have found Him, we must know that all our sins are freely forgiven for His sake. *Ye shall find me when ye seek me with your whole heart.* This is true, for God, who cannot lie, says it."

"LOOKING UNTO JESUS.

"Wherefore droops thy trembling soul?
Wherefore sadden'd is thy brow?
Clouds around thy path may roll,
But thy God is present now.
Raise thine eyes, the cross is there,
Steadfast still, though tempest frown;
Lift up thy head, and make thy prayer,
Claim thy Saviour for thine own;
Make through Him thy deep appeal,
LOOKING UNTO JESUS, *kneel.*

"He, the Author of the faith
Which thy Spirit shall renew,
In His sacred hour of death
Finish'd thy salvation too.
Learn thy Saviour's power to see;
He, the life, the truth, the way,
Interceded e'en for thee,
Ere thy heart had learn'd to pray.
Lift thy heart, and raise thy hand,
LOOKING UNTO JESUS, *stand.*

"When the water-floods of grief
Round thy helpless head shall rise,
When there seemeth no relief,
Look toward the eternal skies:

God is only effectually profitable as it is worked out by the trying providence of God in the soul's deep experience. Head-knowledge will not do. Hearing with the outward ear does but little for the soul, enables it to make no headway towards heaven, or unfolds to us the tenderness of Christ, or the real character of God. The truth as it is in Jesus is more known in one deep trial than a year of smooth sailing. Worldly prosperity is but indifferent soil for the Christian to grow in. It rather stunts the soul; and nothing but an Almighty arm can save from the sleep of death."

Not only was she permitted to see her children, but her children's children, avowing her covenant God as their God and Portion. She thus gratefully records the interesting event:—

From her Diary.—" The work of grace in the family has filled our hearts with wonder and joy. Three of T——'s children, I do trust, have been brought to surrender their hearts to Jesus. The Lord is answering my prayers; He has dropped the mantle of His love upon my grandchildren, and called them into His kingdom. The work in their hearts is a gentle drawing with the cords of love to a Father's reconciled bosom, where, I trust, their precious souls will be screened from all the evil of an evil world, and be prepared to serve Him here and hereafter. Their convictions of sin have not been deep, but God the Spirit works as a Sovereign in all He does; and what they know not now they will know hereafter, as he leads them onward. Perhaps, if they knew what a bed of impiety lies deeply seated in their hearts, they would at once sink into despair, and give up all for lost. But the Lord will, by little and little, make them acquainted with their own hearts in the same proportion as they know His heart. Oh, how wisely He acts in all His dealings with His children! He gives no account of any of His matters, but acts as a Sovereign on His throne."

" In my private reading this morning, went through God's gracious dealings with the children of Israel, in the third chapter of Joshua, in dividing the waters of Jordan, and taking them over in safety to the good land He had promised to Moses. Afterwards, I read the same in the family, and found much liberty in speaking a little from it. It was sweetly encouraging to my own soul; for Joshua's God is my God; and, although I hear no audible voice from heaven, I hear the still small voice of the Spirit speaking to my inmost heart. Blessed be God for the precious revelations of His holy will concerning us! I am in a wilderness, but God is with me. I walk by faith, and not by sight. He is in all things concerning me. I find it the hardest thing to sit still when in difficulties. My busy, unbelieving heart is ever for doing or undoing,—planning and arranging better and quicker than a good and wise God. Oh, to be still and wait patiently on God! this is my wisdom. I thank Him for keeping me from betraying outwardly my spirit, however the storm may have raged within, and thus bringing dishonour on Him whom my soul loveth. I bless him for preventing grace, for restraining grace, for a throne of grace, where I can relieve my burdened heart, and tell Him all, keeping nothing back, good or bad. Oh, is not this a mighty privilege? The God of Heaven, the Creator of all worlds, stooping in love to simple dust! Had sweet access to Him this morning in private. His presence humbled and melted my heart with deep contrition. How I loathe myself, at such favoured seasons, in dust and ashes before Him!"

"Have been forcibly impressed with the truth, that the kingdom of God comes not with observation. A stander-by knows nothing of what is passing within the soul of the believer—the mighty work which God the Spirit is carrying silently on. The hidden evil is revealed—his soul, in sorrow, flees to Jesus—the Comforter applies the blood to the accusing and disturbed conscience—the throne is erected—the King reigns supreme—the soul rejoices;—all this transpires in the believer without any outward sign, and the world knows it not. And so the kingdom of God's grace in the soul worketh secretly and silently, and without observation."

"My memory fails me. . . . . Lord, whatever else fails me, never, oh, never let me forget Thee, nor cease to pray and praise while I have breath to do it! Oh, thou blessed and Eternal Spirit, help my infirmities, and open both my heart and my mouth! Oh, take of the things of Jesus, and show them to me, that I may be enabled to ask and expect great things from Thee for His dear sake ! Lord, teach me to pray! I would sit at Thy feet as a little child and learn of Thee. Lord, help me! Strengthen me, for I am poor and needy! My soul trusteth in Thee; let me not be put to shame. Suffer me not to grieve Thy Holy Spirit, or dishonour Thee before the rising generation! Thou hast promised never to leave nor forsake me, and, even down to hoar hairs, to carry me."

"How wonderful is God in all His great and gracious dealings! He places us, as soon as the spiritual eye is opened, in His school. First, the infant-school; and then onward and upward, from class to class, losing no opportunity of spiritual instruction. Many hard lessons have we to learn and to relearn. But, oh, the unwearied patience and tenderness of our Teacher! Some of His children are slow learners, dull scholars, and require the discipline of the rod to stimulate them to more earnestness, attention, and submission. Some imagine they have arrived at the end of their education, and sit down at their ease: but presently they are called upon to solve some hard problem, and they find that they know less than they thought, and for their boasting are sent back to a lower class, and made to commence where they first began. Such is the school of Christ. Lord, teach me more and more of Thyself, and of my own poverty, misery, and weakness. And, oh, unfold to my longing eyes and heart what there is in Thyself to supply all my need, and in Thy loving, willing heart, to do all for me, and all in me, to fit me for Thy service here, and for Thy presence hereafter! Sanctify abundantly all Thy varying dispensations to the welfare and prosperity of my soul, and increase in me every gift and grace of thy Spirit, that I may show forth Thy praise, and walk humbly and closely with Thee. Thou knowest what a poor, worthless worm I am, and how utterly unworthy of the least mercy from Thy merciful hands; but Thou lovest to bestow Thy favours upon the poor and needy, such as me, thou most precious Lord. Thou hast been a good and gracious, sin-pardoning God to my soul, and a very present help in every time of trouble. Leave me not, nor forsake me, now that old age is overtaking me, and grey hairs thicken upon me. I know Thou wilt not. Thou, who hast been with me all my journey, wilt not leave me now; for Thou art faithful that hast promised. I feel my dependence on Thee more than ever. Without Thee I can do nothing. Helpless as an infant, I hang upon Thee, to do all for me and all in me. Oh, what a Friend is Christ to me!"

"Ill in bed with influenza. The Lord still gracious and kind. All is in love. No good thing does He withhold. Mercy, mercy, mercy, all is mercy. The bush on fire, and not consumed,—such am I. Sin enough in my flesh to kindle a flame that never could be quenched; but the Spirit is there to overcome; and faith, however weak, is always a conqueror. Faith honours God, and God honours faith. Little faith never need to hang its head; it can do wonders with God, and for God. It is His own gift, and given like Himself, full and free, and it is ever pointing to eternity."

CHAPTER XI.

"IF the Lord has ever honoured me in any way by making use of me, it has been in comforting the comfortless, or in speaking a word to the tried and heavy-laden; but never, to my knowledge, in rousing the dead sinner. I must leave that to better hands. God does not honour me much in that way. He fits His people for whatever work He has for them to do, and when they attempt any other they fail. And yet I do feel most anxious for the conversion of sinners. No subject lies so near my heart, and for nothing do I more earnestly pray." Such were the lowly views of herself, as cherished by the subject of this memorial. And what, though her talent was single, and her mission limited? What if God had confided to her no other and costlier gift, or had appointed her to no higher or wider sphere than that of counselling, succouring, and sympathizing with the perplexed, the feeble, and the tried of His family? Surely, it were a gift to which the highest angel in heaven might aspire, and a mission he might pant to discharge. To this work, for which she seemed peculiarly and pre-eminently fitted, she was, in the providence of God, frequently called. Schooled in adversity, she knew how to address herself to those who were tracing the dreary path she had already trod. Having drunk deeply of the cup of grief, she could speak a word of heart-cheer to those whose lips were but just touching its brim. Call we this a feeble gift, a minor mission? Oh, there is no distinction like that of being a *benefactor* of MIND; and there is no privilege like that of expressing *sympathy* with SORROW. But how little is the philosophy of sympathy understood! How few regard and cultivate it as a self-disciplinary feeling, equally as a means of soothing and alleviation to others! And yet there is scarcely a single one in the class of our emotional feelings more peculiarly adapted to work out this grand result. "Sympathy," as an eminent phil-osophical writer justly remarks, "by bringing us in contact with individuals in various forms and degrees of suffering, tends to withdraw us from the power of self-love, and the deluding influence of present things. . . . The due cultivation of the benevolent affections, therefore, is not properly to be considered as the object of moral approbation, but rather as a process of moral culture. They may enable us in some degree to benefit others, but their chief benefit is to ourselves."* Who cannot, from experience, testify to the truth of this? Who that has sought to soothe another's woe has not found a balm for his own lonely grief? Who that has poured out his soul in intercessory supplications for others has not felt the prayer he breathed to Heaven returning into his own bosom laden with its joy and peace? In a word, who, in the indulgence of a sacred benevolence, and with a single eye to the Divine glory, has ever attempted the accomplishment of any good, has not been conscious of a mental enjoyment the most exquisite, and of a moral discipline the most salutary? Such is the reflex influence of true sympathy. It is now our privilege to present a few of Mrs. Winslow's letters of Christian consolation, selected from a large mass, without any particular regard to exact chronological arrangement. The following remarks from her Diary may not be an inappropriate introduction to these epistles :—

"I think, if the believer makes any attainment in the knowledge of God and of himself, or any advance in the Divine life, he must have much to do with the varied and changing providences of God. In this way the Spirit chiefly and mainly worketh in him, and grounds and settles him in the truth. There is not a single truth in God's word which will be of any avail to us, but as it is wrought out in the experience of the soul, by the power of the Holy Ghost, through the varying dispensations of Divine Providence. Thus the Israelites were led through many trials and difficulties in the wilderness, to show them what was in them. We are such obtuse scholars; and I often wonder and wonder again at the patience of a good, gracious, and unchanging God towards us. He varies His dealings, that He might teach us our nothingness, weakness, and total helplessness. Faith, too, is constantly brought into exercise, and is thereby increased in strength, by an in-

* Abercrombie on the Moral Feelings.

CHAPTER XI.

"IF the Lord has ever honoured me in any way by making use of me, it has been in comforting the comfortless, or in speaking a word to the tried and heavy-laden; but never, to my knowledge, in rousing the dead sinner. I must leave that to better hands. God does not honour me much in that way. He fits His people for whatever work He has for them to do, and when they attempt any other they fail. And yet I do feel most anxious for the conversion of sinners. No subject lies so near my heart, and for nothing do I more earnestly pray." Such were the lowly views of herself, as cherished by the subject of this memorial. And what, though her talent was single, and her mission limited? What if God had confided to her no other and costlier gift, or had appointed her to no higher or wider sphere than that of counselling, succouring, and sympathizing with the perplexed, the feeble, and the tried of His family? Surely, it were a gift to which the highest angel in heaven might aspire, and a mission he might pant to discharge. To this work, for which she seemed peculiarly and pre-eminently fitted, she was, in the providence of God, frequently called. Schooled in adversity, she knew how to address herself to those who were tracing the dreary path she had already trod. Having drunk deeply of the cup of grief, she could speak a word of heart-cheer to those whose lips were but just touching its brim. Call we this a feeble gift, a minor mission? Oh, there is no distinction like that of being a *benefactor* of MIND; and there is no privilege like that of expressing *sympathy* with SORROW. But how little is the philosophy of sympathy understood! How few regard and cultivate it as a self-disciplinary feeling, equally as a means of soothing and alleviation to others! And yet there is scarcely a single one in the class of our emotional feelings more peculiarly adapted to work out this grand result. "Sympathy," as an eminent phil-osophical writer justly remarks, "by bringing us in contact with individuals in various forms and degrees of suffering, tends to withdraw us from the power of self-love, and the deluding influence of present things. . . . The due cultivation of the benevolent affections, therefore, is not properly to be considered as the object of moral approbation, but rather as a process of moral culture. They may enable us in some degree to benefit others, but their chief benefit is to ourselves."* Who cannot, from experience, testify to the truth of this? Who that has sought to soothe another's woe has not found a balm for his own lonely grief? Who that has poured out his soul in intercessory supplications for others has not felt the prayer he breathed to Heaven returning into his own bosom laden with its joy and peace? In a word, who, in the indulgence of a sacred benevolence, and with a single eye to the Divine glory, has ever attempted the accomplishment of any good, has not been conscious of a mental enjoyment the most exquisite, and of a moral discipline the most salutary? Such is the reflex influence of true sympathy. It is now our privilege to present a few of Mrs. Winslow's letters of Christian consolation, selected from a large mass, without any particular regard to exact chronological arrangement. The following remarks from her Diary may not be an inappropriate introduction to these epistles :—

"I think, if the believer makes any attainment in the knowledge of God and of himself, or any advance in the Divine life, he must have much to do with the varied and changing providences of God. In this way the Spirit chiefly and mainly worketh in him, and grounds and settles him in the truth. There is not a single truth in God's word which will be of any avail to us, but as it is wrought out in the experience of the soul, by the power of the Holy Ghost, through the varying dispensations of Divine Providence. Thus the Israelites were led through many trials and difficulties in the wilderness, to show them what was in them. We are such obtuse scholars; and I often wonder and wonder again at the patience of a good, gracious, and unchanging God towards us. He varies His dealings, that He might teach us our nothingness, weakness, and total helplessness. Faith, too, is constantly brought into exercise, and is thereby increased in strength, by an in-

---

* Abercrombie on the Moral Feelings.

creasing knowledge of God's veracity, power, and love. We often pray, *Lord, increase our faith.* The Lord, in answering this prayer, places us in such circumstances as call it forth. The little we have (and we often find we have much less than we thought we had) is to set to work with God, with whom alone faith has to do. Providences, adverse and painful, stir up to cry mightily unto God. Then come in the promises. These become unspeakably precious. Faith takes them, as so many promissory notes, to the great Promiser for acceptance. Faith takes them, as so many promissory notes, to the great Promiser for acceptance. Faith knocks and waits, knocks and waits again; thus is it exercised and increased. Presently the hand, the helping hand, is held out, and deliverance comes, and God, the mighty Deliverer, is seen. Then we say, *The Lord is my helper; I will not fear what man can do unto me.* All our journey through, from first to last, the great work of preparation for usefulness in His service here, and for the rich enjoyment of His presence in glory, is thus carrying on in the soul of the believer. When his spiritual education is finished, he is at once put in possession of the inheritance prepared for him from before the foundation of the world. Oh, what a God is ours! Who is like Him in wisdom and goodness, mercy and truth?"

To a beloved friend, endeared by a long and tried friendship, she thus writes, in a season of anxiety:—

"Beloved in the Lord Jesus,—

"I remember you in my poor prayers, and do trust the Lord will be with you, giving all needful grace, wisdom, and above all, precious faith, to cast your burden upon Him, and from whom cometh all our help. Is He not a present help in time of trouble? He will carry you through your labour of love, for His name's sake, and give you to acknowledge, that as your day, so was your strength. Has He not given you a work to do for Him, and will He not fit you for the work, seeing His own glory is connected with it? Fear not, then; Jesus is with you and me. He has laid by one upon whom, perhaps, you depended too much, to show you how easily and blessedly He can work by whatever instruments He chooses to employ. We are so prone to look to the creature; and then He takes our prop away, that we may lean upon Him and upon Him only. . . . Now, beloved sister, be of good courage. God is with you, Christ is with you, the Holy Ghost is with you, and all the host of heaven are with you, and you need not fear. Be not over-anxious. There is an anxiety that borders on unbelief. Get rid of that, and believe that Jesus is really with you in all you have to do for the spiritual welfare of those dear children. I grieve for dear Mr. ——. May the trial be abundantly sanctified to him. If he is to be useful, he must have trials; and, perhaps, God is teaching him some precious truth from soul-experience, for which he will have to praise and bless Him throughout eternity. He does nothing in vain towards His own people, for He loves them too well to afflict them for nought. I shall continue to remember you all; and do not forget your sister in the tribulation and kingdom of Jesus Christ, for I truly need your prayers.

TO MISS L. O——, ON THE DEATH OF HER MOTHER.
"MY DEAR YOUNG FRIEND,—   October 28th, 1851.

"I have been longing to write to you; but although I have not done so yet, you and your dear sisters have been much in my heart and in my thoughts. The Lord has taken from you your dear mother, I humbly hope to His own loving self. If so, you will meet her again; and oh, what a meeting will that be! What a gathering! Your dear mother is now beyond all care and anxiety, hushed to peace in the bosom of Jesus, the Saviour of sinners. Think of her as she *now* is. She has seen the Lord. What a change, from a bed of weariness and a body of suffering, to be in an instant in the presence and within the arms of Christ! Oh, let it be our aim, our chief business, and the desire of our souls, to walk humbly and closely with God! In a little while and we pass away; and oh, how we shall wonder at ourselves that we could have suffered any one thing to divert our minds, even for a moment, from the great, the overwhelming concerns of eternity! . . . And now you are cast, in an especial manner, on the all-protecting care and love of Jesus Himself, who will be both a Father and a Mother to you all. I often think of the last interview I had with your dear mother, Lady O——, when she called upon me at Brighton. How little did I then think I should see her no more on earth! She looked so well, and was in such good spirits. Now she is with Jesus. Oh, the infinite compassion of the Lord! A look, a desire, a sigh He will acknowledge. Great faith will bring great comfort into the soul, but little faith can get to heaven. If no more than as a grain of mustard-seed, it will land the soul safely there. Blessed be God for all His great, rich, and precious promises. They are all like Himself. And now, beloved friend, it is the will of God that you should look to Him, and to Him only. He is a Father to the fatherless. Whatever your care or trouble may be, take it at once to Jesus. Your present position is an enviable one; for, if God be for you, who can be against you? Were your dear father and mother still with you, what could they do for you more than God Himself can do?"

TO THE SAME.

"January 10th.—I am longing to hear how the Lord your God and Father is dealing with you. You are peculiarly His own. When father and mother go, then the Lord will take you up, and carry you in His loving fatherly arms, care for, and lead you through this wilderness; so that you have nothing to fear, and nothing to do but to trust in the Lord with all your heart. Has your brother E—— arrived? and how is he? I feel deeply interested in you all, since your trying and heavy loss. Your orphan state, at present, is one of peculiar and tender interest. May the Lord enable you to take a fresh hold of Him, and he will prove Himself better than ten parents. Why has he dealt thus with you? To bring you to a better acquaintance with Himself, that you might know more of that loving, faithful heart, that says, *I will never leave thee nor forsake thee.* I would not have been without my sad trials for ten thousand worlds. What should I have known, the little I do know, of His wondrous, tender, and unchanging love, but for them? The Lord bless you and your dear sisters, and keep them in the hollow of His hand, and bring them to His heavenly kingdom. And oh, what a meeting we shall have in heaven! This is but a wilderness, and, like the children of Israel, we must pass through it to reach our heavenly home. Live much in holy contemplation of the glory that awaits you. This will enable you to bear the bitter trials that daily cross your path. Carry all your difficulties, small and great, at once to Jesus. His ear is open to your requests, and He will make every crooked path straight, and rough path smooth. We are on a journey, and how soon it terminates! But, oh, how awfully blind are many who call themselves Christians!

Religious formalism is the bane of thousands. They *say* prayers—but never *pray.* They know nothing of the great change from nature to grace—nothing of the new birth. They have no personal, spiritual acquaintance with Christ; nothing of real conversion. Is it not melancholy to see so many whom we love, yet living in the gall of bitterness and in the bond of iniquity, while we know that dying in that state they are lost for ever? Oh, let us pray for them, who know not to pray for themselves. My love to Mrs. F——; to your aunts at Brighton. I love all who love Christ. Also, your brothers and sisters. They are one family. Oh, to be a *whole* family in heaven! Let me hear from you."

TO MRS. F——, ON THE ILLNESS OF HER HUSBAND.

" BELOVED FRIEND,— January 26th, 1852.
"I hear your dear husband is ill. May the Lord heal and comfort him. May he have the enjoyment of His manifested presence. Satan will try hard to harass him, but Jesus is near. His darling attribute is mercy—mercy to the chief of sinners is the delight of His soul. *Call upon me in the day of trouble, and I will deliver thee, and thou shalt glorify me. Look unto me, and be ye saved.* This same Jesus, tell your husband, is waiting to be gracious to him. He listens to hear his voice. I trust he is resting alone in Him. Tell him not to look within for evidence, but to look direct to Jesus only. He is just the same that He was when He trod the streets of Jerusalem. Was He ever known to reject any who came to Him? It is not in the heart of Jesus to turn away from the vilest who call upon Him. It is sinners He came to save, not saints, and *as sinners* we must come. I trust the Lord will comfort you in your present trial. May He manifest Himself to your dear husband! I enclose for you the 'Untrodden Path.' "

TO THE SAME—ON THE DEATH OF HER HUSBAND.

"I only heard of your loss yesterday. The Lord has taken your dear husband from the evil to come, and in a little while you shall meet him again. May He comfort your sorrowing heart with a blessed realization of that glorious truth, *Them also which sleep in Jesus will God bring with Him.* And should He call us away before He comes, we shall still meet them in glory, and join our shouts of praise with theirs. In the meantime, beloved friend, you are the object of His especial care, as His endeared child. You have a double claim on Jesus now, who is the husband to the *widow*. Go to Him with all your fears, your difficulties, your pressures, whatever they may be; great or small, real or imaginary. His loving ear will be ever open to listen to your voice. Your oneness with Jesus makes your cares His cares, your concerns His concerns. He will deny you nothing that will be for your good or comfort. This will make the little space left us on earth less irksome; and constant communion with this precious Friend will tend to conform us to His image. Let me hear how the Lord dealt with your dear departed, and how He is dealing with your bereaved heart. Oh, what an honour put upon us, to have Christ as our Husband; and now that He has written you a widow, this is what He is to you and to me."

TO MRS. E—— B——, ON THE DEATH OF HER CHILD.

" MY DEAR YOUNG FRIEND,—

"I see, by the papers, the Lord has been pleased again to try you in removing, or shall I not rather say, in housing, another of your little ones; it is gone to join the host of those already there. '*Of such*,' says Christ, '*is the kingdom of heaven*.' This has been, no doubt, a severe trial, and your affectionate heart has deeply felt it, as well as your dear husband. But as there is nothing that can take place towards a child of God but what our Heavenly Father designs, in infinite love, for our spiritual advancement, which is closely connected with His own glory, we are to submit to His holy will, and believe that there was a needs-be for it. The Lord loves His children too well to lay upon them the weight of a feather, without an absolute necessity. I hope you have been enabled to say, *Not my will, but Thine be done.* Perhaps, in this affliction, you have felt it hard in God to deal thus with you; and the enemy may have suggested that God could not love you, or He would not so afflict you. Now, the reverse is the case. The Lord chastens those whom He loves; and were we without chastisement, we might well doubt our sonship. Your little ones are not lost, but have only preceded you to glory. They are taken from the evil to come. The Lord loved them better than you could do, or He would not have relieved them so soon from all the ills and temptations of this poor, wicked world. A time of affliction should be a searching time with our hearts. We should see how matters stand between our souls and a heart-trying God. He is jealous of our love. He will occupy the first place. And if, upon investigation, we find that the world or the creature has displaced the Saviour from our affections, what, then, have we to do? Only to acknowledge our iniquity, returning to Him who is willing to receive our confession, and to pardon our sin . . . . May He comfort your heart and bless your soul."

TO MRS. C――――, ON HER ILLNESS.

"MY DEAR FRIEND,—   September 2nd, 1852.

"I was glad to see your handwriting to-day, but how sorry I was to hear you continue so tried in body! Surely the Lord loves you too well to lay the weight of a feather upon you, were it not for some wise and loving purpose He has in view preparing you for the full enjoyment of the glory He has gone to prepare for you. Think of this when resting your afflicted body,—Jesus had no bed on which to rest—no voice to speak a word of kindness; persecuted and reviled, He sought the dark and dreary mountain, and there He rested. He was then paying our debt of sin to Divine Justice, and He paid it to the last mite. . . . . . God, even our own God, deals wisely and graciously with us in all His varying dispensations. God is love, and no one that knows Him can doubt it for a moment. If tears could be shed in heaven, we should weep that we ever mistrusted His goodness in His dealings towards us. Let us, in this world of trial, cling close to Him, and lean more upon Him as little helpless children. Keep a constant intercourse with Him. Tell Him all you feel, or wish or want. Christ and you are one. We are bone of His bone, and flesh of His flesh. . . . . May the Lord's richest blessings rest upon you."

TO THE SAME,—ON THE DEATH OF HER SISTER.

"You have been in trouble, and I knew it not until last evening. And has the Lord at last appeared for His suffering child? Has He taken her out of all her troubles, to her happy, happy home? Long had she been refining in the furnace, and preparing for that place Jesus had gone to take possession of for her. Not one pain did she suffer, or sorrow did she feel, but had in it the tenderest love of Jesus. All was needful. He was preparing her for the full enjoyment of His presence. *Shall not the Judge of all the earth do right?* I wish her joy. She has made her escape from a world of sin and trouble, and from a body, not only of sin and death, but of suffering, and long a clog to her soul. She has broken loose from her cage, and is with Jesus. Oh, the happiness to look upon Him—to behold Him in all His unveiled beauties—to see Him face to face! I rejoice that she is at last released. I feel heaven is very near. Oh, to be ready, *quite* ready! . . . . The recognition of the saints in glory is a sweet thought. Shall we know Abraham, Isaac, and Jacob, and not know those with whom we have had sweet fellowship on earth? Surely we shall; and one of the delightful employments of heaven will be, to trace back the way the Lord led us safely, in spite of ourselves, through the wilderness world; and then shall we see how needful was every cross, and trial, and pain, and dispensation, with which our precious Jesus saw fit to exercise us. And we shall meet where all differences of sentiment will be for ever done away, and we shall see eye to eye, and Christ will be all in all to our unhappy souls. Let us try to be more like Christ, and less like ourselves. May the Lord bless you, and comfort your heart, and the heart of the bereaved widower,* and the motherless children, is my earnest prayer."

TO MRS. C——, AT A TIME OF DEEP AFFLICTION.

"Dear sister in Jesus,— Leamington, May 9th.

"My dear son has permitted me to see your mournful letter; and having myself passed through the dark waters of tribulation, I thought I would drop you a line, to encourage your heart in the Lord. When we recollect that Jesus and His saints are one—*I in you and you in me*—that this blessed union is eternal, and can never be dissolved; then is He in all our afflictions and trials, great and small. Nothing can take place towards us but is especially designed for our advancement in the Divine life. He has now placed you in just that position to prove His faithfulness and love. Watch His tender dealings towards you, and see if He does not prove to you that He is better than ten husbands, or ten thousand friends. He

---

* The late Venerable Archdeacon Hodson, one of the brightest lights of the Church of England, eminent for his sound theological views, as for his earnest piety. He died recently, while making the tour of the Continent.

wants you to be better acquainted with Himself—to know Him more personally. He wants you to have more to do with Him, that you may understand more of His real character, both as to His divine and human natures. These are stately steppings Jesus is now taking with your soul. He says to you, 'Now come nearer to me, My child; look more into My loving heart—see your name written there never to be effaced. Fear not. I will never leave thee, for we are *one*.' You have hitherto loved Christ for saving your soul; now He would have you love Him for what He is in Himself. How can this be, unless you are brought into closer contact with Him? He has taken your husband, to place Himself in the same position. He wants you to live a life of sweet, holy dependence upon Him as your Husband, Friend, Provider, Care-Taker, Benefactor. He designs to be all to you and yours, a Father to the fatherless, and the widow's God. Beloved, you are highly honoured of God; you are now in a position to live a life of faith on the Son of God,—the happiest, the holiest life a mortal can enjoy in this world. You have now a twofold claim upon God, as His adopted and His widowed child. Take Him now as one who has engaged to provide for all your wants, and the wants of your children. Go to him for all you need—not first to the creature, but to Jesus at once. If we honour the creature more than we honour Christ, we must expect He will suffer us to be disappointed. Tell all to Jesus; keep nothing back from Him. Only trust Him fully. Honour Him with your entire confidence. We live at too great a distance from Christ. He wants us to experience more of His sympathy, His boundless love, His nearness to, and His oneness with us. Forgive me if I have presumed in giving this advice to one whom I only know through her sweet letter. I am an aged pilgrim, who has travelled this thorny road before you. I may be permitted to speak a word for Jesus to one who, in some measure, is travelling the same. May the Lord make these few hints a little help to you in your pilgrimage.

TO MISS L. O——, IN BEHALF OF A DISTRESSED CLERGYMAN.

"DEAR YOUNG FRIEND,—

"You will, perhaps, call to mind the circumstance of the Rev. Mr. ——, the clergyman, who has fallen into very distressed and trying circumstances. His health prevents him from labouring as he could wish, and his family is large. I wrote to dear Mr. Noel, and he has sent me a little help; and now I must remind you of your promise to do what you can for this dear afflicted servant of God. *Inasmuch as ye have done it unto one of the least of these, my brethren, ye have done it unto* ME. Do you remember James Montgomery's 'Stranger and his Friend,' which S. C—— used to play with so much feeling, and which always brought Jesus, precious, compassionate Jesus, present to my mind? A verse will remind you of it:—

> 'A poor wayfaring man of grief
> Has often crossed me in my way,
> And sued so humbly for relief,
> That I could never answer, Nay.
>
> 'I had not power to ask his name,
> Whither he went, or whence he came;
> Yet there was something in his eye
> That won my heart, I knew not why.'

I must send you the music. Your dear sister, M——, will sing it with effect. Now, will you endeavour among your friends to assist this dear man? See Christ in His servant, believe and feel that you are doing it *for Him*. Return me the enclosed letters, and what your hand findeth to do, do it *quickly*, as I must hasten to send him all the aid I can. Dear —— has commenced a course of sermons on the Creation. The one last Lord's Day evening was on Genesis i. 2: *And the earth was without form*, &c. The sweetest part was the Spirit of God moving upon the face of the waters—figurative of the Spirit hovering over the dark, chaotic soul of man. The lecture was listened to with breathless silence, and, I hope, was blessed to many a dark, unconverted soul present. Be not long in answering this, as I shall wait impatiently until some help be sent. I am informed they are really suffering from want. My Christian love to all your circle."

TO HER SON, ON THE DEATH OF A CHILD.

"The Lord has mercifully housed our dear little sufferer; has taken it to His garden of perfume above. It was so appointed by Infinite wisdom. I trust you will see it so. If the utmost tenderness and love could have saved her, she would have been saved. . . . She is not lost; she is in the tender bosom of Jesus; and this was designed from eternity.

May your hearts be comforted, and you be enabled to say, '*The Lord gave, and the Lord hath taken away; blessed be the name of the Lord.*'"

TO MRS. G.———, ON THE DEATH OF HER HUSBAND.

"DEAR C———, May, 1849.

"I loved your precious mother, and now that you are in trouble, my heart turns to you in this your hour of deep sorrow. God had need of your dear partner, and has sent for him home. He only lent him for a season; and now look at him where he is. Would he, if he could, return to this poor, wicked world, and again take up that body of sin, and of suffering, and of death? Think of him as a pure spirit in the presence of God, at the feet of Jesus, mingling with that holy, goodly company, your dear sainted mother among them, around the throne. Much as he loved you, would he return? And now, dear C———, fulfil your mission; let your heart be comforted, and say to the Lord, 'Here am I; what wilt thou have me to do?' Be assured He will comfort and soothe your widowed heart, and enable you to give it all to Him. He is a jealous God, and covets the whole heart, and well does He deserve it. Your dear husband never did for you what Jesus did. He paid the full penalty due for all your sins, and now claims you for His own. But still you have your work assigned you. These little ones are given you to bring up for God. I would comfort you with the comfort with which I myself have been comforted of God. . . . And now only have I spoken of myself, but to lead your bleeding heart to the same rich source of consolation. God is love, an ocean of love, nothing but love. His tender, loving eye is upon you, and His loving heart is towards you at this moment. *Ask what ye will and it shall be done unto you.* See what a God and Father He is. He has given you a work for Him; and soon we shall all pass away, and have done with sorrow and sin for ever. A thousand times have I thanked the Lord for all my trials and afflictions. I would not have been without them for worlds. They have been messengers of boundless love and mercy to me and mine. I do trust this will be your rich experience.'

TO THE REV. J. H. E———, ON HIS ILLNESS.

"MY BELOVED BROTHER,— October 18th, 1845.

"The word in my heart at this moment is, 'Praise

God from whom all blessings flow.' Yes, beloved, even your trial, your present trial, shall be to the praise of His dear and holy name. Be of good cheer, God has sent it; it is a messenger of love,—nothing but eternal, boundless, never-ending love. The Lord sent you to preach glad tidings to poor, lost sinners; and to gather in His own sheep, feeding them in rich pastures, and causing them to lie down beside the still waters. But now He has closed your lips for a season. He who sent you to preach, now bids you cease for a time, until again He says, 'Go and preach the preaching that I bid thee.' Well, beloved, is He not as full of love in all this as ever? Just the very same. Only trust Him for all consequences. He is doing all things well. Leave yourself in His blessed hands, and seek more for cheerful submission than for the removal of the trial. Resignation will follow, and then, what a calm! Oh, how soothing is the voice of our Beloved! How it comforts and hushes the restless, agitated feelings to peace! we then lie quiet in His hands, and feel that His will must be best, because He is God, and knows the end from the beginning, while we know nothing. Dear, dear brother, let us rejoice that you and I are in His loving hands, and leave ourselves there. If He says to me, 'Be satisfied to be lame and a cripple for the little remnant of your pilgrimage;'* and if he says to you, 'You have preached My gospel, but now it is my will that you be silent;' what! are we to think hardly or unkindly of this? How restless and earnest I was to be healed; but no healing came, until prompted by the Spirit to ask for *submission;* and in a moment it was given, and all was calm and quiet within. And what then? In due season the cure most unexpectedly came, and I was made whole. So may it be with you, my tried brother. Be assured this affliction is sent for some especial good,—for a great blessing to your soul, and to the church at large. I would not now have been without my trials, no, not for a thousand worlds. Oh, the goodness of God was so richly displayed, that I have no power of language to express it. Wondrous is He in His dealings with us, and He is dealing with us every moment of our existence, and we with Him. How little does the world know of the wondrous transactions that are going on every instant between heaven and earth,—the unceasing intercourse between God

---

* The allusion is to a lameness, which for a time prevented her from walking, and which threatened to render her decrepit for life.

and His chosen and adopted family! But why should I enlarge on a subject to you, who are so much better taught than I am? only you are now in the cloud, and I have just come out of it, and can and may be allowed to speak a word of comfort to your tried soul. May the Lord comfort and guide you in every step, and enable you to lie passive in His loving hands."

TO MRS. H——, ON THE DEATH OF HER HUSBAND.

"DEAR SISTER IN JESUS,— January 9th, 1853.

"I may say, too, in tribulation, for the Lord has written you a widow indeed. Such are His loving dealings towards those, one and all, whom the Father has given Him. We must all pass through much tribulation to the kingdom He has gone to prepare for us. Let us, then, take up the cross, and follow hard after Him. A little while, and we shall be there, and join all who have got there before us. Sweet thought! Oh, let us try and realize it. Heaven is not so far off as we imagine. The world of spirits is all around us. Absent from the body, we are present with the Lord. Dear friend, I do trust this trial will draw you so sensibly near to Jesus as to enable you to go on your way, realizing more and more the gracious manifestations of the Lord to your widowed spirit. Jesus is always near to you, listening to hear what you would say to Him. Take Him now as your Husband, Friend, and Brother,—that Brother born for *your* adversity. Oh, is He not all that you could wish or desire? Take Him for your constant companion; He will never fail you. I feel my time here cannot, in the common course of nature, be very long. But, as I draw nearer and nearer, heaven seems to open with increasing attraction; and the prospect of seeing Jesus, that same Jesus that bore all my sins on the accursed tree, and so many dear to me in the ties of nature, around that glorious throne where Jesus sits, fills me with joy unspeakable and full of glory. It is all true. I can see afar off, as it were; the distance seems to vanish, and the realities of the better world seem sensibly near. Oh, dear friend, live upon your best Friend. There is nothing too small to carry to Jesus. Abroad, at home, in company, or in the street, lift up your heart, and tell Him all you feel and all you desire. Aim to have constant communion with Him. Let Him not be long out of your sight. Oh, to have to do with Jesus, and with

Jesus *only!* Do not make up your mind to do aught before you ask counsel from Him. The heart is deceitful, and will lead us astray. Let us be very jealous over this inward foe, and only consult our dearest and best Friend. . . . If it be pleasant to have fellowship with the saints of the Lord in the midst of much imperfection, what must it be when we get home, and cluster altogether around the feet of Jesus, who lived and died, and rose again for us! Oh, help me to praise Him! You cannot think how often I take my walks above, and how pleasant they are. It is so real. I seem to see so many I have loved, and had fellowship with here, all around the throne; and to see that loving, tender, sympathizing Jesus, who once was a man of sorrows, who bore my sins, paid all my great debt, and ransomed my soul from the destroyer,— now, in all His glory and infinite beauty, waiting to welcome home every new-born soul. Oh, He is an ocean of love,— nothing but love is in His dear heart towards you and me. Who would not serve Him here that knows Him? Follow on, dear friend, to know more and more of Him. Keep up a constant intercourse with Him. I hardly know how to stop, my heart is so full. Pray for me, and may His sweetest blessings be with you."

TO MR. W——, ON THE DEATH OF HIS WIFE.

" . . . The Lord has laid His heavy hand upon you. All is in love. May He open your eye to see it. He loves us too well to afflict us without a need-be. When we get above, we shall see how needful the chastening of Him who loves us, for our preparation for the full enjoyment of that place He has gone to prepare for us. Oh, what a change! from earth to heaven—from a suffering bed to a mansion of glory. *You* are the sufferer; but dry your tears, for home will come at last, and may we receive from His own loving lips a *Well done, good and faithful servant; enter thou into the joy of thy Lord.* I feel for you, and pray you may be sustained and comforted of God. Jesus is very near. He is ordering all things for you. He does not willingly afflict us. It is to wean us from a dying world and from ourselves. We too much grovel here; the Lord sees the encroachment of earthly ties, which leave but half for Him. Let us, then, gird up the loins of our mind, and make a fresh start for heaven. A crown of glory awaits us. Jesus, the very same Jesus, is on the throne, as full of love, compassion, and sympathy as when a man of sorrows here upon earth. And, although He has taken wife and child from you, blessedly housing them near Himself, He has not taken Himself, but is with you, and will comfort your poor sorrowing heart. Soon you will meet again those you love, and be for ever with the Lord. Oh, the glory that awaits the Christian! By all these painful dispensations He is preparing us for the full enjoyment of that glory—glory begun here—glory increasing throughout eternity. This world is not worth a thought; and we should ever bear in mind, it is but a passage to a better. . . . Dear brother, let this fresh trial, like a stormy gale, drive you nearer and still nearer to Jesus. Make Him your all in all. Live upon Him, and you may live with Him even here upon earth. Oh, it is a little taste of heaven below to enjoy the lifting up of His own loving countenance. Covet these gracious manifestations of His presence to your soul. Heaven is all around us. Angels are the Lord's messengers watching over every step. Yes.

'The hour, the hour is hastening,
  Spirit shall with spirit blend,
Frail mortality is wasting,
  Then the secret all shall end.

' Let, then, the thought hold sweet communion,
  Let us breathe the mutual prayer ;
Till in heaven's eternal union
  We meet with those we've loved while here.'

" May this season of sorrow draw you closer to his heart."

TO AN AFFLICTED FRIEND.

" MY DEAR FRIEND,—

" The Lord has tried you of late, and I do feel anxious to speak a word of comfort to you in this affliction. Those whom He loves He invariably tries. The graces of the Spirit are thus brought into holy exercise. Jesus is thereby honoured, and our souls ascend a higher round in that ladder that reaches from earth to heaven. We must sit at His feet, and believe that He does all things well. What we know not now, we shall know hereafter. The Judge of all the earth must do right. Oh, let us cling closer and closer to Him than ever. Let us make Him our all in all. Oh, to live for eternity! Eternity! solemn thought! The eye, the all-searching eye of God is upon us at this moment. May the constraining love of Christ, the eternal love of the Father, and the sanctifying love of the Holy Ghost, rest upon you, guide, and bless you."

TO MISS E. W——, IN TRIAL.

"Dear Friend,—   April 16th.

"You are one of God's tried ones. The trial of your faith is much more precious then gold, for it will appear in the end that it was needful, and that you could not have done without it. Do not think, because I have not written for some time, that I have forgotten you. Ah, no! You have often been in my heart.

"Dear friend, this is our season for the trial of faith, and every fresh trial, under the loving eye of Jesus, and sanctified by the indwelling Spirit, is like a fresh gale wafting us nearer and nearer to our port—to the place He has gone to prepare for us. All these things work together for our prosperity of soul. 'Heaven is a prepared place, for a prepared people,'—the one family of God. Oh, beloved, what must it be to be there! I am now living on the verge of it. A few weary steps more, and I shall be put into my possessions, all prepared by the hand of eternal, unchanging love. We shall never think when we get there that we had one trial too many. We shall see, too, that we could not have done without one of them, for that *all* were so many needful lessons to instruct us in a journey through a wilderness full of temptation; and that Infinite wisdom had chosen them for us. I know your trials are often great, but the loving eye of Jesus is upon you, and your name is deeply engraved upon His heart. Whom He loves He loves unto death. I am near my eternal home. Jesus is very precious and His presence is sensibly with me. I have at times most precious glimpses of the glory of heaven, and of the reality of the resurrection—of Jesus seated on the throne, looking as full of pity, sympathy, and boundless love upon all the weakest of His little flock, as when here below. He is just the same now. Go to Him at once, dear friend, be your trouble what it may. Lift up your heart, though surrounded with company, or sitting by your dear sick sister; only raise it, in silent breathing, and He will hear and answer. It will be the prayer of faith—the faith of one who feels she has no help but Jesus. May his sweetest, richest blessing rest upon you, my dear sister; and if I see you no more here, I will meet and welcome you above.

"P. S.—I live now more as a little helpless child (an infant) upon Christ, than ever I did in my long life."

TO THE REV. B. P———, AT A TIME OF SEVERE DOMESTIC AFFLICTION.

"Leamington, Oct. 26th.

"DEAR BROTHER IN A PRECIOUS JESUS,—

"One in Christ, and in the kingdom of tribulation, I feel a desire to drop you a line, though personally unknown. You are in trouble—this is enough—and having myself passed through the same, I feel doubly anxious to speak a word, if the Lord permit, of comfort to your weary and tried spirit. It is through much tribulation we are to enter the kingdom—how true is this to every saint! . . . Oh, dear brother, it is an honour put upon a saint of God to be called to taste a little of that sorrow through which Jesus, our Elder Brother, passed for us. Deep, awful, and mysterious was His tribulation when our heavy debt was laid upon His righteous soul. What we are called to taste is but to refine and meeten us for the full enjoyment of that place He has gone to prepare for us. Be it so, Lord, only let our tribulation cause us to cling closer and closer to Thyself. I am sure this will find an echo in your soul. Submission to His loving will under trial He only can give. In vain we try ourselves—our reasoning powers will not avail us: our deceitful hearts will argue the point, and leave us as far off its attainment as ever. We must go in all our helplessness to Him who has said, *Without Me ye can do nothing.* Dear brother, this you know better than I do. But this I know, that when a storm comes upon us, often a mist is cast before us by the enemy, and we cannot clearly see our way; then is the time to cast ourselves at the feet of Him who is watching over us with a loving, sleepless eye. We are in the furnace, but not alone; the Son of God is with us, saying, *Be not afraid, it is I.* I have passed through deep, dark waters, but I now feel that these things were sent for my good, and I would not have been without His chastening for ten thousand worlds, and you will have to declare the same. The Lord deals with us with a view of causing us to know more of His wondrous love, and the glorious mystery of fellowship with his suffering. Jesus who loves us has 'done all things well,' and this we shall acknowledge before angels and men. I should never have known so much the tender sympathy, gentleness, and matchless love that there is in the heart of Jesus, nor have enjoyed so much union and communion with Him, or the interchange of a holy recognition, but for His dealings. . . . The Holy Spirit is given since Jesus came to restore, in a measure, the sensible presence of a good and gracious Father to His children. And those who walk closely with God are permitted to hear His voice, evermore speaking to them by the Spirit within. Great is the mystery of godliness! Oh, to hold fast our oneness with Jesus! To come with an open heart, in all our helplessness, and tell Him all. Is not this a mighty privilege for a poor, helpless sinner? What need we fear when He invites us to cast our burden upon Him who is able to bear our burden and sustain us too? We want more childlike simplicity in obeying the commands of Christ. Soon we pass away to our heavenly inheritance, and then we shall see all the way He led us through the wilderness was the right way, and that not one trial or cross could have been dispensed with. Forgive me for troubling you with this, written amidst much interruption; but the Lord laid you on my heart, and I could not refrain from telling you so.

Accompanying the preceding and touching letter, addressed to an honourable servant of Christ, was a copy of the following exquisite lines on Christian sympathy, for which she might have sat as the original to the gifted author:—

> " Must I my brother keep,
>   And share his pains and toil;
> And weep with those that weep,
>   And smile with those that smile?
> And act to each a brother's part,
> And feel his sorrows in my heart?
>
> " Must I his burden bear,
>   As though it were my own,
> And do as I would care
>   Should to myself be done ;
> And faithful to his interests prove,
> And as myself my neighbour love?
>
> " Must I reprove his sin,
>   Must I partake his grief,
> And kindly enter in
>   And minister relief;
> The naked clothe, the hungry feed,
> And love him not in word, but deed?

"Then, Jesus, at thy feet
  A student let me be,
And learn, as it is meet,
  My duty, Lord, of Thee:
For thou didst come on mercy's plan,
And all thy life was LOVE to man.

"Oh, make me as Thou art,
  Thy Spirit, Lord, bestow;
The kind and gentle heart
  That feels another's woe,
That thus I may be like my Head,
And in my Saviour's footsteps tread."*

Such are a few specimens—culled from an extensive correspondence—of her letters of Christian sympathy. The thoughts and feelings they so glowingly express welled up from a heart trained in that most blessed and instructive of all schools—sanctified sorrow. Her posture while penning them would seem to have been that of the 'disciple whom Jesus loved,'—leaning upon the bosom of her Lord; or, to quote her own expressive words, 'taking her walks above,' and dating as from the borders of the Celestial City. Comforted herself by Jesus, she sought to lead all who were in any trouble to the same divine source of consolation. From heartfelt experience she could say, "Oh, taste and see that the Lord is good!" Again we ask, What, though this were her only gift, where, in the Church of Christ, is there one more rare or more precious? And yet what Christian, whose consolation has abounded by Christ, may not go and do likewise? Who that has a wound healed by the Saviour's sympathy, may not gently lead another bleeding heart to Him? It is thus we aid Him in His mission of love to our world. We recur again to her Diary.

"April 23rd.—Surely I have seen an end of all perfection both in myself and in others. But, oh, there is One, and only one, and He is perfect. The Lord be praised for this! The goodness, the long-suffering, the loving-kindness of God surpasses our conceptions. Eternity only can unfold it to us, and we shall be even there learning it out for ever and ever. O Lord Jesus, make me holy—sanctify me for Thyself. Fill me with Thyself, that I may know what it is to be filled with all the fulness of God. Sanctify me, body, soul, and spirit."

* Rev. Dr. Raffles.

"27th.—When disappointed in the creature, I take refuge at once in Jesus. I run to Him, and find Him all my heart could wish. Oh, how precious is a throne of grace to my soul—a meeting-place between a holy God and a poor sinner, sprinkled with the blood of His dear Son, and ever a verdant spot, inviting a poor, needy, trembling sinner at all times and under all circumstances. Lord, how could I live without Thee? Thou art my all in all! my comfort, my joy, my peace, my strengthener, my home for time and eternity."

"30th.—How intricate is often the believer's way! So hedged up that He cannot discern a single step before him. All is dark. He here and there goes too often to the creature for counsel, and, perhaps, for sympathy, but finds all but broken cisterns. But Jesus is at hand—a Fountain of living waters, ever ready to impart all comfort, wisdom, and direction. But, oh, how slow to approach this Fountain! How base and ungrateful the heart, and wretched the unbelief that still lurks within, ever leading us away from Him who is a present help in every time of need. Take up thy rest, oh, my soul, in Him who hath loved thee with an everlasting love, and will love thee unto the end!"

"There is a voice—it comes to me
  On memory's happy wing,
When doubts and dark despondency
  Their fearful shadows fling;
'I am thy Helper, I thy Friend,
I'm with thee always to the end.'

"When trials came, and threat'ning ill,
  And dearest comforts fled,
I look'd above to Zion's hill,
  And the blest promise sped,
To soothe my heart, to chase my fear,
'I'm with thee always—I am near.'

"When duties press'd with heavy weight
  Upon my bosom sore,
My pathway seemed more dark and strait.
  I heard the voice before—
'Take up my cross and follow me,
Soon thou shalt my salvation see.'

"And when the spoiler's cruel dart
  Had touch'd my fairest flowers,
Dear, cherish'd objects of my heart,
  And sadd'ning all my hours,
The voice then came so small and still,
It bow'd me to Jehovah's will.

"'Twas dark upon life's rugged sea,
    And friends who once did shine
In days of fair prosperity,
    I could not claim as mine ;
One then replied, 'I am thy Friend,
I'm with thee always to the end.'

"And oft when sickness, feverish pain,
    Came with relentless power,
Methought I heard the voice again,
    Sustaining in that hour;
'I am thy Saviour, I thy Friend,
I will be with thee to the end.'

"And when the strife of death comes near,
    And darkly rolls cold Jordan's wave,
I'll look to yonder brighter sphere,
    To Him who has the power to save.
Oh! may I trust Him to the end,
The sinner's everlasting Friend!"

CHAPTER XII.

TRUE religion, as we have had occasion to remark, is essentially experimental in its nature. Find it delineated where we may—in the sacred volume, or in the uninspired records of the saints of God—its nature, its phases, and its effects are identically the same. Who can trace the histories of Abraham, of Moses, and of Job—read the psalms of David—glide along the enchanting stream of prophetic truth—listen to the discourses of Jesus—peruse the letters of His apostles, or catch the last tones of inspiration as they float from the lonely Isle of Patmos, and not feel that true Christianity is nothing less than the life of Jesus dwelling in the soul of the believer? But Christian experience varies; it may be more strongly developed in some individuals than in others. One believer may present a more robust type of this essential characteristic of Christianity than another. It is not, perhaps, difficult to account for this difference. He may have been more an object of God's especial dealings, and consequently he has had closer dealings with God. He may have been more variedly tried, more heavily afflicted, more frequently chastened; he may have been led into a deeper insight into his own heart; he may have been permitted more thoroughly to learn his native vileness and weakness, and by a process most painful and humiliating; he has had more to do with providential dispensations—he can tell of blighted hopes, of disappointed schemes, of withered flowers, of broken cisterns; he has become more closely acquainted with God; has learnt more of Jesus, has kept a closer eye upon the hidden work of the Spirit in the heart; and thus, by these varied processes, he has become a more deeply *spiritual* and *experimental* Christian. Of this class was the honoured subject of our memoir. Christian experience, in some of its most holy, lovely, and touching unfoldings, was pre-eminent in her religious life and correspondence. Not merely do we trace it in the recorded exercises of her own soul, but also in the intense, holy concern she felt and expressed for the religious progress of others. To the illustrations already given, a few more are added, gleaned alike from her private journal, and her general correspondence. The following touching *résumé* of past experience is taken from her diary.

"'Faint yet pursuing,' is my present motto. Hitherto has the Lord been with me, and so far has He brought me on my eventful journey. On looking back, I have much to mourn over, and I have much to be thankful for,—mercy and goodness, faithfulness and boundless love, have followed me every step of the way. The Lord has gently and tenderly led me on. Once, and but once, He laid His hand sorely upon me. But it was the rod of the 'covenant, ordered in all things and sure.' It pressed heavily. I could not discern a Father's hand. Overwhelmed, almost stunned, with the suddenness of the affliction, I lost my hold and confidence in Him who had said, '*He would never leave nor forsake me.*' The enemy seemed to sift me as wheat. Bereaved of an affectionate husband—deprived of fortune—friends far away—in a strange land, heart-broken and alone—while the pitiless storm raged over me, I would steal away and weep in secret agony. Such was my state and such my misery, when the Lord sent a man of God to me with a message of love to my soul. He spoke of the unalterable love of Jesus, and of His never-failing compassion, even while He chastened. He opened up and unfolded the precious truths of the gospel with such power accompanying every word, that I once more raised my head, and lifted up my heart to God as my Father still; who though He had chastened me, yet His anger was turned away, and I was comforted. Many, since then, have been the trials I have had to pass through, but the Lord has stood by me, and delivered me out of them all. Strength has been given to me equal to my day. The precept was laid upon my heart, *Owe no man anything;* and I have been enabled to walk in that precept, and God has fulfilled the promise, *Your bread shall be given you, and your water shall be sure.* I was led to walk by faith in an unseen Protector, Provider, and Friend. I never went to bed owing anything but love. I repaired to God for all I wanted, feeling I was His child and doubly so as his widowed child. As such, I called upon Him in every time of need for counsel in difficulty, for strength in weakness, for healing in sickness, for supplies of grace to uphold and keep me near Himself, my best, my only Friend on earth and in heaven. He never, no, never failed me. His ear was ever open to my cry, and His love shed abroad in my heart, was my joy and my comfort by day and by night. My children are grown up —some are walking among those that fear His name; and I still pray and believe that the promise will be fulfilled which He gave me in the early days of my lonely widowhood—*I will be a Father to thy fatherless children.* How can He be a Father, and one be lost? Not so, Lord, for Thy word shall never fail of all that Thou hast put Thy name to."

"How is it with Thee now, O my soul? Is thy God still gracious, and art thou yet upheld and comforted? Has old age overtaken thee, and thy pains thickened upon thee, and is thy God still faithful to His promise? Yes, oh yes! He is all and everything He has said He would be. He is my joy by night and by day. My comfort in sorrow—my stay in trouble—my strength in weakness—the lifter up of my head, and my portion for ever. God be praised! God be praised!"

"Still, I have cause to praise and bless the God of my salvation, and the God of all my comforts. 'His loving-kindness, oh, how great!' I am, however, still called to fight, to watch and pray. The world with its cares, unbelief with its fears, and Satan ever on the watch to tempt, harass, and allure: and yet, in the midst of it all, the Lord indulges me with much nearness to Himself, and a subdued heart at a throne of grace. I pray, and praise, and weep before Him, and feel He is my Father in heaven. Jesus is precious. I felt to-day as if I could say I loved Him better than all created beings, however near and dear to me. But, while thus pouring out my heart to Him, I thought of poor Peter, and remembered how little he knew of his own heart when he said so boldly that he was willing to lay down his life for his beloved Master. I acknowledged my inability to do better than Peter, but could say, I did *desire* to love Him supremely from my very heart, and to prefer His love to every other love beside."

"February 28th.—This day I am nearly three-score years and ten, and during that period the Lord has borne with my manners in the wilderness, while goodness and mercy have followed me all the way. What shall I do, or what can I say to Thee, thou God of love! Oh, for a heart filled with grace, that I may make some little return for such an ocean of goodness! But no, I must still come a poor, needy, unworthy sinner to the throne of grace. The dust is my proper place; there must I lie. But a little space may now be left me; my journey may soon come to an end. How glorious does the gospel appear to my soul! It just suits my case. Blessed be the Father of our Lord Jesus Christ for His unspeakable gift. And oh, the thought, that if I had been the only sinner on the face of the earth to be saved, He must have died—He must have been that Man of sorrows—He must have sunk down to the utmost depth of degradation—He must have grappled with death, hell, and the grave—He must have shed every drop of that rich blood that cleanseth from all sin, ere I could have entered the kingdom of heaven! Oh, then, how vile am I to serve Him so ill, and make so few returns of love for such an ocean! God knows it is my desire to love Him supremely, to live to Him, and to live for Him, and Him only. But oh, this heart of mine! what can I do with it? Lord help me! Help one that is willing to be helped, and looks alone to Thee for that help she so much needs."

"I felt humbled at what passed last evening—too much trifling conversation. I do hope the Lord did bring me to His footstool this morning with a broken heart. I think there is more danger in being with lukewarm professors than with the unconverted. I shed many tears, and abhorred myself before Him. Oh, the exquisite tenderness, compassion, and long-suffering of Jesus towards such a one! Oh, for more wisdom, discretion, and the power of the Spirit within! Blessed be His holy name, for every precious promise He has left to encourage our souls in this incessant warfare. Trying it often is; there is no other help but to run to Jesus, and the Fountain opened for sin. It is there we get the broken and contrite heart, and fresh strength to go on in spite of all that opposes us in our progress homewards. Lord, strengthen Thy poor, aged, feeble one, and keep me moment by moment, as in the hollow of Thy hand. Leave me not to dishonour Thee in old age. Hitherto Thou hast upheld me, and not suffered me outwardly to dishonour Thee. Thine holy eyes have seen enough to cast me off for ever; but oh, for ever blessed be Thy name, though Thou hast in some measure rebuked and chastened, and caused me to see and lament my sin, Thou hast kept my secrets within Thine own loving bosom, thou most precious

Son of God. This it is that breaks my heart, and causes tears to run down my aged cheeks. What, oh what shall I render unto Thee for Thy wondrous goodness and patience towards me? Nothing have I to render. I am poor and needy, and dependent upon Thee moment by moment. God be praised for such a Saviour, just suited in every way to my necessities. Oh, for a heart to praise and bless His holy holy name!"

"There is, in the Christian mind, such a proneness to be satisfied with a little. No pressing onward and upward. We receive a little, and then sit down and live upon it until it is all exhausted, and our very bones stand out from leanness. We forget, that the oftener we apply for more, the more welcome we are, and the holier and happier we become; and not only this, but the more we receive, the more we feel our need of deeper supplies, grow in grace, and in the knowledge of our Lord and Saviour Jesus Christ. We need to know more of Jesus. The more frequently we go to Him, the better we shall know Him. Always welcome. Never will He frown a poor beggar from His footstool. He upbraids us for not coming. *Ye will not come unto Me.* Why should our grace droop, and languish, and die, when we can repair to the Fountain of living water, at all times and under all circumstances? Oh, the blessing of having such an Almighty Friend in glory, waiting to be gracious to us, whose power is infinite in heaven and on earth, and whose love, like Himself, is from everlasting to everlasting!"

"It is a lovely day. Experienced a precious nearness to Jesus in prayer. Felt I loved Him above all earthly love; that to me He was the chiefest among ten thousand, and altogether lovely to my soul. Could recall all His tender dealing, watchful providence, unwearied care, all-protecting hand, from infancy to the present moment. I delight to trace before Him His wondrous, unwearied love, in His providence all my journey through. Oh, what a God has He been—and what returns? Often the basest. How humbling is this! How often does the remembrance of what He has been to me, and what I have been to Him, bring tears to my eyes."

"What a grief it is to me to see those professing Christ, and yet living to the world. *If ye love the world, the love of the Father is not in you.* Oh that all this evil might be subdued in me! Truly can I say, in my flesh dwelleth no good thing. Lord, put thoughts in my heart, and suitable words in my mouth, that I may speak to sinners—*one* word followed with Thy blessing! Only make me a humble instrument of some good where I am. Dear Lord, wilt Thou condescend to use me for Thyself, and for the good of those around me? Often am I afraid of speaking, lest I should do more harm than good by exciting the enmity of the carnal mind. Lord, when I would do good, evil is present with me. Help me. I am Thine, and Thou art mine! Oh, thou blessed Spirit of all grace, truth, and power, work that in me that shall be for Thy glory, and the good of poor dying souls. Never did I more feel my incompetency to do anything, or to speak a word for Christ. I can talk to those who love Thee, and enjoy it; but faithfully and fearlessly to speak to and warn the empty professor and the unrenewed sinner, I shrink from it. Precious and beloved Jesus, help and strengthen Thine unworthy one in doing what is right in Thy sight."

"Oct. 1st.—The Lord has brought me in safety to town through His tender and never-ceasing mercy. What thanks do I owe Him for His watchful providence over me moment by moment. Among other blessings would I praise Him for the affection and devoted love of my children. I have paid the three in the country each a visit; and never did a mother meet with more tenderness and love—anticipating my every wish, and watching over me as a nurse her tender babe. God be praised for all His unmerited favours."

"I cannot see God for one moment out of Christ. I behold Him in all His glorious attributes in Jesus, the Son of His love. *He that hath seen Me hath seen the Father.* I often feel, in drawing near the throne of grace, I need a Father's pity. I go to Him as my Father. At other times I feel I need all the sympathy and tender compassion of Christ's manhood. And, again, I feel I need the power of the Holy Ghost within me, to teach, to sanctify, and to heal. Thus a Triune Jehovah is made known to us through Jesus. And these three—Father, Son, and Holy Ghost—are, one and all, engaged in the glorious work of saving fallen sinners. God be praised for what we do know. God be praised!"

"Had precious nearness to-day in pleading for my children —much sweet, holy liberty in prayer. Oh, how blessed are these opportunities, when heaven seems opened, and God reveals the love of His heart, and His willingness to do all we ask! Felt, too, much brokenness of heart, under a deep sense of my unworthiness of such unbounded love. It is a great comfort to me to think that the Lord knows me altogether. I would have no concealments from Him. He graciously permits me to come with an open heart."

"O Lord, my God, bring salvation to my house again. Make bare Thine holy arm. Remember Thy gracious promise given to Thine handmaid in the time of her deep sorrow. For ever blessed be Thy name for the consolation then afforded her, and for what Thou hast so wonderfully accomplished. But, dear Lord, there is yet to be a fulfilment of Thine own precious word. Remember, too, in great mercy, Lord, ——. Open Thou his eyes to behold himself a sinner in Thy sight, and Thyself able to save to the uttermost. Oh, lay him low in the dust of self-abhorrence at Thy dear feet, there to sue for pardon through that precious blood that can alone cleanse from sin. Have mercy ere he goes hence; and may he leave a testimony behind him to the precious fulness of Thy great salvation."

"*Unto the upright there ariseth light in the darkness.* Oh, to walk with an open, unveiled heart with God. To have no concealments, not the shadow of a wish to conceal; but rather rejoice that He who loves us knows us altogether just as we are. He alone can heal all our diseases, and help all our infirmities. He has graciously undertaken to meeten us for that place He has gone to prepare for us. What a Saviour is ours! God be praised for His unspeakable gift."

"How utterly impossible for me to choose for myself. This is the second time in my life, when in the providence of God, I have had to decide upon a point of some moment, and which might lead to important results. I have carried it again and again to the Lord, but to this moment no light has shone upon my way. I think I feel willing to have no wish to determine for myself. I do desire that the will of the Lord should be done in me. Precious Jesus, my Guide, my Guardian, my unceasing Friend, undertake for me. Still I am to walk by faith through the wilderness."

"I believe that every word of God is only profitable as it is wrought out in the soul, often by trying providences. Head knowledge will not do. Hearing with the outward ear profits not the soul. It makes no headway towards heaven, and knows nothing of the love of Christ, or the real character of God. The truth as it is in Jesus is more known in *one* deep trial than in years of smooth sailing. Worldly prosperity is unfavourable soil for the true Christian to grow in. It benumbs the soul, and nothing but the Almighty power of God can keep it from the sleep of death."

"My posture is still waiting upon God. To know His will is my chief desire. *Be still, and know that I am God.* These words were applied to my soul to-day with much sweetness. I think, small crosses stir up the corruptions of the heart more than deep afflictions. The flesh frets; pride is set in motion; and at once the soul is called to conflict with a host of enemies that lie dormant until roused to strive against the Spirit. Satan, then is busy, and the soul has, with all speed, to betake itself to its stronghold. Oh, it is then the throne of grace is a blessed resource. Jesus is most precious."

"Blessed, thrice blessed, is the prospect of eternal companionship in heaven with those from whom we differ in judgment upon earth."

"What a brittle thing is all the glory, wealth, and honour of this vain world! How empty and what trash does it appear! And yet men sell their souls to grasp it, and at last pass away from it and find it all a phantom. How unceasing is Satan in for ever bringing it before our eyes, in some form or other."

"How much stronger faith it requires to go to the Lord in our little difficulties than when greater troubles press us. I feel, at times, almost ashamed to bring my small trials, and feel as if it required an apology. But, oh, in a moment I am helped, at such a season of temptation, to prostrate myself before the Lord, and humble myself for the pride of my wretched heart; for it is that, aided by the enemy, that creates the suggestion. In one sense, all our circumstances are trifles in the sight of a great Almighty God; but if Christ hath said that the very hairs of our head are numbered, how much more does He condescend to care for what is a trouble to us."

The following presents the "child of the light walking in darkness." This was not often her dreary path; but when so, like her blessed Saviour on the cross, her faith never relinquished its hold on God.

"March 6th.—Good and gracious has been the Lord to me in all outward comforts; but my soul has been led to walk in a dark way, and although I do feel Jesus more precious than ever, I have not that abiding enjoyment of His presence as formerly. I am greatly straitened in myself, and particularly in family prayer am greatly tried. My mind is confused, and my memory fails me, and the presence of so many becomes a snare to me, that I feel I am sinning in attempting to address the heart searching God in such a state of mind. The Lord, the Spirit, has withdrawn His sensible presence, and my soul has been in great trouble. I search for the cause, and the more I search, the plainer I see great cause indeed wherefore He should leave my soul to barrenness and wandering. Surely, I have followed Him of late like sorrowful Mary, and would cry, Oh, that it were with me as in days that are past! And yet, Jesus is not out of sight, and I feel that the wealth of ten thousand worlds could not compensate for the loss of the light of His countenance. I feel, at times, that I am His, and that He is mine; but still there is a want in my soul that He only can meet. Lord, help me, and revive Thy work for Jesus' sake. I never before had such wrestling with God, and never before walked in such a dark, bewildering way. O Lord, show me the why and the wherefore. Subdue my sins, give me deep repentance, and set my soul once more at happy, holy liberty."

"20th.—Bless the Lord, who has heard the voice of my supplication, and though He bore long with me, has again spoken peace and comfort to my troubled, tempest-tossed soul. My soul rejoices in God my Saviour, in whom is all my hope and my salvation."

Let those who fear the Lord, who are walking in darkness and have no light, be encouraged to trust in the Lord. "Light is *sown* for the righteous, and gladness for the upright in heart." We propose following these extracts from her private papers with selections from her general correspondence, as still further illustrating the experimental character of true godliness.

TO LADY B——. ON THE SEALING OF THE SPIRIT.

"DEAR LADY B——, Leamington, March 17th.

". . . . How poor and trifling is everything else, compared with the glory of God in the salvation of His saints—in their well-being and their progress homeward. It is a certain thing, that there is no standing still in our heavenly course. We have too many enemies to contend with to allow of this. We have need, indeed, of all the help we can obtain from

THE SEALING OF THE SPIRIT. 271

above and below, to keep our feet from falling, and our heart steadfast in the way to glory. What is all the pomp, and wealth, and rank of this poor fleeting world, in contrast with the glory that shall soon be revealed in all them that love His appearing? *In whom also after ye believed ye were sealed with that Holy Spirit of promise which is the earnest of our inheritance.* Eph. i. 13, 14. This passage of Scripture is very precious, and it is most important that we should be experimentally and practically acquainted with it. It is not peculiar to the apostles and the disciples of old; but it belongs to you and to me, and it should be a question of great moment to us both? Have I been SEALED with the Holy Spirit of promise? Have I the witness in my soul that I am a child of God? Have I really believed, and am I thus *sealed* as an heir of God, and a joint-heir with Christ Jesus? Have I made my calling and election sure to myself? Oh, are not these important questions to put to ourselves, particularly when we know not how soon we may be called to render in an account to God? One step and we are there—in the very presence of a holy, heart-searching Jehovah. Is there anything upon earth of equal importance to this? Earnestly, then, would I urge you to press onward; and if yet unacquainted with the *sealing* of the Spirit, which is the earnest of your heavenly inheritance, to go again and again until you obtain it. It is for you. It is the certain pledge of God's eternal, unchangeable love to your soul. Oh, do but try for it. Though faint at first, it will increase more and more. It is the image of Christ stamped upon the soul of His redeemed one. Oh, to know this precious Jesus is life eternal. The world is passing away, and we are passing away, but this will never pass away. I feel as if standing on the very verge of the eternal world—full in view before me—and I cannot but say to all I love, The Bible is true—God is true—Jesus is true—all that He has said is *true*. He stands ready to receive, to pardon, to sanctify, and to SEAL as His own, all who come to Him, and has promised that He will cast out none that come. I should like to hear that all is well with you, and that you are making progress heavenward, homeward, and that Jesus is increasingly precious to your soul. Oh, I do love the saints. I have this *one* evidence that I have passed from death unto life, because I love the brethren. All who love Christ, I love. And I shall love them even better when I get above. Heaven's atmosphere is *love.* Christ's heart is an ocean of love. Let us endeavour to have as much as we can of heaven in our souls while here. We have but a brief space left to show our love to Christ. Let us work for Him, live for Him, live to Him, and look forward to living with Him. There is such a thing as a most blessed fellowship and communion with the Saviour. I once heard Mr. Evans say, 'there were some professors of religion who did not know when the Lord was with them, or when He was not.' Is not this a most painful truth? Oh, how can these walk happily or holily in such a state of soul? . . ."

TO THE SAME.—ON A SPIRITUAL MINISTRY.

"Your pastor has been obliged again to leave you; but oh, what a mercy, although the under-shepherd is away, the Chief, faithful Shepherd never leaves his flock. How much the soul needs the constant supplies of spiritual food to sustain it in health and vigour! Christ is the bread of the spiritual life, and Christ is the sum and substance of the gospel; and therefore the gospel is needful, that we may grow in grace. And now, dear friend, you will be without it at——, I fear. Your work, then, is before you. 'Ask anything in My name, and it shall be done unto you.' You want the gospel; it is more needful for you than your necessary food; you want it for yourself, for those you love, for the poor around you. I do not urge you to wander, seeking an under-shepherd that you think will suit; but I do say, go to Jesus, to the compassionate, the Chief Shepherd, and ask Him to send you one after His own heart. Do not be satisfied with going once, or twice, or thrice, but go, and continue to go, taking no denial. The Lord loves importunity. A greater blessing God could not send you than this. You will honour Him by asking, and He will honour you by giving. If the man that comes does not preach Christ from first to last—if he puts anything else in as a substitute—God has not sent him. Then go and tell the Lord. Oh, let this be a grand transaction between God and yourself. . . . ."

TO THE SAME.—ON CONFORMITY TO THE WORLD.

"What a difficult matter it is to be *in* the world, and yet not to be *of* the world! Our Lord has said of his disciples, *They are not of the world, even as I am not of the world.* Christ himself carried out this principle. He passed through the world as one who was not of it. Oh, that we could but imitate His holy example, and aim only, while in it, so to let our light shine, that others may take knowledge of us that we have been with Jesus, and have learned of Him. It should be our whole endeavour to do all the good we can in it and for it, and yet to set at nought its spirit, its principles, and its maxims. 'How can this be?' I think I hear you say. Go to Jesus, and ask of Him strength for any duty that devolves upon us. *Without Me ye can do nothing.* And yet with Christ strengthening us, we can do all things. What a present helper is Jesus! When we are called to go amongst those who know not God, let it be from an absolute duty, and with a desire only to do good to their souls, and after much prayer—honest, sincere prayer—to be preserved from evil. Oh, how much need have we to watch over our hearts, and ask the Lord to purify our motives in all that we do! We have need to keep close to our dearest, our best Friend, and beseech Him to save us from *ourselves.* How can a believer walk through this world safely and securely, but as he is upheld by a strength that is Omnipotent? . . . . I am passing through a world lying in the wicked one. I belong to another kingdom, which is not of this world. I am a subject of the kingdom of Christ; hence it is my duty and my high privilege to obey and to serve. And, oh, His service is no slavery; it is perfect freedom. Dear friend, see, then, our high calling! He has called you and me to come out of the world and to be separate, in principle, in practice, in heart. I once sat by the bedside of a dying saint. She had devoted her life to the Lord, and no one could say but that she walked as a believer should walk. But, oh, her great grief, when she was about to appear before Him was, that she had lived too much to the world. Her sorrow was great; and, although she expressed no fear as to her acceptance in Christ, yet, on looking back upon her past life, she saw so much to deplore of *heart-departures,* that her sorrow in this respect obscured, in a measure, her prospect of the endless glory that doubtless awaited her, and which, I believe, she is now enjoying with Him she loved—'chosen in Christ before the foundation of the world!' . . ."

TO A BELOVED FRIEND.—ON LOOKING TO JESUS FOR EVIDENCES.

"DEAR AND BELOVED FRIEND,— Tuesday Evening.

"I have just returned from service, and found your kind letter. Many, many thanks. I have long wished to write and inquire how it was with your soul, which, I believe, is as dear to Christ as the apple of His eye. . . . Precious friend, look full at Jesus. Look no longer to your own weak, sinful heart. *Look upon Me, and be ye saved. Only believe*, and you shall have eternal life. It is the record God has given of His dear Son we are called to believe; and the moment you believe this with all your heart, you have peace. All your trouble arises from your looking for evidences within; and when Satan blinds your eye, and you cannot find them, directly you think you have no part or lot in this matter. Your salvation does not hinge in the slightest degree upon what is done in you or by you, but what Christ has done for sinners; and if you are a sinner, then Christ has done it for you. Oh, look and live! Keep your eye upon Jesus. Try and realize the simple, plain, matter-of-fact truth that God was in Christ Jesus! that He came into the world for the express purpose of saving sinners, the vilest of the vile; and that He rose from the dead, and is now above, at the right hand of the Father, to fulfil every promise he has left in His last will, signed with His own blood. Now, faith does not consist in believing that I am a believer, but in believing in Jesus Christ; and all the rest—joy, peace, love, hope, and every other blessing—will assuredly follow. Oh, how simple is faith, and how many make a Christ of it, when it is nothing more than believing! But, lest I should mislead here: this faith is a divine operation, and is the gift of God; but all that we have to do is to deal with the matter-of-fact truth of the Gospel. In the Acts of the Apostles, you will find that they invariably stated to sinners the things concerning Jesus, and when they heard they believed and rejoiced. You do not find they looked into their own hearts for evidences when they were called to believe. They received the truth at once, and rejoiced with a joy unspeakable and full of glory. We are to look for comfort only to Christ. The bitten Israelites looked at once and direct to the brazen serpent, and were healed; and when we want (renewed) healing, we must look again and again. Oh, the precious fountain for sin and uncleanness! I am obliged to come again and again to it. May the Lord disperse every dark cloud from your mind; for well I know, Jesus loves not to see His child mourning in unbelief. The weakness of the body often affects the mind; but, let what may be our feelings, Jesus' love is always the same, and *the Lord changes not.* What I have written, you know, beloved friend, as well as I do. And yet often when a cloud comes over the mind, it is the privilege of one who is travelling in a lighter part of the road to speak a word of consolation. Cheer up, beloved of God, it is all right; for God, even our own God, is with you, to do you good; and every trial you now meet with is to make you cling closer to Jesus, that you may know Him better and love Him more. . . . . I am fighting on my way, often sorrowing and rejoicing at the same time,—mourning for my sins, while I can and do rejoice that Christ has made an all-sufficient atonement for all, past, present, and to come; which, while it humbles me in the dust of self-abhorrence, makes me increasingly long to be like Him. Only believe, and it will be well with you through time and throughout an endless eternity."

TO THE SAME.—THE EVERLASTING LOVE OF GOD.

". . . . It is so pleasant to talk of an absent friend,—a friend that one dearly loves, and longs to see; particularly if the person with whom you are conversing is especially interested in the subject. As I sat musing alone, I thought of Christ, and then of you; and as I am too far to hold a conversation, I must write a little about Him we both love; *and we love Him because He first loved us.* If we feel one particle of love to Him, be assured it is a proof that He loves us. But still there are seasons when our hearts are so cold and insensible, that it would not do always to have this as a test of His love to us. What a mercy of mercies to have such a God to deal with, who cannot cease to love, because He cannot change! How much solid comfort is in this thought! How it quiets and soothes all our doubts and fears, and puts Satan's 'ifs' to the blush! There is no uncertainty with God. His thoughts of love towards us have been from everlasting to everlasting. He loved us when we were wandering far from Him, and far from happiness. He loved us when we knew Him not. He loved us out of Satan's kingdom into the kingdom of grace, and He will love us into the kingdom of glory. Our doubts and fears may harass us, but they can make no alteration in His eternal purposes. Jesus is alive; never fear! He is risen and at the right hand of the Majesty of heaven, and is the executor of His own will, entrusting it not to the highest angel in heaven. Let us then encourage our hearts in the Lord, and know that while we are looking to Jesus, He is at that very moment looking on us with a heart overflowing with love, as eternal as Himself. May He draw us nearer to Himself, and conform us to His own lovely image."

TO THE SAME.—SPIRITUAL ENCOURAGEMENT.

" . . . . I was rejoiced to hear that you were enabled (if it was only for a moment) to cast yourself upon Christ. Be assured the time will come when He will enable you to do it wholly. He is leading you by degrees, to see what He is, and what He is to you; and for wise purposes, He is teaching you many hard lessons, that you may be prepared to teach others; and thus He is fitting you for future usefulness. Let me not, in thus speaking, put a stumbling-block in your way. There is such a fulness in the boundless love of Christ's heart, that there is no necessity for staying out of it for one moment. It was framed for sinners; and there is room enough for you, for me, and for ten thousand more. Oh, let us enter in at once and feel at home, no longer strangers, but at home with a loving Father and a precious Christ. This is what I covet for you. I pray you may be led to cease from all teaching but that of the Eternal Spirit, and with the word of God in your hand. May God pour into your soul such a sense of His wondrous love for you, as will enable you to triumph over all the host of foes within and without. And when you see His holy face, and can cast a thought on me, oh, remind Him what a poor one He has in your unworthy sister."

TO LADY L——. ON ANTICIPATION OF HEAVEN.

"BELOVED IN THE LORD,— April 21st.

"I grieve that I was obliged to leave home without seeing you again; but if we meet no more on earth, there is a blessed world where I expect to meet you, and all we love who have preceded us there. Let us keep our eye and our hearts upon it. Earth is but a stage erected as our passage to the place Jesus has gone to prepare for us. And what a place must that be, which Infinite power and love has engaged to provide! Oh, let us not lose sight of heaven for a moment. How prone we are to allow our minds and hearts (treacherous hearts!) to become entangled with the baubles of a dying world. No wonder Christ exhorted us to *watch and pray*. Heaven is our home—our happy home. We are but strangers and pilgrims here. Try and realize it. Let us keep ourselves ready to enter with Him to the marriage supper of the Lamb. In a little while, and we shall see Him, not as the 'Man of sorrows,' but the 'King in his beauty.' Shall we not know Him the moment we get there? Shall we not recognise that blessed countenance, which so often cheered and encouraged us when cast down? Dear friend, we shall. Then, let us fight against earth and all its false attractions, for it passeth away. Let us keep close to Christ; go to Him on all occasions, and never be satisfied without an interview with our best beloved. Were the Queen to invite us to visit her, and we went to the palace, but did not see her, should we return satisfied or pleased? Just so with the King of kings. When we go to Him, let us not come away without having an interview. We must speak to Him, open our whole heart to Him, while He opens His loving heart to us. This is communion, and there is no communion without it. May all your children be led to choose the one thing needful. What a mercy for a family to have a praying mother! Love, tender love to you."

TO MISS M——. THE POWER OF CHRIST'S RESURRECTION.

" DEAR SISTER IN JESUS,— May 4th.

" What shall I say to you for my apparent neglect of your kind and considerate letter, when dear —— was with you? I take shame to myself that I have not before thanked you for it, and trust it is not now too late. . . . God be praised for the precious Gospel, which reveals to us the whole will of God. What should we do without the Bible? and what should we do without Jesus, the source and substance of the Bible? and what should we do without the Spirit's holy teaching? God be praised for all; all is boundless, fathomless love, from first to last. Dear friend, I have often had you in my mind since I saw you at Leamington, and thought I would write and induce you to tell me now and then how gracious

God was dealing with you. He is full of love. No tongue can tell how gracious He is to unworthy me; and is He not so to you, dear friend? Could you live without Him? I cannot. He is the health and joy of my soul. His name is as ointment poured forth. What will heaven be, where we shall see Him face to face? Do you not at times long to be there, a pure spirit, in due time inhabiting a glorified body, mingling with the happy beings, many of whom we knew and loved, around the throne? Mighty are our present privileges. What could we do without a throne of grace? Do we not need it every step we take, and at each turn of Providence? Let us, then, endeavour, dear friend, to live more on high,—more in full expectation of our great change. I believe that a constant looking to the glory that awaits us, will enable us to live above the trials of the way; will strengthen our faith to overcome, and cause us to sit in *heavenly places in Christ Jesus;* realizing in our soul's experience, that all is true that our God has told us and promises us. The resurrection of Christ is to me a blessed confirmation that all else that is revealed is true. If Christ be risen from the grave and is in heaven, then my soul is as safe as if I were there at this moment. Every other revealed truth rests upon this one; and if this is a verity, all else is so. Now we have but to believe this, and joy and gratitude, love and hope, at once spring up in the soul. Then comes the question, *Lord, what wouldst thou have me to do?* The believer will not be satisfied with merely being saved. Though this is a great mercy, there yet are enjoyments, I do believe, experienced as we travel onward in the heavenly journey, that far,—oh, how far!—surpass the paltry glory of this poor passing world; experienced only by those who are united to the living Vine. May the Lord help you to go forward, to know more and more of the power of His resurrection,—to follow on to know the Lord. The more we have to do with Christ the more we shall know of His excellencies, His sympathy, and His exquisite, boundless love. Pray for me, that I may be more anxious to press forward, and not be satisfied to know these things in theory only, but in my soul's sweet experience. In a little while, and we shall be there. I believe, from the signs of the times, we may hope soon to see Him whom we love, coming in the clouds of heaven, to take His weary Church to Himself. Think of me when waiting before our mutual Friend."

TO MRS. T——. JESUS WITH HIS SAINTS IN SICKNESS.

"MY DEAR FRIEND,—

"I hear from dear E——, that your dear husband is very ill. Perhaps this illness is not unto death, and that he will yet be spared to you, and you to him, a little longer in this vale of tears. But oh, when faith is in lively exercise, how sweet is the thought of going home; dropping the weary, worn out body for a season, in full confidence of one day being united to it again! How kind it was in Jesus to give us that promise from His own dear lips, *I will raise it up again at the last day!* That identically same body; but oh, how changed, how beautified! Then soul and body in re-union shall stand before a holy Lord God, and Christ shall fully see and perfectly enjoy the travail of His soul. Tell him that all that Jesus has said is *true;* that He is in heaven who died for sinners; and that no believing soul, however great his sins, can be lost while Christ lives. He has said to him, *Because I live, ye shall live also.* The same Jesus who, a poor and despised Man of sorrows, trod the streets of Jerusalem, is in heaven, as full of goodness, tenderness, and love, as when here below. He is now with you, and is watching beside the sick-bed of your dear husband, saying to him, 'Fear not, it is I. It is I that lived for you, that died for you, that rose again for you, and am now waiting to welcome you home. I have prepared a place for you.' Absent from the body, we shall be present with the Lord. When his eyes close on earth, at that very instant he will open them upon Jesus Himself. Comfort him with these precious truths. May God be with you."

TO THE SAME.—FORESHADOWING OF THE COMING GLORY.

"April 13th.

". . . . We must not lose sight of each other, for the time is shortening. The present signs speak loudly to us, *Prepare to meet thy God!* But oh, what a pleasant prospect is before us, almost in full view. Jesus is at hand, and if He does not soon come to us, we shall soon go to Him, our best and dearest Friend. Oh, to see His face, once so wearied and care-worn, traced with sorrow and with grief,—and that because our sins were laid upon Him,—but now resplendent with glory; His countenance beaming with ineffable delight upon His redeemed, blood-bought family, rescued from the power of hell, death, and the grave. Can we conceive of anything to equal such a scene? The Bridegroom rejoicing over his bride, saints singing, angels admiring. Endeavour to realize this, dear friend. Take your walks in the good land flowing with milk and honey. I am never so happy as when I am able so to do. To hold converse with spirits around the throne; above all, with Him who sits upon it. Nothing in this fading world can equal it. A throne of grace, with a broken heart for sin, and a pardoning Saviour, is a verdant spot in this wilderness...."

TO MRS. A———. ON THE CONFESSION OF SIN.

"DEAR SISTER IN THE LORD,—

".... While I recommend this dear Christian friend, as a companion, sweet it is to think how soon, how very soon, we shall be fitted for the companionship of Jesus Himself, beholding Him in all His unveiled beauties. Does not the thought often gladden your heart, and fill your eyes with tears of joy, and holy contrition for sin? I cannot conceive of holy joy unaccompanied with godly sorrow. Confession of sin should make up one-half of our lives. *Only acknowledge thine iniquity.* And when we remember that we have to do with One so willing and so able to pardon, it becomes then a mingled feeling of pleasure and pain. By confessing sin, we gather strength to resist it; thereby the enemy of our souls is foiled, the conscience is kept tender, the heart is sanctified, and the blood of Jesus becomes increasingly precious. Let us constantly flee to the cleansing fountain; *for if we say we have no sin, we deceive ourselves, and the truth is not in us. If we* CONFESS *our sins, He is faithful and just to forgive us our sins, and to cleanse us from all unrighteousness.* Oh, to go and acknowledge the hidden, concealed evil of our hearts —that sin that no eye has seen or can see but God's holy eye. Is not this a high privilege? And who can subdue sin in us but Jesus? I might as well attempt to remove mountains, as to reason away one corruption of my fallen nature. But if we, the moment we detect it, carry it to Jesus, He will do it all for us. This is one of the most difficult lessons to learn in the school of Christ. I am but just beginning to learn it, and therefore I am placed in the youngest class, travelling to Jesus more as a little helpless child, for Him to do all for and all in me. My fancied strength is all vanished, my boasted reason turned into folly, and now, thus living on Christ in childlike simplicity, my peace, joy, and consolation, are past expression. Oh, the love, the matchless love of Jesus to a poor sinner lying thus at His dear feet, waiting to receive a welcoming smile beaming from His countenance. Dear friend, keep close to Him. Let not the world or its cares come between you and Christ. If there is a cloud, rest not until it withdraws. Go again and again, should there be but a shade, until it is put away, and you see Him who loves you. I think, if it were possible to be sensible of shame in heaven, we should be ashamed of our sins,—above every other, of the sin of *unbelief*. . . . You may, perhaps, wonder why confession of sin should be the subject upon which I have chiefly written. I had just returned, when I took up my pen to address you, from my *confessional*—the throne of grace—so sweetly refreshed and so blessedly pardoned, that I could not refrain from recommending it to all I love and write to, as one of the most hallowed exercises of the Christian. I often repair to it heavily laden, and return as though nestling beneath the wing of the Saviour. I tell Him all that is in my heart, and what I could not tell the dearest friend on earth. He keeps all my secrets; and while I open my sinful heart to Him, He unveils His loving, gracious heart to me. This truly happy intercourse with God, I would urge upon all whom I love, and who love Him. Nothing must be kept back. Descending to particulars, we must deal with God in small as well as in great matters. One lifting up of the heart—one thought darting heavenward, when surrounded by clouds, is sufficient for Jesus. Lord, help us so to live and so to die."

TO MRS. R———. GRATEFUL REVIEWS.

" DEAR FRIEND,— October 5th, 1852.

" My own dear pastor, Mr. Evans, has often said to me, ' Dear sister, what a *poor* world it is !' And such I find it increasingly. We shall soon be gathering up our garments in preparation, I trust, for a better. What folly to wish to stay in a wilderness longer than is needful. You and I are daily nearing our heavenly home, and Jesus stands ready to put us in full possession of our glorious inheritance, prepared for us before the foundation of the world. With adoring gratitude I look back on all the way He has led me, and stand in wondering praise at His long-suffering patience, gentleness, kindness, and forbearance. My heart seems ready to melt into contrition in view of the ten thousand, thousand sins, wilful and aggravating, that I have committed against Him, who loved me with an everlasting love, and with loving-kindness drew me to Himself. I think, were it possible, there would be weeping in heaven. But not so. My tears will be wiped away there. Repentance is not a thing to be once done and then done with. Not so. The more I see of Jesus, the more He opens to me His loving heart, the deeper is the sorrow for sin. I lie down in the dust of His feet closer than ever I did before. I can truly say, I abhor myself in dust and ashes before Him. Sins of early days are brought before me as if just committed—over them I weep. As I get nearer the land of glory, the light dawning from thence shows more vividly the darkness within, and the hatefulness of that which crucified the Lord of life and glory. I am nearing day by day my heavenly inheritance. It seems at times almost in view. It is but a step, and I am *there*. I am led often to live [as it were] my life over again; and how plainly do I see now the why and the wherefore He dealt with me, in leading me through trials and tribulations. How good is the Lord! At present my feelings are blended. I rejoice while I weep. Oh, there is none like Jesus in earth or in heaven. I sometimes long to be there. I am quite sure the nearer we get to glory, the atmosphere becomes clearer, and we can see afar off. Stephen, when departing, saw Him standing at the right hand of God, ready to welcome His first martyr home. What will heaven be! Let us live more in preparation for it, and realize it more than we do. I find nothing so keeps the heart right, as having constant communication with Christ. . . . As soon as we are born again, He puts us to school, the Holy Ghost being our teacher; and many hard lessons we have to learn. Some of us are dull scholars, and require to learn the same lessons over and over again, and often need the rod. The hardest task we have to study is *ourselves*. Another lesson is, to hunger and thirst for more, not satisfied with what we do know, but to follow on to know more of the matchless love that there is in the heart of Jesus. And this, I believe, we shall be learning out through eternity, and never come to the end of it. Oh, let us hold fast our oneness with Christ! And not only pray, but go not away without an answer. The blessed spirit who indites the prayer, responds to it, and thus we know we have the ear of God."

TO MRS. W—— ON ENTERING FULLY INTO CHRIST.
"DEAR FRIEND,—
" . . . . Many years have I laboured with you, and yet you have not arrived at the state in which I have long wished to see you—full of the Holy Ghost and of joy. And why is it? What hinders? All things are ready—the table is spread—Christ invites you. There is everything in the gospel to fill you with gladness and joy, above all with real happiness, such as this poor world knows nothing of. This is what I covet for myself and for all God's redeemed ones. It is a mercy and a great one, to know that we are saved; but this is only the beginning of blessings. Greater blessings await us journeying through the wilderness to the land of glory. Suppose we have faith in Christ, and a good hope through grace, this is but the first round in that ladder that reaches from earth to heaven. We are to ascend higher and higher, always looking upward, never downward, lest we become dizzy and fall. Oh, it is only looking to Jesus that keeps us ascending. *They go from strength to strength, every one of them in Zion appeareth before God.* As I have often said before, we cannot be stationary in the divine life—we are advancing or receding. It must be one way or the other. How many, dear I believe to Christ, do I find, who, after years of profession, are just in the same spot at which they set out! They know no more of Christ than they did at the first. Now in worldly things this would not be so. But, oh, when such riches await us—honour, glory, and immortality—how diligent and earnest should we be to make progress in the way, and so glorify our God! Every stage on the road brings us nearer to our happy home. Oh, the joy of soon being with Jesus! Heaven is very near. The eternal world is all around us. Oh, to realize this continually! We do not dwell sufficiently on these glorious realities; we do not bring them home to ourselves. We are either too much engaged with earthly things, or are looking more within the dark recesses of our hearts, than to the glory that awaits us, and into the possession of which we might be any moment introduced.

" In studying the prophecies, there might be much benefit in our researches, if we found more of Jesus. It is the looking to Jesus—the going to Jesus—the confession of sins to Jesus —the constant application of His blood—disclosing to Him all we fear, all we doubt, all we hope, all that is in our hearts, which, dear friend, I would have you cultivate. Let nothing come between you and your best Friend. Never forget, you and Christ are one—one in time and one in eternity. The world, and all its riches, glories, and honours, is as dross when compared with the blessedness of our union with Jesus. Do not be satisfied unless in prayer you have the presence of God. Rest not in mere prayer. I must feel that I have the ear of God when I draw near to Him; and when I have not a sense of His presence, I am not happy; and I go again and again, until He lifts up upon me the sweet light of His countenance; and if ever I have had the broken and the contrite heart, it has been when He most shone into my soul. Oh, the wondrous condescension of our God! He does even now leave the heavens and come down to bless us. How boundless is the love of God to the feeblest of His little ones! Excuse all my mistakes. I write thus in haste, and I am as busy as an old woman of seventy eight can be. My tender love to your husband. May you both grow daily in grace, and in the knowledge of Christ."

TO THE SAME.—ON HEARING THE VOICE OF JESUS.

". . . . Do you think that you have sought the Lord all these years, and that He has not heard you? But, you will reply, 'He has not answered me.' Well, that is your fault, and not His. You have been looking within yourself, instead of looking full at Jesus. He, who was once a poor despised Man of sorrows, is now risen from the dead, and having paid the full penalty of your sins and mine, is now ready to hear your plea, and to send into your soul a full sense of pardon. Wrestle with Him until He answers. Jesus will speak, and speak comfortably to you. Once I pleaded with Him, and I did not rest until He said, 'I am thy salvation.' I went to my bed unconverted; I rose in the morning a saved sinner—an adopted child of God. I never closed my eyes to sleep until Jesus spoke peace to my longing heart. Oh, how sweet and how wonderful was the voice of Christ to my soul! And this voice I have heard again and again since then. When in deep trouble, often has He spoken words of comfort and rich consolation, allayed my fears, and soothed my sorrows. Oh, such a Jesus is He! He cannot but hear you, and cause you to hear Him. His love transcends the united love of all creatures, as the Infinite exceeds the finite. Do not rest without a sense of it. On my knees this morning, I had such a blessed interview with the Saviour of sinners, as I would not exchange for a thousand interviews with all the kings of the earth. The Spirit seemed to bring you so fresh to my mind afterwards, that I could not help again urging you, in the dear, loving name of Jesus, not to stop short of this blessing, that you too may be enabled to say, '*I sought the Lord, and He heard me, and saved me from all my fears.*' I find confession of sin—sins of heart, lip, life—a season of penitential communion with Jesus, and a time of refreshing from the Lord. He loves to hear your voice. He waits to be gracious. Think of Christ waiting and listening to hear your voice pleading with Him. Jesus never turns away from the broken-hearted sinner, and never can. When you hear the precious voice of Jesus, you must let me know. '*My sheep hear my voice.*' You cannot mistake it. Read the Psalms of David. David's God is the same as He was in David's time. '*I, the Lord, change not.*' Deal with Him as such, and rest not until you can say, 'He has spoken peace to my soul.'

> 'My soul, ask what thou wilt,
> Thou canst not be too bold.
> Since for thy sake His blood was spilt,
> What else will He withhold?'

TO THE REV. J. H. E———. A WORD IN SEASON TO A PASTOR IN ILLNESS.

"BELOVED BROTHER,—

"Has He who is all love, *nothing* but love to you and to me, again laid that loving hand upon you, and taken you aside for a little season, that He might converse with you alone; that He might show you more privately what is in His heart, and lead you deeper and deeper into that mine of unfathomable wealth that is in store for you and me, and all that are His own elect? Oh, what a God is ours! how gracious, how mighty in all His dealings with us! And has He not to do with us moment by moment? His dear loving eye is upon you in your sick chamber, in your retirement. Who can separate you from Christ? not from his love only, but from Himself. He is in you, and you are in Him—a partaker of His nature; one with Him, through time and through eternity. Blessed thought! Oh, to live for Him and Him only! Jesus is watching over you with the tenderest sympathy, such sympathy as mortals know nothing of. He is now most kindly, most mercifully dealing with you. He has some communications to make to your soul, be assured, which can be done in no other way. So the Lord works with His beloved ones. In a little while, and we shall be with Him, see and love Him as we now desire, but cannot. And yet we might have more of heaven below than we have. If we had more constant dealings with Him than we have, how much more real happiness should we experience! To be *with* Jesus is heaven below and above. Heaven itself would be no heaven to me if He were not there. No, though all I loved on earth were there, and He not, it were no heaven to me, nor you either, beloved brother. The presence of our God will make that place of bliss all that it ever will be to us throughout an endless eternity; and when I think how near we are, and how soon we may be there, how trifling does all the glory of the world appear! Oh, to live on high; to get closer and closer to Jesus, and see in a Father's heart all that the feeblest of His tender weaklings can desire! Dear brother, the Lord has brought me to live more as a helpless infant upon Him day by day, and so enter more fully into that truth, *Without Me ye can do nothing*. How sweetly does the spirit work in us after truth; and although we need and acknowledge it, yet it is only by deep experience and by the mighty power of the Holy Spirit we are effectually taught. Dear brother, you know all this a thousand times better than I can tell you; but still it is a comfort to speak together of Christ's doings, and the way He takes with us. There is not a circumstance but infinite wisdom and love are in it. Christ is in the furnace with you now, and not a hair of your head shall be injured. He is at your side moment by moment, and you shall see the wherefore He has laid you aside from your pleasant work. May you listen and hear what the Lord would say unto you in this providence. There is a voice. It is not in the strong wind, it is not in the earthquake, it is not in the fire. It is the 'still small voice' of our Jehovah-Jesus, that will sweetly, blessedly speak to your soul. The voice of His Spirit within. When He speaks comfort, who can, what can give disquietude? When Jesus speaks, all is hushed into silence; for there is no voice like His. Is He not the same who spake to Abraham, to Isaac, to Jacob, and to Moses in the wilderness; and who tabernacled in the flesh for a season here below? Is He not the same who spoke to Saul of Tarsus, after his resurrection, and who stood by him in the storm, to encourage his heart? And is He not the same to you and to me now? I feel He is the same, and I desire to go to Him as such, expecting great things, since He is a great God and a great Saviour. Therefore He says, *Open thy mouth wide, and I will fill it.* I fear I may weary you, though I could write a volume on the subject. Precious, precious Jesus, bless, oh, bless my beloved brother; heal him, and lift up upon him the light of Thy countenance, and draw him nearer and nearer to Thyself.

TO HER SON.—THE LORD THE REFUGE IN THE STORM.

"I wrote to you, that I have had for several days a sore conflict, greatly tried by sin within, and by cross-providences without. I was in a storm, and had no more power to guide it than an infant conflicting with a giant. I went to my stronghold again and again. I felt that Christ could do it. I lay prostrate at His feet, pleading the promises as fast as the Holy Ghost brought them to me. In a short time afterwards I was placed just in that position that was the most trying; but all was calm, peace, and quietness. It was the Lord. Oh, how grateful I felt! I retired to my room, to thank the Lord for His goodness. He tried my faith, and at last brought me down powerless at His feet, who has said, *All power is Mine, in heaven and on earth.* By these things we are taught experimentally wherein our great strength lies. Mere head-knowledge will do no good. The Lord is the helper of His people, and there is no other. Thus the Holy Ghost works in the souls of the redeemed. Precious Jesus! Thou art that Friend that sticketh closer than a brother, or the tenderest and dearest object on earth. I was led this morning to *reason* with the Lord in His own words, *Without Me ye can do nothing.* If you have ever beheld a vessel in a fearful storm, followed by a sudden calm, you can fancy my situation. The Lord be praised for His goodness. My soul desires to give Him the glory."

TO MRS. LIEUT.-COLONEL P—— B——, INDIA,—ON KEEPING AN OPEN HEART WITH GOD.

"DEAR, VERY DEAR FRIEND,—

"Through the kindness of dear Mr. C——, I have obtained your address, and a kind message from you. Thus does the Lord unite His own family in the blessed bonds of

Christian love. Oh, may this be to us a sweet earnest that this union, commenced in the wilderness, will continue throughout a blessed eternity! Since I last saw you, we have made some rapid strides towards the haven of rest. I trust, if we meet no more in this vale of tears, we shall meet there. There will be no wide ocean to separate the one dear family of God, and we shall know as we are known. There will be perfect knowledge, perfect purity, perfect love. Oh, may a view of the blessings awaiting us encourage our hearts to press on to know more and more of the power of the Lord's resurrection in our souls! By faith are we saved, through the finished work of Jesus Christ; and if the Holy Ghost has taken possession of our hearts, we shall manifest it by a holy walk and conversation before a gainsaying world. Oh, that you may follow on to know more and more of the truth as it is in Jesus! Be not satisfied with your present measure of faith. Press on for more. Greater things await you. Jesus stands ready to bestow all you need, all you ask. When you go to Jesus to make known your requests, go in the expectancy of prayer. The importunate prayer will meet with an answer. *Lord, Thou hast heard the desire of the humble; Thou wilt prepare their heart; Thou wilt cause thine ear to hear.* Psa. x. 17. When I go to the throne of grace, I cannot be satisfied unless I *feel* I have the ear of God. I cannot be happy if I have not communion with Him my soul loveth. Perhaps you will reply, 'But I do not know or feel that I love God.' Well, go and tell Jesus that. If your heart appears cold, hard, and insensible, take it to Jesus, and tell Him how it is with you. He will warm, soften, and fill it with His love. Go, under all circumstances, and tell Him all you feel, and all you do not feel. Oh, keep an *open heart* with the Saviour of sinners! Make sure of heaven. Let nothing of an earthly nature come between you and it. Let it be your chief work, and occupy your best thoughts. Look not behind, but press forward, and Christ will give you life and love, joy and peace in believing. Keep close to Jesus, for He is your life. In all your fears, failures, and discouragements, go to Him, and tell Him all. Oh, live for eternity! Realize your adoption into God's family. Never rest until you know you are born of God. Go again and again until He answers your prayer, and satisfies you on this all-important point. *I sought the Lord, and He heard me.* There must be first union, and then communion. I hasten to conclude.

Oh, that I might meet you in heaven! My journey on earth cannot now be much longer. Jesus is ready to receive me, and my prospect at times is bright and glorious. I shall know you then. Perfect knowledge we shall then have. Heaven is worth living for, and it is worth dying for. I commend the loving Saviour to you. He is all that He says He is. His heart is ever towards you, and His eye is ever upon you."

"Dec. 19, 1851.

To the Same.—"Deeply has my heart felt for you, my dear, widowed friend, since I heard how the Lord had dealt with you in removing your dear husband. I know what that widowed heart feels, from having passed through the same myself while in a strange land. I do feel for you; though, long before this reaches you, I trust the Lord has comforted your soul with the consolation which He alone can impart. All these things are to lead you to Himself; and He says now to you, 'Daughter, give me thy heart. I have taken thy husband, but I will be unto thee better than ten husbands, for I am the Husband of the widow. Look unto Me, and be saved from all your fears.' I have heard no particulars of your sad bereavement, and write at a venture. Should you return to this country, how much I should like to see you once more! The Lord is still keeping me here, and preparing me for the great change from earth to heaven. Who would not be a Christian? Dear friend, I do trust that this heavy affliction has brought you nearer to Jesus, and that you can now say, 'He is my Saviour and my God.' The Lord does nothing in vain. All His dispensations are intended to awaken us to a full and just sense of our responsibilities, and of our accountability to Him. He has made us, and made us for Himself; and what a mercy to be brought to know this, and to turn to the Lord! He loves us too well unnecessarily to afflict us. Nestle now under His loving, protecting wing. Get close to Jesus. Open all your heart to Him. His ear is open to all your requests. Take Him as your Husband, Brother, Friend, Counsellor, and present Help in every time of trouble. I have had you much in my thoughts and in my heart. If you can, drop me a line. I may not be long here. Jesus, the very same Jesus that once was on earth, is waiting to welcome all who seek and love Him here into the realms of eternal blessedness. No more tears there—no more sorrow—no more sin; all glory begun and never ending. Make your calling and election sure; and endeavour to induce others to come to Jesus, and partake of the same mighty blessings. Farewell! If you see the dear C——s, give my love to them both."

TO THE HON. F. T——, ON MAKING SURE OF SALVATION.

"MY DEAR FRIEND,— Leamington, March 9, 1853.

"We are still journeying onward, but *where?* is the question. Is it not a solemn thought? Should we not examine well our chart and the way-marks, to see if we are in the right way? Should this be left to an uncertainty by a wise man? Again I repeat the solemn truth, we are on an eventful journey, which must terminate in eternal life or in eternal death. Men, blinded by the enemy, will keep fully occupied with everything and anything but what would conduce to the soul's salvation. Beware of Satan's wiles! Turn in upon your own soul, and ask yourself, 'Am I ready to give in my last account to the Judge of all the earth? Can I stand before His scrutinizing eye? Can He look upon me, and see no spot, or wrinkle, or any such thing? Can I appear in perfect holiness before Him who cannot look upon sin but with the greatest displeasure?' Dear friend let me entreat you to be honest with your own soul. Eternity, eternity, with all its solemn realities, is before us. Flee at once to Jesus, the Saviour of poor sinners, nor leave Him until He speaks peace to your soul. Wrestle with Him for this mighty blessing; for, sure I am, if you do, you will get it. Give no rest to your soul, until you can say, 'My soul is saved! Christ is my surety! Christ is mine, and I am Christ's!' How busy is Satan when a poor sinner is about securing a glorious inheritance! He suggests, 'You *are* saved. You go to church; you say your prayers; you give to the poor; you do no harm; you have often good thoughts in your heart. What more can you do? Are you not in your duty when you attend to your parliamentary concerns—the concerns of the nation? Oh, what a wily foe is he! He will try every means to keep a soul from seeking Jesus as a lost sinner; and you will never find Him until you do. How would it gladden my heart to hear you say, 'I have found Him of whom Moses and the prophets have written.' Leave Him not until He speaks peace to you, and sends you away rejoicing in Him. I long to see you going on your way heavenward, rejoicing in Christ Jesus, and helping on all who may be halting or have got entangled in this world's wilderness. Take this world in its best attire, it is but a wilderness of bitter-sweets. Dear friend, give up your whole heart and soul to Jesus; He will accept you just as you are. He has said, '*I will manifest myself unto you.*' Go and plead this promise. And, now, why has Jesus laid you so near my heart as to cause me to write this long letter? Because He loves you. Ever since the memorable day we met, your salvation has been near my heart, so that I *do* know that the Lord loves you, and that you are dear to Him."

To the Same.—"Wednesday morning. It is vain for me to promise to see you in the evening. I am old and feeble, and cannot do as I could wish. I am nearing my heavenly inheritance; and as this poor body must be laid by for a while, it also is preparing for its quiet resting-place. But, oh, could I but tell you of the blessed prospect that is before me, while I gaze into the better world, and am sometimes favoured with glimpses of the glory that awaits me—of Jesus! If you and I are ever saved, He bore all our sins in that fearful moment when He hung upon the cross. He must have paid the full penalty to the uttermost ere we could get to heaven. Oh, think of this? And how we ought to love Him! Was there ever love like His? And was there ever sorrow like His? It is this that often breaks my heart, and melts it into deep, deep contrition for sin."

To the Same.—"June 15. My Christian brother, as I believe you really are one of Christ's little flock, I wish to say a word, seeing I may not meet you again in this poor, passing world. It *is* a poor world, could we possess the whole of it, with all its hopes and glory. You mentioned having a better record of the Forbes family than mine. My son is preparing a family tree, and I should like your record, if you can spare it. But, oh, dear friend, how much better for you and me to be a living branch of Christ Jesus, the true Vine! According to the regular course of things, we are hastening to the period when the summons must come to each of us, 'Come up hither!' Oh, the change from earth to heaven! The thought of seeing Jesus face to face! Think, the joy of that moment! And yet how few I find are living in the full and joyful expectation of this coming event. And why? because they have so few transactions with Jesus. They have so little to say to Him, so little to do with Him. He may be a friend or an enemy, they are not quite sure. They have a sort of hope, but it is fleeting and uncertain. What a poor life is this! Dear, worthy friend, I am more and more jealous on this subject, and would urge upon all I love not to rest short of knowing their reconciliation to God through Jesus Christ. Aim to walk with God even *now!* To live upon Jesus—to hold sweet, holy converse with Him—to go with an open heart and tell Him all! He will never frown your soul away. He will smile a welcome, and listen to all you have to tell Him. And when, conscious that we fall short of what we ought to be, He says, *Only acknowledge thine iniquity.* Let us set out afresh to run the heavenly race—warmed with the love of Christ in our heart, anointed with the Holy Ghost, heaven in view, a crown of glory awaiting us, and Jesus on the throne ready to bid us welcome. All, all is *true.* Heaven is true, Christ is true. While everything around us appears what it is not, fixing our eyes on the glory that awaits the Christian, we can exclaim to the world lying in the wicked one, Arouse from your slumbers, and come to Jesus. He stands ready to receive all that come to Him, and will in nowise cast out. It is worth ten thousand worlds to know Him, whom to know is life eternal! All would send love, but I am alone in my room, where the Lord has often made himself sweetly, blessedly known to my waiting soul. It has often been a Bethel to me. There is none on earth or in heaven like Jesus—the chiefest among ten thousand, the altogether lovely. Oh, love Him! Give your whole, your undivided heart to Him. If I had a thousand, He should have them all. Adieu.

"Believe me, affectionately, your sincere friend and fellow-traveller to a better, brighter world."

TO LADY L——, ON THE NECESSITY OF THE HOLY SPIRIT.
"MY DEAR FRIEND,—

"How is it, above everything else, with thy soul, that better part, that must live for ever? And yet, though we know this, how much more are our thoughts engaged with this present evil world, and our poor decaying bodies, than concerned to know what awaits us in an endless eternity.

Is not this one of Satan's devices? He will endeavour to engage our thoughts with often the veriest trifles that would shame a child, in order to hide from us the eternal realities of the glory that awaits the believer. Oh, let us beware of Satan's devices! Many hard conflicts have I had with him through my long and chequered life; and, had I not been upheld by Jesus, the sinner's Friend, I should have made shipwreck of my faith long since. But this dear Friend stands ready to help you too. Recollect, He is a present help in every time of need. You are now in a wilderness; but a wealthy land lies before you. Make your calling and election sure. Make sure your acceptance in Christ. Is there, or can there be, anything on earth of equal consequence to this? A soul saved, or a soul lost! Come, just as you are, to Jesus. The prayer, 'God be merciful to me a sinner,' springing from a real sense of our need, and breathed from a heart feeling its awful sinfulness, and the utter impossibility of salvation in any other way, will, in due time, be responded to by the Holy Spirit. We cannot utter one real prayer but by the Holy Ghost. He it is who shows us our iniquity and helplessness, teaches us how to pray, and what to ask for, and then responds to our prayer. Oh, dear friend, pray over your Bible, that this same blessed Spirit (the third Person in the blessed Trinity) may unfold to your mind the precious truths it contains. You do not know how anxious I am for your soul's welfare. I long to see you going on your way rejoicing. Never rest until you can say, 'I have found Jesus, and my soul is saved!' You can go to Jesus, the same as did the disciples when He walked the streets of Jerusalem. He is the same loving, tender, condescending Jesus that He was then, and will never deny Himself to any who feel their need of Him. I am looking forward to my great change. *Absent from the body, present with the Lord.* The only thing worth living for, is to be prepared for the full enjoyment of the glory that is now prepared for all who come to Jesus. Come, just as you are. Be assured of this, if you have one wish in your heart to love Jesus, it is because He has first loved you; and the Holy Spirit is giving you the desire to wish to love Him. Excuse all blunders. Make allowance for poor old *eighty*. I am not far from my happy home, and it looks so inviting. Oh, the welcomes! oh, the joy! oh, the meeting with those that have gone before! We meet to part no more for ever!"

TO MISS S——, ON RUNNING THE CHRISTIAN RACE.

"My dear Friend,—

"I have not forgotten my promise, to drop you a line of remembrance. I have often thought of you, and my hope abideth that you have really and truly set out on your journey heavenward. May the Lord speed you on your way. May He keep you, moment by moment, looking unto Him who is your life. May you be led to see unceasingly that this world is not worthy of one anxious thought. It is all passing away, and we shall soon stand before the great white throne. As you have commenced your journey, so go forward. Do not rest where you are. We are on a race-course. The point from which we start is conversion; the goal to which we run is heaven; the prize for which we contend is a crown of glory, which the righteous Judge will give us at that great day. If, dear friend, you have started in this race, *So run that you may obtain.* How few lay these great things to heart! The world and its trifles so engross the thoughts, that God and Christ, and eternity, with our vast responsibility, are shut out of sight; and Satan, the great foe of mankind, gains his point, unless Sovereign grace interferes, and opens the blind eye to see the danger, and Jesus the Refuge. Oh, what a mercy of mercies to know all this, and to act upon it! Yet how many are satisfied with the form of godliness, while they know nothing of its power. They go to church, repeat many prayers, yet never feel sin a weight, a grievous burden, nor shed one tear before God for having sinned against Him. Oh, it is with a holy, heart-searching God that we have to do. And the soul is of more value than ten million worlds. *What shall it profit a man if he gain the whole world and lose his own soul?* These are solemn, awful truths; but only by a few are they laid to heart. May the Lord enable you to bring your heart to Him, who alone can heal it thoroughly; and may he lead you in the right way. I believe that none will ever come to Jesus until they feel that they are lost and undone in themselves. He came not to call the righteous, but sinners to repentance. Oh, come as you are—blind, wretched, helpless, and in that state cast yourselves at the feet of Jesus, and He will not spurn you from His presence. Read the third chapter of John's gospel to all whom you may find anxious about eternal realities. May you be made a blessing to many. A great work has been done in you, and a great work is to be done by you. All who know the Lord should let their light shine before men, that others might be led to the true light. Oh, the mercy of being in the right road—the narrow road, that leads to life eternal. Dear friend, study your Bible with prayer for the teaching of the Holy Spirit. Read the first and second chapters of Ephesians, and pray over these precious portions of God's word, that the Spirit may lead you into all the richness, fulness, and sweetness therein; that with an assured hope you might not only go on your way rejoicing, but may also be instrumental in leading others to examine for themselves. Oh, what is all the grandeur, wealth, and honour of this fleeting world, compared with the glory that awaits the believer in Jesus? Kings and queens pass away, and leave their crowns; but the Christian goes to his, and wears it through eternity—ever bright, ever pure."

To an aged Christian, whose trembling faith her letters had often nourished, and who, since her own departure, has gone to unite with her in the song of the Lamb, she thus encouragingly writes:—

TO LADY MARY F——, ON WAITING UPON GOD.

"DEAR SISTER IN THE LORD,—   London, May 25, 1848.

" For as such I hail you. We are travelling fast, and are nearing at every step our heavenly home. We shall both see Jesus soon—oh, how soon!—and know even as we are known. All that he has spoken is confirmed *truth*. Then, let us take Him at His word, believe it, and go on rejoicing in Christ Jesus. What a mercy of mercies that He has condescended to call us out of darkness into His marvellous light, and to translate us into the kingdom of His dear Son! What do we not owe Him for this rich display of sovereign mercy? I often have to exclaim, Lord, why me? such a poor sinner as I am to be brought nigh unto God—adopted into His family—made an heir of God, and a joint-heir with Christ Jesus? Such are we in Him. Let us hold fast our oneness with Christ, then we shall be better enabled to walk with God. We are journeying to the inheritance which the Lord our God has given to us, through a world crowded with temptations on either side, which would divert us from the way, if it were possible. Our worst foe, the body of sin and death, we bear about with us. But our Jesus is for us, and withal we can say, *More are they who are for us, than they who are against us.* God the Father, Son, and Holy Ghost, are on our side, and these are *Almighty.* Dear friend, seeing these things are so, what manner of persons ought we to be, in all manner of holy conversation and godliness! God be praised on your behalf, that He has brought you so far. We may not meet in this vale of tears, but I shall meet you above, and shall know you amongst the goodly company that are around the throne upon which Jesus sits, in all the majesty of heaven, waiting to welcome his pilgrims home. Let us endeavour to allure all we love to join us on the way. I have just been bringing all mine, one by one, to Him who is able to save to the uttermost. I know something of His power and unparalleled love towards poor sinners. Let us pray on for those who are dear to us. Our God hears and answers prayer. On him let us wait, and wait unweariedly until He answers. In waiting on Him for those dear to us, we shall receive a blessing for our own soul. We cannot approach Infinite Goodness without getting good. And oh, how blessedly refreshing and invigorating is the lifting up of the light of His countenance upon our weary and tried souls! It is a wonder that we are not oftener at His gracious footstool. What could we do in this poor dying world without a throne of grace, and a God of grace upon the throne, in our every time of need? Oh, let us keep close to Him who loved us with an everlasting love, and with loving-kindness has drawn us to Himself. In waiting upon Him, let us not be satisfied without the feeling that His ear is hearkening to us. This is very important—I must *feel* that he hears me, the blessed Spirit bearing witness with my spirit that God, even my God and Father, hears his poor child's pleadings. This is the privilege of all the dear family of God. To each one He says, *Ask, that your joy may be full.* He upbraids His disciples for asking so little; *Ask what you will in my name, and it shall be done unto you.* There He sits at the right hand of God, to make intercession for us. He is waiting to be gracious. Let us, then, trim our lamps, that at His coming we may be found *quite* ready. The Lord bless you with much of His sensible presence, is my prayer."

TO MRS. W——. ENCOURAGEMENTS TO PRAYER.

"MY DEAR CHRISTIAN FRIEND,— Nov. 24.

". . . I trust the Lord will in due time answer your prayers, as it respects your dear children. *All power is mine*, says Christ, *in heaven and on earth*. Oh, the mighty power of prayer with God our Father, in the name of His beloved Son! We must get to heaven before we know what that power has been in its fullest sense. *Command ye me.* Oh, the luxury of prayer! We have intercourse truly, familiar intercourse with God. To *talk* with God. To go and shut the door, and tell God all, *all* that is in our heart. To feel that He is listening to hear what we have to say to Him; and then to wait and see what He will say to us. Dear friend, such, as you know, is the privilege of all the saints. It may be long ere you see your prayers answered; for faith must be brought into exercise; and often, when we are ready to give all up, *then* the Lord comes, and, although in a very different manner to what we expected, He answers our prayers, and puts our unbelief to the blush. Oh, to have such a God to deal with, and to know that He is always dealing with us in His providence and by His Spirit! Glorious is our high calling in Christ Jesus. It is He who says, '*Ask anything in my name, and I will do it.*' *Is anything too hard for me?* saith *the Lord.* What could I do with such a heavy charge laid upon my heart, if I had not such a God to deal with? Fifty-seven immortals, bearing my name, do I think of, and pray for. Some are converted, others still in nature's darkness. Is there not work enough here for one poor pilgrim? But such is the power of the Most High, and such the fulness of Christ, and such the boundless love of God in Jesus, that I am greatly encouraged to make large demands upon Him in the dear and all-prevailing name of His own Son and of my own Saviour. So you see I would try to encourage you, too, to pray on, and to expect an answer when your faith is fully tried. . . . . I have been greatly exercised as to the path of duty for ——. But I gave myself to prayer, which, in all circumstances, adverse or otherwise, is my stronghold. I can find my way to the heart of God, when I cannot elsewhere do good, or shape things as I would wish. He is, and ever has been, a present help to me in all my troubles, trials, and adversities. I would not now have been without them *all*. It was in love He dealt with me. . . . This is the God I have now to do with, day by day, moment by moment. I rest on His loving, Fatherly care; and no tongue can tell the rich enjoyment of sitting in all the helplessness of infancy at His feet, and know that He is listening to all I would say to Him, and all that I would need to say, though unexpressed. Oh, how few really know God! I meet with many *hearsay* Christians, who have heard of Jesus, as Job did, with the hearing of the ear, but who have no personal acquaintance with Him. They have never come to Christ as poor, wretched, blind and naked; and therefore they know nothing of that peace which the application of the atoning blood alone can impart. They have never come in contact with Christ. They only believe what others say of Him, and know nothing of a blessed recognition, a oneness, and a holy intercourse between Jesus and the poor sinner, saved by sovereign grace, and eternal, everlasting love. Pray on; wrestle with Christ."

TO THE SAME,—ON THE OXFORD TRACTS.

"The Lord, I believe, is answering prayer by all these things that at present alarm us. I have long regarded the church, the one church, composed of all the chosen of God, as comparable to a house out of order, with nothing in its right place; so that it has been my constant prayer, 'Lord, when wilt Thou come and set Thine own hand to the work, putting down the work of men, and causing Thine own ordinances to be duly honoured?' When the 'Oxford Tracts' first made their appearance, I remarked that the Lord was about to commence His own work, in His own way. That Baptismal Regeneration would do it. From that moment I have been watching events: and when the Papal Aggression came, it gave me no alarm. Jesus reigns. Oh, that He would appear in this awful state of confusion, and cause His own people to come out of Babylon, shake off the dust from their feet, and separate themselves from the ungodly. The Lord is about to do a great work, and what we have to do is to humble ourselves before Him on account of the abominations of the land. I believe that His hand is in this 'Aggression,'—in the confusion that confounds our senators, and in all that is now going forward; and if we watch and pray, we shall see it plainer and plainer. My soul rejoices in God my Saviour, and I have no fears nor misgivings. My prayers are about to be answered, and the one elect church will be purified from all the dross, and will stand forth *fair as the moon, clear as the sun, and terrible as an army with banners.* I have had a blessed praying time this morning, and could open my mouth wide, and ask great things concerning His one church. Thirteen ladies have engaged to meet every morning, at eight o'clock, in united prayer for the Queen. Oh, I do know something of the mighty power of prayer, particularly *united prayer.* In the midst of all the public excitement, my little bark is riding serenely through the storm, and soon I shall drop my anchor in the still waters of eternal rest and glory."

". . . I feel that one reason why many real Christians do not go on their way rejoicing, is, that they *deify* the humanity of Christ. They feel they are coming to a holy God, who cannot look at sin without infinite displeasure; and this view of Jesus repels and throws them back. Whereas Jesus is the very same Jesus now that He was when He walked the streets of Jerusalem. Though His body is glorified, He is not altered. His heart is still the same, full of sympathy and love, ready to listen to all we have to say to Him, and to do all we ask Him to do, and in the best possible way. Precious Jesus! is He not altogether lovely? He is everything to my soul. Life were an aching void without Him. Now and then He lifts the veil, and gives me a blessed glimpse of the glory that awaits me and all who love His appearing."

TO MRS. C———, ON HEAVEN, AN INCENTIVE TO PERSEVERANCE.

"DEAR FRIEND,— London, Feb. 10th, 1840.

"How is it with the poor body, and how is it with your precious soul? Looking forward, I trust, to your blessed meeting with Him, who *so* loved you as to *die* that you might live with Him in that place He has gone to prepare for you. Only think of this! Jesus is above, and is ready to welcome you home. Let us hourly realize this,—realize heaven, with all its glories. Your dear sister stands ready, amongst many more, to welcome you there. And more than all, and above all, is Jesus, with a countenance radiant with love, prepared to rejoice over every emancipated soul that leaves this world of sin and sorrow, to enter into the enjoyment of what He has prepared for it. And behold the goodly company around the throne; and believe, that if there is joy in heaven among the angels of God over a sinner that repenteth, there is also a joy among saints and angels over every released saint that reaches heaven at last. Glory to Him who hath done such great things for us! When Lazarus departed, angels attended him, nor left him until they bore him to Abraham's bosom. I believe this is the case with all who love the Saviour. They are absent from the body, and that same moment they are present with the Lord. What rapture to fall at His feet, and to hear Him say, *Come, ye blessed of my Father!* Oh, that the saints of God would live more in the anticipation of the glory that awaits them! There is much of heaven to be enjoyed even on earth. Let us live, too, more in holy familiarity with Jesus. Nothing is too much beneath His notice. As dear old Mr. John Newton says, 'If the buzzing of a fly is an annoyance to us, it is our privilege to carry it to Jesus.'

"The question again recurs, how is it with your soul? Are your prospects growing brighter and brighter as you travel on? Do you find Jesus nearer and more precious day by day? What progress have you and I made? We have had our conflicts, our wanderings and backslidings many; but still onwards we must go. There is no standstill in this journey. We know less or more of Christ than we did a year ago. Tell me when you saw Him last, and how you feel in the prospect of soon being with the beloved One for ever and ever. I am not happy here without Him, and should be miserable indeed, were I not quite sure of seeing and dwelling with Him in glory. Jesus is all in all to my soul, and life would be wearisome indeed were it not so. He makes up the sum of my happiness here, and will be my joy, my life, and my glory hereafter. Dear friend, let us speed more our journey, nor loiter in the way. I must conclude. The Lord is prospering His work amongst us."

TO MISS C———, ON THE INTERCESSION OF CHRIST.

"I am sitting in my quiet room, beloved friend, where I have been blessing and praising God for His ten thousand, thousand mercies, in giving me such an all-sufficient Saviour and precious INTERCESSOR as His beloved Son. Having taken a body like our own, though free from all taint of sin, He is both able and willing to make intercession for us with a holy, holy Lord God, who cannot but behold sin with infinite displeasure. What a mercy for such as we are, who feel the taint of sin in all we do and say, to be enabled to present all our petitions in the dear name of God's Son, with whom the Father is ever well pleased! Such an intercessor was needful. God has said to Jesus, '*If thy children backslide, I will chasten them with the rod; nevertheless my loving-kindness will I not utterly take from them, nor suffer my faithfulness to fail.*' We often sin, and deserve a Father's rod; but Jesus, at the right hand, prays, '*Father, forgive them.*' Such is Jesus to us, making intercession moment by moment, and presenting all our petitions in His own blessed name. Is not this most blessed? Does it not give us an inexpressibly endearing view of Jesus, our elder Brother, our Brother born for adversity? And now I am going to tell you good news. Dear W—— is converted. He has found Jesus precious to his soul. . . . It is a mercy to see any asking their way to Zion, with their faces thitherward. I believe that God is about to work like Himself; and to overturn, overturn, and overturn, to accomplish His own blessed will. Let us, who are of the day, watch and pray. Who would not live for eternity? Is it not strange that we can for one moment lose sight of heaven, and the increasing glory, as long as the existence of God Himself, and grovel in the dust to gather pebbles, for the pleasure of throwing them afterwards away? Man walks in a vain show, and, blindfolded, goes down to the grave unsaved! Join me in praising God for His great and distinguishing mercy to us, in opening our eyes, and leading us to His beloved Son, that we might be saved with a sure and everlasting salvation. Let us keep close to Jesus, and pray for each other. I thank you again for the nice help to my blind eyes. The spectacles are always at my side."

TO THE SAME.

"I have written to you of the Lord's goodness to us in the conversion of W——. The Lord is good indeed. My soul rejoices in God my Saviour. Let us ever trust Him for His unchanging and unchangeable love. From everlasting to everlasting He has loved us; and all the varying dispensations of His loving providence are only to prepare us more completely for the place He is now preparing for us. Let us aim to see Him in all things, and to have Him ever present with us. How sweet to walk through the wilderness with our hand in His hand, feeling that He is leading us safely along the narrow road that leads to everlasting life! Dear friend, may Jesus be more and more precious to you and me. Cannot you repeat from your heart these lines with me?

> Is there a thing beneath the sun
> That strives with thee my heart to share?
> Ah! take it thence, and reign alone,
> The Lord of every motion there.
> Then shall my heart from earth be free,
> When it hath found repose in thee."

"None but Jesus can make us happy here and hereafter. Only believe, and wait the time when we shall more fully understand this great mystery of godliness. Oh, the glorious prospect that is before the feeblest child of God! Look often at your inheritance. Take your walks in the garden of love above. See Jesus there, no longer wearing a crown of thorns, but a diadem of glory, in the very same body He carried up with him. There is your dear sister among the number, and oh, how many that I love who are waiting to welcome me home! Dear friend, *realize* it. It will tend to strengthen your faith, and brighten your hope. My loving love to your cousin."

TO HER SON O——, A MOTHER'S PRAYERS.

". . . . . I have just had an interview with the Lord our God, and a blessed one it has been to my soul. And do you think I forgot you all? Oh, that the Lord might be to you what He was to the family at Bethany—the Martha, and the Mary, and the Lazarus, whom He loved! I have been asking great things for you all; for, while He held out the sceptre, my heart was full, and my mouth opened wide to ask much for you all, and all whom God has given me. Oh, what a mighty privilege is the believer's—to have holy intercourse with, and blessed access to, the God of heaven! May we never lose sight of it, but ask much, and expect what we ask for. God is leading us in a right way to the New Jerusalem above; and all we have to do is, to keep a steady eye upon Him; for, be assured, He will never leave nor forsake us. All is true, as God is true. Keep your eye intently upon Him. Take no step without Him. Beware of forming plans in your own mind, and then coming to ask counsel of God. Never let us forget that God has to do with us every moment of our existence, and we ought to have to do with Him. We are not to be like the world around us, but to walk humbly and closely with God. Blessed be His name, he gives me at times such blessed access to Him, that I can testify it is real, it is true. My soul seems swallowed up in God. I feel heaven so near, that I am almost in the actual presence. Yes, Jesus is above. Our own Joseph lives, and for you and for me He has said it, and I believe it. Oh, I do think He will give us a revival. He will do again what he has once done. What blessed nearness to Himself He gave me one morning when I descended from my room, and said 'Look out for the Lord, for He is near you!' Oh, may He appear once again for us, and revive His work in all our souls, and in His churches! How do I long to see it! To-day He has given me fresh testimony of his unchanging love, and that He is near to us, oh, how near! May he suffer no root of bitterness to spring up among us, and the Spirit be grieved, and the work be hindered. God be gracious to us, and come and bless us! We cannot do without Him, for He is our joy, our life, our all. Without Him, the world, and all it calls good, is a wretched wilderness; with Him, a wilderness can be a paradise to our souls, and a little heaven below."

TO THE SAME—ON CHRISTIAN UNION.

"Wednesday Evening.

"You are just now preaching, and I have been praying for you again and again. I am alone in the drawing-room. I was just thinking, after reading about the Evangelical Alliance, could you not write a work on the Unity of the Church, grounding your subject on the passage, *Love ye one another, as I have loved you?* Love to the brethren springs from the love of God in the renewed soul. This love surpassing all creature love, and enkindled by the indwelling of the Holy Ghost, must necessarily unite the one family of God. If the Holy Spirit dwells in me, when communicating with another, who also is a temple of the Holy Ghost, the Spirit within me will surely acknowledge His own image in the other, and love will necessarily flow out towards the individual. Therefore the apostle says, *We know that we have passed from death unto life, because we love the brethren.* If the Lord lay this subject with power on your mind, and open it to you, so that you can write upon it, it may be a great blessing to the church of God. The love of Christ to His saints is to be the measure of their love to one another."

TO MRS. H——, ON THE INFINITE LOVE OF CHRIST.

"Dear Friend,— January 17.

"I must not forget to wish you a 'happy new year,' in the best sense of the word. Oh, that in this new year, you and I might grow in grace and in the knowledge of Jesus Christ more rapidly than we have hitherto done! Thus we shall grow in meetness for our heavenly inheritance. Christ has gone to take possession of heaven in our behalf. He would not delegate this to the highest angel in glory. He knew that He was the fittest One to do this. It was love, infinite love, that brought Him down to earth. It was infinite love that led Him to pass through the tremendous conflict, when He grappled with death, hell, and the grave. It was infinite love that sustained Him in it, and that brought Him out of it a royal Conqueror. It was infinite love that bore Him back to heaven, where he is now, and where we shall be also. Oh, for this hope, this good hope, through grace, let our hearts abound with holy love towards Him.

"And now, what have we to do here, but to glorify Him who has done such great things for us! The influenza has been raging, and many, strong and healthy, have been summoned into eternity. .... What a stormy life is this! Gale after gale, all to show us that this is not our rest, but that a better awaits us, even a heavenly. Who would live away? Who would desire to dwell on these lower grounds, where sickness and sorrow, the sad consequences of sin, follow in our wake? In heaven, our happy home, we shall enjoy perfect holiness and perfect happiness. Oh, that you and I might live for that, towards which time is so rapidly hurrying us! Dear friend, keep close to Jesus and a throne of grace. If you feel your heart cold, go at once, and He will warm it. If you feel it hard and impenitent, go, and He will soften and awaken it to sweet contrition. Go, under all circumstances and with all frames. All your difficulties, however small or however great, you have a right to bring to Jesus, *casting all your care upon Him, for He careth for you.* Dear friend, Jesus wants you and me to live more upon Him, like little helpless children. I hardly know how to dismiss this darling theme, so full of consolation is it. May the Lord bless and keep you very near Himself."

TO MRS. C. G——, ON THE DEATH OF A CHILD.

"MY DEAR FRIEND,— Sept. 9, 1839.

"I was not aware, until I called to inquire after you this evening, that the Lord had taken your little one. My heart tenderly sympathizes with you; for I know, by sad experience, what the feelings of a bereaved mother are. May the Lord be gracious to you, and whisper sweetly to your heart, 'All is well!' He has mercifully housed your sweet flower, and when you get above you will find him there, blooming in eternal youth. We know not when our little ones are so early removed, from what evil a gracious God has taken them. He sees the end from the beginning; we cannot discern a single step. How much better, then, to leave all in His dear hands, who loves them better than we can, and because He loves them, takes them home. All His dispensations are designed to draw us closer to Himself, and He would remove every object that comes between Him and us. Your faith, as well as mine, has been sharply tried; but Jesus is watching us both, and not one trial too much shall we have. His loving eye is upon you; let yours be up to Him. *Call upon me in the day of trouble, and I will deliver thee, and thou shalt glorify me*, is a promise which has been worth untold gold to me. I never knew it to fail. If He did not remove the trouble in *my* way, He did so in a far better way. I have felt for you, and have brought your case before the Lord. May he sanctify abundantly the discipline of the covenant. Whom he loves He chastens. Let us make sure work for eternity. There are some who take these things for granted. Now in a matter of such tremendous importance, God is too good to leave us to an uncertainty. There is such a thing as *knowing* that our sins are forgiven, and having the witness of the Spirit with ours that this is the case. Look not so much within for evidences, as to Christ, who has done the great, the mighty work for us who believe with all our heart unto salvation. The Lord bless you."

TO MISS B——, ON THE SOLEMNITY OF DEATH.

"MY DEAR FRIEND,— Feb. 17. 1851.

" . . . . I cannot but feel that it is a solemn thing to hear that one is so soon to enter the eternal world before me, so much younger than myself. And yet this awaits us all; and blessed is the thought, that if we are really what we profess to be, we may rejoice when the summons comes to bring us home to God. In a little while, and we shall meet to go no more out for ever. Should not this make us to rejoice in the prospect before us, and cause us to trim our lamps afresh, and be quite ready when the message comes? It is a solemn thing to die; and yet how few are thoroughly prepared for it! May we be found in readiness; this only can be as we are living and walking with the Lord. Death, to the believer, is but passing out of a world of sorrow and sin, and entering upon a world of indescribable glory. If we lived more in anticipation of the happiness that awaits us, earth would have less hold on our heart's best affections. Love to all."

TO MISS M. H.———. LIGHT IN SPIRITUAL DARKNESS.

"Leamington, March 28th.

"DEAR SISTER IN A MOST PRECIOUS JESUS,—

"I must address you thus. Although a stranger to you, I am not a stranger to Him who loves you, nor a stranger to the road you are now treading. As an old pilgrim, who has walked the narrow way for many years, and has passed through many trials and changes, I thought I would drop you a line; and perhaps the Lord may make it a comfort to your soul, which will not prevent my son, when he is more at leisure, from giving you his views of your case. The Holy Ghost is leading us—sees fit to guide us just as, in His own wisdom, He sees best for our advancement in the Divine life. As I have in some measure trodden the dark path you now tread, I may be qualified to speak a word in season to you. The changes—oh, many there are!—through which the believer passes, are richly calculated to mature his graces, to confirm him in the truth of the Bible, and render Jesus more precious. We are to follow on to know the Lord; and, in proportion as we know Him, we shall trust in Him in the dark day as well as in the bright noon-day, when the sun of His blessed countenance is upon us. But although your way is now dark, there is no necessity why you should remain in darkness. The ear of our loving Father is open to the cry of His child, and His heart is ever towards you. He delights to hear you always; and a sigh, a groan, a desire, is *prayer*, though you utter not a word. Besides, a throne of grace is ever at hand; and, as you say you cannot pray, go and tell Jesus. Keep nothing back from your dearest and best Friend. He requires an open heart. He has given you *His*, and He asks *yours* in return. Have no secrets with Him, and He will have no secrets with you. Whatever your feelings, no matter how bad, take them to Him; for He has engaged not only to save you from all evil, but to save you from *yourself*.

"It is no uncommon thing for God's beloved ones, dear to Him as the apple of His eye, to walk sometimes in spiritual darkness. *Who is among you that feareth the Lord, that obeyeth the voice of His servant, that walketh in darkness, and hath no light! Let him trust in the name of the Lord, and stay upon his God.* Not many years ago, I was called to walk in much darkness, after a long and blessed period of sweet, holy, and uninterrupted enjoyment of His presence. I was greatly distressed. I searched diligently for the cause, and I saw clearly enough why the Lord should have hid from me the light of His countenance. In a little while, I felt I must flee from myself to Jesus. I humbled myself before Him, confessed my sins, and gave Him no rest until He appeared for me again, and restored me to the sweet enjoyment of His presence. This He did. Oh, the blessings of importunate prayer! Think of the wonderful condescension of God, to say to us, 'COMMAND ye me.' Will He withhold any good thing from us? You will, perhaps, reply, 'not if we walk uprightly.' Well, if we have not, let us go and tell Him so. *Confession of sin* is one of the sweet, holy, and profitable exercises of the soul. It endears us to Christ, and endears Christ to us. It brings us into a brokenhearted, contrite communion with a loving, sympathizing Saviour, purifies the heart, and keeps the conscience tender and watchful. Have I said enough, without wearying you, to induce you to go at once to Jesus, and lay bare your whole heart before Him? He waits to be gracious. You need not be long in darkness. Fervent, importunate prayer will bring light into your soul, and Jesus, with all the tenderness and compassion of His nature, will show you He is yours, and that you are His through time and eternity. *I, the Lord, change not.* We change, everything around us changes! but our gracious God and Father changes not. Go to Jesus, and all will be well. When He visits you, let me know, that I may praise Him on your behalf."

TO MISS R——. THE SUPERLATIVE EXCELLENCE OF CHRIST.

"DEAR FRIEND,—

"What a high and holy privilege it is to walk in the fear of the Lord all the day long! And not in the fear of God only, but also in the love of the Spirit. I have sensible access to God. To listen to His still, small voice, and to feel an echo to it in our hearts, is not this a mighty privilege, worth a thousand worlds like this? What is all the pomp and glory of this dying world, compared with five minutes' such communion with the Holy Lord God, manifesting Himself in the face of Jehovah-Jesus? Beloved, this is your privilege and mine. God, in His rich mercy, causes us to enjoy it every day, and all the day long. What could we do in this world of manifold temptations, had we not a God to go to, ever ready to be a present help? Suffer no distance to arise between you and your best friend. He has undertaken for us in all things. We want Him as our Counsellor, as our Guide, as our Protector, as our Deliverer, in ten thousand ways. How needful and how sweet to be ever sitting at His feet, looking up and meeting His eye bending down upon us in love! I took my pen to address you, and my thoughts ran into this subject; my heart filled, and I could not but express what was passing there. Jesus is indeed very precious to my soul. All creature love sinks into nothing before it. If ever a mother loved her children, I have; but what are they, or all their love, compared to Jesus? The more I see of the fulness, the boundless love of Christ, the more I sink in the dust of self-abasement before Him.

"And now you are in the house of mourning. If the dear mother is safely landed, blessedly housed in the mansion long prepared for her, should it not be a house of joy? In her Father's house above, at home with God, freed from all pain, sin, and sorrow for ever, saved from the evil to come. What joy were this! Heaven is a *place*, and a place of the most perfect enjoyment; and the presence of Jesus makes it all that an immortal soul can desire. Its happiness, too, is ever increasing, as well as the capacity of the soul expanding, to receive and enjoy an ever-growing knowledge of God. Were our faith but stronger, we should clap our hands when our dear ones were taken to their heavenly home, and say, with Mrs. Isabella Graham, 'I wish you joy!' May the Lord comfort your hearts, and fill up the void He has made amongst you, and cause you to rejoice."

TO HER SON O——.

" London, *Wednesday.*
" . . . We returned yesterday from Taplow. The Lord brought me in safety here again. May He condescend to use me for Himself the little space that is now allotted me here below! It seems as if my time hitherto had gone to waste, and I had been an unprofitable servant. May the Lord forgive, and grant me all the grace I need to do His will! I was glad to find your interesting letter. Mrs. W—— called yesterday. I gave her the work on the 'Recognition of the Saints in Glory,' of which she is doubtful, and fears it leads to carnality. She says the 'Glory of the Redeemer' is a great source of comfort to her. I have just been pleading with the Lord to make the books a great blessing to the ——. All hearts are in the hands of Him with whom we have to do. He can bless them. Oh, how many things I have to ask Him for! and I believe He hears me always. There is never a work to be done, but Satan will endeavour to raise up an adversary. I have just been reading the Lord's deliverance wrought for Hezekiah when the Assyrian king came upon him. He is the same God now, never having changed since Adam fell. Hezekiah's God is our God. Let us encourage our hearts in the Lord, and keep close to a throne of grace. Take care of your health."

TO E. AND M. W——. ON THE NEARNESS OF HEAVENLY SPIRITS.

"DEAR FRIENDS,— March 10.

"Why have I not heard from you for so long a time? How is it with your poor bodies, and, above all, how is it with your precious souls—souls that Jesus loves, and for whom He shed His precious blood? Oh, may we never forget what it cost the Son of God to redeem us from endless perdition. We must remember *from* what we are redeemed, and *to* what we are redeemed. Eternal woe would have been our portion in infinite justice; but now eternal felicity will be our portion, and that, too, on the ground of infinite justice. Bless the Lord for His wondrous goodness in providing such a plan, by which He could be a just God, and a holy God, and yet save lost and rebellious man. Help me to praise, and let us encourage each other to love Him more, day by day. I want to love Him to-day better than I did yesterday, and so through an endless eternity. Dear friends, how little, in general, do we think of these things! The trifles of a day, yea, of an hour, occupy our thoughts, and cause us to grovel here below. Gladly would my soul be on the wing, ready to mount upwards at His bidding. In a little while, and we shall see Him as He is. We know not how soon. The heavenly world is all around us, and could we leave the clay, we should behold the air filled with the heavenly messengers sent down to minister to us, and to guard us from the evil power of darkness. Oh, the care of the Good Shepherd! His wakeful eye is ever upon us, and His loving heart is ever towards us.

" . . . Since I last wrote I have had a severe attack of influenza. It is the Lord, and a part of the discipline of the covenant. . . . And now I must hasten to close. Let us take courage, and press onward, keeping our happy home in view. In a little while, and we shall be there. Let me hear from you both. I hope the dear invalid is better. Never mind. We shall have new bodies, more beauteous than the brightest angel in heaven, and standing, too, nearer to the Saviour than they. Oh, I would encourage you both, dear, *dear* sisters, and myself, too, in anticipating the glory that awaits us! . . ."

TO THE SAME—ON TELLING JESUS.

"I have thought much of you both, beloved in the Lord, and wished to tell you so, but we have been in much anxiety on dear E——'s account, who has had an attack of inflammation on the lungs. . . . O—— was to have accompanied his brother to New York on business, but her illness prevented, and the steamer leaves to-day without them. So the Lord has ordered it. Praise to His holy name, who hedges up our way, sometimes with thorns. Oh, we shall see, when we arrive in heaven, how wonderful has been the wisdom that has guided us in all our journey through! Only realize your oneness to Him, then you may be quite certain that all that takes place, small or great, is in that covenant that is ordered in all things and sure. Nothing is uncertain with God. We walk by faith in Him, and not by sight. Oh, carry all your wants to Him, nothing doubting that He not only hears you, but is every moment watching over you! All is well, and though dark clouds come between, there is a bright light behind them. Go at once with your trouble, be it what it may; nothing is too trivial to carry to Him. In this you honour Christ, showing you believe His words, *Without me ye can do nothing.* Now, then, Jesus will do all things for you, and all things well. A sparrow falls not to the ground without Him. You are of more value than many sparrows. E—— is better. Oh, it has been, I trust, a time of deep searching of heart! She was left alone with God. Solemn thought! We often need be compelled to turn aside with God, and hear what He will say to us. We want no intruders there. We want to speak to God alone. Oh, doubt not that God does even now speak to His saints by the still small voice of His Spirit, so that we can respond, *Speak, Lord, for thy servant heareth. He openeth the ear to discipline;* and how sweet it is to wait and listen, to hear what God would say to us. Be not satisfied with praying, but wait for the *answer,* for it will come in some way. Let me have a line. I always remember you (one time in the day, perhaps,) in my prayers."

TO HER SON O——, ON A GOOD MINISTER OF CHRIST.

"How often it is, that while God is in His own way answering our prayers, unbelief will mist our eyes, and tempt us to fret and repine at His dispensations, not thinking that this is the way He takes to accomplish what we wish. Last Lord's-day was very refreshing to my soul. I went into the sanctuary, and then the Lord gave me a little insight into His doings. . . . Do you recollect what I wrote to you, that a dear, aged Baptist minister once remarked, that 'when God means to make a man rich, He takes away his money?' How often we think we could do the Lord's work better than He can Himself! F—— sent his carriage to take me to Mr. C——'s yesterday, where I spent most of the forenoon. What a dear, precious Christian he is! I think He is one of the most lovely saints I ever met with. His gifts for the ministry are not great, but what he has he honestly lays out in the service of the Lord—his whole heart devoted to Him, and his whole life a constant aim to glorify Him. Holy, upright, walking closely with God, and evidently experiencing much of the approving smiles of the Saviour. And although his holy fear of offending may incline a little at times to legality, it is yet a most lovely spectacle to behold. He will receive a *Well done, good and faithful servant, thou hast been faithful over a few things, enter thou into the joy of thy Lord.*

"... Oh, to look into eternity, and in its light to see the folly and madness of ungodly men. How do I long for the end of all things; for the coming of the Lord to put all things straight! for even the Church of Christ has wandered far from the right way, and has greatly dishonoured her Head. ... I found it very sweet to meet at the Lord's Table. Dear Mr. E—— recognised me, and gave me one or two of his kind looks, but I was too much engaged with Him, who is one ocean of love to my soul, to take much notice. He returned thanks to the Lord for preserving me in the time of danger, and for bringing me among them again. When will the book be out? I long to see it. Love to A—— and the dear chicks."

TO MISS J——, SOOTHING THOUGHTS IN ILLNESS.

"DEAR FRIEND AND SISTER,—

"I hear that you are not well. Do drop me, if only a few lines, and tell me all about yourself. Oh, dear friend, the world is one vast hospital filled with diseased inmates, and only one class can ever hope for a perfect cure. We shall all be well when we get above. This is not our rest, nor our home. We seek a better, and, blessed be God, our best Friend is preparing it for us. When we get there, we shall find it far beyond our highest and most enlarged expectations. Oh, help me to praise and bless His holy, holy name! .... There are seasons when, alone in my little sanctuary in this house, I am favoured with such precious glimpses of the glory that awaits the Christian, that I could shout aloud, *It is all true!* The atmosphere between this world and the other seems clearer and lighter, and but a step and I am there. What a meeting around that great white throne, basking in the glory emanating from the countenance of Him who so loved you and me as to live for us, to die for us, and to live again, and to say, *Because I live ye shall live also.* Oh, let us encourage each other in the way! Our poor bodies, too, will be raised again, glorious bodies, beautified and prepared for the reception of the glorified spirit. The prospect is opening fast before me. Satan would try hard to mystify, or withdraw us from the simplicity of the precious Gospel. But let us come to Jesus, and bring to Him all our cares, large and small, and tell Him all that is in our hearts.

"P.S. I am still at L——, and thank God for giving me such a home for the little while I am here. I am fed with the sincere milk of the precious Gospel, by him whom the Lord gave me in infancy to nurse for Himself. I am watched over with the tenderest care, as a babe that can do little for itself. I have no care. I talk to Jesus, and tell Him all I wish and all I want. Sweet to close the door, and admit Him to my heart, confessing my sins again and again—the sins of my whole life, as the Holy Spirit brings them to remembrance. Repentance, I find, is not a thing once done, and ever after done with. Oh no! I go again and again, as sin arises in the mind, lay myself at the feet of Jesus, there to confess, weep, and love—no rebuke, all pardoned. Oh, the wondrous, the ocean-like love of Jesus! Who can fathom it? Dear friend, we can have some little glimpses elsewhere of Heaven. Cheer up! we shall meet above, and spend an endless eternity together. Oh, what a gathering there! I love to anticipate it, and do, in a measure, realize it. How beautiful they look clothed in the wedding garment, clean and white,—the infinite righteousness of Christ Himself. Why should we not rejoice? Let not the enemy keep you back. When he comes in like a flood, go directly to Jesus, and He will fight your battles. Let us pray for one another. Once more, farewell!

> 'For us the Lord intends
> A bright abode on high;
> The place where sorrow ends,
> And nought is known but joy;
> With such a hope let us rejoice,
> We soon shall hear the Bridegroom's voice.'"

TO MRS. C. W. J——, ON HER CONVERSION.

"MY DEAR FRIEND,—

"Although so lately known to me, yet having seen how blessedly Jesus—my Jesus and your Jesus—has drawn you to Himself, I can and do rejoice over you as one of the redeemed of the Lord, and a willing candidate for a crown of glory. Oh, dear friend, let no man take your crown. Watch and pray that you enter not into temptation. You and Christ are one. You are now called out of the world's wide wilderness, and you have taken up the cross to follow Jesus. You are now a soldier of the cross, and it is written, *Fight the good fight of faith; lay hold of eternal life.* What an honour to be called, as you have been, to own your Lord and Saviour before a gainsaying, Christ denying world! For this you can never be grateful enough.

> "Oh, to grace how great a debtor
> Daily I'm constrain'd to be!
> Let that grace. Lord, like a fetter,
> Bind my wandering heart to thee."

Oh, that Jesus might indeed bind you to Himself with cords of love! Never forget that you and Jesus are one. All your concerns are His concerns. All your cares are equally his cares. Therefore you are to be careful for nothing, for He careth for you. See what an honour it is to be a child of God, and to have grace given to walk boldly forth and own Him as your Saviour, Sovereign, and Friend. I do, indeed, rejoice with you, and rejoice over you. Hold fast your profession. You must expect to meet with scoffers, and those who would lead you far from Jesus. But cling firmly to Him, and hold fast to His word. I would say here, that confession of sin is a most sanctifying exercise of the soul. When you feel in your heart that you have grieved the Spirit, at once confess it to your dearest, best Friend; and He will, by the application of His own precious blood, not only give a sense of pardon, and grace, but will strengthen your faith and confidence in Himself. Do not forget this. It is of consequence that you do not. Let me write to you as a tender mother would to her beloved child. I have felt all this toward you. And oh, the prayers I have offered up for you! You will never know until you get to glory. Let me meet you there, beloved friend. I bear you in my best affections. When you meet with sufferings, remember your dear Lord met with such before you; and it is a great honour put upon you to be as He was in this present evil world. I do not wonder that —— said that you had 'united yourself to a vulgar religion,' for so said the multitude when Jesus was on earth, and when the Apostles went forth to preach Christ. The religion of Christ is not the religion of the world, but is in opposition to the world, and therefore the world will ever hate it and its followers. But there is a cross Christ's true disciples have to take up. Ask the Lord to strengthen, uphold, and comfort you.

"P.S. The following lines, dear friend, suit you:—

SOUL DARKNESS.

'Jesus, I my cross have taken,
  All to leave and follow Thee;
All things else for thee forsaken,
  Thou from hence my all shalt be.

'Perish every fond ambition,
  All I've sought, or hoped, or known,
Yet how rich is my condition,
  God and heaven are still my own!

'Let the world despise and leave me,
  It has left my Saviour too;
Human hearts and looks deceive me,
  Thou art not, like them, untrue.

'And whilst Thou dost smile upon me,
  God of wisdom, love, and might,
Foes may hate, and friends disown me,
  Show Thy face, and all is bright.

Go, thou earthly fame and treasure,
  Come disaster, scorn, and pain,
In Thy service pain is pleasure,
  With Thy favour loss is gain.

'I have call'd Thee, Abba Father,
  I have set my heart on Thee;
Storms may howl, and clouds may gather,
  All must work for good to me.'

"The enclosed Paper on 'Religious Progression,'" I had printed. We are to *go forward*. The Christian's watch-word is—Follow on to know the Lord. You have just commenced your heavenly race. You are to go on to know more of this great and glorious salvation. May the Lord Jesus teach you, and bless you with much of His sensible presence."

TO MR. W. D. L——, IN SOUL DARKNESS.

"DEAR BROTHER IN JESUS,—

"I think I must write a line to you; I have long wished it, but did not know how to intrude myself upon you. My dear son has sometimes given me a sight of your kind letters, which has led me to lift up my heart to the Lord in heaven to bless you, and to cause His face to shine upon you, filling you with joy and peace in believing. The love of God's saints to each other is as far superior to the natural love of relationship, or to the common friendship of the world, as the heavens are higher than the earth. This love emanates from God. It is a Divine cement that unites the one family of heaven. *We know we have passed from death unto life, because we love the brethren.* How sweet is this most precious evidence of our sonship! Hail it, dear friend, as a grand evidence of God's eternal, everlasting love to you. I have passed my threescore years and ten, and am looking out for the messenger from my Father's house to bring me to my happy, blessed home. It is almost in sight. I am favoured with some precious glimpses of the glory that awaits me. . . . Oh, to come to Jesus just as we would have done when He walked with His disciples here below! 'Precious Jesus, Thou Son of God, bless my young friend, and lift up upon him the light of Thy countenance, and say, *It is I, be not afraid.*' My heart is full of love towards you. I think I know a little of the road by which the Lord is leading you at this moment. Oh, let us bow our neck to the cross, for Jesus is walking with us every step of the way! . . . When tried, rush at once into the very bosom of Christ, and feel the warm pulsations of His own loving heart, and rest your head there. All will be well. He is with you now, and will never leave nor forsake you. Pray for us, and may the richest blessings rest upon you, beloved friend.'

TO E. S——. ENCOURAGEMENT TO COME TO JESUS.

"DEAR SUFFERER,—

"How have I thought of you since last evening; you looked so ill! My long letter, written some days ago, would not, I fear, be of much comfort to your heart. But Jesus loves you, and He will comfort you, I know. One glance of His loving eye beaming upon your inmost soul will be all-sufficient for your peace, and rich consolation under your present suffering of body. The body is but the casement to the jewel, which is rich and valuable enough to place in the crown of Him who died and who rose again, and who at this moment is seated on His throne in glory, waiting to welcome all who feel their need of Him, and can do nothing for themselves. It is upon such, Jesus has His loving eye. While you think you will try and do your best to please God, you will find you will come short, and will be weary of your efforts. But when you cast yourself, in all your helplessness, upon His mercy and power, and His word which says, *Come unto me, all ye that labour and are heavy laden, and I will give you rest,* then, my beloved friend, you will find Jesus, the Saviour of sinners, all that He has said He is, and ever will be, to every needy one who looks to Him for help. A glance, a sigh, a desire, He never, no never will overlook. His heart is one ocean of love—love to sinners, as sinners, not as saints. He loves the saints too, but He first loves them as poor, lost sinners, that can do nothing for themselves, and who come to Him to be saved. Oh, how welcome you are now, just in your present state of mind, to the heart of Jesus! His heart is yearning over you at this present moment. I will say no more. I have been to prayer for you, dear friend, for you are laid much upon my heart."

TO THE SAME.—THE DESIRE TO LOVE CHRIST PRECIOUS.

"Do not attempt to answer my note of yesterday; there is no necessity for it. I only thought I would give a word of comfort in your trouble. The poor body's necessities call for all your energies and patience, without having to write and answer notes. Be assured of this truth,—you would never have had a wish to love Jesus if He had not first loved you. That love is divine in its character, and springs from the power of the Holy Spirit. It never grew in nature's soil—it is above and beyond fallen nature. It comes from Christ, and quick returns are made to Christ. And if we have but one spark in our souls, it will kindle into a holy flame. Oh, to be a living member of Christ's living body! We are the members, and He is the Head. These are great mysteries, which you will better understand as you travel on in the narrow road that leads to the land of glory. Go with all you want to Jesus— keep nothing back. Go with all the simplicity of a babe, and tell Jesus. He will bow down His loving ear, and listen to all you have to say to Him. I must not weary you, but finish with what I began with—that if you have the faintest wish throbbing in your heart to love Jesus, it is one of the sweetest evidences that you can have that He first loved you. Now, the more you know Him, and have to do with Him, the more you will love Him."

TO HER SON O——, ON THE SUDDEN DEATH OF A DEAR FRIEND.

"Saturday Evening.

"I received yours this afternoon. I saw, by the papers this morning, that Mrs. ALERS HANKEY had gone to her happy home, and immediately wrote, as the Spirit led me, a word of comfort to the afflicted daughters. She is safe, I have not the shadow of a doubt. She is with Jesus. Little faith can get to heaven. It was a happy dismissal, just such a one as, in all her weakness and trembling, suited her, sparing her much bodily and mental suffering. How much do I see the tender love and sympathy of Christ in dealing with her thus! He knew all her feebleness, and how Satan would attempt to harass her in a lingering illness; and so He took her away as in a deep sleep; and before she knew that she was dying she was safely lodged within His loving bosom. Oh, the goodness and gentleness of Jesus—our God-man Mediator! How beautiful does the tender sympathy of the *manhood* appear in its union with the power and glory of the Godhead! Such is Christ to me. . . . Every now and then, the thought of the gracious dealings of our God towards dear Mrs. Hankey, as it respects her sudden and gentle dismissal, passes over me with much sweetness! What a realizing view it gives me of the exquisite character of Jesus—His gentleness, tenderness, and sympathy! Oh, how enviable such a death! *Let me die the death of the righteous, and let my last end be*—just as He would have it. Only would I say, 'Let me see Thy face all through the dark valley.' My soul at this moment rejoices in God my Saviour. He is all to me, living or dying. The last time I saw dear Mrs. Hankey, she sat listening with the deepest attention, and with tearful eyes. And when we parted, she kindly drew me towards her, and kissed me affectionately."

"Lord's-day.—This clause in one of the Psalms has been very sweet to me to-day: *For God is for me*. What, then, need the believer fear, here or hereafter? This is His comfort. Christ and he are one in time and in eternity. Looking into 'Bridge on Faith,' these words met my eye: 'Suffering times are self-recollecting times.' And we may add, suffering times are, or ought to be, fruitful, growing times. *Every branch that beareth fruit, He purgeth it that it may bring forth more fruit.* Oh, that it may be so with dear E—— and me! I have followed you with my prayers to-day, that the Lord might heal the sick, strengthen the weak, and bless His own word to saints and sinners. Love to all."

What pen could have given so faithful a delineation of her elevated Christianity as her own has unconsciously presented in the foregoing utterances of her heart? The impression on the mind of the reader must be, how *real* is true religion, and how *earnest* is its spirit! And yet there is nothing in that religion, as thus exhibited, that the lowliest subject of grace may not experience. Precious is the sentiment with which the chapter closes—"LITTLE FAITH CAN GET TO HEAVEN."

CHAPTER XIII.

"As the sunbeams united in a burning glass to a point have greater force than when they are darted from a plain superfice, so the virtues and actions of one individual, drawn together into a single story, strike upon our minds a stronger and more lively impression than the scattered relations of many men and many actions."* It is upon this principle of concentration, for whose discovery we are indebted to the Bible, that God has condescended to reveal Himself to man. In the person of His Son He has so embodied the perfections of His nature, and has so concentrated the beams of His majesty, as to present in focal grandeur the "light of the knowledge of the glory of God in the face of Jesus Christ." In picturing the sunset of a life so prolonged and honoured of God as that which these pages record, it will be our endeavour, as that life approaches its close, thus to collect and concentrate its retiring beams, intercepting them only so far as a gentle hand may be required to guide them to the focus. It is a rich autumnal sunset we are about to contemplate. The 'sear and yellow leaf' is falling thick and fast; but in the lingering freshness and fertility, the reader will be reminded of the character appertaining to the aged godly, so beautifully delineated by the sacred penman,—" The righteous shall flourish like the palm tree: he shall grow like a cedar in Lebanon. Those that be planted in the house of the Lord shall flourish in the courts of our God. They shall still bring forth fruit in old age; they shall be fat and flourishing; to shew that the Lord is upright." It is the remark of an elegant writer, and the sentiment is not less true than beautiful,—" Cheerful piety in the decline of life, is like a tree which the storm has shattered, but which yet retains much of the verdure of summer, and is still the resort of the birds which sing among the branches."

* Addison.

These pleasant characteristics of religion in old age will be recognised in the extracts we proceed to make from Mrs. Winslow's diary and correspondence, indicating an extraordinary elevation of spiritual feeling, blended with a solemn yet radiant consciousness of her nearness to the glory within which she was soon to pass. Our first quotations are from the private journal which has supplied us with so much rich material, but which, alas! is soon to receive its final record of a pilgrimage from earth to heaven.

"*Leamington.*—I could never have believed that I should have such nearness to Jesus, as I now, at times, enjoy. Read this morning the twenty-first of John, from the 4th, particularly pausing at the 12th verse, *Jesus saith unto them, Come and dine.* His care, His forethought of His disciples, is now just what it was when this circumstance took place. He had watched the fruitless labour of His disciples through the night —they had caught nothing. Just at this juncture, when weary, discouraged, and hungry, He appeared. They needed refreshment—He was not unmindful of it. Coals were kindled—fish was laid thereon, bread was provided—nothing omitted suitable to their wants. And then they were invited to dine. They need not ask, *Who art thou?* The multitude of fishes they had caught at His word, the repast He had provided—the invitation He had given—all proclaimed who He was—their dearest friend. Is it not so with thee, O my soul? Has Jesus ever been unmindful of thy wants? Never, no *never.* Always ready to supply my need, He has gone before me in the wilderness, and prepared a table for me. Remembering the thorn and the briar, He has made a narrow road for my feet, saying, *Follow thou me!* Had I ever need to inquire, *Who art thou, Lord?* Did I not know Him? Yes! Even now I feel His presence. I know the person, and I hear the voice. How sweet, how cheering, how comforting! To be with Jesus, and to know it! With such a visit have I been favoured this day. Oh, what little things do worlds appear, when so blessed! Wondrous in all His dealings has Christ been to me. Chosen in Him before the foundation of the world, in due time called, justified, sanctified, and shall be soon and eternally glorified."

"The Lord does wonderfully seem to let heaven down into my soul. I have no power to describe it. Then does heaven itself seem so inviting, so attractive. I feel it but a step, and

I am in the midst of happiness, perfect and supreme. I have asked the Lord not to send the grim, pale messenger for me, unless he comes with him. I must see His own, well-known face, ere I can welcome the summons. Oh, to be in His bosom, there to rest without a fear or misgiving—to pass through that dark valley in His own loving, Almighty arms, reposing upon His very heart! May this be my case. He so condescendingly answers my poor prayers, and in a way so remarkable, that were I to tell some individuals, they would declare it a delusion. But I know otherwise. Every precious word He has spoken is *true*. My soul rejoices in God my Saviour, my Friend, my Father. I shall see Him—see Him as He is; be like Him; dwell with Him through eternity, in perfect knowledge, perfect purity, perfect happiness, perfect glory. Precious Jesus, Thou knowest all things; Thou knowest that I love Thee. And though, like Peter, I have often wandered from Thee, yet Thou hast never left me, nor denied Thyself. Glory be to thy dear and holy name."

"How gracious, how transcendently good has the Lord been to me this day! The 20th Psalm was made a rich blessing to my soul. How wonderfully does the Lord reveal Himself through His own word to the heart and conscience of His children! Truly is His loving ear open to the faintest cry of His feeble ones—such condescension in stooping to catch their faintest breath of prayer! Language seems to fail, when the heart is thus filled with the Spirit, to express its deep emotions—the feelings of a broken and a contrite spirit. Never, no never, does sin appear so hateful as when the Lord comes down to bless. Prostrate at His feet I fall, love and sorrow so strangely mingled that they cannot be separated. Oh, for a close walk throughout this day, my eyes and heart fixed upon Jesus—Jesus risen! He that was dead, is now alive, and reigns upon the throne above; all power on earth and in heaven is His. With Him I shall dwell throughout eternity—blessed thought! Precious Jesus! heaven would be no heaven, wert Thou not there. Not all I love on earth, were I to meet them, could compensate for the loss of Thyself. Lord, help me this day to pass through its cares without contamination, upheld by the Spirit. I am all weakness; with Thee is all power. Help Thy weak one, and leave me not to myself. Take my whole heart and soul in Thy hands, and order all my goings, for Thine honour's sake."

"Tuesday.—The text this morning was from Song of Solomon ii. 10: *My beloved spake, and said unto me, Rise up, my love, my fair one, and come away.* . . . The Lord is pleased to enable me to hear without excitement. Surely He has heard my prayer, and answered it. And not only so, but in blessing the word to my soul. Every word seems to tell; and to all my heart can echo its sincere *Amen.* Oh, what cause for thankfulness is this! His dear name shall have all the glory."

"Wednesday Evening.—The text this evening was from Phil. iv. 19: *My God shall supply all your need according to His riches in glory by Christ Jesus.* . . . A word to the rich and the poor of the flock. We have a spiritual and a temporal need; both supplied in and by Christ Jesus, in whom God has treasured up a fulness adequate to all the wants of His bride, His beloved, His fair one, whom He invites to rise up and come away. Glory is prepared for her—a mansion suitable to her dignity and station as the bride of the Lamb and the Heir of God. Who can tell what this will be? We grovel so much here, we can hardly raise our poor ideas to that inheritance that awaits us. Oh, for an eagle's wings to mount higher toward heaven! How trifling would then everything appear here, but that which was connected with things above! Lord, help Thy creature to live more on high—more in communion with Jesus—more looking to a *risen* Christ.

"10th.—I have met with the following excellent observations from the pen of the Rev. Dr. Stone, Rector of Christ's Church, Brooklyn, which are in close accordance with my own views: 'The object of God, in the revelation of His will, and in the incarnation of His Son, is to save men from sin, and to bring them to eternal life. Every one in whom the required faith is found has a direct and personal union with Christ; so that He draws his spiritual life, not by succession from another believer, but immediately from the Saviour Himself. Nothing, however thin, intervenes between the two. By faith the believer is in Christ, and by the same faith Christ dwells in the believer's heart.* This mystic union between Christ and each individual Christian is as close and as perfect as though Christ and each individual were the only ones in all the world concerned in that union. As a foundation, Christ is as broad as

* Would it not be more correct to say, that Christ dwells in the believer's heart *by the in-being of the Holy Ghost?*—EDITOR.

the realm of sin, and as long as the age of grace; so that every true believer touches, immediately and for himself, that on which he builds. Each single character holds this living connexion and communion with the Saviour as immediately and as closely, and draws life therefrom as largely and as perfectly, as though himself and the Saviour were the only beings concerned in the Divine affinity. There are, then, in the world, and there have been from the beginning, and will be to the end, a steadily growing, and at length a very great company of human beings, maintaining the character which I have just explained—the character of true believers in Christ, and the relations of a holy, individual union with Christ. These, as represented in the Bible, and as found in fact, are an exceedingly "peculiar people." There are none like them in all the world. If what has been wrought in them could be laid open to the eye of sense, they would instantly be known from other men all over the earth.' Thus writes Dr. Stone. Oh, how precious is this union! How closely it draws the heart to Jesus; and how the heart entwines around its better part, and exults in the thought, that nothing, not death itself, shall separate it from its dearest and best Friend. This is my highest joy."

Following this extract from an American divine we find transcribed in her journal an appropriate poetic piece of touching beauty. The lines are suggested by the words of Jesus, "The foxes have holes, and the birds of the air have nests, but the Son of man hath not where to lay His head."

"Birds have their quiet nest,
Foxes their holes, and man his peaceful bed;
All creatures have their rest,—
But Jesus had not where to lay His head.

"Winds have their hour of calm,
And waves, to slumber on the voiceless deep;
Eve hath its breath of balm,
To hush all senses and all sounds to sleep.

"The wild deer hath his lair,
The homeward flocks the shelter of their shed;
All have their rest from care,—
But Jesus had not where to lay His head.

"And yet He came to give
The weary and the heavy-laden rest,
To bid the sinner live,
And soothe our griefs to slumber on His breast.

"What, then, am I, my God,
Permitted thus the path of peace to tread?
Peace, purchased by the blood
Of Him who had not where to lay His head?

"I, who once made Him grieve;
I, who once bid His gentle spirit mourn;
Whose hand essay'd to weave
For His meek brow the cruel crown of thorn—

"Oh, why should I have peace?
Why? but for that unchanged, undying love,
Which would not, could not cease
Until it made me heir of joys above?

"Yes! but for pardoning grace
I feel I never should in glory see
The brightness of that face
That once was pale and agonized for me!

"Let the birds seek their nest,
Foxes their holes, and man his peaceful bed;
Come, Saviour, in my breast
Deign to repose Thine oft-rejected head!

"Come! give me rest, and take
The only rest on earth thou lovest—within
A heart, that for Thy sake
Lies bleeding, broken, penitent for sin."

"Still going on my way, leaning on my Beloved. Jesus is very precious. No tongue can tell how precious. Language often fails, when on my knees, to tell Him how much I love Him. My soul is kept near Him. I often have Him full in view. If a cloud intervenes, I cannot rest until it be withdrawn. Oh, for more of the wrestling power of prayer! How sensibly is He then present, lifting up the light of His countenance, and bending low His ear. When thus He shines, I then see what sin really is, and I weep. The sin pardoned, the sinner beloved—this it is that breaks the heart, if anything can. What an honour put upon a poor vile sinner, to be permitted to love Jesus—to be invited to come to Him just as we are. No wonder there is joy in heaven, and there ought to be more joy on earth. Him truly we now only see through a glass darkly. And yet there are times when the vail seems a little withdrawn. I believe this is often the case at a dying hour, just at the instant when the soul departs, and leaves its clay behind. Lord Jesus, be a present help to me then. Let no misgivings come over my mind. Keep Satan far from me.

Remember Thy weak, Thy aged one. Speak to my struggling soul. Speak holy words of comfort. Be near, and let me hear Thy well-known voice. Let not the conflict be long. Give me a speedy dismissal, and an abundant entrance into Thy kingdom above. Oh, to be for ever with Thee; that will be heaven enough for me! To gaze upon Thy ineffable face for ever—to love Thee as I long to do—oh, it is worth dying for!"

"The Lord has most preciously drawn sensibly near to my soul. This morning, held sweet communion with Him. My mouth was opened wide, to make great demands on His love. I felt I had not only His ear, but His blessed countenance shone upon me. How did I feel that to be with Jesus would be heaven! I longed to be with Him—wanted to get nearer, and still nearer. I wept in an agony of love. How little did the world, and all that was in it, appear to me! Seemed as if I could with ease have left the body, and mount up on high. Felt overwhelmed with shame that I could ever have harboured one unkind thought of such a Being. He is all love, nothing but love. Not one cold, upbraiding look has He ever given me. Go as I will, and when I will, His ever-benignant face smiles a welcome. Blessed Saviour, may I never, no never, mistrust Thee, nor grieve Thy Spirit. Keep, oh, keep me near Thee. Keep thine own blood-bought child from departing from Thee now. Let me not lose sight of Thee, no, not for one moment. Be Thou in all my thoughts day and night, and let my thought, wish and desire centre in Thyself."

"What communion can a formalist have with God? Communion is supposed to be an interchange of sentiment, feeling, and expression. What communion could one have with a statue? You may speak to it, question it; but there is no response, no intimation of feeling, no communion. So is it with the mere religious formalist. He regularly says his prayers, but it is to an *unknown God*. He repeats the same again and again, but he knows not the Being he addresses. There is no response, no interchange of feeling, above all, of love. There is no answer from the Lord, no bending down of His ear, no lifting up of His countenance, no cheering welcome; and the formalist is satisfied. He does what he thinks is his duty. He repeats his lifeless, heartless prayers, and thinks he has done well; and so he lives and dies with a lie in his right hand, unless God, in his sovereign mercy, awakens him from his awful delusion, and shows him his lost and undone condition. But oh, how great are the believer's privileges! He draws near to a reconciled God and Father. Unless he has communion, he cannot be happy. He pleads in the name of Jesus, opens all his heart to One who loves him, and whom he loves. He finds a response in the heart of God. He knows God hears him, and will withhold no good thing from him. He makes all his requests known with thanksgiving. He often goes heavy laden, and returns with a lightsome heart, overflowing with love. God has whispered peace to his troubled soul, and the Spirit within has borne the witness that God loves him. *This* is communion. Oh, what a mercy to know it!"

"Text, *Men wondered at.* May the Lord bless it, and give him who preached it strength of soul and strength of body to go onward and live upward; to gather all his supplies of grace and providence from Him who is God all-sufficient, ready to bestow all needful good for body, soul, and spirit. Text on Sabbath morning, Psalm xviii. 35: *Thy gentleness hath made me great.* In the evening, Luke xv. 2: *This man receiveth sinners, and eateth with them.*"

"This is the Lord's day. Confined to the house. Dear —— is now standing up in the name of the Lord, proclaiming the glorious gospel of a precious Saviour. I have been to prayer for a blessing upon it. Oh, that the Lord would pour out a mighty blessing on the church! Oh, that He would be pleased to bow the heavens, and come down in the power of the Holy Ghost, and encourage the heart of His tried servant! Lord, do be pleased to bless him throughout the day, and made him the honoured instrument of great good. Oh, that to-day sinners may be converted, and saints *re*-converted; for how many such are but half-awake, alas! 'resting on their lees.'"

"The Lord has a controversy with this sinful land, this ungodly nation. The famine and the pestilence is sweeping away its hundreds and its thousands in Ireland and in Scotland. The land may indeed be clothed with sackcloth. But do the ungodly take knowledge of this? Are the churches of Christ humbling themselves? Is not the famine in Ireland sent as a messenger of woe to proud and haughty England? Are we not partakers of the sins of Ireland? Are we less criminal than they? No; not one whit less. Equally guilty are we of trampling upon every precious precept, and of substituting our own views of truth, formed to please and honour the flesh, instead of the pure and precious gospel! Oh, when will men *be wise, and consider their latter end?* When will they obey God? The world, the world is in their hearts, and the god of this world reigns supreme, and there is no room for Jesus. Precious Saviour! still I pant for a closer walk with Thee. The more man sets Thee at nought, the dearer art Thou to my soul. I could weep to think how little Thou art thought of by the world at large, and how little even by the professing church. What a corrupted Christianity spreads, what cold, heartless formality prevails! How many are saying, 'Lord, Lord!' who know Thee not! How many are standing up this very day in the name of the Lord, to preach a gospel—which yet is no gospel—of their own invention!"

"Spent the evening at ——. Had much to mourn over afterwards. Lord, help me! keep me humble, meek, and lowly in heart! I am powerless! all power is Thine. With Thy strengthening arm I can do all things. Be with dear —— in his study to-day. Prepare him to preach a full gospel this evening, and accompany it with the power of the Holy Ghost to every one that heareth. Fill the place with true worshippers. Oh, that sinners may be converted, and saints sanctified! Glorify Thyself in the midst."

"*I cried unto the Lord with my voice; with my voice unto the Lord did I make my supplication. I poured out my complaint before Him; I showed before Him my trouble.* How often has this been my case! I, too, have cried unto the Lord in my trouble, and He has heard me. He has bent low His ear, and listened to my cry, and, oh, how graciously has He answered my request, and done more and better for me than I asked! The Lord always exceeds our requests, and is better than our fears."

"The Lord laid His hand upon me a few nights ago, and brought me very low. My children did all that could be done to alleviate my suffering; but I lifted up my heart to God while fainting and sinking, and He heard me, and I am now slowly recovering. *When my spirit was overwhelmed within me, then Thou knewest my path.*"

> "My God, whose gracious pity I may claim,
>   Calling thee 'Father,' sweet endearing name,
>   **The sufferings of this weak and weary frame**
>   All, all are known to Thee.

"'From human eyes 'tis better to conceal
Much that I suffer, much I hourly feel;
But oh! this thought does tranquillize and heal,—
    All, all is known to Thee.

" When in the morning unrefresh'd I wake
Or in the night but little rest I take,
This brief appeal submissively I make,—
    All, all is known to Thee.

" And this continued feebleness, this state
Which seems to unnerve and incapacitate,
Will work the cure my hopes and fears await;
    That cure I leave to Thee.

"Nor will the bitter draught distasteful prove,
While I recall the Son of Thy dear love;
The cup Thou wouldst not, for our sakes, remove,
    That cup He drank for me.

" He drank it to the dregs. no drop remain'd
Of wrath, whose cup of woe he drain'd,
Man ne'er can know what that sad cup contain'd,—
    All, all is known to Thee.

" And welcome, precious can His Spirit make
My little drop of suffering for His sake.
Father, the cup I drink, the path I take,
    All, all is known to Thee."

" Dr. Chalmers was found dead in his bed a few days ago. How ready we all should be for the summons! Blessed Jesus, keep Thine handmaid in perfect preparedness, looking and longing for Thy coming. 'What,' says Bishop Hall, 'is death, but the taking down of these sticks whereof this earthly tent is composed. The separation of two great and old friends till they meet again. The great gaol-deliverer of a long prisoner. Our journey into the other world, for what we, and this thoroughfare, were made. Our payment of our first debt to nature. The sleep of the body, the awakening of the soul.' Lord, come Thou with the last enemy, and let me see Thy smiling face all through the dark valley.

" How often, when a difficulty or trial has arisen, either from feelings within or from circumstances without, helpless as an infant, I have shut to my door, and come to the Lord, and laid it before Him, pleading the promise—*Cast the burden on the Lord, and He shall sustain thee.* In a short time I have risen from my knees, not only with my pressure entirely gone, but with such a sense of His faithfulness and abounding love towards me, as has caused me to rejoice even to tears. At other times, when a similar necessity has arisen, and I have sat down to consider what I ought to do in the matter—thus trusting my own heart, and leaning to my own understanding—and afterwards have carried it to the Lord, I have been left still to bear my burden, attended with much discomfort the while, the Lord having left me to my own way. All events are in His hands to direct, and overrule, and bless to His own redeemed people. I say not that we are to fold our arms and do nothing; but I do say, that after carrying our care in simple faith and obedience to His commands, we are to wait and watch the leadings of His infinitely wise providence, which is always at work for us."

"Yesterday was much tried. The Lord seemed to withdraw His blessed countenance. I had not, as usual, a sense of His presence. My heart failed me, I missed Him, and was troubled. But it was not long. I cried unto Him with my voice, and He heard me. The cloud, the dark cloud that veiled His face, was removed, and He again appeared. I wept for joy. Oh, how inexpressibly kind and indulgent He is to all to whom He is the centre of all happiness, joy, and comfort! How sweet the fresh recognition, the inward whisper, 'I am thine, and thou art mine. Why didst thou doubt?' O Lord, I did not doubt Thy faithfulness, but feared I had displeased Thee, and that Thou hadst put Thy child away from Thy presence. Now I know that Thou art pacified towards me, and my heart is glad in Thee. Hide not Thy face from Thy aged one, and put not Thy servant from Thee; for Thou art my chief joy, my life, my all. Without Thee this world were wretchedness itself. I would not live always here, though blessed with Thy presence. I want to see Thee as Thou art, in all Thy glory, surrounded by the pure spirits redeemed from the curse, and to join my song of praise with theirs. Keep, oh keep me near Thyself, nearer, *nearer* still; and suffer no earthly love to occupy Thy place in my heart."

'Jesus, first-born Priest and Brother,
   Changing not as others change;
 Wherefore should we seek another?
   Whither should our spirits range?

"While thy gracious arms enfold us,
   Should we seek another rest?

Could another stay uphold us,
Like our Saviour's faithful breast?

"Earthly love, how fitful, gleaming,
O'er life's tossing, troubled tide;
Thine the lamp for ever beaming,
With the golden oil supplied.

"Jesus, come, our strength renewing
Blessed, living Fountain Head;
Bid our souls to cease from hewing
Broken cisterns in Thy stead."

The few incidents of her subsequent sojourn upon earth, and much of the spiritual exercises of her mind, will be gleaned from extracts from her correspondence.

TO MISS R——, ON HER RETURN FROM AMERICA.

"MY DEAR MISS R——,

"I have heard a report that you have arrived safely in England once more. But I should much like to receive the intelligence from yourself, and to hear all about our friends on the other side of the water,—some dear to me as well as yourself in that happy land. I love America, and always shall be interested in the welfare of that country. For though my deepest trials were there, so there also I experienced some of my richest consolations, and much Christian love and fellowship. It is good to feel that we are in the Lord's hands, and that all our trials, small and great, are designed by Him for the furthering His work in our souls. They are great blessings in disguise to a child of God. Nothing takes place, within or without, but is designed for our especial benefit and the glory of His own dear name. We shall have to thank Him for all, when we see Him face to face. What a blessed time will that be! Oh, that we did but live more in holy anticipation of that event, to which all things else are subservient! How much do we need of weaning from this poor disappointing world,—a world lying in the wicked one; and yet so closely do we cling to it, He who loves us is compelled to give us many a wrench to tear us from it. Oh, to be on the wing for our blessed inheritance above, looking to those things that are eternal! *Love not the world, neither the things that are in the world.* With what hearts of unbelief do we read the Bible; and how prone are we to forget its commands, precepts, and promises; and so we call down a Father's gentle rod, to awaken us to a sense of our folly and our sin. But, oh, it is all in love to our souls that He thus acts towards us. He is now trying my faith in this dispensation. I have been some weeks confined to the house, and with but little prospect of being able to walk again soon, if ever. I needed it, I doubt not. Now write me a long letter; it will cheer me in my sick room. My love to your nieces."

The bodily infirmity alluded to in the preceding letter threatened at one time the most serious consequences. It sprung from a weakness, which increased to such a degree, as not only to occasion at times intense suffering, but also entirely to prevent the use of the limb. For some months she was dependent upon others, and could only move from place to place in a wheel chair. After having the best surgical advice in town, she was carried to Leamington, relinquishing all hope of ever again being able to walk. The temper of her mind under this severe trial, and the details of its removal, we gather from one of her familiar letters to a friend.

"Leamington, March 24th.

". . . . I have thought much of you lately in your painful position. There was an expression in my last to you that has worried me, because I feared it might wound you. I remarked, among other things, that the Christian should suppress that murmuring spirit that adheres so closely to us. Now, beloved, I feel in your case it is quite a different thing; and that in expressing your daily sufferings, there may be no murmuring against a good and gracious God who loves you, and is trying your faith to the utmost. May the Lord enable us more and more to look alone to Him, for he is a present help in every time of need. His heart overflows with tenderness, sympathy and love. But there are real believers who do, too often, repine at the providence of God. If all things do not go as they wish, they fret and are dissatisfied. This state of mind I believe is injurious to them and dishonouring to God. Oh, for a stronger confidence in Jesus! Whatever draws or drives us to Him is good. The oftener we go the better; and the Lord frequently places us in such peculiar circumstances, as compel us to apply to Him for the help we can get nowhere else. You will remember my trouble in the loss of the use of my limb. I was obliged to be carried about like an infant. Then often I went to the Lord, and earnestly besought Him to restore to me its use. I filled my mouth with arguments, and told Him He had but to speak the word, and I should be whole. I felt he could as easily heal me as He did the lame man that lay at the pool of Bethesda. I reminded Him again and again of this, and my faith was strong in His power to do now as He did then. But still my lameness continued, and I was totally helpless. And now Satan took advantage of this to upbraid me,—' Where is the answer to your prayers? You asked not to be left to be a burden to yourself or to others,—where is now the answer of which you so often boast?' But still I clung to the Lord, and believed, bad as my case was, He would heal me. One day these words came powerfully to my mind—'Ask for *submission*.' I immediately obeyed the heavenly admonition, and turned my prayer into an earnest petition for this grace. At that very moment it was given. I felt in an instant quieted down, and all my restlessness of spirit and anxiety to be healed was gone, and I was cheerful and composed. I was satisfied to be borne about like an infant, if it were the Lord's will. A fortnight after this my medical man called, and seeing me in the drawing-room in my wheel chair, inquired the cause. I told him. He asked to examine the limb, which presented a highly inflamed appearance. He said nothing then, but called the following day. Finding me down, he took my arm, and insisted, against my remonstrance, that I should walk round the room. This I did three times; and from that hour the healing process commenced, and I was perfectly restored. Was not this of the Lord? He first gave me submission to His will, and then answered my prayer by restoring my limb, and I was no longer a burden. Thus does He try the faith He gives. Oh, for faith in the power of God! Why have I detailed this long story? Simply to encourage your confidence in the Lord, who has said, *Is anything too hard for Me?* . . . I am, through mercy, well, and go on my way rejoicing in the Lord. Live much in heaven, and earth will grow less attractive. Realize what awaits you, and go fully into the good land. There are many borderers; they go not up to possess and enjoy their inheritance. They follow not on to know the Lord. They do not know what close fellowship with Christ is. They do not come with the expectation of being absolutely heard and answered. They are satisfied to go away without a response. If we have the Spirit of Christ within, He indites our prayers; *for we know not what we should pray for as we ought; but the*

Spirit itself maketh intercession for us according to the will of God; and that self-same Spirit will respond to our petitions. . . The present times are momentous. The Lord himself is showing us that He is about to deal with His one church, for He has but *one*, composed of all that are born of the Spirit, and are thus new creatures in Christ Jesus. This is His bride, His spouse. This one church He is about to sift. It needs it, for there is much chaff with the wheat. Let our eye and our hearts be up unto Him, and see what He designs in all the great movements around us. I sit quiet as a babe, and can say, 'It is my Father, let Him do as it seemeth Him good.' He will do us all possible good, and no harm. I hope I have not wearied you. May the Lord heal, comfort, and bless you."

Another domestic sorrow was darkling over her path. The alarming illness, and its fatal termination, of a much-loved daughter-in-law, the wife of her son, the Rev. Isaac Deblois Winslow, Vicar of Napton,* bowed her aged frame with sorrow to the earth. Endeared, through many long years of tried affection, by a character of peculiar excellence, by an amiability of disposition as rare as it was charming, and by sincere and simple piety, her loss was a sore bereavement to her family. Mrs. Winslow's diary and letters describe her thoughts and feelings in this keenly-felt affliction. We quote from her journal:—

"Feb. 11th.—Dear F—— has been seriously ill, and at times not expected to recover. G—— is with her, and so is E——. I am feeble and depressed. My threescore years and ten have expired, and I feel everything a burden and a sorrow. But the Lord is very gracious, and at times my heart is overwhelmed with a sense of His unmerited love towards one so utterly unworthy. I long to be with Him. The thought of heaven is very sweet. And when I can realize it, my soul feels as if upon the wing. I long to see Him in glory, who has so frequently and tenderly dealt with me. Even to old age has He carried me, and I believe will never leave nor forsake me, but land me safely in glory."

"14th.—Still the accounts of dear F—— are far from being encouraging. I fear for her life. I pray the Lord will be graciously pleased to spare the mother to her children, and

---

*Now Vicar of Bucklington, Warwick.

sanctify the affliction to herself and to all her family. How needful to be ready! What a constant source of temptation the world is, in some shape or other, to the believer all through his journey homeward! Its cares and its pursuits, its pleasures and its claims, lawful though they be,. yet, through the weakness of the flesh, are constantly a snare to the heavenly pilgrim. Its principles and its pursuits are adverse to the prosperity of the soul, which struggles on through a host of foes from within and from without, and often exclaiming, 'How shall I ever maintain my standing to the end? Lord, hold Thou me up, and I shall be safe. Thou, who hast delivered my soul from death, wilt Thou not deliver my feet from falling, that I may walk before Thee in the land of the living?' A patient waiting upon God, and a constant application to the Fountain, is the safest way to glory. Precious Jesus, strengthen thy poor dust, and enable me to cling closer and closer to Thee. Increase my faith, and sanctify me for Thyself. Be with the dear sufferer to-night, and give some refreshing sleep, and keep dear E—— from over-fatigue. Lord bless, heal, sanctify, and restore!

"15th.—Dear F—— has fallen asleep in Jesus."

To her pastor she thus unfolds her sorrow:—

". . . The Lord has again laid upon me His afflictive hand. My heart has been sorely tried, and my soul cast down. God has taken another from me, very dear, and I cannot describe how greatly it has oppressed me. I am sad, very sad, and have not been able to rise above it, as on former occasions. Pray for me. The Lord is good, I know; in the midst of it all, there is a reason for all that He does, and He will make it plain in His own time. The sufferings of the dear departed one still press me down; but at times I get a glimpse of her pure spirit above, and I weep for joy, but much oftener for sorrow. See how much I need your sympathy just now. Dear E—— has been deeply tried. She watched by this dear departed one, untiringly and devotedly, day and night, for weeks, scarcely in all that time having one night's rest; and at last her sister, as she wished, expired in her arms. Beloved brother, do not forget us. My soul is cast down, but in the midst of all I can say, 'Thy will, O my Father, and not mine, be done.' Pray for us and the motherless ones."

"Dear Miss D——.

". . . This has been a severe trial to us all. Dear Fanny was tenderly beloved by my whole family, who have known her from almost a girl. Her sufferings were severe, and from the first she resigned all expectation of recovery, and said, 'I shall die.' Her mind, in the early part of her illness, was much exercised and greatly tried in view of eternity; and she lamented she had not cultivated a closer walk with God. Dear E—— reminded her that Jesus was ready to receive her now, even *now*, just as she was. She replied, 'Yes, I must come, as a poor wretched sinner, now.' The Lord, however, appeared, and her mind became stayed upon Christ. A day or two before she died, she sang the whole night such hymns as these—

'Rock of ages, cleft for me.'
'Jesus, lover of my soul.'

And on one occasion said, 'Oh, that I might recover to tell you what the Lord has done for my soul on this sick bed.' . . . Dear friend, how these things should remind us of the uncertainty of life, and the necessity of living prepared to meet the Lord in the clouds of heaven, at His second coming, or when he sees fit to summon us to Himself! To be with Jesus, let that be as it may, is heaven. How precious is the thought, to be for ever with the Lord!—to see Him in all His glory, to mingle with the pure spirits around the throne, and be a pure spirit too. Oh, I think the very purity of heaven is its sweetest attraction! Dear friend, ere long I hope to meet you there. Blessed hope, beaming with immortality, which I sometimes long to realize. Let it be our chief aim to glorify Him— to live upon Him, and live for Him. Oh, he is most precious, so tender, so full of love, so watchful over our interests, caring for us in all things, and entering into all our poor concerns! He is one with us in our tribulations, one with us in suffering, one in time and in eternity; for there is no separating Christ and His saints."

The following interesting extracts are from her diary while at Napton Vicarage, the scene of her recent bereavement. The brief record of her visit to the grave of the dear departed one, evinces the triumph of real faith in the living, as in the dying Christian, over its gloom and sadness. "O grave, where is thy victory?" might well now have been her challenge. Let us, who repair to the graves of the holy dead who sleep in Jesus, to weep there, cherish the feeling and indulge the hope she thus so touchingly describes.

"Napton.—I had often wished, during my visit at Napton,

to see the spot where the dear body lay, but for fear of exciting my feelings and producing illness, I refrained. After the lapse of some weeks, still cherishing a strong desire to go there, accompanied by H——, I ascended the hill to the church. I drew near and looked at it, and as I stood bending over it, these words sounded in my ears, as distinctly as if audibly spoken, 'She is not *here*.' 'Oh yes,' I replied aloud, 'she is not *here*, she is THERE,' looking up.. It was the well-known voice of my Beloved. Oh, to know His voice! May I hear it again and again, speaking words of comfort when I am called to pass through the dark valley. The Lord is ever near; He is about our path. We have not far to go to seek Him. I think I know something of the still, small voice of the Spirit within, and desire so to walk as to be better acquainted with God, and to feel that He is always with me, and that I am not alone."

"Called to see a young woman in the village, dying of a consumption. She does not know Christ. Read and prayed with her. She begged me to come again. Spoke to the woman who has the care of her; found her quite ignorant. This sick woman has three young children, one a suffering cripple, and another not expected to live, and her husband scarcely able, by hard labor, to maintain them all. What a suffering world is this, and how little anxious poor sinners are to secure a better! Went into another room, and talked to an old woman, poor but respectable, seventy-five years old. She does not know Jesus. Spoke faithfully to her, at which she seemed to feel and expressed herself thankful. Called at an adjoining cottage, and had a long conversation with another aged woman, who acknowledged she was not converted. Exhorted her to lose no time in applying to One, who alone could save her soul. While speaking loud to her, as she was deaf, I found a young woman in the next room, with a family of children about her, heard me. She was rejoiced to see me, expressed herself as happy in the Lord, and while speaking of Christ her heart seemed to overflow with love. She had known Jesus for some years. Returned to the Vicarage, comforted that I had seen one who knew Him whom my soul loveth."

"How difficult it is, at least for me, to sustain anything like spiritual conversation when many are present, even though they are religious professors! The interest languishes. I find it more profitable to speak to one or two alone; and but seldom feel refreshed when the conversation descends to generals. Oh, to keep close to Christ, to talk of Christ, to encourage one another to believe, to get more of heaven in our souls, more of the power of Jesus within, to believe with all the heart— that is what we want!"

'Have been unwell, but am better, though still feeble. H—— is with me, and is very careful and tender. After a little walk upon the lawn, was tired, and glad to rest. What a mercy to be able to look beyond this dying world, to the prospect of meeting Him who has pardoned all my transgressions, and of being with Him for ever!—to meet again those we have loved here, mingling with their pure spirits, and uniting in their eternal anthems of praise to Him who brought us there. And shall I, the unworthiest of the unworthy, see Him face to face, against whom I have so often sinned, whose Spirit I have so often grieved? Shall I be near Him, and be permitted to love Him as my soul wishes now to do, but cannot? Oh, glorious prospect! My heart is humbled while I rejoice in the wondrous goodness of a sin-pardoning God, who could, and does, love such a one as I. How I long to be holy even as He is holy! And will it not be so? When I drop this vile body, shall I not awake in His righteousness? When I see Him, shall I not be like Him? Everything in this house reminds me of dear F——. She is with Christ. Her little faith would take her within the gate of heaven. She mourned over her short-comings, wept that she had not walked closer with God. But her end was peace, and that was enough. O—— returns from the Evangelical Alliance Conference tomorrow. I hear, the Lord has been graciously pleased to be with the dear brethren. Oh, for a greater outpouring of His Spirit before the close! Lord, set Thy seal of approval afresh to this great movement of Thy one church, for thine own name's sake."

For the works of the old divines she had imbibed an early taste. Their sound theology, depth of thought, and elevated spirituality, harmonized with the peculiar order of her own mind. She was wont to remark, that there was more of Christ, more of the marrow of the gospel, and more of Christian experience in a single page of such authors as Owen and Charnock, Leighton, Bates, and Newton, than in entire volumes of some modern theological writers. Interwoven with her diary, we find the following extract from one of her favorite

authors. Its perusal may be a word in season to some tried reader of this volume, as it was to her when transcribed:—
"On the subject of *faith*, Bridge has these striking and excellent remarks:—'God doth so give blessings and mercies unto His own people, as that He may be most of all seen in them. Beloved, God doth not only give us these outward creature comforts to supply our wants, but to bear up the honor of His own greatness. When He gives to His people, He gives in such a way as He may most of all unfold Himself. If it were only to supply their wants, then, possibly, the sentence of death would never come upon the second cause; but it is also to bear up His own name, and the honor of His own greatness, and that is done this way. Hereby God is known to be the *living* God. So long as there is life in the means, God is not so well known to be the *living* God; but when all means are dead, and yet the mercy comes, 'Oh,' says the soul, 'now I see that God is the living God.' Hereby the power of God is made known. He must needs be great in power, that can say to things that are not, 'Be,' and give a resurrection to dead things. So long as there is strength and ability in the means, the soul doth not so much consider the power and the all-sufficiency of God; but when all means are strengthless, and all means are dead, and yet the mercy comes, 'Oh,' says the soul, 'now I see that God is Almighty, God all-sufficient.' Secondly, God goes to work this way with His people, that they may learn to *trust* more in Him, and in Him alone. The apostle says, 'She that is a widow and desolate trusteth in God.' We seldom trust in God till a desolation comes upon the means; then we learn to trust in God. So long as one who is learning to swim, can touch earth with his feet, he does not commit himself to the stream. So long as the soul can stand upon second causes, he does not commit himself to the stream of mercy. Again, God is pleased thus to order things that the comforts of His people may be more sure and steadfast. If our comforts hang at the girdle of the creature, they are most uncertain; but if they are all laid upon God, His promise and His power, they are certain. Again: A mere rational considering of the means—their straitness, narrowness, and scantiness—is a great enemy to the act of believing. The Scriptures have laid a flat opposition between faith and sense. We live by faith, and not by sense. The reasons drawn from sense are sense. If you live by faith, you do not live by sense.

They are two buckets—the life of sense and the life of faith, when one goes up, the other goes down. The higher faith rises, the lower sense and reason sink. If you would believe, you must crucify that question, 'Why?' God would not have us so full of wherefores. And if you would believe, you must go blindfold into God's command. Abraham subscribed to a blank when the Lord called him out of his own country. It is the privilege of all the children of Abraham to believe when means fail. It is exceeding pleasing to God, and most acceptable. Oh, what encouragement is here to believe above hope and against hope, and when death sits upon the life of the second cause! Some there are that can believe for the bodies, but they cannot trust God for their souls when means fail. Some say they can trust God for their souls when means fail, but they cannot trust Him for their bodies. Some say they can trust God for themselves, but they cannot trust Him for their families. O my soul, trust thou upon God!"*

TO MRS. C——.   TRIALS, A HEAVENLY DISCIPLINE.

"Very dear Friend,   "Napton, August 22d.

"The Lord has brought me here, I trust, for some service He has for me to do. If His servants, we ought to be doing His work; and it is so sweet to work when love turns the wheel. It is the love of God in the heart that sets us all in motion. I am persuaded it is irksome where this is not the case. To work for God as a hireling is one thing, and to work for Him as a son is another. Dear E—— is one of the most efficient curates a parish minister need have. She is up and doing the will of the Lord in everything to which he points. I—— is from home, and she is doing his work, all but going into the pulpit; and this she gets properly supplied, and has this morning gone ten miles to procure a clergyman who she knows loves and preaches the gospel. . . . I was glad to hear dear Mr. C—— was better in health. We must not expect much here; all our richest blessings are to come, reserved for us who are kept for them. This time-state is but a preparatory state. We are disciplining and preparing for the glorious inheritance above; but how often, through wretched unbelief, we seem to wish to have our all here. And although, from bitter experience, we feel and acknowledge it is polluted, and

* Rev. William Bridge died 1670.

is not our rest, yet more or less we go on, often repining, because we cannot have things just as we wish. Oh, to leave ourselves in a loving, tender Father's hands! He knows what we need, and what we ought to have, and will deny us no good thing. But He must judge for us, who are but as babes, who cannot judge for ourselves. . . . You are in His hands, and although He tries your faith, in due time, if you look alone to Him, He will appear for you, and show you the why and the wherefore He has tried you. Blessed is the man that trusteth in the Lord: may this blessing rest upon you. It is so difficult to keep from looking to an arm of flesh, and yet say, we must make use of the means. I do not plead for indolence, nor would encourage inactivity; but I would not work out a way for myself, but leave it to Him, who sees the end from the beginning, to work for me. It is a happy position for a believer to be in, when he is brought to that point to see he can do nothing for himself, then to rest and wait patiently for the Lord, fully believing He will do all things in the best possible way. Whatever the Lord does in this way for us, is the best, the very best, better than with all our wisdom and management we could have done for ourselves. I am persuaded, the more we live by faith, the holier and the happier we are. Is it not written, *Casting all your care upon Him, for He careth for you?* What, then, need I care, when my Saviour is caring for me? Am I not one with Christ, and is He not one with me? Then, are not my concerns His concerns, and has He ever failed me? Then, O my soul, why not trust Him now? May He increase our faith; this will more glorify Him than all our fleshly burnt-offerings and sacrifices.

"How do you both feel towards the 'Evangelical Alliance,' now assembled in London? I consider it one of the grandest movements of the one church below since the apostles' time. One of Christ's last commands was, *Love ye one another, as I have loved you.* Now we are always anxious to fulfil the dying requests of one we love, and everything then said seems of the greatest moment to us. *This* was one of our dying Lord's last requests to His church. These dear men are carrying it out on the broad foundation, simply of love to all who love Him, and who hold Him the Head; while all minor things are laid aside, and they agree on the fundamental truths of the gospel. I believe this movement is of God Himself, and that already He has put upon it His seal of approbation. Satan will endeavor to hinder it; but be assured the Lord will bless it, for it is a holy attempt to obey His command, which has been too much neglected. Many will say, who stand aloof from the Alliance, 'But I do love all God's people.' We answer, 'Show your love by *uniting* with these men of God as one in Christ.' God is love. The atmosphere of heaven is love. When we arrive there, we shall swim in an ocean of love; then why not have as much of heaven here as we can? Why not try to be as much like what we shall be, while journeying towards that ocean of bliss and love? I think, were I upon my dying bed, and were called upon to address them, I should say, 'Go on, my beloved brethren, to show your love to Jesus, by exhibiting your love to every member of His own body; for you are all members of that Body, and members one of another. *Love ye one another, as I have loved you.*' I believe that popery is working its silent way, and that the last effort of the 'beast' will soon be manifest. No wonder that the Lord is calling his people to unite together in a holy confederacy to resist the common foe. It will require the united force of God's church to withstand this arch enemy. I believe that this 'Alliance' is preparatory to the great onset; that the work is the Lord's, and that He will bless it. I can and do pray for it, nor can I express to you in language the measure the Saviour permits me to enjoy of His sensible presence while pleading on its behalf. Oh, there is a truth in the religion of Jesus! There is an enjoyment in communion with the holy God, of which the worldling knows nothing. It is foolishness with the wisest of men; but the sincere, lowly follower of Christ Jesus, loved of God, regenerated by the Holy Ghost, is made to sit in heavenly places in Christ Jesus. Oh, the infinite value of a throne of grace!" ..

"Dear beloved Friend, "Leamington, 27th, 1851.

"It is long since I heard from you. We are both nearing our port, where we are to cast anchor for ever. Sweet thought! What a mercy for you and me that we have known Jesus; a still greater mercy that He has condescended to know and acknowledge us as His! Let us rejoice together in the goodness and loving-kindness of our God. My heart is often overwhelmed at the thought of His avowing such a worthless worm as myself as one of His sheep for whom He shed His precious blood. Dear friend, let us never for a moment forget what we were, and what we now are—candidates for a crown of glory, heirs of God, and joint-heirs with Christ. Is not this worth living for, and worth dying for? Let us now aim to walk humbly and confidingly with Him, and never suffer Him to be out of our sight. Oh, to travel on, leaning upon our Beloved! His arm will support us in our feebleness; His eye will guide us in our blindness; He will strengthen, uphold, and comfort us, and never leave nor forsake us. I cannot express to you on paper, hardly in language, how graciously the Lord does at times enable me to anticipate the heaven of glory that awaits the believer in Jesus. There sits Jesus, He who was once despised and rejected of men; who suffered, the innocent for the guilty; who paid the full demand to stern justice for our sins; He who had no place to lay His weary head, though Maker of all things; there He now is, enthroned in the majesty of heaven, and encircled by that goodly company who have escaped from earth, and are now hymning His praises, and *standing nearer His throne* than the highest angel in heaven. I sometimes so realize the blessedness of the believer, that I could shout to the whole world that all is true, the Bible true, Christ true, heaven true. May the Lord bless you with much of His sensible presence; and when we get above, we will unite our praises to Him who loved us, and washed us in His own most precious blood."

We continue extracts from her family correspondence, as exhibiting a yet greater variety of topic:—

TO HER DAUGHTER.

". . . . Oh, to look fully to Jesus, not with a half-heart, but to carry all our every varying care to Him, and plead the promise. Sure I am, if we walk in the precept, He will fulfil to us the promise. May He continually give us grace to do so! Oh, the luxury of living upon Him; to be constantly depending upon our covenant Father in Christ Jesus! But faith has, and must have, hard travail to bring forth, and to press through the crowd of difficulties and impossibilities that lie in the way to the kingdom of glory. Thus faith fights all the journey through, and upholds the poor, trembling believer; and not only so, but brings him off victorious at last. The life of faith in the soul of man is wonderful, and is, I believe, a wonder to the angels in heaven; and I am sure we are often a wonder to ourselves,—at least I am. Oh, what a God we

have to do with! so full of love and compassion; and although
He tries us, it is all in love to bring us to know Him more,
that we might love Him better. Should we not give our undivided hearts to this gracious God and Father in Christ
Jesus? The last chapter of the Gospel of John is so full,
precious, and abounding in the love of the Triune-Jehovah,
from the 14th to the 18th verse. Read it with prayer, and
see how certain and secure is our salvation, what a firm foundation it rests upon. What is the world, or the glory of a
thousand such perishing worlds as this, when compared with the
glory that shall be revealed in them that love His appearing?"

"What a mercy to have a good and gracious God to look
to, and ask what you will, and to know that He always hears
and stands ready to answer! Think what an honour put upon
a poor worm, to have the ear and the heart of the mighty
God! to know that He loves you, and cannot cease to love,
because He cannot change. He knows what we were, and
what we should be to the end; and yet He loved us, and will
love throughout eternity. And what does He require? Only
our *heart*—just as it is, with all its imperfections. He asks the
gift, and that it may be His, and His only. He loves not a di
vided heart—He will not share it with the creature. . . . He can
never do aught but good to you, because you are His—His child,
His *own* child by adoption—His child by regeneration—His child
by an especial promise. *I will be a Father to thy fatherless chil
dren*, says God to you. So you see what a claim you have upon
God. Remind Him of this. He loves to be reminded of His
promises, though He never forgets them; but He loves to see
that we remember them too. Oh, what a holy endearing intercourse there is between a child of God and his heavenly
Father! No earthly parent could have loved you as He does.
There is something so precious in coming to Him, your Father
in Jesus. These two names are better and sweeter than all
the names on earth and in heaven; *a name which is above
every name;* and these are yours made over to you by an everlasting covenant of grace, which will finally end in glory to all
eternity. Be not over careful about earthly things; get above
them as much as you can. Look to Jesus for help when they
press upon you, and He will not fail you, for He knows that
without Him you can do nothing. All power is His in heaven
and on earth. Go to Him for little things, in little straits and
difficulties, at home or abroad, in a crowd or when alone; raise

your heart to your Father who heareth alway, and will never leave nor forsake His own child; for He will be with you even unto the end. Look at the scenes of a busy world, how they pass away; it is but as the buzzing of a summer fly, and all is gone. Therefore, set your affections on things above, where friends pass not away. Oh, for stronger faith, to give full credit to what the Lord says, to act upon it, and carry it out in every department of life!"

". . . How have I thought of you all this day, travelling to a strange place, and the weather so cold! You have not been a moment, I think, out of my mind. I thought, and prayed, and could have wept. I trust the Lord heard my prayer and strengthened you, and shielded you from the severity of the weather, and caused you to see His own loving hand. If you do not find Clifton to suit you, try Torquay, or Ventnor. Oh, that the Lord may lend a gracious ear, and cause us to see all was directed in a special way by Himself! . . . But I must again advert to the great mercy of having such a Helper as our loving Lord to do all for us, and far better than we could think of or imagine for ourselves. I trust, when He places us in such peculiar situations, it is to make us see and feel there is a reality and power in faith in God. Write as soon as you can, if it is only a few lines. O—— is in his study; H—— and P—— are reading Miss Grant's Memoir, written by her mother. Good night. May you enjoy much of the presence of the Lord, and feel you are not alone, but that you have the best Friend that mortal can have to watch over you, and to whom you can open your whole heart, and talk to Him as a man talketh with his fellow."

To her son, in acknowledging a small work on the Resurrection, she thus touches upon her favorite theme:—

"Blessed is the pen, blessed the hand that holds and the heart that indites, that gives one cheering view of the mighty blessing that awaits the sleeping, holy dead! The dust of the Christian reposes in quietude until the voice of Jesus shall bid the slumberer arise in perfect beauty, in His own likeness, and suited to the happy spirit, and both now joyfully mingling with the blessed of the Lord in the kingdom prepared from the foundation of the world. Happy Christian! Your journey here was thorny, and the last enemy may even now be looking upon you; but, take courage; the time will come when this very body shall rise again to life immortal, and soul and body be ever with the Lord, increasing in beauty, growing in knowledge and glory through eternity. Happy saint! Oh, to meet, too, with those we love, the dear departed ones for whom we have mourned! We shall meet again. Jesus on the throne will rejoice with us when He beholds our happiness complete, Himself its sole author and finisher. Oh, the glory of that moment! Preach much on the resurrection of the believer. It will encourage, perhaps, many a timid, sorrowful spirit. I find it so when able to glance at it myself. How wearisome is now the poor body, creeping to the grave, and Satan ever ready to suggest his 'ifs' and 'buts!' It is a dying body, but it shall rise again. Jesus has said it. Lord, increase my faith."

"I was so thankful to-day, so refreshed and comforted, in reading your welcome letter, that it led me with a heart full of love to a throne of grace. I closed my door, and kneeling before my chair, gave vent to my grateful and deep emotions to Him who heareth His own redeemed, bought with His precious blood, always. Oh, the matchless love that is in our reconciled Father's heart! Can we suppose for a moment that He sees not our trials, temptations, and conflicts; and that He is not caring for, and watching over us? Oh, no; God is with us and for us, working all things, even now, for our good and His glory."

"Saturday morning.—I have just been praying for you, and I do feel I have the ear of the most blessed, the most precious, most loving God and Saviour that ever poor sinner had to deal with. I am often overwhelmed with such a sense of His wonderful condescension, that language fails me, and I can do little else than weep. Oh, how strange that He should listen, and *so* listen, as if He said, *Yes, yes,* to every request I make! He overcomes me with His love. He breaks my heart, then heals it again. It is His love that does it. He gives godly sorrow; puts forth His hand and draws me near to Himself, and then says, *What is thy petition, and what is thy request?* Then I hasten to tell Him all, *all,* as if I feared He would withdraw before I could do so. But He lingers and listens, and then sends me away rejoicing that I have such a Friend in heaven, and longing to drop this body of sin and death, that I might be with Him. Oh, God is such an ocean of love to me! The more His wondrous love is manifested, the more I hate and abhor myself. This is your God, too. And though

He tries the faith of His people, He will appear. Remember, Joseph was two long years in prison, after he had got the promise from the chief butler; and no doubt his faith was sharply tried, for God had partly given him the promise, by enabling him to interpret the dream. But, at last, the promise was fulfilled, and the blessing came in rich abundance. Take courage, He is the same now that He ever was."

"This morning while the children were surrounding my breakfast table, I spoke to them of some of the providential dealings of God with me, passing through this wilderness-world, by land and by sea. Among others, was brought to my recollection the circumstance of my embarking on board ship on a long voyage to Bermuda, in ill-health, going to join the regiment to which we belonged. Our provisions were nearly exhausted; and there was little else on board but salt meat, fit only for the hardy sailors, and most unsuitable for me, an invalid just recovering from a severe illness. But the Lord sent a calm, and with the calm a shoal of dolphins alongside, which followed us from that time a great part of the passage, affording us a wholesome meal every day, of great delicacy. Oh, how wonderful is our God in all His dealings with the children of men! My soul is refreshed, and I have been on my knees to thank Him for bringing these incidents to my remembrance. It is good to call to mind the many deliverances we have met with from the hand of our God. Shall we not often think of them, and tell them to our children, and recount them by the way? Lord, pardon my heartless sin of unbelief, and let my whole heart sweetly, safely confide in Thee. I am afraid your health is not as good as it was. Try and cast this burden on the Lord, and He will help you. I know He is willing as He is able. Only believe, and let the precept be as precious as the promise, and the Lord will appear for you in His own good time. Wait on the Lord. The Lord exercises faith, and this is needful to conform us to His own lovely likeness. We want to be like Christ, but we do not like the way He takes to make us so. What a mercy it is that He takes His own way, and not ours! *Fear not*, is the dear Redeemer's watchword to His saints. Why should we fear? Are not our worthless names written in the Lamb's book of life? If He is ours, and we are His, will He withhold anything that is really good for us? No, not even the *rod;* for that is often for our good. I wonder how it is that Christians do not fear the rod more than they do. They think that God is altogether such as themselves, and will not chasten His beloved child when He sees he needs it. But He will chasten, because he is His child; and that, too, should make us hate sin, and watch against its risings in our hearts; though *love* is a more influential grace than *fear*."

"I had one of my alarming fainting fits, and often think I may go off in one of them. And if indeed ready, which I trust I am, what a mercy would this be! Absent from the body, I should be present with the Lord.* I am better, but feeble. God be praised for all His love-tokens. These visitations are nothing more. They are designed to prepare us for our glorious inheritance above. The oftener the gold is put in the furnace, the more the dross is consumed, and the brighter it shines. In the trial, we cling closer to Jesus; we see more of His loving heart, and imbibe more of His holy image. We cannot come in close contact with Christ, and not get good. Touch but the hem of His garment, and virtue flows. Last night I rode to the Episcopal Chapel, West-street, to hear one of a course of twelve sermons on the New Covenant. Some of these sermons have been excellent, but this last evening was rather prosy. I could not see with the good man, and think he overstrained the Scriptures. However, the subject is well worth close investigation. There is a volume just out, composed of twelve sermons, one of which is by Mr. James Haldane Stewart, on the present signs of the times, which are considered very ominous. They are looking for judgment on the Gentile church, and the restoration of God's ancient people; and certainly there is a moving of the waters in that quarter just now. Oh, that God might give us a right judgment in all things! May he keep you steady to your principles, and enable you to hold fast that which you have received and been taught by the Holy Ghost! Trying times are coming upon the church of Christ; men's souls will be tried as gold is tried in the furnace."

"The way the Lord is teaching you is the right way. To be well acquainted with our own hearts, is to bring us nearer

---

* " Better a thousand times live under the government and tutory of Christ, than to your own, and live at will. Live in Christ, and you are in the suburbs of heaven; there is but a thin wall between you and the land of praises,—ye are within an hour's sailing of the shore of the new Canaan.—*Rutherford.*

to Jesus, and to make us more firmly cling to the Cross. Your poor heart is the same as it was years ago, but there was no light to show its evil. But as you grow in grace, you will see more and more the goodness of God in the gift of His dear Son, to make an all-sufficient atonement for sinners so vile and utterly helpless as we are. It is a great mercy that, while the Holy Ghost opens up the deep fountain of iniquity within to our view, He also, at the same time, shows us the Fountain open, always open, in which we may wash and be clean. This makes Jesus so precious to the deeply-taught Christian. To be well acquainted with your own heart is worth all the pain you may be called to suffer. I am often tempted to say to you, make the most of your time now to acquaint yourself with God. A time of affliction is like material thrown into the ground to enrich it, that it produce a good harvest in good time. This is rather a homely way of expressing what I mean; nevertheless, I refer you to the whole tenor of Scripture for the truth of this. Sweet affliction, that brings us near to God."

"Oh, to have the heart right with God! It is so awfully deceitful, and we are so continually more or less deceived by it, that we fancy all is right, when, in fact, all may be wrong. Then comes the trial. The rod our all-wise Father will not withhold. And what a mercy it is to be able to bear the rod, and to see the cause! But how often do we close our ears, and go on in our crooked way until he speaks by some louder and yet heavier blow! and then it is our mercy to run at once into the tender, loving bosom of God, confess our sin, and beg for renewed grace, to enable us to *forsake* it. I do not think there was ever one of His own dear children who more required this discipline than myself. I seem to need the rod all the way to heaven. Well, if I can only see a Father's loving hand in it all, and it does but endear Christ to me, it is *well*."

"Lord's-day.—I am still poorly, and kept at home. You are now in the midst of your sermons. May the Lord's sensible presence be with you. May you preach as if the Lord's eye, not the eyes of the people, were full upon you. May the Holy Ghost clothe His truth with power, that every soul may hear and feel it, and that great good may be done in the name of Jesus, sinners converted, and saints re-converted; the one is as much needed as the other. Nature sometimes puts on a show of religion, and will go a great way while the heart is not changed, and the fear of God and the love of the Spirit is not there, and is not known. Thousands, I fear, deceive themselves into this resemblance of religion; and it is a great mercy, if, when death looks them in the face, the Lord divests them of all false confidence, and brings them guilty to the Fountain open for sin and uncleanness. Then, and then only, do they know what real conversion is—sorrow for sin, and joy in God."

"Yesterday I was enabled to go twice to the House of God, and the Lord did bless the truths I heard, and sweetly drew out my heart's best affections to Himself, particularly at the Supper, and during the reading and singing of the hymns. As dear Mrs. Graham says, 'My memory fails me as to the text, &c., and yet my soul is fed and strengthened by the word.'"

The illness and death of one who had sustained to her for above twenty years the closest relation of a friend, and the yet more sacred and enduring relation of a pastor—during which period not a wavelet had ruffled the surface, nor a cloud had shaded the glow of a friendship which God had made the channel of so much mutual blessing—would naturally elicit some of the tenderest features of her Christianity. Hearing of the illness of the Rev. J. H. Evans, she thus seeks to comfort and cheer him:—

". . . . . Yes, beloved, even your present trial shall be to the praise of His dear and holy name. Be of good cheer! God has commissioned it as a message of love, nothing but love,—eternal, never-ending love. The Lord sent you to preach glad tidings to poor, lost sinners, to gather in His own sheep, feeding them in rich pastures, and causing them to lie down by the side of still waters. But now He has closed your lips for a season. He who sent you to preach, now bids you cease until He says, 'Go again, and preach the preaching that I bid thee.' Well, beloved, is He not as full of love in all this as ever? Just the very same. Only trust Him for all consequences. He is doing all things well. Leave yourself in His blessed hands, and seek more for cheerful submission than for the removal of the trial. Be earnest for submission, and He will give it, and resignation will follow, and then, what a calm! Oh, how soothing is the voice of the Beloved! How it hushes to rest all the agitated feelings! To be quiet in His hands, and feel that His will must be best, because He is God, and knows the end from the beginning, while we know nothing! All our wisdom is in our adorable Head. How earnest and restless I was to be healed (when lame), but no healing came, until prompted by the Spirit to ask for *submission*, and in a moment it was given! God the Holy Ghost indited the petition, and God the Father heard it, and all was peace within. And what then? After awhile the healing most unexpectedly came, and I was made whole. So may it be with you, my tried and beloved brother. Be assured this affliction is sent for some special good, and a great blessing to your own soul and to the church at large. I would not now have been without my trial for a thousand worlds. Oh, the goodness of God! His name is love, and wondrous is He in all His dealings with us; and He is dealing with us every moment of our brief existence, and we are dealing with Him. How little does the world know of the wonderful transaction that is going on every instant between earth and heaven—the constant intercourse between God and His chosen and adopted family! But why should I enlarge upon this subject to one so much better taught than I am? Only you are now in the trial, and I have just come out of it, and may be allowed to speak a word of comfort to your dear and tried soul. Be assured it will be well, it must be well, for it is the Lord who doth all things well. *Many are the afflictions of the righteous: but the Lord delivereth him out of them all.* I believe, though the Lord may try your faith to the utmost, yet that He will appear for you; only leave yourself in His loving hands. Some great good will come out of this trial. It is much more difficult to be quiet and passive than to labour. We want always to be doing; but the Lord says, *Be still, and know that I am God.* Farewell! May the Lord comfort, heal, and guide you in every step you take, and enable you to repose passive in His dear hands, is the prayer of your affectionate sister in a precious Jesus."

"Beloved brother and fellow-traveller in the kingdom of God, it is through much tribulation we are to enter into His kingdom of glory above. I have heard of the late trial your Father has sent in much love. When we arrive at home, and trace our steps through this wilderness, we shall see that every trial, cross, and disappointment was needful, and that the work would not have been complete without all, even the least. Our loving God and Father takes no pleasure in afflicting us; but it is by these things we are brought to be better acquainted with ourselves and with Him. He does it all. Even this fall from the carriage is designed to produce some great good. . . . Can anything happen to you or to me but what God does in love to our souls? Oh, that He may remove every wish contrary to His present dispensation towards you, giving you cheerful submission! He will take care of His own church. John-street church is His, not yours. Be not any more careful about it. The Lord wants to have you to himself; and oh, you will find it sweet to be alone with Jesus! Is it not a great and might privilege to be shut out from labor, and to be shut in with God? You will yet see the goodness and loving-kindness of God in thus setting you aside from your work, pleasant as it was to you, and keeping you for Himself. I feel quite sure, dear and beloved brother, that you will have to bless and praise Him for all His present dealings with you. He will open his ever-loving heart to you, and you shall see more of the heart of God than ever you have done before. . . . Oh, that we could always believe all that He says of Himself! He is the same God that He was to Abraham, Isaac and Jacob. Does He not often speak to us now by the still, small voice of His Spirit, and does He not allow us often to speak to Him as a man would to his dearest friend? Will He not do us all the good we need? Are we not in His heart, and can anything happen to us but what He designs, and comes to us with a blessing? Are we not one with Christ, and is not Christ one with us? And now, dear, precious brother, if you have had patience to wade through this, accept my thanks, and be assured I often have you in my mind and on my heart. Cast all your care on Him, for He careth for you. He will do all things for you and for John-street church too. He is better able to bear the burden than you are. Lie contented in His loving hands, and let Him take His own way with you. You would be working for Him, but He says to you, 'Be still, and know that I am the best Judge of what is good for you!' Heaven will be no idle place. God has a work for you there. I love to think of heaven. What a change! To see and be with Jesus—to be like Him—a pure spirit mingling with pure spirits—perfect holiness—perfect love. Let us take courage and look up. My love to your dear wife. Let us join to praise and bless our God that He has spared your life, and may you be able to trust Him fully to the end."

About three months after the preceding letters were written, we find the following mournful record in her diary:—

"December 4, 1849.—Heard to-day of dear Mr. Evan's escape from a body of suffering to a land of glory. It took place on the 1st, at about six o'clock in the morning. He died in Scotland, and the remains are to be brought to town for interment on the 6th. Praise God for the blessed and good hope, through grace, of life eternal beyond the grave. A letter, addressed to the church, thus speaks of some of his closing moments: 'I said to him, I felt sure that prayer was made for him that day, and that I had written to the church that he was worse.' He said, 'You should tell them the state of my mind.' I then asked him if he had any message, and he answered, 'Tell them I stand accepted in the Beloved, notwithstanding all my sins and infirmity.' In a minute after, he proceeded, 'I never felt more than now my sins, but in Jesus I stand, Jesus is a panacea.' It being previously remarked how soon he would be with Jesus, in a few minutes he said, 'And am I so near eternal glory, and not more rejoicing in it?' It was replied, 'But do you;' to which he answered, 'In a measure.' When sympathy and tenderness were expressed to him, he said, 'But soon to be with Jesus, whom I love—who loved me before I loved Him.' And now *he is with Jesus*, partaking of His fulness of joy, happiness and glory. The days of his mourning are ended for ever."

This deeply-felt bereavement elicited the following characteristic letter of sacred sympathy, addressed to the widow of her lamented pastor:—

December 15, 1849.

"MY DEAR AND PRECIOUS SISTER IN THE LORD,—

"I think I wrote you such an unfeeling letter yesterday, that I have been quite distressed about it; but I did so fully and truly realize the joy, the glory, the full, overflowing cup of happiness of the dear departed one, that I did not, as I ought to have done, sufficiently consider your loneliness, deep sorrow, and long dreary nights of watching, while looking upon suffering you had no power to alleviate; and now those sorrowful hours and scenes are passing before your imagination, and Satan will be busy in bringing them to your recollection, for he seeks to harass those whom God loves. May faith be given to you to enable you to look above, and in due time to rejoice with him in spirit, who now no longer is a sufferer here in this vale of tears, and who would say to you, 'Weep no more for me, for the days of my mourning are ended, and 1 have entered into the joy of my Lord. I have seen Jesus whom I loved, and lo! the half of His glory, His goodness, and His love, was not told me while below.' Dear sister, ere long, and we shall both be away too, and we shall see him again, and all spend a glorious and an endless eternity together."

"There is so much lurking infidelity in our fallen nature, that we little realize what God has said in His blessed word, and therefore we do so little go on our way rejoicing. It will be according to our faith, here and there too. It is faith that enables us to realize what the Lord has promised, and brings us into close contact with Christ here; and in the same proportion as we have Christ in our souls here, we shall have Christ in our souls there. And although there will be no lack to any—for every vessel will be full—yet the larger vessels will hold more in the very same proportion they did here below. So that we need, not only for our present comfort and usefulness, to live upon Christ as much as we can here, but with the blessed hope before us of enjoying Him to the utmost when we hereafter shall arrive in the regions of the blessed. Such is *now* my dear brother's complete felicity. He is with Jesus, and Jesus is with him. His vessel is full, and it will be enlarging through eternity, capable of holding more and more of God, and that throughout the existence of God Himself. I am persuaded we are great losers by not fully realizing what God has promised us, and by not dwelling more on the glorious realities of the world to come, and also by losing sight of our nearness to Christ. Christ has been with you in all your late deep trial, and He is with you now. See what a Friend you have by your side—to talk to in your solitude—to tell Him all you feel and fear, all you wish and want! Oh, what a Friend is Jesus! He is better than ten thousand husbands and children. What a Friend has he been to worthless me! I could not live without Him here, nor in heaven either. He is the chief of all my joys, and my comfort by day and by night. Dear, precious sister, such will He be to you. The Lord says to you, 'Cleave to Me. I am thine, and thou art mine. Ask what you will, and I will do it. Ask, that your joy may be full. I will never leave thee nor forsake thee. Keep thy steadfast eye upon thine inheritance; a few more days of trial, and thou shalt be with Me.' I would fain comfort you with the comfort with which God has comforted me. This life is a dark passage to a world of light and glory above. Many whom we love are there, having outrun us in the race; but we shall meet them again, and recount together all the way He has led us through the wilderness; and, if there could be weeping in heaven, we should weep there, that we so faintly believed all He told us while here."

But two unpublished notes addressed to her by Mr. Evans, remain. They are so beautifully characteristic of the writer, that they may form a befitting close to the reference which this volume has so frequently and necessarily made to this eminent Christian, and beloved and lamented minister of Christ.

"MY BELOVED FRIEND,—

"Grace, mercy, and peace be with you and yours. All things are in the hands of that Jesus whom we love, and who, wonderful thought! loves us. He bears us and our low concerns upon His heart, and into those hands would I ever commit myself and mine. He who has borne my sins, must bear my sorrows and cares, great and small. . . . However sweet the stream, the channel down which it flows and the source from whence it springs give it a double sweetness. On the Lord will I wait, and for Him too. My dear sister, we shall soon be in the eternal world—with Jesus—eternally happy, and infinitely, in Him. This may well lift us above all anxiety. I last night preached Balch's funeral sermon. The chapel was crowded, and the subject was deeply solemn, and I *as usual*, was alas! alas! very much below the occasion. But the Lord will humble me in the pulpit. It is my dispensation—in tender love does He it—and I need it. With kind Christian regards, and affectionate remembrance to your daughther, ever believe me, dear sister,

"Your ever affectionate,
"J. H. EVANS."

"MY DEAR AND BELOVED SISTER IN A PRECIOUS SAVIOUR,—

"How great is our mercy that we know Christ, or rather, are known of Him! and how cheering is the thought that we, through wondrous grace, shall soon see Him whom our soul loveth! Your letter refreshed our souls. It was sweet to us. It had the savour of His name in it; and by the power of the same Spirit who indited it, was it made as ointment to our souls. Dear and precious sister, we are but slow learners of the two great truths of the gospel; the one, that 'by grace ye are saved;' the other, 'Christ is all.' And I believe that they are but half learned, even at the last. Oh, how deep is the power of sin and Satan, ignorance and unbelief, in our poor hearts! all working together to hide this precious object from our sight. How often do even lawful things, and things which in themselves He approves of, still tend to this, except the blessed Spirit breaks through all and shows Him to us!

"And yet amidst all our neglects, and coldness, and ingratitude, still He bears with us, comes over the mountains of our base forgetfulness, and restoreth our souls. I am sometimes led to think, that even in heaven one shall weep to think of the returns which He has received from our treatment of Him; but all tears shall be wiped away, if any are shed there, by His own blessed hands.

"It will rejoice you, I am well assured, to be told by me, that I am wonderfully better than I was; and, although the complaint has not quite left me, yet, through the tender mercy of our God and Father, it has nearly done so. For fourteen nights I was quite unable to lie down in my bed, and they were generally sleepless nights. But I was not alone, and I felt it. I fully believe dear sister, that this attack has an especial message in it. May the Eternal Spirit cause me to learn it, yea, all of it; unimproved mercies—and such are trials, overlooked; the loving hand which sends them, and the infinite necessity there was for them; the secret sins they are meant to detect; and the gracious discoveries they are intended to disclose of the unutterable fulness of Jesus and the Divine goodness,—are very serious things.

"I have lost much by this in past days. May He who is able, give me full possession of this especial dispensation. With my very kindest love to dear O——, and every affectionate remembrance to all his, and especial affection to E——; and with every prayer that your own soul may be filled with all the fulness of God,

"Ever yours, with truest affection,
"J. H. Evans."

How unconsciously did she betray her own spiritual progress in her anxiety for the advance of Christ's kingdom in the souls of others! Writing to a beloved family whose parent preceded her only a few weeks previous to her own departure to the "rest that remaineth for the people of God," she earnestly inquires:—

"How is it, dear, dear friends, with your precious souls? Are you speeding on your way? I have not heard from you of late. Is there not one among you to tell me how matters stand between you and our best Friend? Are there no new communications from above? Have you nothing to say to a poor weary traveller, on the same road with yourself? Well, I must say a little about it to you, which may encourage us all,—me to write, and you to join me to praise and bless His holy name who is preparing us all for that happy, blessed place He has gone to prepare for us. How little, beloved, do we think of this as we ought! How faintly we realize it! How little do we believe what God has promised us. Oh, for a stronger faith to give full credit to what we read of God's word! We are travelling home to God. This is not, and never was intended to be, our rest. It is a wilderness we are passing through, and shame, shame to us, that we so often want to sit down amidst its weeds and briers, and amuse ourselves with the trifles of a fallen world lying in the wicked one. All here is polluted and tainted by sin, therefore does Christ say, *Arise, my love, my fair one, and come away.* Dear friends, tell me how it fares with your souls. Do you find Christ more precious day by day. Let us keep very near to Him, *sensibly* so. Oh, there is a joy unspeakable in walking *near* to Jesus— in having daily, sweet holy intercourse with Him—never satisfied to have our best Friend out of sight!"

"6th.—Beloved in the Lord, I do love you all most tenderly, not only in Christ, but for your own sakes too, and cannot be reconciled to lose sight of you; so do let hear. I have this one evidence, if I have no other, of my election of God—I love all the saints in the bowels of Jesus Christ. I feel a oneness to them that I feel to no other. But oh, what will that love be when we get above? It is there I am looking. There is my only, my best Friend, and there is my heart. Behold Him seated on His throne, and all the goodly company of the redeemed around Him. Oh, the blessedness of beholding all His unveiled beauties, and of basking in the sunshine of His countenance! Does not your heart burn within you when you think of these things—these glorious realities? My heart is full to overflowing; for I have just been at His blessed footstool, and had a few holy, precious moments of intercourse with Him. But I must tell you of two sermons yesterday. In the morning, from the words, *He endured as seeing Him who is invisible.*—Heb. xi. 27. In this discourse Jehovah was exhibited as revealed in Jesus. Jesus, the *visible* manifestation of the *invisible* God. In the evening, from the words, *But we see Jesus*, Heb. ii. 9. I cannot express to you how my heart rejoiced in God my Saviour, while listening to such an exhibition of His glory, though robed in humanity for our redemption. I wept for joy; my heart was overflowing. Well beloved, we shall all soon see Him eye to eye, face to face. Do not let us lose sight of Him altogether. There is much of heaven to be enjoyed while here, a foretaste of what we shall realize through eternity. *Let us hold fast the profession of our faith, without wavering.* We are pretty well. Dear little E——, from her spinal affection, is still reclining upon her back. This is a trial of faith, but we must all have them; they are good for us—are disguised blessings. Nothing but good from the hands of Him who loved us unto the death. He could do no more than die for us. Yes, He rose again. Blessed be His dear name, He did all that He could to save us from eternal woe, and bring us to eternal glory. Farewell, beloved sister in a beloved Lord. May you enjoy much of His presence."

TO HER SON O——.

" .... I went, according to invitation, to the T——'s yesterday. The admiral led me down to lunch, and afterwards left, to meet an engagement. We retired to the drawing-room, and had a sweet conversation. I think Christ was there, for our communion was of Him. You will be amused to hear that Lady C—— (Lady T——'s mother) and myself met at a dinner-party in Bermuda, fifty-seven years ago, both of us then young, and but recently married! Now we meet as old ladies, but, best of all, as followers of the Lamb, saved and sanctified by sovereign grace. How strangely people are thrown together in this wide, wide, wilderness world! But, oh, the home of the blessed, where all the saints shall meet, and know as they are known! I am reading your book, every now and then; may the Lord bless it to the quickening of saints and sinners. I cannot but think it would be better to place quotations from God's word in italics.* I had a sweet, refreshing, and heartbreaking view of the infinite goodness of God on first rising this morning. It was a melting of love to my soul, so plainly could I read my interest in Christ, and my title to my home in heaven. I have not lost its richness yet, nor the deep sense of my worthlessness. Truly, *the goodness of God leadeth to repentance.* I did not forget you. May the Lord's choicest blessings rest upon you all!"

"Sabbath Morning.—I have just been praying for you. Oh, that He might answer the prayer, and put strength in body and soul, and the fulness of the Spirit in the word preached, that all may feel that the Lord of a truth has sent you with a message of mercy to all who hear it! . . . This is another cause of gratitude to Him who deals so lovingly and graciously towards us. Let us praise Him now, and praise not only with our lips, but may our *lives* show forth His praise, by walking before Him in all the holy precepts of the Gospel. *If ye love Me, keep my commandments.* Not one nor two only, but *all.* It is not given us to choose which we shall keep, and which we shall break. Oh, for a closer walk! To walk in company with Jesus—side by side—my hand in His hand—my eye on His eye—my heart ever toward Him; this is *fellowship* with God's dear Son. How have I been wrestling for you to day! May He give you a holy, happy Sabbath! May the word be attended with the power of the Holy Ghost to every soul present! I have prayed for quietness of soul, and for healing for the poor head."

Her pen, always at home in the Lord's work, was never

---

* A striking coincidence of opinion on this point with that of Mrs. Isabella Graham, whom she personally knew, and whom in so many features she resembled, may be worthy of note. "Mrs. Graham," observes her biographer, "was very partial to the works of Dr. John Owen, the Rev. W. Romaine, and the Rev. John Newton, and read them with pleasure and profit. One day she remarked to Mr. Bethune, that she preferred the ancient writers on theology to the modern, because they dealt more in italics. 'Dear mother,' he replied, 'what religion can there be in italics?' 'You know,' said she, "that old writers expected credit for the doctrines they taught by proving them, from the word of God, to be correct; they inserted the Scripture passages in italics, and their works have been sometimes one-half in italics. Modern writers on theology, on the contrary, give us a long train of reasoning to persuade us to their opinions, but very little in italics.' This remark of hers has great force in it, and deserves the attention of those who write, and those who read, on theological subjects."—*Life of Mrs. Isabella Graham.*

more appropriately or usefully employed than in imparting spiritual instruction and encouragement to individuals anxiously and earnestly seeking the Saviour. To her own heart He was so truly precious, and to her mind to believe in Him was so exceedingly simple, that it was her peculiar delight to meet and aid a soul earnestly asking the way of salvation. To specimens of her letters addressed to the unconverted—to those of Christian sympathy—and to others appropriate to various circumstances and states of mind, we add a few selections from her correspondence, especially illustrating her peculiar gift in leading the anxious, tremulous mind to a full repose in Christ.

TO LADY A. DE CAPEL B——.

"DEAR LADY B—— April 20.
"How kind of you to write to me that little note, when your suffering head must have rendered it an exertion! It is a mercy for you and me that there is a Head which is always right, and a heart, too, that is ever disposed to do us all possible good. Oh, to have such a Friend as Jesus is in the court of heaven, who feels all our sorrows, carries all our burdens, and has promised to bring us safely through this trying world, and place us at last at His own right hand, where neither sickness nor sorrow shall ever come! Dear friend, let me commend you to keep close to this precious Friend, who can only be spiritually known and seen by the eye of faith. To all others he is invisible. Faith can discern Him when sense utterly fails. But it is our mercy, that, though this world knows and sees Him not, yet He does and will make Himself known to those who seek Him with their whole heart. Oh, the kindness, the loving-kindness that fills the heart of Jesus towards one poor feeble soul who can but waft a sigh, a wish, a desire towards Him! To such, His heart in a moment responds. Oh, how attentively He listens to hear, and how eager to respond to the first pulsation that arises in the soul towards Himself! That desire to know and love Him is the blessed work of His own Holy Spirit. Dear friend, go to Him just as you are, nor rest short of a holy, familiar, abiding sense of His presence. To know Him is life, and life eternal. He says, *I am the way, the truth, and the life.* How sweetly and lovingly He invites us, *Come unto me, all ye that labour and are heavy laden, and I will give you rest.* If you and I have come and cast ourselves at His blessed feet, we need fear nothing, for

He will do all things well for us, here and hereafter. I could fill a dozen sheets on this precious subject, but will not fatigue you to read more than is needful to assure you of my sincere desire and good wishes for returning health, and that body and soul may prosper. My Christian love to dear Miss T——. She belongs to Jesus, and is one of His fold. *My sheep hear my voice, and I know them, and they follow me. I know my sheep, and am known of mine.* Oh, it is a mercy of mercies to know Jesus as *my* Shepherd. May he draw you nearer and nearer to Himself."

TO H. AND E. S——.

"MY BELOVED FRIENDS,—

"I have been thinking of you, and thinking of Jesus too. What a heart has Christ! Do you know what it is made of? It is an ocean of goodness. It is a sea, fathomless and shoreless, of matchless love—love to poor sinners who but look to Him or sigh for Him. It is the joy of His heart to save sinners. This was His express mission to our world. Then would I have you look, not to your evidences, or to your own goodness, or to your unworthiness, but to Jesus, with a believing heart, and you shall be saved in Christ and for Christ. By simply believing in the Lord Jesus, He becomes one with you, and you one with Him, the Holy Spirit taking possession of your souls for Himself. In a little while, and we pass away, and one thing only is needful. Come, then, to Jesus, and be saved; and give Him no rest until He manifests Himself to you, as He has promised. *We will come and manifest ourselves unto you.* This manifestation of the Lord Jesus Christ to your souls, when you experience it, will be worth more than millions of worlds to you. I am convinced you will echo this when you receive the blessing. He waits to be gracious, lingers for your coming, just as you are, not waiting to make yourselves more acceptable. He undertakes to make you all you ought to be, and will work in you *to will and to do*, and all that is pleasing in His sight."

"If you will cultivate the habit of going and telling Jesus all you wish or fear, you will find in Him a hearkening ear; and thus you will become acquainted with God and His peace. Your desire is to know Jesus, to believe in Jesus, to be assured of your interest in Jesus. Can there be a better way of accomplishing this than by going to Him in all simplicity, and opening freely and fully your whole heart to Him? Put from you all cold formality, and deal with Christ as if He were now what you read of Him when upon earth. He is the same that He was then. He was never known to reject any that came to Him for help; nor will He turn Himself away from you. Go to Him, and continue going until you can say, *I have found Him of whom Moses and the prophets did write.* Oh, the joy and hope that will then spring up in your heart, when thus you have found Him! He is not far from you now. In one moment you may make acquaintance with Jesus, and a precious Saviour you will find Him. And what a mercy it will be to have such a Friend always near you, to guide, protect, and bless you, and make you, in return, a *blessing* to others! Remember wrestling Jacob, who said, *I will not let Thee go until Thou bless me.* This was that same Jesus with whom the patriarch wrestled, who afterwards was manifested in a body like ours, to pay to Divine justice our mighty debt, to suffer in our stead, and who rose again from the dead, appeared to Mary, and now waits to be gracious unto *you.*"

"*The Lord taketh pleasure in them that fear Him, in them that hope in His mercy.* On opening my Bible this morning, my eye rested upon these words, and I thought, beloved friends, of you. I felt they suited your state of mind. The Lord your God, manifest in the flesh, taketh pleasure in you. Go alone, and thank Him for this precious word, with a heart fully open to His view. Have no concealments from your best Friend. He loves an open, candid heart. He wants you to approach Him with your low frames, with your bad feelings, with your cold affections, with your wandering minds, with your unbelieving hearts. He will listen to your voice, and regard your wants, and do all that you can possibly think of, and more than your highest thought or imagination can conceive. *The Lord is nigh unto all them that call upon Him, unto all that call upon Him in truth.* You shall never seek His face in vain. One loving look from Christ will dissolve your heart into love and sweet contrition. His invitation is, *Look unto Me, all ye ends of the earth, and be ye saved.* And when the Holy Ghost shall take of the things of Christ and show them unto you, you will then say, 'Not half has been told me; now we know Him, not because you have told us, but because He has made Himself known to us.' I long to see you rejoicing in Christ, as if you were a part of myself. I hope to welcome you in heaven. Think of the meeting there! Who would not strive for it? Tarry not, nor stop, until you are quite *sure that you are saved.*"

"It seems to me that the chief concern of life is to get to heaven. This, the grand object of our brief sojourn in this vale of tears, should engross our every thought, and enlist our utmost aim. Is not everything else that would allure us from this great concern a device of the enemy, plying his efforts and powers to divert us from our eternal interests? My beloved friends, keep your eyes open to the ten thousand temptations of the enemy of souls, and cultivate a readiness to obey the summons, which at any moment may come, *Prepare to meet thy God.* The subject upon which I write is of the first moment. How stands the matter between God and your souls? Have you the sealing of the Holy Ghost? Has Jesus manifested Himself to you? Press the question upon your consciences, and, oh, may the answer be an honest one! A heaven, with all its glory, or a hell, with all its horrors, is dependent upon your present decision. A soul saved, or a soul lost! A soul eternally happy, or a soul eternally wretched! But Jesus stands ready to receive to his loving bosom every poor sinner that comes to Him, in all his helplessness, for salvation. May this be your happy case!"

"I wish, my beloved friends, to quote a passage from God's word, for your comfort, which arrested my attention in the course of my reading, and my thoughts wandered to you in a moment; and may the Lord Jesus make it a quickening, comforting, refreshing portion to your precious souls. *I know the thoughts that I think towards you, saith the Lord, thoughts of peace and not of evil, to give you an expected end. Then shall ye call upon Me, and ye shall go and pray unto Me, and I will* HEARKEN *unto you. And ye shall seek Me, and find Me, when ye search for Me with all your heart.* Jer. xxix. 11. Is not this worth wrestling for? Can you go a day or an hour without receiving it? Seek earnestly, then, until you find the Lord, and He says to you, *I am thy salvation.* The blessing is *without money and without price.* My soul travails in birth for you, until Christ is formed within you, the hope of glory. There is nothing in this poor, passing world that is to you, at this present moment, of such vast consequence. Dear, very dear are you to me, and I do feel that you are dear to the heart of Jesus. You have my fervent, earnest prayers: and how will it gladden my heart to see you rejoicing in Christ Jesus; and when you do, come and tell me, that we may rejoice together."

". . . Many thanks, dear, loved friends, for the flowers, and also for the lights. I had some, but yours eclipse them entirely, and burn beautifully at night, when mine are quenched in darkness. Oh, that your *spiritual light*, and mine too, may shine brighter and brighter unto the perfect day! How brightly will that light shine, when once introduced into the glories of the upper world. No night there, for Jesus will be the light and glory thereof. Beloved friends, press onward to know more of this most precious Friend. I am very feeble; pray for me."

In the following extracts we trace the application of divine truth to a more mature stage of Christian experience:—

TO MRS. H——.

". . . . . Yesterday we had a day full of Christ—His death and glorious resurrection. The Fast-day was a day of feasting with our souls. The word was full of manna and fatness; from seven o'clock in the morning until half-past nine in the evening, we were more or less in the sanctuary, humbling ourselves at the feet of Jesus for the sins of the nation, and for our own. The Lord was most blessedly with ——. The word came with power, and accompanied with the unction of the Spirit. It was a day long to be remembered by us. Dear friend, what could we do without the Gospel? It is bread to the soul, the living soul,—for a dead soul does not value it; but we need it, that we may grow in grace and in the knowledge of Jesus Christ, who is its sum and substance. We must feed upon him.

'None but Jesus can do helpless sinners good.'

". . . . How important it is that we should be quite sure that we are on the right foundation. Is there, or can there be, anything of equal importance to this? And yet, how many are wasting their precious time on the things of this poor world they are so soon to leave, and are risking the never dying soul, yet hastening on to the bar of God, unprepared for that great day for which all other days were made! Is not this madness? May the Lord make us faithful to them and to others, urging all we love to flee from the wrath to come, pointing them to the Lamb of God, whose blood, while it cleanses us from all sin, sanctifies the heart. We often shrink from this duty, and Satan endeavours to hinder us; but Jesus requires it at our hands, and by coming to Him, and telling Him our weakness, He will strengthen us, and help us to do His will. The text yesterday was, *Who shall roll us away the stone from the door of the sepulchre? And when they looked, they saw that the stone was rolled away, for it was very great.* How often we have our stones of difficulty lying in our path; and as often, when we come to the difficulty, we find that the stone has been rolled away by a hand invisible to mortal eye. But the saint of God knows whose it is."

TO MRS. W——.

"I was just thinking of Jesus, our dearest, best, and never-failing Friend, and I thought I should like to talk to you about Him. It is so sweet to talk of one dear to us who is absent. Bless God with me, that we are both so near our home, each day's travel bringing us nearer and nearer. Our eyes shall behold Him whom our souls love beyond all created good. What a prospect is before us! For ever with the Lord! Oh, for stronger faith, to give full credit to all we profess to believe! You will recollect I told you, I have more communion with the saints above than with the saints below. Many whom I meet seem to have so little to do with Him, and their acquaintance with Him is so slight. Precious Jesus! who would not know Thee? and in knowing Thee, who would not love Thee? I long to see Him, to tell Him how much I love Him. Is He not all in all to us? Are we not His, and is He not ours? Does He not sit enthroned upon our heart's best affections. Do we not commune with Him as a Friend to whom we can open our entire heart, tell Him all, and listen to his gracious response? Oh, how precious this intercourse with One we love, and who loves us! My thoughts are, more or less, in heaven. There is Jesus; the same gentleness, sympathy, and goodness, portrayed on His blessed countenance, every feature beaming with love, as when on earth. Oh, beloved, let us join to praise Him! Help me to love Him better. We should be helpers of each other's joy. Our journey is drawing to an end. Look forward, look upward. Jesu's eye is upon you; His heart is towards you. A few more severe trials, a few more staggering steps—and we are *there!*"

TO HER SON, REV. G—— L—— W——.

"..... I was grieved to hear —— was of a sceptical turn. Oh, what a mercy to have godly parents! and how much have they to answer for, who have brought up their children to rest their happiness only on a world that is passing away, and is bearing them on to another. Godly parents cannot convert their children; God alone can do this. But they can lead them to Jesus, and bring them up in the fear of the Lord; and when they have done this, they have done all they can do; for the Holy Ghost alone can change the heart, and this is what we have to pray for, until we see them safe within the ark. Every moment they are without it, is replete with danger. They must be born again. Christ has said it. It is not a change of sentiment, nor an outward reformation of life; it is a new heart imparted by the Holy Ghost; and when they have it, they will know it. May we, who do know our sins are pardoned, be fully sanctified, body, soul, and spirit for the Lord. We want more devotedness of heart, more of the single eye to His glory, and to feel more the value of precious souls. Oh, think of lost souls—of the eternal woe, where the worm dieth not, and the fire is not quenched! Do we believe God? And has He not said this? Let us, then, put far from us all the false charity that leaves sinners to stand upon the precipice, because we will not disturb their carnal security."

TO HER SON O——.

"...... I have been feeble; but this I must expect, according to the course of things in this changing, fading world. And when I look back upon, and think of all that I have passed through, I have cause to bless and praise the Lord, that I am as well as I am. I was glad to hear of the arrival of Captain B——'s vessel in Australia. I have felt anxious for their safety, and have seldom forgotten them in my prayers. Would they all knew the value of prayer! Oh, to live upon Jesus—to live for Him—and in a measure, even now, to live *with* Him! But I must not write you a long letter, for I know you have but little time to read it. I bless the Lord you were carried comfortably through your labours yesterday. It is a mercy to have the Lord's blessing, even in a small way; to be quite assured that His presence is with us, though all the world should be against us. It is a narrow road the followers of Christ walk; but it is the foothpath He Himself travelled, and it is a great honour put upon a follower of Him, to tread in the same. In all my helplessness, I lean upon Him. I must not detain you, though my heart is full."

"E—— has been unwell. What frail bodies we carry about with us for a season! and bless God, it is but for a season, and a short one, when, if in Christ, all will be, must be, well in the end. . . . . . I constantly repair to my stronghold on your behalf. There is none like Jesus, the once despised Nazarene, who trod this earth in loneliness and poverty, despised and rejected of men. Oh, to walk as He walked, waiting, as He patiently waited, for the crown of glory prepared for all who follow in His blessed footsteps! The honours of this poor world are not worth a thought. May the Lord keep you more than merely satisfied; may you always *rejoice* that He has called you to take up a cross for Him who bore so heavy a one for you, that you may hereafter, in a little while wear a crown. I am increasingly feeble. Old age is infancy again. Who would live alway? Oh, for the eye of faith to look within the vail, and see Jesus there, in full possession of His kingdom, waiting to welcome every weary pilgrim home with, *Come, ye blessed of my Father!* Humanly speaking, I think this will be my last summer on earth. Well, be it so; the Lord knows the best time, and He will take care of His own. Do not let 'Octavius, jun.,' forget grandmamma."

Soon after the letters were penned from which the above extracts are made, and while still on a visit to her son in town, she was seized with an illness which filled her family with the greatest alarm. Her advanced age and enfeebled constitution, combined with the severity of the attack, left but faint hope of her rallying. It were needless to say, that the most skilful medical aid that London could afford was obtained, the responsibility being too great for a near relative to sustain. It was an especial and signal kindness of God's providence, that the physician thus summoned to her couch should be the late Dr. GOLDING BIRD, of Russell-square. Never, perhaps, did two individuals meet in the relation of patient and physician, between whom, in some of the finest points of natural, as in many of the higher features of Christian character, there existed a closer resemblance, or a stronger sympathy. They met,

"New as if come from other spheres,
Yet welcome as if loved for years."

Until then they were entirely unknown to each other. In a short time, however, they discerned that a powerful and responsive sympathy existed between them; that, taught by the same Spirit, their hearts fashioned alike by the same Divine hand, they were "no more strangers, but fellow-citizens with the saints, and of the household of God." The tender interest with which Dr. Golding Bird became at once inspired in his venerable patient—the anxiety, skill, and gentleness, with which he watched her case—could not have been surpassed by the devotion of the oldest friend, or the tenderness of the fondest son. It was a touching spectacle,—and it would have formed a fine study for the pencil,—which met the eye of the writer, on his return from Switzerland (from whence he had been summoned by the illness of his parent,) when for the first time, he saw Dr. Golding Bird. On entering the room, Mrs. Winslow was seated on a sofa, then convalescent, her beloved physician at her side. His pale, intellectual countenance was bent over her with an expression of the profoundest interest and veneration, while she was expatiating with her wonted energy and earnestness on her favourite themes—the preciousness of the Saviour, and the glorious hope of the Christian beyond the tomb. The grateful and affectionate regard which the recovered patient cherished for the Christian physician—himself then battling with an insidious and rapidly-ripening disease—by whose skill and care, under God, her invaluable life had been reclaimed as from the grave, found expression in the following letters addressed to Dr. Bird:—

"39, Upper Bedford-place, Sept. 24, 1853.

"TO THE BELOVED PHYSICIAN.

"DEAR BROTHER IN JESUS,—

"How can I sufficiently thank you for all your Christian kindness, tenderness, and love to a stranger, to whom you came in an hour of suffering? I am convinced the Lord sent you; and may the life He has spared be increasingly devoted to Him, and may the sweetest, richest blessing rest upon you. *Inasmuch*, says our Lord, *as ye have done it unto one of the least of these my brethren, ye have done it unto Me.* It is one of the strongest evidences of our adoption, the love which the

Spirit creates, and which cements and binds together the one family of God. By this we know our election of God, and that we have passed from death unto life. I am leaving town, but could not go without one word to you, as we may not meet again until we meet above. And oh, the meeting then! What will it be? We shall behold that same Jesus who trod this lower world, now enthroned in glory, as full of love, tenderness, and sympathy as ever, saying to us then—to you, beloved brother, and to unworthy me—*Enter into the joy of thy Lord!* Oh, for that blessed recognition! May we have stronger faith to realize our high calling, and to live in more constant intercourse with Jesus here, even amidst all that would fain turn us aside. It must and it will be a fight of faith; but if, in childlike simplicity, we keep our eye intent upon Jesus, travelling to Him for all we need, we shall be able to go on our way rejoicing. My own dear brother, in the best sense, I must now bid you farewell. I am better than I ever expected to be in this vale of tears. Heaven is my home, my happy home. Where Jesus is, there you and I must be. Again let me thank you for all your kind attentions; and ever believe me your grateful sister in Jesus."

"January 9th, 1854.

". . . It is in my heart to enclose you a little work, which you may read when resting from your labours on the sofa. To me it has been a rich repast, a sweet morsel for a weary, aged traveller through a wilderness world, which, take it at its best, is nothing else, and God designed that it should be nothing else. But the prospect beyond, oh, how glorious! A Father's house—a house not made with hands, eternal in the heavens! Dear friend, the Lord sent you to me at a time of suffering. He blessed what you did for me, and I was brought back when I expected soon to be with Him whom my soul loveth, and have done with sin and sorrow for ever. 'Not yet,' said the Saviour; 'a little longer trial and conflict in the wilderness.' I have something more to learn of my helplessness and weakness. It is but a little, and we shall pass away; all our sicknesses, trials, and disappointments, are needful to fit us for it. I have, through a long-protracted life, waded through much tribulation, and now feel that I have not had one sorrow amiss. **The port is almost in view, and how** pleasant it looks! Let me send my Christian love to your dear wife, and believe me most gratefully yours in Jesus."

"April 18th, 1854.

". . . And now we are both nearing day by day, hour by hour, our glorious inheritance. It is all ready for us, and Jesus, whom we both love, because He first loved us, stands prepared to bid us welcome. Fear not, dear brother; you have a right to the inheritance; it was purchased for you, and the full price paid down, before you had existence, save in the foreknowledge of God. I shall meet you there, and recognize you too. There will be a perfection of knowledge, as of everything else. We have been for years pressing on through a wilderness, and now, through the weakness of our faith, we are loth to leave it. But be of good cheer, for it is all true, all real. Our best Friend, He who loved us unto the death, is there, and at times so very near does it seem to me, I can hardly contain the joy that fills my whole soul. Truly, it has not entered into the heart of man to conceive the things that God has prepared for them that love Him. Sometimes He draws the curtain back a little, and gives me a glimpse, and then, overpowered with the sight, I can but weep for joy,— yes, and weep for sin too. Oh, the wondrous love of God in the gift of His beloved Son, to suffer, bleed, and die for such poor, wretched sinners! Only believe. I have had such a view this morning of the glory that awaits the believer, that I could not bear much more. I write now to encourage you in the conflict. I may be there to bid you welcome. Who can tell? The Lord sent you to my bedside, as His messenger, to bring me back again to earth, to see the conversion of several of my grandchildren, in answer to my many prayers, and also to witness, even in this poor world of sorrow, some glimpses of the glory that awaits the believer. When Stephen was dying, the curtain of heaven was drawn, and he saw Jesus *standing* ready to receive him. He is the very same now,—*the same yesterday, to-day, and for ever.* I will not, dear friend, trouble you longer, but will ask the Lord to bless you, to encourage your heart, to comfort your dear wife, and to prepare all you love to follow you into the land of glory. Oh, to spend eternity together with all we have loved on earth! That glory shall be increasing through the countless ages of an endless existence."

The warm response which these utterances awoke, was worthy of him on whose Christian heart they fell like the soft breath of evening on the sweet Æolian. The finest chords of his gentle nature were touched, and trembled with holy ecstasy.* A brief note, penned from his couch of languor, survives to complete and close the record of a friendship too sacred and too brief for earth:—

"48, Russell-square, Feb. 3rd, 1854.

"I must, my dear Mrs. Winslow, write a few lines to you, to thank you gratefully for your last kind letter. I cherish all your letters, but the last was very genial and comforting to me. It came just as I began to feel again the pressure of the burden of my work on my feeble frame; and although I have not been quite laid aside, I have been obliged to limit myself to my home practice, so as to rest for the other part of the day. It was comforting to be reminded by you, who had so long tasted that the Lord is gracious, that we should go to Him even with our small cares, as without Him we could do nothing. I fear I have too much reason often to say, with the trembling suppliant of old, 'Lord, I believe; help Thou my *unbelief!*' My dear wife, who deeply enjoyed your letter—for we regard it as common property—desires to unite with me in earnest prayers for your preservation during the perils of the winter, and that you may yet long be spared as an example of one who in this world is enabled, by grace, to live in the land of Beulah.

"Do give my affectionate regards to Miss W——, and your dear son O——, and

"Believe me to remain, ever your friend,

"GOLDING BIRD."

"To Mrs. Winslow."

"I shall never forget," adds one who survives to mourn, as none others can, his irreparable loss—"I shall never forget his reading the last letter sent. Tears of joy fell from his eyes at the sweet mention of that dear Saviour whom he so loved. His love for your dear parent amounted to a kind of reverence." Religion mourned the loss of one of her brightest ornaments,

---

* " His fine toned heart, like the harp of the winds,
 Answers in sweetness each breeze that sings;
 And the storms of grief, and the breath of joy,
 Draw nothing but music from its strings."

and science one of her noblest sons, when Dr. Golding Bird was numbered with the dead. Seldom have more brilliant powers or brighter hopes become suddenly quenched in the darkness of the sepulchre, than when this accomplished scholar and eminent physician succumbed to the power of a disease accelerated, if not caused, by his extreme devotion to his profession, on the loftiest summit of which he stood when death's dart laid him low. But distinguished as were his talents, and successful as was his career, the highest encomium of Dr. Golding Bird is,—that he was *a believer in the Lord Jesus Christ.* Nature made him great, Providence made him useful, religion made him good; and nature, Providence, and grace, unite to accomplish the purposes of Him "who is wonderful in counsel, and excellent in working." The grace of God was "exceeding abundant" in him. He was not "ashamed of Christ and of His words," but everywhere, and on all occasions,—whether lecturing from the chair of the professor, or administering in the sick room of the patient,—he invariably exhibited the character, maintained the dignity, and exerted the influence, of the—CHRISTIAN PHYSICIAN.*

It was soon after her recovery from the illness just referred

* "On one point," remarks the elegant pen of his biographer, "he entertained a strong opinion, regarding it an unpardonable fault, to delude the dying patient with false hopes, when all earthly means of relief had failed, and death remained inevitable. Whilst rational hope existed, he encouraged it; but when it was shut out for ever, he always told the truth. He spoke emphatically on this subject some years ago, when called by a late eminent member of his profession to the bedside of a dying physician. He was assured that their suffering brother did not know his danger, and had not been told of it. 'Then be it my task,' was the reply, 'to tell him. If we cannot preserve his life here, we must not let him hazard life hereafter.' . . He had always pursued his profession under the conviction that the spiritual and practical physician was inseparable: that between them a kindred tie existed, a union often to be usefully employed, and which it was an important duty to preserve and strengthen. By him it was never broken. At the risk of being deemed sometimes intrusive, he never failed, when he felt that it was necessary, to direct the attention of the dying to that reliance on the Divine sacrifice which, when his own voice was hushed in the silence of death, and his worn-out and suffering body was at rest, graced his thin features with a smile of tranquillity and peace."--*Biographical Notice of the late Dr. Golding Bird, A.M., M.D., F.R.S., F.L.S.*

While thus touching upon the union of the medical profession with Christianity—the connexion of science with religion—as illustrated by the life of Dr. GOLDING BIRD, it may not be inappropriate to quote some observations, yet further and more ably elucidating this important and to, that the following letters were penned, the elevated, heavenly tone of which would alone indicate that she had been so near to her eternal home as to have gazed within the

interesting question, by Dr. FORBES WINSLOW, the youngest son of the subject of this Memoir. The extract is taken from a volume, entitled " Lettsomian Lectures on Insanity, by FORBES WINSLOW, M.D., D.C.L., 1856."

When speaking of the psychological vocation of the physician, Dr. Forbes Winslow observes:—"I claim for the cultivators of medical science higher and more exalted functions than those usually assigned to the physician. We form but a low and grovelling estimate of the high destination, and of the solemn duties of our dignified vocation, if we conceive, that the operations of the physician are limited to the successful application of mere physical agents. The physician is daily called to witness the powerful effect of *mental* influences and *moral* emotions upon the *material* organization. He perceives that such causes engender disease, destroy life, retard recovery, and often interfere with the successful actions of the most potent remedial means exhibited for the alleviation and cure of bodily disease and suffering. Although such influences are admitted to play an important part. either for good or evil, I do not conceive that the practitioners of medicine have had a sufficient appreciation of their great importance. The physician is often called upon, in the exercise of his responsible duties, to discharge medico-theological functions. It is occasionally his painful duty to sit by the couch of the dying, and witness the last sad conflict between *mind* and *matter*. It is on such occasions that he has, either in co-operation with the recognised minister, or in his temporary absence, an opportunity of whispering words of comfort, hope and consolation to the wounded spirit, and of directing the attention of the patient, and those immediately about him, to the only true and legitimate source of the Christian's hope. Let the physician not lightly esteem or neglect the solemn functions thus imposed upon him.

" Our position as medical philosophers, occupied in the investigation of the phenomena of life, of mind, and of disease, entails upon us anxious, solemn, and responsible duties. In the hour of pain. when the spirit is humbled by suffering—in the day of distress - in the solemn moment of dissolution—it is our high and noble privilege, iike guardian angels, to hover about the couch of the sick and dying. We enter the chamber of the man writhing with agony, bereft, perhaps, of that which alone made existence pleasurable, the right exercise of the mental powers, and loud and affectionate demands are made upon our sagacity and skill. Life—the silken thread,—the fragile chord of life—depends upon our rapid appreciation of the phenomena of disease, and ready administration of remedial agents for their relief and cure. Our profession is a noble one—a most dignified, exalted, and honourable calling While feeling that the best of our works are imperfect, and that we must rely for our future happiness upon the mercy of God, in Christ Jesus, and not upon our own merits. I cannot be forgetful how great is our responsibility, for the right use of our talents, and the faithful discharge of our solemn and anxious duties."

vail, and to have felt and heard what it was not possible fully to utter.

TO MRS. C——.

"My dear Friend,—   Nov. 25th, 1853.

"I have often thought of you, and have inquired of those who knew, how you were. But when we get above, we shall not have far to seek each other. Oh, *that*, not this, is our home! Here all is tainted, defiled with sin; God has something better in store for us. Make your calling and election sure for that better land. *I go to prepare a place for you.* I have lately been brought by severe illness almost in view of my glorious inheritance. My children were weeping around me, and all thought my time was come, I felt quite ready. In a few moments I expected to be in the presence of Him my soul loved. But it was not to be so; and here I am still in this vale of tears, kept for a season out of my eternal inheritance, and, for some wise and gracious purpose, have been wonderfully raised up again. The will of the Lord be done. And now, my dear friend, I feel I must live more than ever upon Jesus. He is alone able to counsel, direct, and overrule all our concerns, and in the best possible way. Why, then, should you and I be over anxious about any one thing, when we can cast *all* our cares upon Him? Oh, it is sweet living when we thus live upon Jesus! Go often and talk with Christ, and tell Him all you feel and desire. The smaller the case you take to Him, the more you honour Him! for in this act you acknowledge your belief in what He says that, *Without me ye can do nothing.* I am with ——, and greatly enjoy his ministry. When he was an infant I fed him, and now in my old age he is permitted to feed me with the sincere milk of the word, which is very sweet and refreshing to my waiting soul. The Lord Jesus draw you nearer and yet nearer to Himself, and make Himself more sensibly known to you. Do not lose sight of Him; He is your Helper in this vale of tears, and has promised that He will never leave nor forsake you. And oh, to see Him in all his glory above, and be acknowledged there, in the midst of all the host of heaven, as His beloved, this is worth living and is worth dying for! In a little moment, and eternity will burst upon our view. Lean upon Jesus for everything, and you will find you cannot do without Him here or hereafter."

TO MRS. C.——.

"... Since I last heard from you, I have been brought almost in full view of my eternal home. My physician gave me up, and my children, who were all about me but dear O——, who was abroad for his health, were expecting my departure. But the Lord said, 'Not yet;' and so I was raised up, and brought back to suffer a little more of earth's trials. I felt peaceful and satisfied that I was safe. There was not that rejoicing that I sometimes have had, but a calm, trusting, confiding state of mind; not the shadow of a doubt, nor a cloud between my soul and Him whom my soul loveth. Oh, dear friend, let us often meditate on heaven; it will assist us to bear more serenely the ills of life. Our Jesus is there, the self-same Jesus who dwelt in the flesh. Was it not sweet and lovely in Him to lead His disciples out to the spot from whence he ascended to glory, in order that they might see that the identically same body He had borne about with Him on earth, He bore up with Him to heaven? I am quite sure that if we dwelt more in all godly simplicity in the full expectation of seeing and being with Jesus for ever, we should be found oftener rejoicing in the prospect before us. Have, my dear friend, constant transactions with this precious Saviour. A holy familiarity with Him will tend much to conform us to His likeness. But few go to Jesus just as they are, and with no price in their hand. A poor, needy sinner, empty and helpless as a babe, is inconceivably welcome to Christ. From such He will never, no never, turn away. This simple, believing living upon Christ has a most sanctifying, purifying tendency upon the whole inner man; and thus sin grows more hateful, and the world less attractive, and the pleasures of sense increasingly distasteful, and we are better fitted to sustain the trials of life. I must now conclude, but my heart is so full of this glorious theme, that, were it possible, I could proclaim to the whole world the willingness there is in the heart of Jesus to receive and save sinners, *as sinners*, and not as saints. Let me hear from you."

How often in the Christian's deepening experience are old and long-familiar truths brought to the soul with all the power, and clothed with all the freshness and beauty, of a new revelation! What an evidence this of the divinity of the Bible, and what a touching unfolding of the love of the Spirit!

It is thus she confirms, by her own personal experience, this thought:—

"DEAREST O——, Sabbath Afternoon.

"I am still confined to bed, quite unable to exert myself. I have prayed for you again and again, many times to-day. Oh, what a mighty privilege it is to have to do immediately with God, with God Himself, the mighty God in Christ! How could we have known anything of God, had He not stooped to reveal Himself in Jesus? I have been thinking much to-day of this wondrous stoop. It has opened in my mind a new spring of thought, has given me a fresh view of God, to an extent I have never had before. For, although I have often read and spoken of God revealing Himself in my nature, yet it has never appeared so vividly true, so blessedly real as to-day. Oh, as I travel on to my heavenly home, and near the time when the vail will be drawn altogether, how increasingly wonderful are the glorious realities of eternity! wonder upon wonder opening up to the astonished sight, almost overwhelming. Praise our God. What could I do without Jesus! Old age, with its untold infirmities, would be a serious drag if He were not by me, and had I not the privilege of leaning upon Him with all the weight of care, pain, sin, and sorrow. Again would I say, how inexpressibly precious the incarnation of the Son of God has been to my soul to-day, the Holy Ghost unfolding it in a new light, and giving me to take a more simple, direct hold upon it as a matter-of-fact truth! I ask you now to help me to praise Him for the depth of love, matchless, wondrous love, it has unfolded to me, and to urge you to preach more and more of God, the mighty God, dwelling in Jesus, in a body like our own. I have been praying that the Holy Ghost may help you to-day, and carry the word home to the hearts of all, that many poor sinners may be brought to the feet of Jesus. It has not been a barren Sabbath to me, although I have been kept at home. Oh, the goodness of God, the wonders of His matchless love! Eternity will be only long enough to tell of it. Love to all."

It was a pleasing interpretation of the design of God in thus turning her back again into the wilderness, after giving her so close and vivid a view of the good land, to the borders of which He seemed to bring her, that she was spared to behold several of her children's children avow her God and Father to be theirs,—thus permitted to sickle, ere she departed, a "kind of first fruits" of the golden harvest of her long-sown prayers. We have space but for a few extracts only of the many instructive and encouraging letters her pen addressed to them on this occasion, all breathing much holy joy in their conversion, and godly jealousy for their consistent walk.

TO HER GRANDSON, T. E. W——.

"Dearest T——,

"Dearer to me now than ever, since you came into this world of trial and sorrow. The love of Jesus acts as a holy cement, uniting the one family of God to Himself and to each other. Bless the Lord for His great goodness and His tender love to you all, not forgetting the dear departed one, the father of you all. So eternal and deep, so sovereign and boundless is the love of God, angels cannot fathom it. And I believe that a sigh, sincere and deep, coming from the chief of sinners, even at a dying hour, the loving, sympathising heart of Jesus could not resist it. Oh, the wondrous love of God in giving us such a Saviour, able to save to the uttermost all who feel their need of Him! Now is the Lord answering my ten thousand poor prayers, and these, I think, when I was so near my happy home, almost in sight, He brought me back to see. Oh, He is a God who loves to answer prayer, and is faithful to His every word! You cannot ask too much of Him. The more you ask, the better is He pleased. Go with large demands. *Ask anything in My name, and I will do it. Ask, that your joy might be full.* We heard from W——, who gives as a reason for not writing sooner, that they had set apart one evening in the week, H—— S—— and himself, for reading the Bible and for prayer. A young man whom they have met in the University, and who is a dear Christian, and advanced in the ways of God, has joined them, and is a great acquisition. My love to your wife. Oh, that we might be a whole family in heaven!"

TO HER GRAND-DAUGHTER S——.

"No one can tell how my soul rejoiceth over you, my beloved child. Now do I see why the Lord brought me back to earth; it was to cause me to see the answer, before I left, of my poor prayers. And now I shall hope to meet and dwell with you throughout a blessed eternity, and many more so dear to us both. How grateful I am to Him for all His abundant goodness and tender mercy to us as a family! God be praised. My heart has been melted in love to-day to Him, who is all over and all within, nothing but love unfeigned, constant, and unabating, to the weakest, the most unworthy of all His little flock. And now let me urge you to live upon Him as a young child, going to Him for all you want and with all you fear. You will find Him ready to respond to your request by the still small voice of His Spirit. *Hear me, O Lord, when I cry with my voice: have mercy also upon me, and answer me.* Psalm xxvii. 7. Oh, that He may go on in His own loving way until all we love are *born again*, and set out on their heavenly race to the land of glory!"

"Oh, how my heart rejoices over you, my beloved child, doubly dear to me now! Oh, the mercy of mercies, to be beloved of Christ! The Lord has at last condescended to bow the heavens, and listen to my ten thousand prayers for you all. May the great and mighty work go on among the others still to be called into the kingdom! Oh, the wondrous power of prayer when we come in the name of Jesus, God's dear and beloved Son! My heart is brimful of joy on your account and dear Octavia's. I wish you would both come and see me. The Lord has raised me up from the borders of the grave, to see the fruit of my prayers. I wondered what I was spared for, but I see it now. Keep an open heart with Jesus. Remember He is bone of your bone, and flesh of your flesh. He can enter into all your fears and hopes, desires and difficulties. Having once been in the body, He knows how to pity and to succour you, and to be a present help in time of need. Thank dear E—— for her kind letter, giving me such precious news."

"I bless God, dear child, often on your behalf; but now remember, you have but just begun to run the race—a race for a crown of glory. *So run that you may obtain.* Many I have seen set out well in this race, but I have lived to see them fall short at last of the prize. They forsook their first love, and sought their enjoyment in the poor wretched trifles of time and sense. May it not be so with you, darling child. Keep close to Jesus. How do I pray for you and for dear Octavia too, and for all those who have truly set out on their heavenly journey! You are in a world full of temptation. Satan, the foe of Christ and the enemy of souls, goeth about to draw away Christ's lambs from closely following their Shepherd.

He has a thousand ways to allure and entrap them to do and say that which will grieve the Spirit, and dishonour the Saviour. He will say to you, 'This is no sin, and that is no sin; other Christians do it, and why may not you?' And what can you do, thus assailed by the arch enemy? You have no more self-power to resist him than an infant has over an elephant. But Jesus, who loves you, and has all power in heaven and on earth, invites you to come to Him, and be saved from all your enemies, from the power of Satan, and from the evil that is in the world, and from the corrupt tendencies of your own sinful nature. And although you are now saved, and your name is written in the Lamb's book of life, yet you are still in the body, and have daily and hourly to contend with the world, the flesh, and Satan. And Satan is sure to find a hidden foe in your heart, ready to betray you into his power. And what can a feeble child do in such a case, but run at once to Jesus? Be where you may, in company, in the street, or at home, lift up your heart to Jesus for aid, and He will prove a present help in your time of need. He listens to the feeblest breathings of the heart. He requires not the voice; a wish, a faint desire, will be all-sufficient. Wherever you are, there is Jesus. And may the Holy Ghost write upon your heart the precept, *Grieve not the Holy Spirit, whereby you are sealed unto the day of redemption.* One wrong step in the early part of your Christianity may lead to an eventual going back far to the world. Remember, you are commanded to come out of the world, and to touch not the unclean thing. I wish you to be much in the study of the Bible, before you unite yourself with any particular church. See what your Lord says as respects the ordinances of His house, for it is most important that we walk in the right ways of the Lord; this you can do, and still, if you prefer it, attend the ministry of Mr. Jarman."

"Go nowhere where you cannot take Christ with you. Put your hand, as it were, in His hand, and whatever you do, let your whole aim be to please Him, who suffered, bled, and died that you might live for Him, and with Him for ever. Let me hear often from you. It is but a little while that I shall be here. Pray for dear H—— and P——. Encourage dear S—— and H—— in maintaining the worship of the Lord in the family. Make it a point to take the younger children in to hear God's word and to pray. May the Lord bless you, my own beloved child, make you useful, and keep you near to

Himself. Let darling Octavia read this; it is for you both. Pray, pray, pray without ceasing. God listens to your faintest breathing. Oh, the marvellous potency of prayer, when we plead the name of Jesus! Thank dear E—— for her precious letter; but you must not any of you *cross* your letters, as I cannot make it all out, and then I am *cross* too!"

A name occurs in one of the preceding extracts which it may be proper, in this part of the Memoir, to introduce. It was her privilege, during her visits to town, and as the close of life drew on, to wait occasionally on the ministry of the late REV. DAVID FENTON JARMAN, incumbent of Bedford Episcopal Chapel, Bloomsbury. It was just the character of ministration that her soul needed to nourish and strengthen it for its passage over Jordan. Often would she repair to his sanctuary when scarcely able to walk from the carriage to the pew, and when more than once compelled to retire, from faintness, before the service closed, and as frequently has she returned refreshed by, and rejoicing in, the glorious truths that had fallen with so much power from the lips of this honoured servant of Christ. Grateful for the soul-help thus derived, and sympathizing with the impaired health from which he was a constant sufferer, she would occasionally visit his apartment adjoining the chapel, and seek to cheer and strengthen his lone and depressed heart. But not to her only were the labours of Mr. Jarman blest. It pleased God to own his ministry, in the conversion of several members of her family; and this circumstance was well calculated to deepen her affectionate and prayerful interest in this tried minister, and draw yet closer the bond that linked in holy fellowship two kindred spirits destined so soon to meet together before the throne of God and of the Lamb. We venture upon a few extracts of the correspondence which resulted from this hallowed friendship. It is thus she seeks to convey the richest comfort that an earnest, faithful minister of Christ can possibly desire or receive:—

TO THE REV. D. F. JARMAN.

"MY DEAR BROTHER IN JESUS,— Leamington, Dec. 13th.

"You will rejoice, I am sure, to hear that the Lord has made your ministry a blessing to several of my very dear grandchildren, and thus has answered my ten thousand prayers for them. They have sought and found Christ precious to their souls, and are going on their way rejoicing. Thus you see, beloved brother, you are not labouring in vain for the Lord; for, although these dear ones have heard and known the gospel as from infancy, yet the seed has laid dormant until now, and God has blessed your ministry to the enkindling of a flame of holy love to the precious Saviour of sinners in their hearts. I could not refrain from telling you this. Since I saw you I have been very near to the kingdom of glory, but the Lord has detained me here a little longer. Yes, it is but a little while, and we pass away to better things prepared for us, and then you will hear the words, *Well done, good and faithful servant; enter into the joy of your Lord.* God be praised that this is not our rest; better things are prepared for us. He will make amends for all your sorest trials and discomforts. Oh, to be there!

"Many thanks, dear brother, for your kind note of yesterday. How unspeakably sweet is that love which unites the members of the one body—Jesus Himself the Head! *Ye are all one in Christ Jesus.* This love is one of the strongest evidences of our adoption, and one of the most sweet unfoldings of our spiritual life. Christ has but one church, but one spouse—all born of one Spirit, and by that self-same Spirit educating for the place Jesus has gone to prepare. Is not this a blessed thought? I seem to stand upon the margin, ready to pass over; and, standing where I do, can affirm that all is true, gloriously true. Oh, the thought of realizing the whole truth! Dear brother, this life of sickness and suffering is worth ten thousand worlds, for it brings us to live more as helpless children on God, and more readily to realize the world to come. Be of good cheer, and work on; the more you are made to feel your weakness, the more welcome are you to Christ."

"Ever varying are the dealings of our God, but they are all in wisdom and in love. He knows the windings and the wants of our immortal souls, and so fits His dispensations as to accomplish the great work to be carried on there. Oh, it is a great work, for it is to glorify a great King! Had we our way, how should we mar this work; and yet how often are we tempted to dictate to Him who is so skilfully carrying it on! Deeply do I feel for you. You love your work; and yet the Lord, who loves you better than you love yourself, is laying you aside from it. Oh, could we but take a glimpse within the vail, we should see how intent the eye of Jesus was upon the progress of His own mighty work in our souls; and in the midst of the many infirmities of body from which you suffer, you would see that even in that state what great things He was accomplishing in and by you! You are now in the furnace, but Christ is with you. But I know something of the working of the heart, the sighs, the regrets, perhaps the repinings, and the ten thousand drawbacks springing out of the flesh; and Satan making the most of them to cause us to murmur, and vainly to suppose that we could manage better for ourselves. But, beloved, though you know all these things, you will not be offended with an old warrior, who has had a thousand battles with this arch foe, and should have fallen a prey to his devices, had not Jesus interposed His shield, and quenched the fiery darts. 'Does God love me? Is He my reconciled Father? If so, why these afflictions, why these temptations?' Thus is the believer often tempted to reason. Thus have I been tried, and thus too have argued. But now that I am hastening to my happy home, I can look back and testify to you and to others, that *the trial of your faith is much more precious than gold, though it be tried with fire.* Jesus was a tried stone, the apostles were tried men,—as soon as a sinner is born of the Spirit, he enters upon a school of trial, and this is the path to the kingdom."

The following is the last letter she penned to this beloved and afflicted minister of the Lord Jesus, written at the commencement of her final illness, and dated as from the confines of glory.

"My dear brother in Jesus, I am ill, preparing to obey the summons, 'Come up hither.' And oh, how blessed is the prospect! Eternal love! eternal glory! To be ever with the Lord, basking in the sunshine of his blessed countenance! I shall be there to welcome you home. Take courage, dear brother, for it is all true and all glorious. The more I am enabled to realize the mission of Jesus to this lower world, the more my whole soul is filled with joy and hope. *I know the thoughts that I think towards you, saith the Lord! thoughts of peace, and not of evil, to give you an expected end.* Reading this passage to-day filled my heart with a blessed conviction that, both in the Old and in the New Testaments, Jesus was the speaker, and that what He was then He is now. Be of good courage, dear brother; we shall surely see Him and dwell with Him for ever and ever. Amen and Amen."

How soon was this blessed hope realized! A few brief

months of increased suffering intervened, and Mr. Jarman finished his course, and went to join her glorified spirit before the throne. She had preceded him, as she desired, and was there to 'welcome him home.' And now that he is gone, it may not be inappropriate to embody in this work a brief quotation from a letter, the publication of which, while he lived, might have grieved the lowliness of his affectionate spirit. In forwarding her Correspondence, Mr. Jarman thus remarks:—

".... Not only are they highly characteristic of dear Mrs. Winslow's elevation and spirituality of mind, but, being among her last letters, they exhibit her at her very highest stage of Christian attainment and proximity to heaven. They show, too, how she united practical godliness with the blessed visions of her home and her glorified Saviour. Rapture never made her forgetful of her own daily duties, or the human trials and cares of others. She was never exalted above measure by the abundance of the revelation given unto her; but you cannot help observing that she constantly employs, in her letters, these bright visions of Christ which she enjoyed to the enforcement of greater activity and patience in the believer's warfare. To have known a spirit who could pen such words and such truths, is one of the greatest privileges of my life. I feel it has done me good. I trust it has drawn me much nearer to God. I believe it has elevated my faith, and introduced me to clearer views of my rest and of my glorified Saviour. I never shall forget her or her heavenly conversation. In my case, the influence of acquaintance was not the only one she produced on me. Most powerfully did I feel attracted towards her even in our first interview, and before any letters had passed between us. I think, and I believe I may say, that attraction ripened into the deepest regard on both sides; and I cannot read the expressions of love and sympathy in her precious letters, without deeply feeling that I have lost a very dear mother in Israel. Oh, that God's Spirit may so sanctify the regard she felt towards me, that it may daily draw me upwards to her, and may give force and power to her kind and invaluable advice! Oh, that the remembrance of what she was may help to prepare me for beholding, with increased love and closer communion, what she is! I commit the enclosed to your careful keeping. Do not mislay them in the very perplexing work of selecting examples of her correspondence for the memoir, for very precious are her words to me, and the truths they contain. May God bless your effort, and make it very useful.

"Yours, with every expression of regard and sympathy,

"DAVID FENTON JARMAN."

But her work was not yet finished. Gently led back to earth, as from the gates of the celestial city, she was not only to be the recipient of a new joy enkindled by a work of grace in those so dear to her, but she was still to scatter around her the golden fruit of her rich and matured experience as she passed to her eternal home. We glean a few of the riper ears.

"DEAR-BELOVED FRIEND,—   Leamington, July 28.

"How glad was I to see your well-known handwriting, for it was long since I had either heard of, or from you! Think you that all this time I could forget you? Oh no, dear, dear friend; the remembrance of you is as dear as ever; and we shall meet above in our Father's house. And, oh, that meeting! to be always together, and to go no more out for ever. Cheer up, Jesus is there, your Jesus and mine. And, next to Him, I may be ready to bid you welcome. He is risen from the dead, and He will raise our dead bodies, and, vile and troublesome as they now are, yet shall they be renewed like unto His glorious body, and we shall be ever with the Lord. I have been a great sufferer for a long time, and, in my eighty-first year, it is hard to bear. And yet Jesus sweetens every care, and His kindness, oh, how great! He has favoured me at times with such glimpses of the glory that is round about the great white throne, on which He is seated, that it seems as if I could not have much more while in the flesh. Help me to praise Him. . . . . And now, my dear friend, I feel my strength failing, and must lay down my pen. Tender love to your dear sister, and to dear Mr. P——. I cannot tell you how dear you are to me. Can I ever forget you, on earth or in heaven? No, never, never. May the Lord bless you with much of His spirit. One word on the blessed manifestation of Jesus to our longing souls. Let us never be satisfied without this precious recognition. I meet with many professing Christians who appear to know nothing about it, and therefore know not what it is to rejoice with joy unspeakable and full of glory. But I seem as if I could not stop. I will meet you above. I do so love you."

TO MISS A——. ON CLOSENESS OF SPIRITUAL WALK.

"MY DEAR YOUNG FRIEND,— Leamington, June 9.
"Many thanks for your kind letters, which I have been too ill to answer. Through much tender mercy, the Lord has again raised me from a bed of severe suffering; and may this painful dispensation be abundantly sanctified to the soul. There was a needs-be for it all. The Lord does not willingly afflict the children of men, but for their profit. This is designed to be the place where God's children are disciplined for their bright and better home above. And, oh, dear friend, what must be that place which infinite love and power are preparing for us, unworthy though we are! Oh, the boundless love of Jesus, our own Jesus, who lived and suffered, died and rose triumphant from the grave, and is now seated on His throne, ready to receive every poor, needy sinner that comes to Him for salvation, or for grace to help in time of need! This is the precious Friend I would recommend. Remember, you are not coming to a stranger. When you come to Jesus, you come to one who is bone of your bone, and flesh of your flesh. Be not afraid of taking all your concerns to Him, however trifling they may be. He has an ear to listen to the feeblest request you have to make. You cannot go to God, the mighty God, but in Christ, the man Christ Jesus. Now, this is the Jesus whose ear listens to our smallest requests; and when we carry them to Him, we the more honour Him, seeing that we believe what He affirms to be true—*Without me ye can do nothing.* Dear friend, let us all agree to live more decidedly for a glorious eternity. We are here but for a little while and then we pass away. Live more upon Him. Do not walk at a distance. The more you go to Him, the better you will become acquainted with Him, and feel you really cannot do without Him. Hold fast your oneness. You are a partaker of His nature, and He of yours, sin only excepted. Make sure your calling and election. Keep near to your best Friend, who has heaven and earth at His command. A crown of glory awaits the poor sinner that clings to Jesus. Who would not live, and die too, for a crown of glory? Oh, let us entreat all we love to cast in their lot with us, and surely we will do them good! My tender love to your very dear mother and sisters. Ever think of me as one who prays for

your best interests, and hopes to meet you in that better world to which we are so rapidly approaching."

TO MISS M. C——, ON THE ILLNESS OF HER SON O——.

"BELOVED FRIEND,—   Leamington, July 24

"Unite your prayers with ours for dear O——, who is very ill in Paris. We only heard last evening: and the moment he can be moved, he will be with us, if God so wills it. We are greatly tried. Jesus is now my stronghold. He can heal, and He only."

"Monday.—By the last accounts, —— was a shade better. Oh, that it may be abundantly sanctified to us all! An especial prayer-meeting was held on Saturday evening. Major T——, who was there, says he never heard more earnest, fervent petitions offered up as then. My soul is able to rest in Jesus, and my eye is continually up to Him. Oh, the mercy of having such a Friend in Heaven, who is able to do all we call upon Him for! They leave Paris for Dover on Tuesday, where we go to meet them." May the Lord bless you for all the tender expressions of your love to me and mine."

"Wednesday morning.—Oh, what a God we have to do with—so slow to anger, so ready to forgive! Help me to praise and adore His holy name. I have just had a blessed interview with Him whom my soul loveth, and He will do all things well for me and mine. I did not forget you, and I know he heard me, and listened to all I had to say and to ask at His blessed hands. Oh, there is a needs-be for every trial! He loves us too well to grieve us; but we need sharp discipline to cause us to know the wondrous love He bears towards us, and in order to bring us to cling closer to Him. No tongue can tell how much I have enjoyed of nearness and holy manifestation, and endearing intercourse of Jesus, in this late trial. Beloved, we shall have to thank Him through eternity for every sorrow we have had while training us, as it does, for that full enjoyment that awaits us above. This late trial has loosened another peg of my earthly tent, and unfolded to me more of the heart of Him who once on earth was the Man of sorrows and acquainted with grief. And now you will be impatient to hear more of our invalid; but my heart was so brimful of love to *Jesus*—for that's the name I most love— that I was obliged to lodge a little of its overflowing in your loving bosom before I could come down to the creature, however dear. Dear —— is better, and they are preparing to leave Paris for Dover. How thankful I am dear E—— was able to nurse him, and he could not have had a better!"

"*Dover.*—I know you will join your praises with mine to the Giver of all good, for His great mercy in so far restoring ——. Oh, these frail bodies! How all these thing should remind us that God has some better thing in store for His chosen, while He constantly says to us, *Arise, my love, my fair one, and come away.* And yet how closely do we cling to earth and to earthly creatures. But who would not love Him, whose ear bends down to listen to our requests, saying to us, *What is thy petition, and what is thy request? Open thy mouth wide, and I will fill it.* Oh, let us draw largely upon this treasure-house of blessing! The oftener we come, the more welcome. Why does the Lord try us, but that we may try Him, and prove that he is able and willing to do all that He has promised? We often ask with so much unbelief in our hearts, the wonder is that He condescends to hear or answer us at all. We have met with some dear saints here, richly taught of God. The Lord bless you."

TO THE REV. E. C. W——.

"DEAR BROTHER,— Leamington, May 12.
"For this I believe you to be. My reason for addressing you now is to acknowledge the receipt of your kind letter to my dear son, who is just hurrying to town, and has not a moment to write. Your letter was a sweet word of encouragement to him, and I promised to drop you a line of thanks on his behalf. Your note was so like a loving disciple of a loving Saviour. How truly does the Eternal Spirit knit the children of God to each other! This is one of the most incontestable evidences of their sonship. Although I have not seen you or your dear wife, as soon as I read your letter, my heart went out towards you. The Lord Jesus has but one church, and this is composed of all who are born of the Spirit. They may be scattered up and down through the wilderness, but He knows where to find them, and will make no mistakes. As it respects myself, my pilgrimage may soon terminate, but the prospect brightens as it draws near. It is my wish to encourage all that are journeying to heaven, to get much of Christ in their souls while here, not only for their present comfort, but believing that, in the same proportion, they will

enjoy the glory of heaven hereafter. There every vessel will be full; but the soul enlarged while here will contain the same proportion there. There will be no lack felt, for every vessel will be full. God be praised for the hope, the blessed hope of eternal life beyond a poor dying world. I perceive you are one of his tried ones. It is all right. I have waded through seas of sorrow, but *now* bless the Lord for all. I do believe He loves us so that He would not lay the weight of a finger upon us, but for some special good, and to bring us to know Him better. . . . . . May the Lord heal you, dear Christian brother and sister in the Lord. If we do not meet here, we shall above. Let us realize what awaits us. Oh, help me to praise and adore Him who has given us such a hope, such a blessed hope! How we will sing in heaven! Live, dear friends, in anticipation of the glory to come. . . . I often think, if anything will make us ashamed in heaven, it will be the recollection of our unbelieving prayers. Oh, for the spirit of prayer, and for the faith of prayer! This brings heaven down into the soul, and lifts the soul towards heaven. We ought to have to do with Jesus all the day long, and the more we have to do with Him, the more we shall resemble Him."

TO G. M——, ESQ., ON THE LOSS OF HIS CHILD.

" . . . I have only within a few moments heard of your loss. May the Lord comfort your heart, and make this affliction a stepping-stone to lift you nearer to Himself, and a little higher towards your heavenly home. This is not our rest, and the Lord causes us to find it so. The Lord, who loves you better than you love yourself, knows how and when to pour the balm of consolation into your soul, saying to you as He once did to me, 'I have done it.' Oh, to live so with God as to listen to the still small voice of His Spirit, responding, 'Speak, Lord, for thy servant heareth!' This He often does in His providence, and still oftener when interceding with Him in earnest prayer. Sin, dear brother, threw us at an immense distance from God, but Christ came to bring us back again, and the Spirit is given to draw us sensibly near. May He speak to you in this trying dispensation, and comfort you as mortal cannot. It is inexpressibly delightful to know that in all our tribulations we have access to the ear of God, and His heart, too, is ready to answer. Let not the enemy suggest to your sorrowing heart that the Lord does not love you, or He would not chasten you in this way. The Lord does chasten those whom He loves, and for wise and gracious purposes too. Let us lie passive in His hands, leaving ourselves to be dealt with according to His infinite wisdom and love. Nestle in the bosom of Jesus, and wait until He speaks peace to you. Our dear pastor has arrived safe, and is now with Jesus, and ere long we shall join Him there. Let us, then, live more for eternity, and less for this poor dying world. I know you have your cares; but if you would carry them simply to Christ, He would make the rough places plain, and the crooked straight. In every difficulty, go at once to Jesus, before you decide in your own mind, or listen to the dictates of your own heart. Seeing you are shut up to God, let this trying dispensation result in a closer fellowship with Him; for I am persuaded He so loves you, that He would not lay the weight of a feather upon you more than is needful. The love of Jesus passeth all knowledge, here and hereafter. We shall never be able to fathom or come to the end of it. You may know these things better than I; but when unexpected trial comes, Satan endeavours to fill the mind with misgivings and doubts about our interest in our best beloved, our dearest Friend in heaven; and it is for this I venture to send you these few lines."

TO A CHRISTIAN FRIEND.

" . . . . Thus has the Lord tried us; but His goodness has been manifested all through. He has heard and answered prayer again and again; and I have often thought it was worth a few trials to experience the blessedness of having constantly to do with One who is so ready to do all we call upon Him for, so able, so willing, so blessedly true to His own word. We must try the Lord before we can know Him; but first He must try us, before we will ever try Him. In this way our trust and faith in God is increased, and our souls established in the truth. I have written to dear Mrs. W——, and I do hope, and indeed I do believe, she will have to say this was one of the richest and most fruitful seasons of spiritual blessing of her whole life. *The just shall live by faith.* The Lord has now placed her in such a position as to compel her to know more of Himself and more of her own heart, and to put her trust in His faithfulness to the test. I could say to her, if it did not appear unsympathizing, I wish you joy! I did not know, dear sister, of your own illness. I trust you are better and nearly restored by this time. I feel at times feeble, but still travel on, sometimes rejoicing, and sometimes sorrowing over the evil within. I would be holy as God is holy; but, oh, the conflict makes one long to depart and be with Christ, which will be far better; so we think! But the Lord is more glorified by the exercise of our faith while battling with, and overcoming the host of evil without, and with a host yet more formidable within. How easy were it for Him to remove all sin in a moment; but is it not more for His glory that the work of the Holy Spirit should be made more manifest in our souls in subduing, counteracting, and overruling; overruling that for good which would be otherwise dire destruction? And, oh, is it not *that* thing that lays us low and keeps us humble at his feet? I am longing and praying for a gracious revival. Often do I go to the Lord and say, ' What hinders, what restrains the blessing? Why not here? What was done, and is still doing in America, and what has been done in Scotland, why have we not in England? Lord Jesus, send us, in much mercy, a gracious revival in our churches.' Join your prayers to mine for this blessing. The signs of the times are, at present, most significant. Is the Lord on His way? Is *He* coming whom we look for? It is a time for much prayer and looking up. Oh for lamps trimmed and brightly burning, that we may go out to meet the Bridegroom! Soon we shall be in glory. A little while and we pass away, and are for ever with the Lord. He that was dead is *alive*, and because He lives we shall live also. He lives for us, and we shall live together with Him."

TO HER DAUGHTER.

" . . . What a resource is prayer—prayer to that God who loves and hears us always! We do know when we have the ear of God, when prayer is *prayer*. Oh, that these things might be made plain by the inward teaching of the Holy Ghost to those we love! No wonder Paul could say, *Pray without ceasing*. It is my greatest comfort and richest employment. I often have so much to ask, I know not how to stop. The golden sceptre is held out, and my mouth is open to make large demands upon infinite power and love. Oh, this holy intercourse! Oh, that all we love knew more about it! I only intended to write a few lines, but now I feel as if I could fill a sheet. It is a mercy to have the heart right with God—

to have an open heart, no hindrances, to confess and forsake. I think there is nothing on earth like it. No happiness that all the glory of this world could produce is equal to that of a broken heart at the feet of Jesus. It is sweet to creep into the very bosom of Christ, while we feel how utterly worthless and unworthy, yet how welcome we are."

"The poor woman that you are anxious about, dearest E——, continues the same. No hope yet, but still anxious. At evening time it may be light to her soul. I read and prayed; she groaned, and seemed to feel; that was all the encouragement I could get. It is in the Lord's hands. Oh, what a wretched thing to leave the concerns of the soul to the last! . . . The Lord is good and gracious, slow to anger, and of great kindness. May He, dear child, make you useful where you are, and keep you near Himself. Remember, you are not your own, but belong to Christ. You are to do His work, and have no will but His; for be assured of this one thing, His will is best at all times. For the world, I would not be left to have my own way in any one thing. God grant you may feel the same, and much more than your unworthy mother."

"I received your letter, and am thankful you continue well. May the Lord keep you so, in his own tender mercy, and direct your every step, and mine, too. The providence of God is a sure direction to the believer now, as the pillar of cloud and of fire was to the Jews of old; although I must say it requires more caution and prayer, and much reliance on God, to discern His will. We must be *honest* when we ask to be kept from our own way; and if we are honest, the Lord will be our guide; and a safe guide He is to all who trust in Him."

"We had rather a cold ride, but the country to me never appeared more beautiful. When I looked around me, and thought of His goodness in leaving this world (which, for man's sin, is under the curse) with so much of its present grandeur and loveliness, and recollected that the very creatures he was thus mindful of, really *hated* Him in their hearts, and returned Him nothing but evil for His good, I could have wept, and did not wonder at the Prophet's speaking of rivers of tears flowing from his eye as he thought of man's rebellion against God."

". . . What a poor creature I am, within and without! What a mercy to have a blessed hope of a thorough renewing, both of soul and body; and what is still more glorious, both to exist in union through a vast, an interminable existence! Praise be to God for this thrice-blessed hope, worth a million of worlds. Hold fast, dearest E——, your confidence, and grow in grace and in the knowledge of God your Saviour. May the Lord keep you from all evil, and your eye up to Him, that you may call upon Him in every time of need, making known your requests with thanksgiving. The best of blessings rest upon you."

"It is wintry cold. Oh, what a mercy to have the love of Christ keeping the heart warm within! May it never, precious child, be dreary winter with your soul and mine; and the only way to prevent this is to keep close to Jesus, and bask in the sunshine of His blessed countenance. When the heart glows with the love of God, everything looks pleasant and happy. Happiness felt within, makes a pleasant prospect without. When Christ smiles, all is light and lightsome. May the Lord give you health of body and prosperity of soul, and enable you to cast all care upon Him, who has cared, and who ever will care for us. It were heathenism to doubt, when God Himself declares it."

"My beloved child, is it not an inexpressible mercy to be enabled to see God in everything, and in everything connected with us individually? We do not sufficiently realize this grand truth, that we are in Christ, and Christ in us. We acknowledge it with our lips, but do not fully from the heart believe it! and, in consequence, we lose a rich enjoyment, and fall far below our privilege."

TO HER SON O——.

". . . I hope you received my note, informing you that I was better, and again in the drawing-room. So the Lord graciously deals with your poor mother—every now and then giving me a love-admonition to remind me that this is not my rest, but that another and a better is in reserve for me. And if the prospect sometimes appears to the imagination so inviting, 'what must it be to be there!' How great is His goodness, that even here, in this vale of weeping, He should at times afford precious glimpses of the coming glory, and a calm assurance that it is all ready for us, waiting but our full preparedness for its enjoyment. Last evening I joined the family circle, and enjoyed some sweet hymns. I am quite certain that for some special purpose I have been sent back when so near my home, almost in sight of it. A little while, yea, a *little* while, and then ——! May I *then* be better prepared for the glory that shall be revealed to all those who love his appearing. Oh, for stronger, more abiding, increasing faith! I am just expecting Mrs. General F——. Lady L—— and Miss M—— called yesterday, and I was able to see them. I tell you this that your mind may be easy on my account, and that you may enjoy your visit. . . . Tell dear Mrs. R—— she must learn the beautiful piece, 'Jesus wept,' and play it for me when we again meet, if permitted, in this vale of tears. No weeping in heaven! Blessed be God for the hope He has given us beyond this scene of sin and sorrow. Let us arise, and travel on, and 'Forward!' be our countersign. The Christian life is a warfare, a conflict of faith! and, as good soldiers of Christ, we are to fight our way to glory under the banner of the Captain of our Salvation, who, as the Mighty Conqueror, has overcome for Himself, and has paved the way for us to follow. *Is* it not a fight, the flesh, the world, and Satan, all withstanding us at every step? But Jesus stands ready to be a present help in our every time of need. I am increasingly persuaded that it is alone by constant intercourse with Jesus we can attain to anything like progression in the divine life. Oh, preach Jesus more and more, and you will never labour in vain! In this warfare to which I have alluded, there must be no truce, no cessation. Think of a valiant soldier in an enemy's country, and in the heat of the battle, resting on his arms before he has gained the victory! The battle never ceases until we enter heaven *more than conquerors, through Him that hath loved us.* But I am sorry to say, we often meet with what we call in the army, *stragglers*—men who grow weary of following the troops, who linger behind, and sit down by the wayside. These are hinderers to those who are engaged in the heavenly warfare, and are a dishonour to their glorious leader. Stir up such, wherever you meet with them. Only think of the crown of glory, and the '*Well done, good and faithful servant,*' that awaits the overcoming saint, the faithful follower of Christ! This subject seems to grow upon me as I travel on; but I must stop. I meet with so few that seem to be in right-down earnest in this holy, heavenly warfare. And yet what is there on earth that can compare with this? A warfare it is of vast importance. But

I will close. Let me charge you to avoid everything that may injure your head, and thus unfit you for your holy engagements. A true soldier in this eventful battle may be enfeebled by long exhaustion, but his Captain is no hard taskmaster, and provides rest for His weary and wounded ones. But I must conclude, although this subject opens upon me. My love to the dear heads of the R—— family, and to ——. Overlook all vain repetitions in my letters; remember the aged cannot do what they have done. There is more in my heart than it can well contain. Oh, what will heaven be! There, and there only will there be a continuous emptying and filling again of the renewed, sanctified vessel of mercy. Write to me soon."

"P.S. I have written to Forbes to offer my proper congratulations upon the Oxford University honour,* which, through his indefatigable exertions, has been conferred upon him, not forgetting the goodness of God in it."

The following extract should have appeared in an earlier part of the volume, but the sentiments it contains are too valuable and precious to be omitted:—

"Lord Lyndhurst is now able to see, the operation having proved entirely successful. Oh, to give the glory of all our blessings not to man, but to God! How needful is the long-suffering patience of a good and gracious God to us! How slow to anger, how ready to forgive! How *we* ought to love Him, and by our love make up the deficiency of all that is lacking in those that love Him not! How sweet it is to go and tell Him how much we love Him, and then to feel that we love Him because He first loved us! What a stupendous privilege, this holy union and communion with Jesus—God-man Mediator—God-with-us! How blessed it is to open our heart just as it is, with all its coldness, deadness, and sinfulness, to Him, keeping nothing back, but telling Him all! What a relief, under any circumstances, is the mighty privilege! Though the whole world were to turn its back upon us, and clouds gathered thick and darkened around, yet here is a shelter, a pavilion, and a hiding-place, full of comfort and safety, in the very heart of Jesus, God's dear and well-beloved Son.

---

* At the installation of the Earl of Derby, the honorary degree of D.C.L. was conferred upon her son, DR. FORBES WINSLOW.

"Oh, the mercy of mercies to know Him, even were there not an endless hereafter, when we expect to see and enjoy Him through an endless eternity! Shall these eyes see Jesus? Yes, those very eyes shall behold Him whom my soul loveth. Let it be our aim to glorify Him here, and when we fall short, hasten to acknowledge at once. Keep nothing back from Christ. Have no concealments. Let us carry our failures and misdoings, our seen and unseen evil—evil within and fears without—all, *all* at once to Jesus. He has engaged to heal all our diseases, to help all our infirmities, and to give us every possible good for time and for eternity. Oh, do help me to praise Him—help me to love Him! I think if I had ten thousand hearts, I could give them all to Him. Good-bye. Do not go where there is fever, nor expose yourself to the heat of the day, nor overwork yourself. Remember, the body is redeemed as well as the soul, and that both belong to Christ."

CHAPTER XIV.

THE *last* epoch of the Christian's life—*such* a life as these pages have attempted to portray—cannot but be peculiarly interesting and impressive. It were, perhaps, incorrect to speak of it as the most *instructive* part of his history. A prolonged course of unreserved consecration to Christ, the record of which would be but a continuous testimony to the truth of the Bible, the character of God, and the power of the Saviour's grace in upholding and succouring, sanctifying and comforting the believer, must necessarily constitute a volume of instruction, such as the most triumphant departure could scarcely supply. If this be so, of how much greater moment, then, is it that the Christian should be solicitous how he should *live*, rather than forestall, by vain and fruitless speculations, the question how he shall *die!* It is the *life*, and not the death, that supplies the most satisfactory and assured evidence of real conversion. "Tell me not," says the excellent John Newton, "how a man died; rather tell me how he *lived.*" Let but the religion of an individual be a living, practical embodiment of the noble sentiment of Paul, "For me to *live* is Christ," and he need not be unduly anxious about his final change; that change, be it whatever God appoints, must be his gain. It is not always that a life of such transcendant beauty—'the beauty of holiness'—as that which we have sought to delineate, is closed by a departure of such corresponding interest and grandeur. As if to illustrate the importance, and to enforce the lesson of a holy life, as a thing of essential moment, God has sometimes disappointed a too eager and, perhaps, too curious expectation, and has taken home His child, not in a chariot of fire, but of *cloud*. We are now, however, to trace the harmony between an eminently godly life, and a singularly happy death. Indeed, so strangely and beautifully alike were the two, it were difficult to decide which the most became her, and which brought most honour to God—the *dying life* or the *living death*. Both were emphatically—*life in Jesus*.

The reader, as he unfolds the closing leaves of this volume, will not fail to mark, we will not say the growing spirituality of its subject, but the deepening glory into which she was so soon to enter. Every thought and word, every look and action, now indicated the nearness of the soul to a higher, nobler, and more genial state of being. While the 'weary wheels of life' moved slower and slower, the 'deathless principle' within gathered fresh strength, and with uplifted pinions and panting bosom, waited and watched the signal for its flight.* Unconsciously to herself, but visibly to all around her, she grew still more heavenly. And as each day some crumbling fragment of the earthly house gave way, the opening chinks let in upon her soul richer streams of the light and blessedness of the upper world, imparting to her countenance inimitable beauty, and to her conversation an indescribable charm. And now she wearied to be gone. As pines the fond child for its home, as sighs the way-worn traveller for his rest, as longs the storm-tossed voyager for the port, so panted she to depart and be with Christ.

Nothing could now exceed the hallowed, elevating tone of her conversation. Many flocked to her, as much to be instructed by her holy counsels, to be comforted by her heavenly words, and to be encouraged and stimulated by her trustful, cheerful piety, as to watch the growing splendor of her setting sun. All who now heard her testify of God, of Christ, and of heaven, irresistibly felt what a reality was vital religion, how beautiful was gospel holiness, how glorious was a risen Saviour, and how solemnly true, and strangely near, was the eternal world! Turn we now to some of her precious thoughts gathered from her closing remains, and recorded in her journal a short time preceding her last illness.

"*There remaineth, therefore, a rest for the people of God.* Oh, what a rest that will be! Sitting down to rest awhile this aged body, I am reminded of that blessed, eternal rest prepared for both soul and body. Lord, let me even here find THYSELF

---

* " The nearer still she draws to land,
 The more her sacred joys expand;
 With steady helm, and well-bent sail,
 Her anchor drops within the vail :
 Triumphant now she claps her wings,
 And her celestial sonnet sings,
  Glory to God ! "

my sweetest resting-place. Oh, to rest in Thy exceeding great and precious promises—to rest in Thy tender, unchanging love —to rest in Thy Almighty power and Godhead—to rest in Jesus, my own Jesus, who has made Himself over to me as my Saviour, my Redeemer, and Friend, and who has promised never to leave nor forsake me! Then He is here; and while I rest this weary frame, He is present with me. Bless the Lord O my soul!"

"Texts last Sabbath: morning—*Now, our Lord Jesus Christ Himself, and God, even our Father, which hath loved us, and hath given us everlasting consolation and good hope through grace, comfort your hearts, and stablish you in every good word and work.* 2 Thess. ii. 16, 17. Evening—*Thy sun shall no more go down, neither shall thy moon withdraw itself; for the Lord shall be thine everlasting light, and the days of thy mourning shall be ended.* Isaiah lx. 20. These precious portions have been each a word of rich consolation to my soul, drawing forth my heart to the Lord in gratitude and love. Blessed, for ever blessed, be His name for all His great goodness to me and mine. What a God has He been to me, *who hath loved me and given me everlasting consolation and good hope through grace*, no tongue, no, not that of the highest angel in heaven can tell. They know not, nor can they enter into my feelings; nor have they any cognizance of what is passing between a broken heart for sin and a sin-forgiving God. My sins, which are mountains high, are all pardoned, blotted out of the book of God's remembrance by the precious blood of His dear and well-beloved Son. Praise God for His marvellous goodness to me a sinner."

"A most refreshing view of Jesus this morning has filled my heart with love, and joy, and hope—love to Him who has done so much for unworthy me. What shall I render unto Him for all the benefits received at His hands? He draws me sensibly near to Himself, and indulges me with precious views of that glory that will be revealed in me and in all them also who love his appearing."

"My heart within me leapeth,
It cannot be downcast;
In sunshine bright it keepeth
A never-ending feast.

"The sun which, smiling, lights me,
To Jesus Christ alone,

And what to sing invites me,
Is heaven on earth begun?"

"The Lord is most gracious in permitting me so sensibly to approach him, to talk with Him by the way, to lift up upon me the light of his ineffable countenance. I have been pleading with Him to-day to be especially near to me in a dying hour; to come with the pale messenger, and let me see the uplifting of his face, irradiated with beams of love, as I tread that dark valley. Oh, to feel Jesus with me then, applying His precious blood to my conscience, speaking pardon, peace, love, full and complete! May I be enabled to triumph over my last enemy, and exclaim, *O Death, where is thy sting? O Grave, where is thy victory?* Bonar remarks, 'Our life throughout is one unceasing battle with death, until, for a season, death conquers us, and we fall beneath his power; but the prey shall be taken from the mighty, and his victim rescued for ever. The trumpet shall sound, and the dead shall arise triumphant over death, hell, and the grave.'"

"What a blessing it is to have such a Friend to go to as Jesus, with all our difficulties, small and great, transferring them to His hands who is infinite in wisdom and in power, and will do all things well. Is not this a mercy worth recording in letters of gold, to be written in the deep recesses of every believing heart? May I have stronger faith and deeper views of truth. Lord, impart to me more of Thyself. Fill this heart with Thy love, engrave Thine image there, and let me not lose sight of Thee for one small moment."

"Thou Lamb of God, Thou Prince of Peace!
For Thee my thirsty soul doth pine;
My longing heart implores Thy grace,
Oh, make me in Thy likeness shine.

"With guileless, ever-humble mind,
Thy will in all things may I see;
In love be every wish resign'd,
And hallow'd my whole heart to Thee.

"Close by thy side still may I keep,
Howe'er life's various currents flow;
With steadfast eye mark every step,
And follow Thee where'er Thou go."

"How can I ever recount the wonders of His love! Wondrous are, and ever have been, all His doings with me. His whole heart is love, and nothing but love; nor will eternity see its end. Thou beloved of my soul, tell, oh, tell me, how I can show forth Thy praise, and best speak of Thy wondrous goodness to me, the chief of sinners. I think of what Thou didst suffer for me—Thy night of watching, Thy day of grief, the trial, the cruel mockings, the thorny crown, the breaking heart—all, all for me, my sins, my cruel sins, charged to Thy account. Jesus, precious Jesus, put such a heart within me as shall never let me forget for one moment what it cost Thee to save my soul. Hell would have been my portion, hadst thou not died that I might live for ever. And now, what returns! Often the worst. Often have I forgotten Thee, though Thou hast never once lost sight of me. Dear Jesus, give me a heart like Thine own. I cannot be satisfied without one cast in Thy mould, reflecting Thy own likeness. How precious Thou art to me, language fails to express. I cannot even tell Thee. I can but weep out my love at Thy feet, and there would I lie to all eternity. When, dear Lord, shall I see Thee face to face? Prepare me for the last struggle. And should the enemy come in like a flood, arraying my sins before me, oh, manifest Thyself then, and fill the gloomy valley with the brightness of Thy presence! When heart and flesh are failing, leave me not. Be gracious, be merciful, and say to my panting spirit, *It is I, be not afraid;* and let me leave a testimony behind to Thy unceasing faithfulness. Oh, blessed prospect of soon being with Thee whom my soul loveth! How my heart bounds at the thought. And shall I behold that dear, that blessed face without a veil, that has so often beamed upon me its ineffable love and sympathy? Lord, I love Thee with a love so ardent, all language fails me."

"Have been much impressed with some remarks on the sight of the dying. 'The late —— remarked, when he was dying, "Mother, I can see a great distance." Doubtless this is the experience, beautifully expressed, by every one who comes with a chastened faith to a calm deathbed. In his progress through ordinary life, the vapors that float in his mental atmosphere render the vision imperfect, and he cannot see afar off; but as he draws near eternity, the air grows purer, the light brighter, the vision clearer, and serenity pervades the whole being; the vista of futurity opens to the eyes of the soul; he beholds the gate of heaven, and the river of life, its glad waters kissing the footstool of the throne of God; the glories of the new world grow brighter upon him; with Stephen, he beholds Jesus at the right hand of the Father; and as he dwells with rapture on these entrancing sights, the earth and all its scenery grows dim about him, and like Elisha's servant at the gate of Damascus, he is instantly environed with troops of angels who come to take him up over the everlasting hills in the chariot of the Lord of Hosts.' Oh, that this might be my experience! Then, when my eyes are closing in death, may I have these refreshing, far-seeing views of Jesus, my best, my dearest Friend."

"*Blessed be the Lord, my strength, which teacheth my hands to war, and my fingers to fight; my goodness and my fortress, my high tower, my shield, and He in whom I trust.* Such is God, my God, to his unworthy handmaid. Without Him, life were an aching void, earth a wilderness of woe and sorrow. He it is who maketh my heart glad, and in Him I confide. And if thus He can transform this wilderness into a little heaven, making it radiant with His presence, what must heaven itself be!"

"*I will sing of Thy power; yea, I will sing aloud of Thy mercy in the morning; for Thou hast been my defence and refuge in the day of my trouble. Unto Thee, O my strength, will I sing; for God is my defence and the God of my mercy.* Psa. lix. 16, 17. This has God been to me throughout my eventful pilgrimage; and so is he now that that pilgrimage is drawing to its close. How can I praise Him as my heart desires? Language fails me, and thought is too big for utterance. Vast as eternity are His mercies, infinite His perfections, and wonderful all His ways. What will eternity disclose to my astonished sight, my eyes then unveiled to see what now I understand not! O God my Lord, draw me sensibly nearer to Thyself. Reveal to me Thy hidden love, and conform me closer to Thy image. My soul longeth to behold Thee, to see Thy face unveiled. Surely I shall know Thee; for have I not, even in this vale of tears, been favoured with precious glimpses of Thy countenance, radiant with love and sympathy? When trouble has threatened to overwhelm me, then Thou hast condescended to speak comfortable words to Thy sorrowing child. May I never forget it! May I be humbled, even to the dust, for my base returns; for how often, when fresh trouble has arisen, I have so little remembered past deliverances. Oh, the baseness of man; the goodness of God!"

"Religion should be the whole business of a man's life. Nothing is of such vast, such paramount importance. And is not the thought appalling, that it is one of the *last* things the generality of men think of, if left to themselves? Then how ought we to pray for and exhort sinners to repent and turn to God! Should we not thus reason with them—'You have departed from God: repent and believe the Gospel; for why will ye die?' This should be our expostulation with every unconverted person we meet. May the Lord make us faithful and diligent! God be praised for the boundless love treasured up in Jesus for every poor sinner that seeks it with the whole heart. Let us who believe, pray, and exhort, and employ every opportunity to arouse, to instruct, and win all to Christ, who has life, yea, eternal life, to give to all who seek it sincerely and earnestly, even with the whole heart."

"When I go hence, shall not my ten thousands of prayers be answered in the salvation of my seed and of my seed's seed to the latest generation? Is he not a God bound by His own word to answer prayer? and did He not promise me in the days of my deep sorrow, 'I will be a Father to thy fatherless?' And oh, how blessedly, in spite of all my baseness and unworthiness, has He fulfilled that promise? *As for Me, this is my covenant with thee, saith the Lord. My Spirit that is upon thee, and my words which I have put in thy mouth, shall not depart out of thy mouth, nor out of the mouth of thy seed, nor out of the mouth of thy seed's seed saith the Lord, from henceforth and for ever.* Isa. lix. 21. May I not take this promise to myself?"

"Confined to my bed. All my thinkings, and all my doings, are now with God. I have to deal most clearly with God in Jesus now. He is all in all to me. I feel a blessed nearness to Jesus, to heaven. My soul holds converse with Him, and sweet I find it to lie as a helpless infant at His feet; yea, passive in his loving hands, knowing no will but His. Holy and distinguished is the privilege of talking with Him as a man talketh with his friend, without restraint or concealment. What a mercy, thus to unburden the whole heart—the tried and weary, the tempted and sorrowful heart—tried by sin, tried by Satan, tried by those you love! What a mercy to have a loving bosom to flee to, one truly loving heart to confide in, which responds to the faintest breathing of the Spirit. Precious Jesus, how inexpressibly dear art Thou to me at this moment! Keep sensibly near to me. Lift up upon me thy heavenly countenance, for it is sweeter, dearer, better than life."

"Oh, the abounding, superabounding mercies of my God and Father, my reconciled Father, to my soul! How amply has He met my every exigence, and cared for my necessities, body, soul, and spirit, and manifests Himself to me in this pleasant, quiet room. Precious Jesus, Thou hast put love in the hearts of all, who are so tender, kind and loving to Thine aged one; bearing with her many infirmities, and helping me patiently to endure my weakness. Blessed be Thy name for placing me beneath this roof to breathe out my last moments on earth here, until I exchange earth for heaven with dear —— to watch over me, and finally close my eyes, when I shall re-open them in glory. Oh, to be there! Oh, to see Jesus face to face! To behold Him whom my soul loveth, and be with Him for ever! But a little while, and I am there."

"Beyond the smiling, and the weeping,
I shall be soon.
Beyond the waking, and the sleeping,
Beyond the sowing, and the reaping,
I shall be soon.
Love, rest, and home,
Sweet hope!
Lord, tarry not, but come!

"Beyond the blooming, and the fading,
I shall be soon.
Beyond the shining, and the shading,
Beyond the hoping, and the dreading.
I shall be soon.
Love, rest, and home,
Sweet hope!
Lord, tarry not, but come!

"Beyond the rising, and the setting,
I shall be soon.
Beyond the soothing, and the fretting,
Beyond remembering, and forgetting,
I shall soon be.
Love, rest, and home,
Sweet hope!
Lord, tarry not, but come!

"Beyond the gathering, and the strowing,
I shall be soon.
Beyond the ebbing, and the flowing,
Beyond the coming, and the going,

>   I shall be soon.
>   Love, rest, and home,
>   Sweet hope!
>   Lord, tarry not, but come!
>
> "Beyond the parting, and the meeting,
>   I shall be soon.
>   Beyond the farewell, and the greeting,
>   Hearts fainting now, and now high beating,
>   I shall be soon.
>   Love, rest, and home,
>   Sweet hope!
>   Lord, tarry not, but come!
>
> "Beyond the frost-chain, and the fever,
>   I shall be soon.
>   Beyond the rock-waste and the river,
>   Beyond the ever, and the never,
>   I shall be soon.
>   Love, rest, and home,
>   Sweet hope!
>   Lord, tarry not, but come!"

"There are periods in one's eventful history when one sees, and yet does not see, hears, and yet does not hear. Thus, when I see and hear what I would not, and cannot remedy, I go to Jesus and disclose my impotence to Him, beseeching Him to undertake. Oh, the unspeakable privilege of having such a resort, a resort so accessible to a poor, weary, oft-tried pilgrim, moving on through a wilderness thronged with the thorn and the briar, and often echoing with the howlings of that roaring lion who seeks to devour, and yet cannot touch the saints, since the *Lion of the tribe of Judah* has chained him fast. How true that it is a life of faith the Christian has to live while passing to his crown of glory! Many are the trials, disappointments, and vexations he is to meet with by the way; but these are things which keep the life of faith in vigorous exercise, work the soul's best interest, and glorify God. Whatever drives or allures us to Jesus is a blessing. The great welfare of the soul is the concern of heaven. All the heavenly host are deeply interested and absorbed in the salvation of Christ's little flock, whom the Shepherd that died for them is conducting to the fold above. Oh, to be ever looking forward to what is to come!"

"How sweet and sacred is broken-hearted communion with Jesus, God's dear Son, crucified for our sins, and risen again for our justification! It is a mercy of mercies to be permitted to draw near to Him with an open, confiding, though a contrite heart—telling him all one feels, and desires, and fears. What an inestimable privilege to have such a friend always so near! We have not to ascend into heaven, nor have we to descend into the deep, to seek for Him; for He always is near, one with us, one in us, yea, a part of ourselves. How constantly is the Lord seeking to withdraw us from the arm of flesh, to a more simple and unbounded confidence in Himself! To whom shall we look? He answers, LOOK UNTO ME, *and be ye saved, all the ends of the earth; for I am God, and there is none else.* Blessed be God, even my God, for every precious word written in that Book of Books—the BIBLE. Oh, that it may be unceasingly precious to my soul. It is good for me to have been tried, though it scarcely can be called a trial, since so sweetly and blessedly has the Lord dealt with me in it. When I can call Jesus mine (as I can at this moment,) trials are no trials. Yes, Jesus is mine, He is sensibly near; and all I need and all I desire is in Him, in comparison of whom all the glory, and honour, and riches of the world are as dross. How sweetly and confidingly can I rest in His faithfulness and love. He lives, and I shall live, because my life is bound up with His life. BLESSED REALITY! Lord, my time now is short; I would fain be useful in encouraging others to come to Thee, thou Fountain, yea, thou Ocean of living waters, that they, too, may draw supplies from Thine infinite, inexhaustible fulness. Oh, the mightiness of the privilege of having, not the hearkening ear only, but the loving heart of God towards and upon us! And if He has set His heart upon us, making us His people, redeeming us from all evil, past, present, and to come, should we not set our hearts upon Him, and upon Him only and confidently? Lord, here is my heart, my poor heart; take it just as it is, and make it all that Thou wouldst have it to be; cast it into Thy mould, and let it receive and reflect Thine image, Thou Son of God, thou inexpressibly, precious Jesus, thou Saviour of sinners, thou Redeemer of my never-dying soul!"

"Oh, that the Lord would descend, and give us a gracious revival in our souls, and in the congregation. We need an especial outpouring of the Holy Spirit. Lord, send down gracious answers to our prayers. Come Thou among us, and do us good; for none but Thyself can do us good. Follow the letter that I have written to Lord —— with Thy blessing. Direct in all our poor concerns. Make us upright before Thee.

Let Thy fear rule, and Thy love constrain us to do Thy will. Search all our hearts, and cast out that which is wrong in Thy sight. May we live upon Thee, and for Thee, and rejoice and be glad that Thou seest us always, desiring to have no concealments from Thee, our best and dearest Friend. Be with Thine handmaid throughout this day, directing in all that lies before her, giving wisdom and grace, a right judgment and an upright heart, and withholding not thy presence. Amen and amen."

"Nothing in my hands I bring,
Yet all things from thy hand receive."

"The apostle, speaking of those who separated themselves from the true Church of Christ, says, *They went out from us, but they were not of us; for if they had been of us, they would no doubt have continued with us! but they went out that they might be manifest that they were not all of us.* 1 John ii. 19. It strikes me, these are the real dissentients, those who separate themselves from the church of God. We are evidently drawing near the time which will mark the consummation of all things. The light of the glorious gospel of the blessed God will shine brighter and brighter, and then will be more clearly revealed—only to be entirely and for ever effaced—the dark spots that now obscure the beauty of the Lord's church; and then will she, freed from all that is now dishonouring to her Head, stand forth a *glorious church*, complete in all her loveliness, in the presence of a holy God. Oh, then, let us, who really and truly are the Lord's, unite together in bands of Christian love to *contend earnestly for the faith once delivered to the saints*, and aim in all things to return to the beautiful simplicity of Christ. Lord, pour out Thy Spirit upon Thy people, enlightening, healing, and sanctifying; and hasten the time when, coming in all Thy glory, the glory of the Father and of the holy angels, Thou wilt claim Thy bride, Thy one church, and present her *without spot, or wrinkle, or any such thing*.

"*Give ear to my prayer, O God; and hide not Thyself from my supplications.* Oh, that my children might live before Thee! This is my daily prayer, that to the latest generation they may be a seed to serve Thee. O Lord, incline Thine ear to my request, and deny me not, for Jesus' sake. I am Thine, and Thou art mine. Jesus has said it, and I believe it. God be praised for His wondrous goodness to me, as poor and needy a sinner as ever lived; and yet I shall live for ever, and rejoice in God my Saviour through an endless eternity."

"When Christians meet together, do they not too much talk *about* religion, preachers and sermons? I cannot but think, that if they communed less about religion, and more of Jesus, it would give a higher tone of spirituality to their conversation, and prove more refreshing to the soul. He would then oftener draw near, and make Himself one in their midst, and talk with them by the way."

"Jesus, Thou art unspeakably precious to my soul. How precious, Thou knowest. Do not I love Thee? Search my heart, for Thou canst read its every thought and feeling, and see if I do love Thee. Blessed by Thy name for Thy love to worthless me. I love Thee, because Thou first loved me. *I am He that liveth and was dead, and, behold I am alive for evermore.*"

> "'Tis past - the dark and dreary night,
> And, Lord, we hail Thee now,
> Our morning star, without a cloud
> Of sadness on thy brow.
>
> "Thy path on earth, the cross, the grave,
> Thy sorrows, all are o'er;
> And, O sweet thought! Thine eyes shall weep,
> Thy heart shall break, no more.
>
> "Deep were those sorrows; deeper still
> The love that brought thee low—
> That bade the stream of life from Thee,
> A lifeless victim, flow.
>
> "The soldier, as he pierced Thee, proved
> Man's hatred, Lord, to Thee;
> While in the blood that stain'd the spear,
> Love, only love, we see."

"Heaven in prospect is very sweet to me. My happiest moments are spent in its contemplation. My soul holds unseen communion with Christ and with the pure spirits around the throne, now in the full enjoyment of His unveiled beauties. I think I can behold their joy, and seem at times to be so near that but a transparent vail separates me from them, and that with one step I am there. I delight to contemplate some near and dear to me (dearer and nearer now than ever,) who have recently passed away from a world of sin and sorrow. Happy spirits! ye are safe at last. Ye have outrun me in the race, have reached the goal, and are at home before me."

"BELOVED ONES, WHOM I HOPE THROUGH INFINITE
MERCY, TO MEET IN HEAVEN,—

"First and chiefest, my own most precious Redeemer, enthroned in all His glory, His countenance radiant with ineffable love, and a welcome beaming from every feature. So shall I behold Him who loved me with an everlasting love, and landed me at last in the kingdom of glory. Then I shall meet my beloved husband, his little faith at the eleventh hour saving him for ever. Then my eyes will be fixed upon my precious mother, saying to me, as she welcomes me home, 'Here, my child, the weary find eternal rest.' And then dear H——, whose simple faith, more costly than the most splendid gifts, placed him beyond the reach of life's stormy winds. And then will come dear S—— and dear F——, whose sincere, childlike confidence in Jesus gave them the victory, and lodged them safely within His arms. There, too, shall I greet many whom I knew and loved below. Dear Mr. Evans and his wife, dear Mr. Whitmore, and a host of others, all encircling the throne, and basking in the full sunshine of the Redeemer's countenance, while I shall lie prostrate at His feet in wondering joy and adoring love at the matchless grace that brought *me* there. Hallelujah! hallelujah! praise, endless praise to God!"

With indescribable solemnity and tenderness of feeling, we thus have transcribed the *last* record of her journal. It was with a trembling hand we lifted the vail that disclosed to other eyes the most sacred thoughts and feelings of her soul. We drop the vail—for we can disclose no more! Bearing us through many years of daily walk with God, to the threshold of heaven, she disappears within its unapproachable glory, and the last notes we catch from her closing lips are, 'Praise, endless PRAISE to God! And then she laid aside her harp below, because she could rouse it to no sweeter, loftier strain.

"Death darken'd her eye, and folded her wings,
And the sweetest note is the *last* that she sings."

It was in the early part of the year 1854, that the indications of a gradual decay of nature became apparent. To those who watched with wakeful eye each new symptom of waning power, the evidences were painfully unmistakable that she was nearing her long desired haven. She still, however, persisted in attending the public means of grace—for she 'loved the habitation of God's house, and the place where His honour dwelt'—often when the state of the weather and her own-felt weakness might have pleaded her exemption. Her *last* service in the sanctuary of God below, was on Lord's-day morning, July 30th. The subject of the discourse could scarcely have been more in harmony with the affecting occasion, had the sad truth been known, that her next mingling with the great congregation would be in the New Jersualem above, of which the Lord God Almighty and the Lamb are the temple. The text was selected from the tenth chapter of John's gospel, and the first clause of the twenty-eighth verse— "I GIVE UNTO THEM ETERNAL LIFE." The varied aspects of the theme,—the glorious truths which it developed, the bright visions of future blessedness which it necessarily brought before the mind, were well calculated to afford nourishment for passing over Jordan. And so she acknowledged. Returning from this her final public service on earth, she expressed in affecting language the refreshment her spirit had experienced, and gave vent to her full heart of thanksgiving and praise for the glorious gospel of Christ, and for the assured hope of eternal life which it revealed.

As the sea air—her native air—always acted upon her constitution like a charm, it was hoped that a few weeks' sojourn at Brighton would prove a restorative. It failed, however, to realize the hope cherished; and finding her powers rapidly failing, she expressed an earnest desire to return to her home. Most grateful was she to find herself once more in her own quiet chamber, which had been to her so often, as she expressed it, 'a Bethel to her soul,' the very walls of which might be said

> The quiet chamber where the Christian sleeps,
> And where, from year to year, he prays and weeps;
> Whence, in the midnight watch, his thoughts arise
> To those bright mansions where his treasure lies;
> How near it is to all his faith can see!
> How short and peaceful may the passage be!
> One beating pulse—one feeble struggle o'er,
> May open wide the everlasting door.
> Yes, for that bliss unspeakable, unseen,
> Is ready, and the vail of flesh between
> A gentle sigh may rend—and then display
> The broad, full splendour of an endless day.
> This bright conviction elevates his mind,
> He presses forward, leaving all behind.
> Thus from the throne the tyrant foe is hurl'd,—
> This is the faith that overcomes the world."--JANE TAYLOR.

to have been tinted with her prayers.* She was not, however, entirely confined to her room. Until within a few weeks of her translation—for such we must designate her departure—she was enabled, occasionally, to join the family circle, unite in its devotions, and listen to some of her favourite hymns upon the piano, often affected to tears while they were sung. During intervals of her illness, supported in bed, she still employed her pen in brief, holy exhortations, a few quotations from which are subjoined.

". . . Oh, to live for eternity! To live to-day, as if to-morrow we should be there. Eternity! eternity! Oh, solemn thought! The eye, the all-searching eye of God is upon us at this moment. Let us, then, dear brother, act for eternity. May the constraining love of Christ—the eternal love of the Holy Ghost, rest upon you, keep, direct, and bless you!"

In a solemn entreaty to an unconverted individual, her love of souls,—the ruling passion of her life,—never appeared more earnest.

". . . And are these things so, dear friend? Yes, they are. Jesus Christ is risen indeed, and has gone up on high, and has opened the kingdom of heaven to all believers. Oh, then, why not live? Jesus stands ready to receive, is prepared to welcome you. He will cast none out who repair to Him for help and safety. Oh, I could stand upon the housetop, and cry aloud, Come to Jesus—come now—come at once. He is all-sufficient to save, and is as willing as He is able. In a little while, and whether rich or poor, high or low, learned or unlearned, *one thing* will be of infinite moment—your calling and election made sure to you. Lose no time in this great, this greatest of all great transactions—the salvation of your soul. Delay not, lest the enemy take possession of you, and you are lost for ever. *Why will ye die?*"

A temporary reviving of her strength elicited in a brief note to a friend some grateful, holy thoughts.

"Through the unchanging mercies of a good and gracious God, I am yet spared a little longer in this vale of tears. My education for a crown of glory is not yet complete. When it is, I shall be called to behold Him whom my soul loveth, and go no more out for ever. O eternity! eternity! An endless life of never-ceasing glory awaits the feeblest follower of that same Jesus, who suffered, bled, and died on Calvary, and who now, in that very same body (though glorified), is enthroned, prepared to welcome home the feeblest of his little flock. Oh, to live, while here, in close intercourse with Him! This is our mighty privilege. Do not let us, dear friend, lose sight of Jesus. Daily intercourse will bring us more to partake of His lovely likeness. I can write no more, my strength fails. Friends so kind—children so tender—a little while, and I shall be with those above, who are waiting to bid me welcome. Realize more and more your glorious inheritance, and covet not the poor trifles of time and sense."

The following touching and solemn counsels are supposed to be nearly the *last* sacred words her pen ever traced. They were written in acknowledgment of a kind note of affectionate sympathy addressed to her a few weeks before her departure:—

TO MISS L—— M—— T——.

"DEAR YOUNG FRIEND,—

"I am sorry to have let your kind letter remain so long unanswered; and also that I am thoroughly unable to say all that is in my heart to say. Young travellers to the glorious kingdom need often a little counsel from those who have waded through trials and tribulations, and have had many hard lessons to learn, preparatory to the full enjoyment of the coming glory. Oh, prepare to meet your God! A little while, and we pass away—all is uncertain. Oh, to be *quite* ready! The enemy is ever on the alert to entangle the young Christian, and draw him into sin. Sin darkens the eye, and hardens the heart. Keep close to Jesus. Oh, the compassion that is in His heart! Never more welcome than when we come with an open heart to tell Him all our failures, all our sins—sins of omission and sins of commission. Always welcome to Jesus—not a feature, not a look in that blessed face to grieve us. 'Oh, how He loves!' Keep close to Jesus. Carry all your little things to Him, as well as greater matters. He will bow His ear, and listen to all that you have to say. Let your walk and conversation be such as to commend Him to all you meet with. *Be ye holy, for I am holy.* Oh, dear young friend, I have been very ill; my happy home almost in sight! It looks lovely—oh, how lovely! Make Jesus your *chief* FRIEND, and look more to the things that are not seen and eternal. I can write no more, sitting in bed supported by pillows. My Christian love, to your worthy father. Oh, may I meet you in heaven! Make sure of heaven. You may make many mistakes as it respects this poor world, but I beseech you, make no mistake as it respects a *vast eternity.*"

An unfinished note, inscribed to one of her sons, was found amongst her last records. Almost too sacred for publicity, and yet too characteristic to be suppressed, we venture to subjoin it. After referring to her deep maternal affection, she proceeds: "This love emanates from the love, the pure, holy love of God's dear Son, shed abroad in my heart. I know you will go forth and preach Jesus Christ to poor sinners. I believe He will make you a blessing. God grant it! When I am gone home, may you live long to do the will of the Lord, and may I be one of the first to bid you welcome, when your work is finished. I feel almost too ill to write, and must lay this by."

It was but within a short period of her happy release that all hope of prolonging on earth a life so holy and precious, yielded to the agonizing conviction that she would soon leave us. The conflict between the desire for her full enjoyment of the heaven for which she longed, and the affection that would still detain her here, was painfully severe; nor was it until a few moments before the last fetter was dissolved, that we could find it in our hearts to comply with her often-made request, and ask of God to release her from her extreme suffering, and take her to Himself.* Her chamber was now literally the gate of heaven. A visitor to that privileged spot might have supposed himself in communion with a being standing within the precincts of glory. So entirely abstracted were now all her thoughts from time, and so concentrated were they upon eternal things—so filled was she with the Holy Ghost—so glowing with the love of Christ—so spiritual her conversation, and so tender and affecting her expressions of love to all around her, nothing could equal the tenderness and unearthliness of the scene. It pleased God that her bodily suffering should at times be severe, but the unimpaired vigour, to the last, of her mental faculties was graciously vouchsafed. During the few months of her last illness, as might be supposed, many holy and precious observations fell from her lips, some of which

---

* " Me, let the tender office long engage,
  To rock the cradle of declining age;
  With lenient acts relieve a mother's breath,
  Make languor smile, and smoothe the bed of death;
  Explore the thought, explain the asking eye,
  And keep awhile one parent from the sky."
  POPE ON OLD AGE.

were noted down at the time, but many others, it is to be regretted, were not preserved. We present them rather in a fragmentary and detached form, than interwoven with the narrative of the closing scene :—

"I am so happy—I cannot tell you how happy I am! Not a ruffle, not a cloud."

"Oh, how graciously the Lord is taking down the tent, pin by pin. What an eventful life mine has been! I have lived much in camp, and have seen the tents struck, and the regiment move off. Such is life. Jesus is all to my soul. Oh, how I realize His presence! I have a full view of Him at this moment. Heaven is a reality. We mystify heaven; it is a *place*. I am going to my family, and I shall see those whom I ought to love as my family. Dear Mr. E——, and a countless throng of others, as dear to me as my own loved family—or, who ought to be, for they have been purchased by the precious blood of Jesus."

"I wonder if we shall not go over our eventful lives in heaven? I think we shall."

"I wish you to keep my poor wandering mind fixed upon that one blessed truth—Christ's glorious *resurrection;* for if Christ rose again and is alive, I shall certainly rise and live with Him for ever."

Portions of the 15th chapter of the First Epistle to the Corinthians were frequently read to her, together with much that fell from our Lord on the subject of the Resurrection.

"I shall enter heaven a poor sinner saved by grace. I seem to have done nothing for the Lord, who has done so much for me." On being reminded that she had been a faithful parent to her children, and had also been a succorer to many in affliction, she replied :—" Ah! faithless, faithless have I been to my trust.

"'Nothing in my hand I bring,
Simply to Thy cross I cling.'"

"I think many Christians dishonour Christ by refusing to obey Him. Oh, keep close to Jesus, and neglect none of His commandments. Whatever your hands find to do, do it with all your might."

"Shall soon be with Jesus—shall see Him face to face. Oh, glorious prospect! Who would not be a Christian?"

To her daughter she said :—

"Go and tell Jesus all your sorrows; keep back nothing

from Him. You will soon be an orphan, but remember, you are Christ's orphan, and will be His especial care. When your father and your mother forsake you, then the Lord will take you up. When you feel desolate, remember that Jesus lives, and you cannot grieve alone, for He dwells within you. Oh, how have I, throughout my pilgrimage, proved the Lord, and ever found Him faithful to his promises! He has never failed me in any one thing, giving me more than He promised, and far more than I had asked. I asked Him to restore you to health, that you might comfort me in my old age, and attend me in my dying hours. What should I have done now, if He had not answered me? I am such a poor dependent creature, I cannot think for myself. When you come to your last sickness, I trust and pray that the Lord will raise you up one who will be as tender a nurse to you as you have been to me. May Jesus make all your bed in your sickness. He is the best friend to trust; He changes not. Oh, how full His heart is of love, I cannot express to you! And if I had millions of tongues, I could not tell you how precious He is at this moment to my soul. I feel His sensible presence. He is near to me; *so near*, that I feel as if I could embrace Him."

"What a glorious prospect I have in view! Who can picture it? No tongue can tell how I love Jesus; not because it is my duty to love Him, but because I cannot help loving Him. He is the chiefest among ten thousand, and the One altogether lovely."

"This is Wednesday evening (the weekly lecture). Oh, may the Holy Ghost rest upon the people! How have I prayed for the church. Lord, pour out Thy Spirit upon that little flock, and upon ——, its under-shepherd."

"Talk to me of the glorious Resurrection; I wish my mind stayed upon that fact." Upon being reminded of the transporting view Stephen had of glory, seeing Jesus standing as if rising to welcome His first martyr, she replied, "Beautiful! beautiful! and you will perhaps say, 'Mamma thinks herself of much importance,' when I say that I believe Jesus will stand to receive me, even me. I am the chief of sinners, but am dear, very dear to the heart of Jesus, who shed His blood to save me, even me, as if there were not another soul to be saved." In this elevated frame she continued several days, frequently observing, that "as she neared eternity, the **atmosphere of heaven became brighter and brighter.**"

That the enemy should not allow her to pass away unchallenged to a final conflict, is not surprising; but it was permitted by Him who loved her, only to render his defeat the more signal, and her own victory the more complete. All one long night she battled with the foe, and when morning dawned she exclaimed:—

"Oh, pray for me! pray for me! I am under a cloud. Oh, what a night of conflict I have passed!—a conflict with death, hell, and the grave. The enemy would conquer me, if he could." She was reminded that all these were conquered foes, and that Jesus had promised that no one should pluck His people out of His hands. She replied, "True, true; but Jesus prayed, did He not?" The words were repeated, "Oh, my Father, if it be possible, let this cup pass away." She answered, "Oh, then, is it any wonder that if the incarnate God should thus pray, I should feel the need of prayer? It is one thing to talk of death; it is quite another thing when it becomes a reality to grapple with it. It is an easy thing to speak of the war in the East—perhaps to plan an attack upon the enemy; but it is quite a different thing to be in the heat of the conflict, the mighty foe contending with you foot by foot. Some go out of the world without a fear, but they know not and feel not the magnitude of sin. To have one's sins all in review before the mind's eye, and eternity in view—*this* is a reality, and it needs the TRINITY to comfort and support the sinking soul." She then referred to Bunyan's Christian passing over the river, and said, "How long, Lord, wilt Thou keep me in the valley of the shadow of death? Why are His chariot-wheels so long in coming?" Various passages of Scripture were read, which appeared to afford her much consolation; to which she responded, "The Lord will comfort me through His truth."

It was delightful to hear her exclaim soon after:—

"The gloom has all passed, and I have a full view of the glory that awaits me. I shall soon see all the dear ones that have gone before me. Dear F——! I shall never forget, when visiting her grave, the words that came to me as with an audible voice: *She is not here, she is risen.* You were (addressing her daughter) a great blessing to her, and you have been equally so to me. The Lord will take care of you. Thousands, oh, thousands of times have I committed you to His keeping." On her asking her daughter if there was anything she could do for her, before the Lord took her, it was replied, only that she would pray that grace might be given to follow her, as she had followed Jesus. She answered, "No, not as I have followed Jesus; for I have come so far short of His example. But I will pray that you may follow Jesus *wholly.*"

On being asked by her daughter, on Lord's-day evening, if she felt able to spare her just to go and partake of the communion, she replied, "By all means; and may Jesus, our Head, meet you there, and speak comfortably to all His dear saints. I shall not partake of it again until I drink of the new wine with Jesus in our Father's kingdom. There we shall sit down together at the marriage-supper of the Lamb."

"This night is long and weary. Come and let us talk together of the better land, then the time will pass sweetly. Oh, how often has Jesus comforted us when cast down, upheld us when ready to give up our hope! And when trouble came, how often has He spoken sweet peace, and delivered us out of it unhurt. Oh, to see Him in all His unvailed glory, and then to turn and behold the many we have loved in the flesh around the throne, shining bright and lovely in their milk-white robes; Oh, the hope of heaven! when shall I be there? I was almost in sight of it, and brought back again, seeing my meetness was not complete. Even so, Thy will, not mine, O my Father, be done."

"You must pass through tribulations, as I have done. We require to be taught by various trials that this is not our rest. And then come the results—the weanings, the heart-searchings, the drawing of the spirit nearer to God, the sweet, encouraging recognitions, the gracious whispers of Jesus' love. His voice saying, 'Fear not, it is I; I will come and receive you to Myself, that where I am, ye may be also.' And then comes the last enemy, and the final conflict; and the happy spirit, freed from the body of sin and of death, trembling and panting, is at the feet of Jesus. Oh, the bliss, the unutterable bliss of that moment! Absent from the body, it is present with the Lord. Oh, the glory! To see Jesus, once a Man of sorrows, now enthroned; that very same Jesus who was upon earth, and who has often spoken words of comfort when others could not comfort."

"Lord, I weary, I weary, I *weary,* to be gone. Keep me, patient, waiting Thy will. I must be perfected through suffering; not one pang too severe, nor one sorrow too much."

"My faith is still strong and confident that I shall meet all my dear children in heaven. The Lord promised to be a Father to my family. It was not for this poor world that He gave me that promise, but for that world which is to come. He is my Father, and He will be my children's Father. Oh, I cannot find words sufficiently expressive of His loving kindness to me. I enter heaven as a poor sinner, saved by grace."

"Read to me the precious words of Jesus. Endeavour to keep my mind upon His truth. Christ is the Rock upon which my feet are placed."

"Keep close intimacies with Jesus. We must live upon Christ, and we must die upon Christ."

To her daughter she said,—

"A mother's blessing rest upon you. Oh, what loving-kindness has the Lord shown to me! He has denied me nothing. I have every comfort I need. I am just where I would wish to die. This room has been so often a Bethel to my soul. I have seemed to commune here with God face to face. I am so thankful that I am *here*."

"How sweet is the sympathy of Jesus; *Jesus wept.* He mingled His tears with Mary and Martha, and yet he met Calvary without a tear."

"Oh, live for eternity! This poor world is passing away; the reality is to come, and a glorious reality it is. How important it is to walk so as to please God in all things."

"Little faith will bring the soul to heaven; great faith will bring heaven into the soul."

"My *first* joy in heaven will be to see Jesus!"

"I am passing away, but not a single cloud veils Christ from my view. Language cannot express how happy, happy I am. Words fail to describe the preciousness of Jesus to my soul. I seem as if Christ were beckoning me to come, saying, 'Why do ye delay? Come up hither!'"

"Your prayers detain me here."

"It ought to be to you a joyous thought that I am going home—*going home!* A welcome home. I have not a want, nor care, nor trouble."

"You are going to the prayer-meeting; oh, be faithful to *professors*."

"I never so felt my dependence upon the power of the Holy Ghost as I now do. I have not honoured Him as I should have done. One in the Godhead, he is worthy of equal honour and praise. The power of the Holy Ghost carried Christ through all of His work. In the saints, it is first seen in quickening and calling them; then, in teaching, sanctifying, and comforting them all their journey through. I repeat it; I never so much felt my dependence upon the Holy Ghost as I do now. My first prayer in the morning when I awake is addressed to the Holy Spirit, that He would take possession of my thoughts, my imagination, my heart, my words, throughout the day, directing, controlling, and sanctifying them all."

"Dwell more prominently and earnestly, in your preaching, upon the truth that nothing but the power of the Holy Ghost can convert the soul."

"You have a great work before you, and I shall be in heaven to welcome you home. Be faithful unto death. *My God shall supply all your need, according to His riches in glory by Christ Jesus.*"

"Oh, for a revival of religion! perhaps the Lord is keeping me here to see it. Wrestle with God for it. If there is a spot upon earth more blessed than another, it is the mercy-seat. None can tell the joy that springs from it."

"Few people are aware of the communications that are going on between earth and heaven. I do not wish to be visionary, but many such manifestations have I had."

"This is the hour to test the *reality* of the gospel. It *is* a reality, a most blessed reality."

"There is a service in heaven for Christ."

"I wish 'Praise God from whom all blessings flow,' to echo through this house when I am gone."

"Soon I shall be singing His high praises in heaven. Oh, how great His love? How can He love so vile a sinner as I? Yet he loves me. I have nothing of my own goodness to bring in my hand,—all, *all* I cast away."

"What will the music of heaven be!"

"Many people say to those going to another place, 'You talk so much about it, you will be disappointed;' but oh, heaven will transcend our highest expectations!"

Gazing one evening from her bed upon a magnificent sunset, she remarked, "Oh, if the *outside* of heaven is so beautiful, what must it be *within!*"

"I never take a glass of cold water, but I think of Jesus' words—'I thirst.' Lord, shall I not weep when I fix my eyes upon Thy blessed face, and remember that my sins caused Thy sufferings? Oh, if there were a thought of my heart for which Jesus did not atone, I should never enter heaven!"

"I long, I weary to be gone; but I would not be impatient."

After a day of extreme languor, she said, "The Lord has fed me to-day with drops of honey. Do not grieve after me."

"Note this.—There is a buoyancy, a vitality in the principle of the renewed soul, which in dying, cannot be depressed. The more the body decays and sinks, the higher it rises to its native heaven."

"If ever there were one graciously, gently, wisely led, it is I. Would that I had kept a more perfect record of all His dealings with me. He would not have me a spoilt child, therefore He has employed the rod; but all His corrections and rebukes have been in *love*."

On her grandson asking her, if he should read to her from a delightful little book, entitled, "Words of Jesus," placing her hand upon her heart, she replied:—

"I have them all *here*. The Holy Ghost administers to me like a little child. My loving Shepherd cherishes the lambs as well as the sheep; and He will come and take me to Himself. I shall not go alone. I want to go—I want to go."

"Oh, why are His chariot-wheels so long in coming? Why does He delay? I am longing to depart, to be with Christ. All is *real*. If Christ is risen from the dead, then I am safe. If He is alive, then I shall be with Him for ever. I long to end this mortal struggle, and can truly say—

"'Jesus, lover of my soul,
Let me to thy bosom fly.'"

On the draught being brought to her, which had so often revived her sinking powers, she said, "Is it wrong to take the draught that detains me here? No, it is not wrong. I would not be impatient, but I long to end the conflict, and be with Jesus. Oh, how precious He is to my soul!" On the passage being repeated to her, "Our light affliction, which is but for a moment, worketh for us a far more exceeding and eternal weight of glory," she replied, "Oh, yes! that glory is to behold the face of Jesus. The glory of heaven is *Christ*. It has been a hard conflict through life to hold fast my confidence. Oh, how far have I come short even as a professor! But I rest upon the finished work of Jesus. I am complete in Him. Stephen when dying, in such painful circumstances, saw Jesus at the right hand of God. That is a sure evidence that He is alive."

It was on Tuesday evening, October 3, 1854, that she departed to her rest. At six o'clock in the morning of that day, she had sunk into a state of exhaustion so extreme as scarcely to betray any signs of life. Observing the alarm this produced, she rallied her feeble powers, and indicated her perfect consciousness, and recognition of all around her. One of her sons then took his position at the head of her bed, and as the Holy Spirit aided his memory, repeated for three hours such passages of Scripture as were appropriate to her solemn circumstances. To nothing were her quick sensibilities more responsive than this. The occasional elevation of her attenuated hand—the heaven-cast glance of her dim eye—the soft whisper of her faint voice indicated her felt preciousness of God's word, and the support it was imparting to her soul, around which the deep waters were now swelling. Soon after, while another of her sons was holding her hand, she raised them both, still retaining his, and fixing her eyes upon his face, with a look of the profoundest solemnity and tenderness, pointed upward. The act was too significant not to be understood. "Meet me in heaven!" was her dying charge. And then, when her lips were thought for ever sealed—lips that had testified so long and so faithfully of Jesus—she exclaimed, with a voice of wondrous energy and power, "A cloudless death!—a cloudless death!—a cloudless death!" So resplendent was the glory now surrounding her—so sacred and awe-struck the feelings of all who gazed upon the scene—the spot where the last conflict was waging seemed more like the vestibule of heaven, than the chamber of death. And now her oft urged prayer was answered, her utmost wishes were fulfilled; Jesus, "that very same Jesus who once trod this earth, had come with the pale messenger," lightening the dreary valley with His presence, and manifesting Himself, as once He did to Stephen, as her own risen, living Saviour, waiting to welcome her to her long-wished-for home. While her gathered children were surrounding her dying bed, watching the closing scene, expecting each moment to catch her last sigh, her eyes partly opened, her lips moved, and with a low yet distinct voice, she rapidly repeated the words, "I see Thee!—I see Thee!—I see Thee!—I see

Thee!" The unearthly grandeur of the scene transcends all description. We felt that heaven was opened—that Christ was there—that the eternal world enclosed us.

"What do you see, dearest Mamma? "The only reply was, "*I see Thee!*—I SEE THEE! And as her voice grew fainter and fainter, and the words died softly upon her lips, she ceased to move—a holy quiet reigned—a solemn calm ensued—her sanctified spirit was in the bosom of her Lord.

"The long yearnings of her heart were still'd."

She lay like a conqueror—as more than conquerer she was—surrounded with the spoils of victory. By the power of a simple faith in a living Saviour, she had wrested the dart from the King of Terrors on the confines of the eternal world, and death was swallowed up in victory. Her countenance was the image of repose—the sublime of tranquillity. No statue from the master's hand was ever chiselled as were those fixed and marble features. From the mental emotion, the soul-ecstasy through which she had but just passed—wrapt in the vision of her living Lord—there still lingered a lustre in the eye, a smile upon the parted lips, and a glow, like that of sunset, upon the countenance, which formed a picture of inimitable beauty and grandeur.

"There lived no trace on that pale brow
  Of wishes unfulfill'd;
The only hope of answer'd prayer,
The calm of perfect peace, was there,
  The saint's last sleep to gild;
'Twere more than crime to mar a rest
So tranquil, so supremely blest."

Our work is nearly done. With a deep feeling of regret—for the preparation of the last few pages of the volume has rendered us quite unequal to the task—we relinquish a feature which entered into the original plan of this Memoir, of presenting a minute analysis of the Christian character and experience it has attempted to delineate. We trust, however, the reader will have no difficulty in forming a just estimate of the principal characteristics of its subject, and of gleaning for himself those practical lessons which may be learnt from the history we have thus recorded. A few observations are all that we can attempt in briefly suggesting those points which appear to be worthy of especial study.

Constituted although she was by God with a mind of superior order, and possessing remarkable strength and decision of character, great energy, and promptness of action, it yet will not be her mental, so much as her *spiritual* endowments, upon which the Christian reader will most delight to dwell. The grace of our Lord was exceedingly abundant in her, with faith and love. That grace, by the side of whose perennial stream she perpetually dwelt, imparted inspiration to her thoughts, a mould to her actions, and invested her whole habit of life with a sanctity and charm indescribably impressive and heavenly. None but those who saw her in all the relations and phases of domestic and every-day life, can form an adequate conception of the beautiful proportions and exquisite symmetry of her Christian character and course. They alone could testify how practical godliness was exhibited, not in fitful and impulsive throes, but as a principle suffused over her whole character, shedding everywhere the bloom and fragrance of spiritual life—noiseless and uniform as the light of day. Reader, the same grace by which she was what she was, is alike accessible to you. By this grace you may be assimilated with the Divine will, may be transformed into the Divine image, may be trained for active toil, or for passive endurance, as was, in an eminent degree, her sacred privilege. Limit not a Divine blessing so inexhaustible in its resources, and so free in its bestowment; but out of the Saviour's fulness receive grace for grace, that in all things "the name of our Lord Jesus may be glorified in you, and ye in Him, according to the grace of our God and the Lord Jesus Christ."

Her power of *faith* and *prayer*—the two distinctive features of her Christianity—are suggestive of deep practical instruction. Her faith was of the most simple character, and in its simplicity may be found the secret of its mightiness. She was "strong in faith, giving glory to God." She took Him at His word, believing Him because He was God. This childlike, unquestioning faith, purified her heart, sustained her under present trial, enabled her to triumph over things seen, and brought eternal realities vividly and constantly before her mind. Her faith honoured God by believing, and God honoured her faith by bestowing. With this vigorous grace of faith, was naturally connected great power in *prayer*. She cherished the most exalted views of the prevalence of prayer with God. With this weapon, wielded by the arm of faith, she felt nothing was too difficult of accomplishment, since with God all things were possible. She was a woman *mighty in prayer*. Apart from all figure of speech, and without any exaggerated conception of the idea, it might be said, she literally "WALKED WITH GOD." She seemed to live, and move, and have her being in fellowship and communion with the Invisible. Her habit was,—be the errand trivial or momentous,—to use her own simple and expressive language, a continuous "going and telling Jesus." She remembered his own words, "Without me ye can do *nothing*," and so she lived, as a little child, upon His guardian, incessant care. The closeness of her walk, and the holy familiarity of her intercourse with God may astonish some, but so it was. She seemed to have her home in His very heart, and thus to have penetrated its infinite depths, and to have unveiled its hidden love to an extent startling to those whose transactions with God are distant, cold, and unfrequent. God was all in all to her. No thought nor wish, no want nor plan, did she cherish or devise, with which His counsel and glory were not sought. "The Lord direct," was always the calm, submissive response to every question of doubt and perplexity. In this impressive feature of her Christian life, how powerfully does she speak! Could her living voice now be heard addressing each tried reader of this volume, with what earnestness of manner, and persuasiveness of tone, would she still say,—"Go, AND TELL JESUS."

How forcibly do these pages illustrate the essential relation of strong faith, full assurance of hope, and elevated rapture of pious feeling, with profound humility of heart, and an almost entire negation of self! When Isaiah, in the heavenly vision, "saw the Lord sitting upon a throne, high and lifted up, and His train filling the temple," and heard the seraphim cry, "Holy, holy, holy is the Lord of hosts!" overwhelmed by the glory of the Lord, he exclaimed, "Woe is me, for I am undone; because I am a man of unclean lips!" And when the believer obtains a near view of the "glory of God in the face of Jesus Christ," he, too, falls prostrate at His feet, lost in a sense of His vileness. It is in the light of the Divine countenance the exceeding sinfulness of sin is seen, and seen but to whelm the soul in self-abhorrence. Before the deepening glory of Christ, the glory of self pales, as the morning star retires before the ascending sun. The closer the acquaintance with Jesus, and the stronger the assurance of Divine forgiveness, the more softly and lowlily will the spirit walk with God. "There is FORGIVENESS with Thee, *that Thou mayest be feared.*" As the vessel more heavily laden sinks deeper into the water, so the soul, the more that it is filled with Divine grace, sinks the lowest into self-annihilation. Almost painfully humiliating, at times, were her views and expressions of herself; and yet, in the deepest, gloomiest vale of soul-humiliation which she trod, she appeared never to lose sight of her completeness in Christ. Her *self*-denial never betrayed her into *grace*-denial.

Let the *widow's* desolate heart be cheered as she reads these pages. They are the records of one who, perhaps, like herself, was early bereft of the husband of her youth, and left to tread the remainder of life's journey in lonely widowhood, and, single-handed, to rear a family for God. Did that God, the widow's God, forsake her? Did any single promise of His word, upon which He caused her soul to hope, fail? Did He, as a God of providence, or as a God of grace, betray the confidence He asked, disappoint the trust he invited, or leave unhealed the wound, unsoothed the sorrow, unaided the burden, His own hands had made? No; not in a solitary instance. Then, all that He has been, He still is, and ever will be—the God of the widow who putteth her trust in Him.

The *aged Christian*, too, will gather much to encourage her heart and strengthen her hands in God from the life under review. A saint of God, closing her pilgrimage of toil and conflict, in her *eighty first* year, bears her dying testimony, that His aged ones are the especial objects of His loving, tender, faithful care. Lean in all the decrepitude of years, in all the weakness, pain, and tremulousness of advanced age, in all the fears, misgivings, and becloudings of life's close, upon this Divine rod and staff. Now that thou art old and grey-headed, thy God will not forsake thee. Rest in the faithfulness of God, lean upon the finished work of Jesus, and hope on for the glory so soon to be revealed. Let thy believing *prayer* be, "Cast me not off in the time of old age; forsake me not when my strength faileth." And God's faithful *answer* will be, "Even to your old age I am He; and even to hoar hairs will I carry you."

How great the power and charm of a *holy life!* Such is the lesson these pages impressively teach. The world is replete with beauty. There is beauty in nature, and beauty in art, and beauty in countless forms; but there is no beauty like "the *beauty of holiness.*" The brightness which gleams through a good man's life outshines the sun in its meridian splendour. The world, too, is mighty in its forces. There is the power of intellect, and the power of learning, and the power of genius, and the power of wealth, and the power of rank; but there is no power so commanding and so effective as the *power of holiness.* The power it wields is omnipotent for the achievement of good. And a more precious and enduring legacy parental affluence and affection cannot bequeath to posterity, than the record of a life traced by the sanctifying influence of faith, the achievements of prayer, and the adornments of holiness. Such a life is a living demonstration of the Divinity of the Bible, and does more to confirm its veracity, and spread its truths through the world, than all that has ever been spoken or written on the evidences of Christianity.

How measureless the *loss* of such a saint of God! To her family and friends, to the church of Christ and the world, the withdrawal for ever from earth of her living piety and fervent prayers, her holy conversation and consistent example, is a serious and far-reaching calamity. And yet she still lives amongst us, not in our hearts and memories only, but in the undying influence of her holy life. "The righteous shall be had in *everlasting* remembrance." The grave hides them from sight, but not from memory. Neither the green turf nor the salt wave can bury the still surviving, and still moulding recollections of the holy dead. In the embalmed remembrance of their graces, their prayers, and their actions, they still live to guide, to stimulate, and cheer us in our homeward march. Nor do we cease to live with them! They remember and love us still. Bearing their friendships with them to the skies, purified, sublimated, and enlarged, they yet think of us, yearn over us, and long to have us with them there, with a tenderness of interest, and an intensity of affection, such as they never felt on earth. For aught that we know, they still hover around our persons, encompassing our path to the abodes of bliss. Angels are ministering agents to the heirs of salvation; and may we not suppose that many of the glorified spirits of "just men made perfect" are clothed with a like embassy? "They serve Him day and night in His temple;" and who will say that it does not enter essentially into that service for the Lord, to administer in some unknown way to their former companions in tribulation, and the expectant sharers of their glory? But until we rejoin them in the home of the Father, we should think of them but to follow their holy example, to gather encouragement from their faith and patience, to learn lessons from their failings, and to take up and carry forward the work of the Lord, which dropped from their dying hands, until we, too, are summoned to rest from our labours, and receive our reward.

Such is *her* happiness, whose sacred memorials we close. She has reached, at last, the heaven of glory, for which her panting thoughts and heaving heart so yearned. She has looked upon Christ, whom her soul adored with an affection so absorbing and intense—has seen angels, and talked with those she once knew and loved below. And now she feels that all indeed is *true!* Mysteries which the hoary sages of antiquity should never know,—glories which the human eye could never see,—joys which human thought could never conceive,—and music such as earth never heard, have burst upon her wondering, blissful spirit. At His feet, who died for her, and who rose again, adoringly she casts her crown, exclaiming, "WORTHY IS THE LAMB!" Ascribing to the TRIUNE JEHOVAH—as we now devoutly do—the praise and the glory of all that she was, as a partaker of LIFE IN JESUS, we will rejoice that, through His sovereign grace, she "fought a good fight, finished her course, kept the faith;" and that now—

SHE IS GONE TO THE MOUNTAIN OF MYRRH, AND TO THE HILL OF FRANKINCENSE, UNTIL THE DAY BREAK, AND THE SHADOWS FLEE AWAY.

THE END.

www.ingramcontent.com/pod-product-compliance
Lightning Source LLC
Chambersburg PA
CBHW020546300426
44111CB00008B/812